German Poetry 1910-1975

German Poetry
1910-1975

An Anthology Translated and
Edited by Michael Hamburger

Urizen Books   New York

Translations © 1976 by Michael Hamburger. For permission to reprint the original German texts and a number of Michael Hamburger's translations we gratefully acknowledge permission from the following Publishers and Authors:

AICHINGER, ILSE
Wo ich wohne
© 1958 S. Fischer Verlag, Frankfurt am Main

ARP, HANS
Opus Null
Sekundenzeiger
Der gordische Schlüssel
Das Tagesgerippe
Das Lied des Roten Haeuser
from Hans Arp *Gesammelte Gedichte I* © 1963 (Gedichte 1903-1939) and Hans Arp *Gesammelte Gedichte II* © 1974 (1939-1957) by Verlags AG "Die Arche," Peter Schifferli, Zürich

Das Rad
© 1963 Hans Arp

ARTMANN, HANS CARL
der graf mit dem einglas
ich bin ein polares gestirn
© Walter Verlag, Olten & Freiburg

ATABY, CYRUS
Besitznahme
Libelle, grünes Feuer
Fourough zum Gedaechtnis
© Claassen Verlag GmbH, Düsseldorf

BACHMANN, INGEBORG
An die Sonne
Nebelland
Alle Tage
Die gestundete Zeit
Exil
© Ingeborg Bachmann's Heirs, c/o Piper Verlag, Munich

BARTSCH, KURT
Brechts Tod
Der Humanist
Elan
© Klaus Wagenbach, Berlin

BAUER, WALTER
Der Weg zaehlt, nicht die Herberge
© Ernst Tessloff Verlag, Hamburg

BAYER, KONRAD
Fuer Judith
© Rowohlt Verlag GmbH, Reinbek bei Hamburg, 1966

BECHER, JOHANNES R.
Die neue Syntax
© Aufbau Verlag, East Berlin

BECKER, JÜRGEN
Bildbeschreibung
You are leaving the American Sector
Berlin-London
Shakespeare's Land
from *Das Ende der Landschaftsmalerei* © Suhrkamp Verlag, Frankfurt/Main 1974

BENN, GOTTFRIED
Karyatide
Nachtcafe
Ikarus
Untergrundbahn
Palau
Ideelles Weiterleben
© Limes Verlag, Muenchen

Nachzeichnung
© 1948 Verlags AG "Die Arche," Peter Schifferli, Zürich

BERND, JENTZSCH
Terezin, das Gräberfeld
From: *Lyrik der DDR* © Aufbau Verlag, East Berlin

BERNHARD, THOMAS
Jetzt im Frühling
An H.W.
© Otto Müller Verlag, Salzburg

BIENEK, HORST
Per sempre
© Horst Bienek

BIERMANN, WOLF
Brecht, deine Nachgeborenen
© Klaus Wagenbach Verlag, Berlin

BOBROWSKI, JOHANNES
Osten
Pferde
Trakl
Steh. Sprich. Die Stimme
© Deutsche Verlagsanstalt, Stuttgart
Entfremdung
Mobile von Calder
© Klaus Wagenbach Verlag, Berlin

BORCHERS, ELISABETH
Jemand schweigt
© Luchterhand Verlag, Neuwied

BORN, NICOLAS
Drei Wünsche
*Das Verschwinden aller im Tod
eines Einzelnen*
© Rowohlt Taschenbuch Verlag
GmbH, Reinbek bei Hamburg
BRAMBACH, RAINER
Der Baum
Granit
From *Ich Fand Keinen Namen
Dafür* © Diogenes Verlag AG
Zürich 1969
BRAUN, VOLKER
Landwüst
© Reclam, Leipzig
BRECHT, BERTOLT
Vom armen B.B.
From *Gedichte,* Band 1: © Copyright Suhrkamp Verlag, Frankfurt/Main 1960
Von den Resten älterer Zeiten
From *Gedichte,* Band 2: © Copyright Suhrkamp Verlag, Frankfurt/Main 1960
Von allen Werken die liebsten
From *Gedichte,* Band 3: © Copyright Suhrkamp Verlag, Frankfurt/Main 1961
*Fahrend in einem bequemen
Wagen*
From *Gedichte,* Band 5: © Copyright Suhrkamp Verlag, Frankfurt/Main 1964
An die Nachgeborenen
From *Gedichte* Band 4: © Copyright Suhrkamp Verlag, Frankfurt/Main 1961
*Legende von der Entstehung
des Buches Taoteking auf dem
Werk des Laotse in die
Emigration*
From *Gedichte,* Band 4: © Copyright Suhrkamp Verlag, Frankfurt/Main 1961
Die Maske des Bösen
Vom Sprengen des Gartens
From *Gedichte im Exil:* © Copyright Stefan S. Brecht 1964. Alle Rechte vorbehalten durch Suhrkamp Verlag, Frankfurt/Main
Überall Freunde
From *Gedichte,* Band 6: © Copyright Suhrkamp Verlag, Frankfurt/Main 1964
BRINKMANN, ROLF DIETER
Die Orangensaftmaschine

Einen jener Klassischen
© Rowohlt Taschenbuch Verlag
GmbH, Reinbek bei Hamburg
BUSTA, CHRISTINE
Die Schüne der Vögel
Unterwegs zu älteren Feuern
© Otto Müller Verlag, Salzburg
CELAN, PAUL
Fadensonnen
Weggebeizt von
from *Atemwende* © Suhrkamp
Verlag, Frankfurt/Main, 1967
Schaltjahrhunderte
from *Lichtzwang* © Suhrkamp
Verlag, Frankfurt/Main, 1970
Mapesbury Road
from *Schneepart* ©Suhrkamp Verlag, Frankfurt/Main, 1971
Mit wechselndem Schlüssel
Tenebrae
Allerseelen
Psalm
Radix, Matrix
© Deutsche Verlagsanstalt
COHN, HANS WERNER
Schlaf
Fall
Das Loch
© H.W. Cohn
CZECHOWSKI, HEINZ
Liebesgespräch
from *Lyrik der DDR* © Aufbau
Verlag, Berlin
DELIUS, FRIEDRICH CHRISTIAN
Geburtstag
Gedicht für Katzen
© Rotbuch Verlag GmbH, Berlin
DEMUS, KLAUS
Steil aufwärts
Hier wo der Bach
©Günter Neske Verlag, Pfullingen
Der Bodhibaum
from *Das schwere Land* © 1958
S. Fischer Verlag, Frankfurt am
Main
DOMIN, HILDE
Makabrer Wettlauf
from *Nur eine Rose als Stütze,* ©
1969 S. Fischer Verlag GmbH,
Frankfurt am Main
Exil
from *Hier,* © 1964 S. Fischer Verlag GmbH, Frankfurt am Main
EICH, GÜNTER
Inventur

CONTENTS

xv

JÜRGEN THEOBALDY

INTRODUCTION

This anthology sprang out of two needs: to collect scattered translations done over the decades and to replace the earlier anthology *Modern German Poetry 1910-1960*, which has been both out of print and out of date for some years. The earlier anthology was compiled in collaboration with Christopher Middleton, who chose not to take on the work of co-editing this one. Since the additional texts—poems published in the last fifteen years, but also earlier poems omitted for one reason or another—called for a reappraisal and rebalancing of all the contents, it seemed best to begin again. In the editing of a bilingual anthology, selection and translation are so closely linked as to become very nearly inseparable. When it became clear that I should do the selecting on my own I decided to do all the translating also. This meant the loss of many good translations by Christopher Middleton; but at least the new anthology would have the consistency of being the work of one selector, one translator.

That decision alone accounts for the absence of a number of poems, and a number of poets, included in the earlier anthology. I could have chosen in principle to include this or that poem because its author ought to be represented in an anthology devoted to the sixty-five years in question, and I did try to include quite a few poets who are missing here; but simply to reprint a text is an incomparably easier matter than to translate it. In the end I had to confine myself to poems and poets not only translatable in the abstract but translatable by me. That, too, proved part of the price to be paid for the consistency I had opted for. My justification is that no anthology, however balanced and far-ranging, can be representative of a whole period, especially if that period is as heterogeneous as the one in question; and least of all a bilingual anthology. One reason is that poetry and history, including the history of poetry, are two different things. An historical anthology of the poems written over any particular period would have to include the mediocre and less than mediocre, since these are more representative of a period than the best work done in it. A strictly qualitative anthology, on the other hand, would convey little or nothing of the range and variety of work written over that period: the major poets would not only dominate but drive out the minor ones. In practice, then, all anthologies pretending to "cover" a particular period can be no more than a compromise between the two procedures. At best, they can aim at a balance between two kinds of representativeness; and one man's taste and sympathies, stretched as far as they will go, are as good a criterion as any. It goes without saying that prejudice, blind spots, and ignorance are other restricting factors; and that these are not eliminated when two or more selectors put their heads together.

One result of the reappraisal I have mentioned is that the word "modern" has been dropped from the title. It goes without saying, too, that I have included no text encapsulated in the conventions of an earlier age to the point of failing to come to life as language. Beyond that, the word "modern" has become so fraught with ambiguities and contradictions as to be very nearly meaningless. It has become harder, for instance, to be as excited as Christopher Middleton and I were fifteen years ago by all the German varieties of modernism that were lumped together as "Expressionism." Most of our Introduction to the earlier anthology was an attempt to define the diverse phenomena thrown together under this label, and to relate them to modernist practice in other parts of the world. The more imitable features of Expressionism itself became a convention very soon after publication of the work done by its initiators before the outbreak of the First World War. The initiators are as prominent in the new anthology as in the old one; but I have found it impossible to translate the rhetoric of the many imitators and fellow travelers, a rhetoric quite as facile and obfuscating as any taken over by other poets of the time from the nineteenth century. What is more, the late Expressionist manner became a convention that could be adopted or discarded at will, as the later development of Johannes R. Becher—or of Franz Werfel—proves with a conclusiveness that raises serious questions about the manner itself. If the plain unfigurative diction of the latter Brecht was just as distinctly modern a phenomenon as the metaphorical luxuriance and broken syntax of late Expressionism—and it would make nonsense of the word "modern" to argue that it was not—the modernism of all but a few of the so-called Expressionists reveals a pathetically old-fashioned core. Brecht took the trouble to study the social and political institutions of his time, instead of merely responding to them emotionally. True, his purge of poetry's emotive diction was at once a revolution and a restoration; and the neoclassical trend in twentieth-century modernism—often close to pastiche or parody, as in some of Gottfried Benn's late poems, for all his Expressionist past, or in some of Stravinsky's music—is pervasive and inescapable. Above all, the notion of linear progress in the arts—or outside the arts, for that matter—has become very dubious indeed. If any pattern emerges from what actually happens, it is one of simultaneous advances and retreats, of leaps and falls, of consolidations and dead ends, of amalgamated extremes, of reverses, reprises, catastrophes. The game of snakes and ladders offers a crude analogy; but that game has a fixed starting-point, a fixed finishing-point, and a winner. The real thing has none of these.

For "modern," then, I substitute a criterion quite as vague in itself, but meaningful as soon as it is applied to specific poems, specific poets: the criterion of authenticity, an authenticity usually bound up with novelty of one kind or another, simply because the authentic poet does not merely repeat or imitate what has been done before, though repetition or imitation may enter into the very novelty and uniqueness of what he is doing. This criterion of authenticity has the advantage of cutting through false distinctions of stature, major or minor, and of being as applicable to poems as to the fiction called "poetry" or to the authors of poems. It is perfectly possible for one and the same poet to write certain poems that are authentic to a degree that others of his poems are not. Where that is the case it matters little whether that poet is judged to be a minor poet who has written major poems, or vice versa. Some of the poets included in this anthology—Trakl is an outstanding instance—have left a small body of work rather narrow in range, yet so generally recognized to be authentic that it has been treated as major poetry—even as one of Heidegger's paradigms of poetry as revelation. Other poets, such as Rilke—another of Heidegger's paradigms—found it necessary to run through a whole gamut of modes, styles, and kinds of poetry, with varying degrees of authenticity, but an overall consistency of concern. To do justice to his variety and consistency I should have needed to include many more poems by him than was compatible with the balance of the anthology; and I should have needed to include extracts from the *Duino Elegies* and *Sonnets to Orpheus*, the later sequences to which he owes his standing as a major poet. The "minor" poems by which Rilke is represented here have the advantage of being less well known, of being more or less complete in themselves—though a peculiar fragmentariness is essential to much of Rilke's later work—and of opening up areas of freedom and adventurousness beyond the bounds of those "major" sequences. To me, they are quite as authentic as the works that Rilke chose to publish in book form as being all of a piece and coming up to his own conception of what "major" poetry ought to be like.

A few extraneous considerations also affected my choice of poems. Christian Morgenstern, for instance, is distinctly underrepresented, certainly not because he was best as a writer of comic—hence "minor"—verse, nor even because many of his comic poems are hard or impossible to translate, but rather because he has been widely translated elsewhere, and his philosophical wit makes little sense outside the confines of specifically German preoccupations which he shared as a serious writer. In the later period I was somewhat inhibited by the wish not to encroach too shamelessly on the terrain of other translators, including my former co-editor, Christopher Middleton. Otherwise I might have produced yet another version of Paul Celan's *Todesfuge*, though in the last years of his life Celan had come to feel that this poem should not continue to be anthologized at the expense of his later work; and I should have translated poems by Johannes Bobrowski already published in versions by Ruth and Matthew Mean, instead of choosing poems from his posthumous collections only. Yet Bobrowski, like Trakl and Celan, was so wholly and authentically himself in everything he wrote that the restriction scarcely matters.

East German poetry, other than Bobrowski's, presented a special problem of selection, due to the recent publication of a separate bilingual anthology I have devoted to it. (*East German Poetry*. Carcanet Press, Manchester, and E. P. Dutton, New York, 1972.) Its contents were not to be duplicated, only supplemented, by the present anthology. Many of the younger East German poets, therefore, were given less space here than they would otherwise have been given. Readers can make up for the deficiency by referring to *East German Poetry*, in which they will also find poems by Brecht written in the last decade of his life, more poems by Bobrowski, and poems by Peter Huchel earlier than the still uncollected ones included here.

"Concrete" poetry is another special case. At its purest it either cannot be translated or does not need to be translated, because it aspires to the condition either of music or of visual art. Although I have included texts that owe something to the procedures of concrete poetry, I have not attempted to jump that formidable hurdle.

The word "poetry" could hardly be avoided in the title; but my concern was with poems, not with an institutional collective to be proportionally represented, much as "the people," another hypothetical entity, is supposed to be represented by elected or appointed deputies. It happens that most of the major movements and trends of the period can be traced in the contents of this anthology; but they could be traced, too, in the development of a few individual poets many-sided enough to have grappled with the conflicting potentialities of their time. Wherever ascertainable, the date of composition or first publication is provided for each poem. Together with the biographical notes on each poet these dates should satisfy historical curiosity. All classification of poets by movements or ostensible subject matter like "nature" or "politics" should be approached with the utmost distrust. Poets themselves are scarcely aware of such divisions when they write. At their best they will write nature poems that are about politics or political poems that are about love. Oskar Loerke and Wilhelm Lehmann, the histories of literature tell us, were the initiators of a new nature poetry widely written by younger poets during and after the last war. So they were, amongst other things; but each, in his way, was something else as well, as their city poems in this anthology will suggest. As for movements, poets may unite to fight a battle, as the Dadaists did at a particular historical moment; when that battle is over they get back to their real business of writing, by which they should be judged. The Dada movement lost its impetus after a few years. Hans Arp continued to develop as a poet for another four decades, remaining true only to one tenet of Dada, the principle of fortuitousness, and that neither slavishly nor always to the same degree.

The diversity and complexity of trends throughout the whole period is such that to attempt a summary of them in the abstract would do more harm than good. I have already touched on the diverse practices that have been lumped together as "Expressionist." Readers of this anthology can arrive at their own judgment of what "Expressionism" was and was not by comparing the poems written in successive decades by Stramm, Trakl, Heym, Lichtenstein, Stadler, Benn, and Goll, to mention only those "Expressionists" whose work I was able to translate. (Werfel's single contribution here is not typical of the manner that made him prominent as a later "Expressionist," but rather points to those derivations and allegiances that caused him to reject Expressionism in later years; and Becher's sonnet was chosen because it is a kind of manifesto of later Expressionist practice, with the redeeming virtue, to me, that it can be read as a poem intended to be funny.)

The biographical notes, on the other hand, may help to make necessary connections between the purely literary or formal diversity of the work done in this period and the political divisions relevant to it. In 1910 Germany and Austria were Empires, in 1918 they became Republics, between 1933 and 1938 most of the more significant German and Austrian literature went into exile or "inner emigration," since 1949 there have been two separate German Republics. Those bare, and simplified, facts cover a multitude of circumstances affecting each of the poets included in this book. Else Lasker-Schüler, the oldest of those poets, was born in the Wupper Valley at the height of the German Industrial Revolution, lived mainly in Berlin, and emigrated via Switzerland to Palestine, where she died. Rilke was born in a part of the Austrian Empire that was to become Czechoslovakia, never became a Czechoslovak citizen, moved about all over Europe, between Russia and Spain, and spent his last years in Switzerland, where he died. Each personal history of that kind has social, ethnic, religious, or ideological aspects more intimately and intricately bound up with a poet's work than mere geographical or national location. In a period of outward instability each poet is not only placed in this or that complex of circumstances but also related himself to them by an interaction that amounts to a placing of himself. Rilke's middle-class background did not prevent him from drawing up a noble pedigree for himself and identifying now with the ''insulted and injured,'' the pariahs, now with the privileged, the aristocracy. Brecht's middle-class background did not prevent him from assuming a working-class persona which, by various stages and by very hard work, became so distinct and genuine a quality of his poetic voice as to be of exemplary use to successors whose background was truly working-class. One reason why poets tend to conflict with totalitarian systems, though they may have worked for the establishment of such systems, is that totalitarian systems depend for their survival on simplistic notions of personal identity and function, making no allowance for the imaginative self-definition as essential to a poet's identity and function as the given circumstances of class, descent, nationality, and inculcated beliefs. The postwar period, too, abounds in extreme anomalies, such as that of Paul Celan, a German poet born in Rumania who spent the greater part of his life in France, never lived in a German-speaking country for any considerable length of time, and owed his peculiar mastery of the language to those very circumstances.

It may well be that an awareness of the historical complexities and anomalies entered into my choice of poems. The inclusion of a little-known, indisputably "minor" poet, Eduard Saenger, occurs to me as a possible instance. The experience of exile or emigration, out of which these poems sprang, informed so much German poetry written between 1933 and 1945—and even later, since many poets never returned, and others, such as Walter Bauer, chose to emigrate after the war because they could not live with their country's past—that there is no lack of work by poets far more eminent than Saenger. What I like about Saenger's poems is that they respond so vividly to the foreign scene, London in his case, without the self-pity conspicuous in poems by many of the displaced writers more conscious of their former eminence. Saenger's poems may lack the political and moral stringency of his fellow exiles in London, Max Herrmann-Neisse and Theodor Kramer—distinguished poets I was unable to translate—but their innocence and delicacy are rarer gifts. Considerations of space forbade the inclusion of Franz Baermann Steiner's admirable poem *Gebet im Garten* (*Prayer in the Garden*), a poem I have translated and should have liked to include.

Outward divisions alone would explain why German poetry after 1945 is as varied as that of the pre-1914 or interwar periods. A number of poems in this anthology have been regarded as landmarks in post-1945 developments. One of these is Günter Eich's *Inventur*, a West German counterpart of the "language-washing" carried out by Brecht over the previous decades, but independent of it, and amounting to a reduction of poetic diction to a plain, unfigurative and unrhetorical iron ration of words. A similar bareness and ordinariness of diction is to be found even in some of Gottfried Benn's poems of the 'fifties, such as *Ideelles Weiterleben?*, though to the last Benn's pronouncements and influence tended in the opposite direction of "absolute" or hermetic poetry. Poets writing in German have been divided between these directions to this day. In the 'sixties the minimal near-epigram seemed to become a favoured medium in both Germanys, but a different kind of reduction was practiced at the same time by Paul Celan, Ernst Meister, and by Günter Eich himself, for the purpose not of formulating a satirical or critical aperçu in words immediately intelligible but of a highly individual mode of vision, feeling, and perception. Concrete poetry, once more, has its own procedures and problems, though its purely linguistic and analytical processes could be applied to social criticism and satire, as by Helmut Heissenbüttel in poems included here, or by Ernst Jandl in sound poems not included. Since the 'sixties the predominance of political and social concerns throughout the German-speaking world—a predominance reflected even in the development of so idiosyncratic and imaginative a poet as Günter Grass—has begun to be felt as a constraint. Immediate experience, rather than its processed end-products that can be labeled "social" or "political" or "private," is apparent in the work of Born, Becker, Handke, Brinkmann, and Theobaldy, to name only poets with work in this anthology.

To say more than that would be to fall into the generalizations and classifications I mistrust. The contents of this anthology do not represent the whole of German, Austrian, and Swiss poetry written over a period of sixty-five years, and could not possibly have done so even if it were twice or three times as long as it is, or extended to poets altogether beyond its scope. Certain of my choices and omissions will be judged to be eccentric or worse. What I can claim on the positive side is that it does contain good and remarkable poems of as many kinds as I could respond to as a translator. Like all my translations, these take no more liberties than are needed to come as close as possible to the original texts, that is, to their tone, gesture, tension, dynamic of feeling as much as their surface "meaning." My hope is that they will convey something of the quiddity of each poem, not of my quiddity, to readers who cannot begin to grasp it in the facing texts, as well as readers who can grasp it with the help of translations.

M. H.
London, August, 1975

German Poetry
1910-1975

ELSE LASKER-SCHÜLER:

Geboren 1876 in Elberfeld. Sie war eine Zeitlang mit Herwarth Walden, dem Herausgeber der Avant-garde-Zeitschrift *Der Sturm* verheiratet und hatte Liaisons mit mehreren bekannten Lyrikern und Künstlern der Zeit, unter anderem mit Gottfried Benn. Sie gehörte zur Prominenz der Berliner Boheme zwischen 1910 und 1930, wurde als Vorläufer der Expressionisten angesehen und war bekannt für ihre exzentrik. Viele Personen, die sie in ihr Werk und Leben aufnahm, waren orientalisch oder exotisch. Sie schrieb Stücke und Prosaphantasien; daneben vorwiegend religiöse und bekenntnishafte Gedichte an Freunde, die sie mythologisierte. Sie emigrierte zunächst in die Schweiz, dann nach Palästina und starb 1945 in Jerusalem. Ihr erster Gedichtband *Styx* erschien 1902; ihr letzter, *Mein blaues Klavier*, 1943 in Jerusalem. Ihre gesammelten Werke wurden zwischen 1959 und 1962, dann nocheinmal 1966 veröffentlicht.

[handwritten left margin: lebte immer in Sehnsucht / jüdisch / Durchdrungen von Gefühl der Obdachlosigkeit]

MEIN VOLK
[handwritten: Das Volk (jüdisch)]
[handwritten: eigenwillige Sprachbildung / nicht sehr formbewußt]

Der Fels wird morsch, *[handwritten: Zustand des Verfalls - Volk befindet sich im Verfall - ist alt]*

Dem ich entspringe *[handwritten: Neologismus - Exp.]*

Und meine Gotteslieder singe . . .
[handwritten: Moment von beten - von Gott]

Jäh stürz ich vom Weg *[handwritten: s Enjambment - verbindet Sätze flüßig zusammen / r Zeilensprung]*

Und riesele ganz in mir

Fernab, allein über Klagegestein *[handwritten: macht das Gedicht schwebender leichter poetischer]*

Dem Meer zu. *[handwritten: Klagemauer]*

Hab mich so abgeströmt

Von meines Blutes

Mostvergorenheit. *[handwritten: nicht mehr viel Kraft]*

Und immer, immer noch der Widerhall

In mir,

Wenn schauerlich gen Ost *[handwritten: ⇒ Sehnsucht nach ihrem Volk]*

Das morsche Felsgebein,

Mein Volk, *[handwritten: braucht Hilfe, ist in Not]*

Zu Gott schreit.
[handwritten: sehr gefühlsbetont]

HEIMWEH

Ich kann die Sprache

Dieses kühlen Landes nicht, *[handwritten: Dtld. - fühlt sich]*

Und seinen Schritt nicht gehn. *[handwritten: nicht zu Hause - möchte lieber das Orientalische]*

< 2 >

[handwritten bottom: s Metrum = s Versmaß]

ELSE LASKER-SCHÜLER:

Born in 1876 in Elberfeld. She was married for a while to Herwarth Walden, editor of the avant-garde periodical *Der Sturm*, and had liaisons with several well-known poets and artists of the time, including Gottfried Benn. She was prominent in the Berlin bohemia of the period 1910-1930, was regarded as a precursor of the Expressionists, and was notorious for her eccentric dress and behavior. Many of the personae she assumed in her work and life were oriental or exotic. She wrote plays and prose fantasies, as well as poems, mainly religious and confessional, many addressed to friends whom she mythologized. She emigrated first to Switzerland, then to Palestine, and died in Jerusalem in 1945. Her first book of poems, *Styx*, appeared in 1902; her last, *Mein blaues Klavier*, in 1943, in Jerusalem. Her collected works were published in 1959-1962, and again in 1966.

MY PEOPLE

The rock grows brittle
From which I spring,
To which my canticles I sing . . .
Down I rush from the track
And inwardly only ripple
Far off, alone over wailing stone
Toward the sea.

Have flowed so much away
From the wine ferment
Of my blood.
Yet endlessly, yet even now that echo
In me,
When eastward, awesomely,
The brittle rock of bone,
My people,
Cries out to God.

1905: *Der siebente Tag* 1913: *Hebräische Balladen*

HOMESICK

I don't know the language
Of this cool country

< 3 >

Auch die Wolken, die vorbeiziehn,
Weiss ich nicht zu deuten.
Die Nacht ist etwas Bedrohliches
Die Nacht ist eine Stiefkönigin.

Märchenbereich
Immer muss ich an die Pharaonenwälder denken
Und küsse die Bilder meiner Sterne.

Meine Lippen leuchten schon
Und sprechen Fernes,

Und bin ein buntes Bilderbuch
Auf deinem Schoss.

Aber dein Antlitz spinnt
Einen Schleier aus Weinen.

Meinen schillernden Vögeln
Sind die Korallen ausgestochen,

An den Hecken der Gärten
Versteinern sich ihre weichen Nester.

Wer salbt meine toten Paläste—
Sie trugen die Kronen meiner Väter,
Ihre Gebete versanken im heiligen Fluss.

*Keine logischen Zusammenhänge
nur Fragmente*

< 4 >

And its pace is not mine.

Nor can I interpret
The clouds that pass.

The night is a step-queen.

Always I have to think of the Pharaoh forests
And kiss the images of my stars.

Already my lips are luminous
And speak far things,

And I am a gaudy picture book
On your lap.

But your face weaves
A veil made of weeping.

My glittering birds
Have had their corals ripped out,

In the garden hedges
Their soft nests turn to stone.

Who anoints my dead palaces—
They bore the crowns of my forefathers,
Their prayers have gone down in the holy river.

                              1914: *Meine Wunder* ·

< 5 >

CHRISTIAN MORGENSTERN:

Geboren 1871 in München. Morgenstern ist bekannt vor allem durch seine komische, freilich sehr kritische, manchmal auch metaphysische Lyrik. Seine ernste Lyrik, die kaum gelesen wird, ist offener philosophisch im Ton, was ihr zum Nachteil ausschlägt. Sie ist eine Ideenlyrik unter dem Einfluß besonders Nietzsches und Rudolf Steiners. In Norwegen traf Morgenstern Ibsen und wurde sein Übersetzer. Er veröffentlichte auch Essays und Aphorismen. Seine komische Lyrik wurde in großem Maßstab ins Englische übersetzt. Morgenstern, der von Jugend an schwindsüchtig war, starb 1914 in Meran. Seine komische Lyrik ist in *Alle Galgenlieder* (1956) gesammelt, die *Gesammelten Werke* erschienen 1966 in einem Band. 1972 folgte der Band *Sämtliche Dichtungen*.

ENTWURF ZU EINEM TRAUERSPIELE

Ein Fluss, namens Elster,
besinnt sich auf seine wahre Gestalt
und fliegt eines Abends
einfach weg.

Ein Mann, namens Anton,
erblickt ihn auf seinem Acker und schiesst
ihn mit seiner Flinte
einfach tot.

Das Tier, namens Elster,
bereut zu spät seine selbstische Tat
(denn—Wassernot tritt
einfach ein).

Der Mann, namens Anton
(und das ist leider kein Wunder), weiss
von seiner Mitschuld
einfach nichts.

Der Mann, namens Anton
(und das versöhnt in einigem Mass),
verdurstet gleichwohl
einfach auch.

< 6 >

CHRISTIAN MORGENSTERN:

Born in Munich in 1871, Morgenstern is best known for his comic, but highly critical, at times metaphysical, verse. His serious verse, which is little read, is more overtly philosophical, to its detriment. It is a poetry of ideas, influenced first by Nietzsche, then by Rudolf Steiner's anthroposophy In Norway Morgenstern met Ibsen and became his translator. He also published essays and aphorisms. His comic verse has been widely translated into English. A consumptive since his youth, Morgenstern died at Merano in 1914. His comic verse was collected as *Alle Galgenlieder* in 1956, and his collected works were published in one volume, *Gesammelte Werke*, 1966. This was followed by a collected *Sämtliche Dichtungen* (1972).

SKETCH FOR A TRAGEDY

A river called Magpie
remembers its true shape
and one evening simply
flies away.

A man called Anthony
catches sight of it on his field
and with his shotgun simply
shoots it dead.

The animal called Magpie
too late regrets its selfish act
(for a serious drought simply
occurs.)

The man called Anthony
(and that, alas, is not strange) of
his share of the blame is simply
not aware.

The man called Anthony
(and there's some comfort in that)
like everyone there simply
dies of thirst.

     1916: *Palma Kunkel*

< 7 >

AUGUST STRAMM:

Geboren 1874 in Münster in Westfalen. Er wurde Postamtsverwalter in Bremen, dann in Berlin, wo er ins Hauptministerium befördert wurde. In seiner Freizeit studierte er in Halle und promovierte. Mit Herwarth Walden zusammen gab er die Avant-garde-Zeitschrift *Der Sturm* heraus, in der die meisten seiner Gedichte erschienen. Er war einer der radikalsten Neuerer der Zeit, dessen Lyrik reduziert ist auf elementare Bewegungen und Gesten, im Widerspruch nicht nur zu den Konventionen lyrischer Diktion, sondern auch zu denen normaler Grammatik. In vieler Hinsicht war er der Archetyp des Expressionisten, der nicht Ideen, sondern Geistes-und Gefühlszustände im vor-artikulatorischen Stadium ausdrückt. Er fiel im Kampf an der Ostfront im September 1915. Seine *Gesammelten Gedichte* wurden 1956 veröffentlicht, gefolgt von seinen gesammelten Werken mit dem Titel *Das Werk*, die 1963 erschienen. Eine neue Gedichtsammlung erschien 1976 mit dem Titel *Zweiter Klasse*.

BEGEGNUNG

Grenze der Spracheinsparung kann man das noch verstehen

Dein Gehen lächelt in mich über
und
reisst das Herz. *Aufforderung*
Das Nicken hakt und spannt.
Im Schatten deines Rocks
verhaspelt
schlingern
schleudert
klatscht!
Du wiegst und wiegst
mein Greifen haschet blind.
Die Sonne lacht!
Und
blödes Zagen lahmet fort
beraubt beraubt!

Wir sollen seine Aussage intuitiv erfassen.

Rhythmus
Intuitives Erfassen
neue Sprachbehandlung

< 8 >

AUGUST STRAMM:

Born in 1874 in Münster, Westphalia. He became a post office administrator in Bremen, then in Berlin, where he was promoted to the central ministry. In his spare time he studied at Halle and obtained a Ph.D. He was co-editor along with Herwarth Walden of the avant-garde magazine *Der Sturm*, in which most of his poems appeared. He was one of the most radical innovators of the period, writing a poetry stripped down to basic kinetic gestures, contrary not only to conventions of poetic diction but also to those of normal grammar. In many ways he was the archetypal Expressionist, expressing not ideas but states of mind and feeling at their pre-articulated stage. He was killed in action on the Eastern Front in September, 1915. His collected poems, *Gesammelte Gedichte*, were published in 1956, followed by his collected works, *Das Werk*, which appeared in 1963. A new collection of poems, *Zweiter Klasse,* appeared in 1976.

ENCOUNTER

Your walking smiles across to me
and
jerks the heart.
Your nodding hooks and tenses.
In the shadow of your skirt
entangled
flinging
flillips
flaps!
You sway and sway.
My grasping blindly snatches.
The sun laughs!
And
timid wavering limps away
bereft bereft!

November, 1914

SCHWERMUT

Schreiten Streben
Leben sehnt
Schauern Stehen
Blicke suchen
Sterben wächst
das Kommen
schreit!
Tief
stummen
wir.

[handwritten marginalia: "Übertragung eines Gefühls in Worte", "keine Visionen", "Eigenwillige Behandlung der Sprache wird ge-", "Um das Notwendigste schreiben", "können alles mögliche hinein legen", "wenn", "Wortschöpfung"]

SCHLACHTFELD

Schollenmürbe schläfert ein das Eisen
Blute filzen Sickerflecke
Roste Krumen
Fleische schleimen
Saugen brünstet um Zerfallen
Mordesmorde
blinzen
Kinderblicke

[handwritten marginalia: "überzeichnet zu extrem", "Sprache ist Gerippe"]

FROSTFEUER

Die Zehen sterben
Atem schmilzt zu Blei
In den Fingern sielen heisse Nadeln.
Der Rücken schneckt
Die Ohren summen Tee
Das Feuer
Klotzt
Und
Hoch vom Himmel
Schlürft
Dein kochig Herz
Verschrumplig

< 10 >

MELANCHOLY

Striding striving
living longs
shuddering standing
glances look for
dying grows
the coming
screams!
Deeply
we
dumb.

December, 1914

BATTLEFIELD

Yielding clod lulls iron off to sleep
bloods clot the patches where they oozed
rusts crumble
fleshes slime
sucking lusts around decay.
Murder on murder
blinks
in childish eyes.

January, 1915

FROST FIRE

Our toes die
breath melts to lead
in our fingers hot needles drain.
Our backs snail
our hearts hum tea
the fire
logs
and
high from the sky
your simmery heart
shrinkily

< 11 >

Knistrig
Wohlig
Sieden Schlaf.

< 12 >

cracklingly
snugly
laps up
seethy sleep.

February, 1915

< 13 >

RAINER MARIA RILKE:

Geboren 1875 in Prag als Kind deutschsprachiger Eltern. Von 1886 bis 1891 besuchte er Militärakademien. Einmal verkaufte er seine frühen Gedichte in den Straßen von Prag. 1899 und 1900 besuchte er Rußland zusammen mit Lou Andréas-Salomé, um deren Hand einst Nietzsche angehalten hatte, und die später mit Freud in Verbindung stand. In Rußland traf Rilke Tolstoj. Der russische Einfluß zeigte sich stark in seinem *Stundenbuch*. Bald nach seiner Heirat mit der Bildhauerin Clara Westhoff im Jahr 1901 ging er nach Paris, um ein Buch über Rodin zu schreiben, dessen Sekretär er 1905 und 1906 war. Sein späteres Leben verbrachte er mit Reisen in ganz Europa, oft als Gast seiner vielen Bewunderer. Die *Neuen Gedichte*, nach der Verbindung mit Rodin geschrieben, markieren eine Wende in seinem Werk—in Richtung auf bildliche oder bildhauerische "Objektivität." Eine weitere Wende trat kurz vor dem ersten Weltkrieg ein, als er unter einer Lebenskrise litt, die mit dem Hervorteten neuer Kunststile, wie z.B. dem Expressionismus, zusammenfiel. Er verbrachte die letzten Jahre seines Lebens in Muzot in der Schweiz und starb 1926 an Leukämie. Er schrieb einen Großteil seiner späten Lyrik in französischer Sprache. Die bekanntesten späteren Gedichte sind die *Duineser Elegien* (1912-1922) und die *Sonette an Orpheus* (1922). Er ist der am weitesten und vollständigsten übersetzte Autor unseres Jahrhunderts. Seine *Sämtlichen Werke* erschienen in fünf Bänden zwischen 1955 und 1963.

[handwritten annotations:] Stufen   1. zuerst Dinggedichte - impressionistisch 2. "Neue Gedichte" - das Wesentliche wird erfaßt - Verbindung zum Meta-physischen - Symbolism 3. "Wendung"

WENDUNG

Der Weg von der Innigkeit zur Grösse geht
durch das Opfet.—Rudolf Kassner

Lange errang ers im Anschaun.
Sterne brachen ins Knie
unter dem ringenden Aufblick.
Oder er anschaute knieend,
und seines Instands Duft
machte ein Göttliches müd,
dass es ihm lächelte schlafend.

Türme schaute er so,
dass sie erschraken:
wieder sie bauend, hinan, plötzlich, in Einem!

< 14 >

RAINER MARIA RILKE:

Born in Prague in 1875 of German-speaking parents. He attended military schools in 1886-1891. At one time he sold his early poems on the streets of Prague. In 1899 and 1900 he visited Russia with Lou Andreas-Salomé, to whom Nietzsche had once proposed marriage and who later became an associate of Freud's. In Russia Rilke met Tolstoy. The Russian influence was strong in his *Stundenbuch*. Soon after his marriage in 1901 to Clara Westhoff, the sculptress, he went to Paris to write a book on Rodin, whose secretary he was in 1905 and 1906. His later life was spent in travels all over Europe, often as the guest of his many admirers. His *Neue Gedichte*, written after his association with Rodin, marked one change in his work—toward a pictorial or sculptural "objectivity." Another occurred just before the First World War, when he suffered a crisis in his life that coincided with the emergence of new styles in the arts, such as Expressionism. He spent his last years at Muzot in Switzerland and died of leukemia in 1926. He also wrote a good deal of his later verse in French. The best-known of his later poems are the *Duineser Elegien* (1912-1922) and the *Sonette an Orpheus* (1922). He is the most widely and fully translated German poet of the century. His *Sämtliche Werke* appeared in five volumes between 1955 and 1963.

TURNING-POINT

The way from intense inwardness to
greatness leads through sacrifice.—
—Rudolf Kassner

Long he attained it by looking.
Stars would fall on their knees
under his strenuous up-glance.
Or he would look at it kneeling,
and his urgency's odour
made a divine being tired
so that it smiled at him, sleeping.

Towers he would gaze at so
that they were startled:
building them up again, suddenly, sweeping them up!
But how often the landscape
overburdened by day
ebbed to rest in his quiet perceiving, at nightfall.

< 15 >

Aber wie oft, die vom Tag
überladene Landschaft
ruhete hin in sein stilles Gewahren, abends.

Tiere traten getrost
in den offenen Blick, weidende,
und die gefangenen Löwen
starrten hinein wie in unbegreifliche Freiheit;
Vögel durchflogen ihn grad,
den gemütigen; Blumen
wiederschauten in ihn
gross wie in Kinder.

Und das Gerücht, dass ein Schauender sei,
rührte die minder,
fraglicher Sichtbaren,
rührte die Frauen.

Schauend wie lang?
Seit wie lange schon innig entbehrend,
flehend im Grunde des Blicks?

*Es fehlt der
eigene Ausdruck
des Inneren*

Wenn er, ein Wartender, sass in der Fremde; des Gasthofs
zerstreutes, abgewendetes Zimmer
mürrisch um sich, und im vermiedenen Spiegel
wieder das Zimmer
und später vom quälenden Bett aus
wieder:
da beriets in der Luft,
unfassbar beriet es
über sein fühlbares Herz,
über sein durch den schmerzhaft verschütteten Körper
dennoch fühlbares Herz
beriet es und richtete:
dass er der Liebe nicht habe.

(Und verwehrte ihm weitere Weihen.)

< 16 >

Animals trustingly stepped
into his open gaze, grazing ones,
even the captive lions
stared in, as though into incomprehensible freedom;
birds flew through it unswerving,
it that could feel them; and flowers
met and returned his gaze,
great as in children.

And the rumour that here was a seeing man
moved the more faintly,
dubiously visible,
moved the women.

Seeing how long?
How long now profoundly deprived,
beseeching deep down in his glance?

When he, a waiting one, sat in strange towns; the hotel's
distracted, preoccupied bedroom
morose about him, and in the avoided mirror
that room once more
and later, from the tormenting bedstead
once more:
then in the air it pronounced
beyond his grasping pronounced
on his heart that was still to be felt
through his painfully buried body,
on his heart nonetheless to be felt
something pronounced then, and judged:
that it was lacking in love.

(And forbade him further communions.)

For looking, you see, has a limit.
And the more looked-at world
wants to be nourished by love.

Denn des Anschauns, siehe, ist eine Grenze.
Und die geschautere Welt ✕
will in der Liebe gedeihn. ✕

Werk des Gesichts ist getan,
tue nun Herz-Werk
an den Bildern in dir, jenen gefangenen; denn du *Bilder hat*
überwältigtest sie: aber nun kennst du sie nicht. *er durch das Schauen, muß aber noch mehr damit machen —*
Siehe, innerer Mann, dein inneres Mädchen, *Herz-Werk*
dieses errungene aus
tausend Naturen, dieses
erst nur errungene, nie
noch geliebte Geschöpf.

er sucht

KLAGE

Wem willst du klagen, Herz? Immer gemiedener
ringt sich dein Weg durch die unbegreiflichen
Menschen. Mehr noch vergebens vielleicht,
da er die Richtung behält,
Richtung zur Zukunft behält,
zu der verlorenen.

Früher. Klagtest? Was wars? Eine gefallene
Beere des Jubels, unreife.
Jetzt aber bricht mir mein Jubel-Baum,
bricht mir im Sturme mein langsamer
Jubel-Baum.
Schönster in meiner unsichtbaren
Landschaft, der du mich kenntlicher
machtest Engeln, unsichtbaren.

AN DIE MUSIK

(Aus dem Besitz der Frau Hanna Wolff)

Musik: Atem der Statuen. Vielleicht:
Stille der Bilder. Du Sprache wo Sprachen
enden. Du Zeit,
die senkrecht steht auf der Richtung vergehender Herzen.

Musik ist festgehaltene Zeit

< 18 >

Work of seeing is done,
now practice heart-work
upon those images captive within you; for you
overpowered them only: but now do not know them.
Look, inward man, look at your inward maiden,
her the laboriously wrested
from a thousand natures, at her the
creature till now only
wrested, never yet loved.

June, 1914

COMPLAINT

To whom, heart, would you complain? Ever more unfrequented
your way grapples on through incomprehensible
human kind. All the more vainly perhaps
for keeping to its direction,
direction toward the future,
the future that's lost.

Before. You complained? What was it? A fallen
berry of joy, an unripe one.
But now it's my tree of joy that is breaking,
what breaks in the gale is my slow
tree of joy.
Loveliest in my invisible
landscape, you that brought me more close to the
ken of angels, invisible.

July, 1914

TO MUSIC

Music: breathing of statues. Perhaps
stillness of pictures. You language where languages
end. You time
that stands perpendicular on the course of transient hearts.

Feelings for whom? O you the mutation
of feelings to what?—: to audible landscape.

< 19 >

Gefühle zu wem? O du der Gefühle
Wandlung in was?—: in hörbare Landschaft.
Du Fremde: Musik. Du uns entwachsender
Herzraum. Innigstes unser,
das, uns übersteigend, hinausdrängt,—
heiliger Abschied:
da uns das Innre umsteht
als geübteste Ferne, als andre
Seite der Luft:
rein,
riesig,
nicht mehr bewohnbar.

vom Inneren zum Äußeren

*— kommt vom Herzen
Gefühlsausdruck*

*vom Inneren nach
außen transponiert*

DIE HAND

Siehe die kleine Meise,
hereinverirrte ins Zimmer:
zwanzig Herzschläge lang
lag sie in einer Hand.
Menschenhand. Einer zu schützen entschlossenen.
Unbesitzend beschützenden.
Aber
jetzt auf dem Fensterbrett
frei
bleibt sie noch immer im Schrecken
sich selber
und dem Umgebenden fremd,
dem Weltall, erkennts nicht.
Ach so beirrend ist Hand
selbst noch im Retten.
In der beiständigsten Hand
ist noch Todes genug
und war Geld.

HANDINNERES

Innres der Hand. Sohle, die nicht mehr geht
als auf Gefühl. Die sich nach oben hält

< 20 >

You stranger: music. You heart-space
grown out of us. Innermost of us
that, rising above us, seeks the way out—
holy departure:
when what is inward surrounds us
as the most mastered distance, as
the other side of the air:
pure,
immense,
beyond habitation.

January, 1918

THE HAND

Look at the little titmouse,
astray in this room:
ten heartbeats long
it lay within a hand.
Human hand. One resolved to protect.
Unpossessing protect.
But
now on the windowsill
free
in its fear it remains
estranged
from itself and what surrounds it,
the cosmos, unrecognizing.
Ah, so confusing a hand is
even when out to save.
In the most helpful of hands
there is death enough still
and there has been money.

1921

PALM OF THE HAND

Palm of the hand. Sole that has ceased to walk
on anything but feeling. That faces up

< 21 >

und im Spiegel
himmlische Strassen empfängt, die selber
wandelnden.
Die gelernt hat, auf Wasser zu gehn,
wenn sie schöpft,
die auf den Brunnen geht,
aller Wege Verwandlerin.
Die auftritt in anderen Händen,
die ihresgleichen
zur Landschaft macht:
wandert und ankommt in ihnen,
sie anfüllt mit Ankunft.

Aus dem Umkreis: NÄCHTE

Nacht. Oh du in Tiefe gelöstes
Gesicht an meinem Gesicht.
Du, meines staunenden Anschauns grösstes
Übergewicht.

Nacht, in meinem Blicke erschauernd,
aber in sich so fest;
unerschöpfliche Schöpfung, dauernd
über dem Erdenrest;

voll von jungen Gestirnen, die Feuer
aus der Flucht ihres Saums
schleudern ins lautlose Abenteuer
des Zwischenraums:

wie, durch dein blosses Dasein, erschein ich,
Übertrefferin, klein—;
doch, mit der dunkelen Erde einig,
wag ich es, in dir zu sein.

SCHWERKRAFT

Mitte, wie du aus allen

< 22 >

and in the mirror
receives heavenly streets, in themselves
mutable.
That has learnt to walk on water
when it fetches water,
that walks over wells,
transmuter of every way.
That appears in other hands,
turning its own kind
into a landscape:
wanders, arrives in them,
with arrival fills them.

October, 1924

From the cycle, NIGHTS

Night. O face against my face
dissolved into deepness.
You my wondering look's most immense
preponderance.

Night, in my gaze a spasm,
in yourself made so fast;
inexhaustible genesis, outlasting
earthly remains;

full of young planets that hurl
fire from the flight of their seams
into the soundless adventure
of the space between:

by your mere existence, exceeder,
how small I grow—;
but at one with the darkened earth
I dare be in you.

October, 1924

< 23 >

dich ziehst, auch noch aus Fliegenden dich
wiedergewinnst, Mitte, du Stärkste.

Stehender: wie ein Trank den Durst
durchstürzt ihn den Schwerkraft.

Doch aus dem Schlafendem fällt,
wie aus lagernder Wolke,
reichlicher Regen der Schwere.

JETZT WÄR ES ZEIT . . .

Jetzt wär es Zeit, dass Götter träten aus
bewohnten Dingen . . .
Und dass sie jede Wand in meinem Haus
umschlügen. Neue Seite. Nur der Wind,
den solches Blatt im Wenden würfe, reichte hin,
die Luft, wie eine Scholle, umzuschaufeln:
ein neues Atemfeld. Oh Götter, Götter!
Ihr Oftgekommnen, Schläfer in den Dingen,
die heiter aufstehn, die sich an den Brunnen,
die wir vermuten, Hals und Antlitz waschen
und die ihr Ausgeruhtsein leicht hinzutun
zu dem, was voll scheint, unserm vollen Leben.
Noch einmal sei es euer Morgen, Götter.
Wir wiederholen. Ihr allein seid Ursprung.
Die Welt steht auf mit euch, und Anfang glänzt
an allen Bruchstelln unseres Misslingens . . .

IDOL

Gott oder Göttin des Katzenschlafs,
kostende Gottheit, die in dem dunkeln
Mund reife Augen-Beeren zerdrückt,
süssgewordnen Schauns Traubensaft,
ewiges Licht in der Krypta des Gaumens.
Schlaf-Lied nicht,—Gong! Gong!
Was die anderen Götter beschwört,

< 24 >

GRAVITY

Center, how from them all
you draw yourself, even from flying creatures
win back yourself, center, the strongest.

The standing man: as drink through thirst
gravity rushes through him.

But from the sleeper falls,
as from a cloud at rest,
gravity's plentiful rain.

October, 1924

NOW IT IS TIME . . .

Now it is time that gods came walking out
of things inhabited . . .
And then demolished every wall inside
my house. New page. For nothing but the wind
that would be raised by such a wind in turning
could turn the air as sods are by a shovel:
a brand-new field of air. O gods, you gods,
the often come, who are asleep in things,
cheerfully rise, at wells that we conjecture
wash wide awake their faces and their necks
and add their restedness to that which seems
full as it is, our lives already full.
Another morning make your morning, gods!
We're the repeaters, only you the source.
Your rising is the world's, beginning shines
from every crack within our patched-up failure . . .

October, 1925

IDOL

God or goddess of the sleep of cats,
savouring deity that in the dark
mouth crushes ripe eye-berries,

< 25 >

entläss diesen verlisteten Gott
an seine einwärts fallende Macht.

GONG

Nicht mehr für Ohren. . . : Klang,
der, wie ein tieferes Ohr,
uns, scheinbar Hörende, hört.
Umkehr der Räume. Entwurf
innerer Welten im Frein. . . ,
Tempel vor ihrer Geburt,
Lösung, gesättigt mit schwer
löslichen Göttern. . . : Gong!

Summe des Schweigenden, das
sich zu sich selber bekennt,
brausende Einkehr in sich
dessen, das an sich verstummt,
Dauer, aus Ablauf gepresst,
um-gegossener Stern. . . : Gong!

Du, die man niemals vergisst,
die sich gebar im Verlust,
nichtmehr begriffenes Fest,
Wein an unsichtbarem Mund,
Sturm in der Säule, die trägt,
Wanderers Sturz in den Weg,
unser, an Alles, Verrat. . . : Gong!

<   26   >

grape-juice of seeing grown sweet,
everlasting light in the palate's crypt.
Not a lullaby—gong! gong!
What conjures other gods
lets him go, this wily god,
to his power that collapses inwards.

November, 1925

GONG

Not meant for ears. . . : boom
that like a deeper ear
hears us, the seemingly hearing.
Reversal of spaces. Draft
of inner worlds outside . . .
temple before her birth,
dissolution, sated with gods
hard to dissolve . . . : gong!

Sum of what's silent, to
itself only committed,
buzzing return to itself
of that by itself struck silent,
duration squeezed out of motion,
star re-cast . . . : gong!

She whom one never forgets,
who gave birth to herself in loss,
celebration no longer grasped,
wine on invisible lips,
gale in the pillar that bears,
rambler's fall to the path,
our treason, to all . . . : gong!

November, 1925

< 27 >

ROBERT WALSER:

Geboren 1878 in Biel in der Schweiz. Das hier abgedruckte Gedicht kann als Biographie und zugleich als Muster seines wunderlichen, exzentrischen und unvergleichlichen Stils dienen. Seine besten Arbeiten sind in Prosa—drei äußerst originelle Romane (ein vierter ging im Manuskript vorloren) und viele Sammlungen von Kurzgeschichten, Prosa-Sketchen, Essay-Erzählungen und schwer zu klassifizierenden Prosagedichten. Sein Roman *Jakob von Gunten* (1908) wurde in der englischen Übersetzung von Christopher Middleton 1969 veröffentlicht; eine Auswahl des gleichen Übersetzers aus den kurzen Prosastücken *The Walk* erschien 1957. Von 1905 bis 1913 lebte Walser als Schriftsteller in Berlin, angezogen durch seinen Bruder Karl, einen hervorragenden Buchillustrator und Bühnenbildner bei Max Reinhardt. Nach seiner Rückkehr in die Schweiz schrieb er weiter, produzierte auch vier kleine Stücke, fand es aber immer schwieriger, einen Lebensunterhalt zu finden. 1920 arbeitete er kurz als Archivar in Bern, gab diese Tätigkeit aber bald wieder auf. 1929 ging er in eine psychiatrische Klinik und wurde 1933 in die Irrenanstalt Herisau gebracht. Er gab das Schreiben auf und war fast in Vergessenheit geraten, als er auf einem Spaziergang am Weihnachtstag des Jahres 1956 starb. Ein großer Teil seines Werks ist verloren oder nicht zu entziffern, aber zwei Sammlungen seiner Werke erschienen posthum im Lauf der fünfziger und sechziger Jahre. Kafka gehörte zu den Bewunderern von Walsers Prosa. Seine Gesammelten Werke sind in West Deutschland und der Schweiz erhältlich.

DER FÜNFZIGSTE GEBURTSTAG

Geboren bin ich im April in einem
Städtchen mit reizender Umgebung, wo ich
Zur Schule ging; Pfarrer und Lehrer waren
Zum Teil mit mir zufrieden. Mit den Jahren
Kam ich als Lehrling hübsch auf eine Bank.
Wonach ich Städte sah wie Basel, Stuttgart
Und Zürich. Hier macht' ich Bekanntschaft mit
Einer gar gütigen und lieben Frau,
Die bald die Stadt und bald die Landschaft, je
Wie es ihr förderlich schien, bewohnte,
Und die auf Heinrich Heine aufmerksam
Mich machte, den ich sicher erst viel später
In seinem weiten Wert begreifen lernte.
Die Frau hiess, wie nur ich imstand wär', es

< 28 >

ROBERT WALSER:

Born in 1878 in Biel, Switzerland. The poem by him included here can serve as a biography as well as being a specimen of his whimsical, eccentric, and incomparable manner. His best work was written in prose—three most original novels (a fourth was lost in ms.) and many collections of short stories, prose sketches, essay-stories, prose poems difficult to classify. His novel, *Jakob von Gunten* (1908), was published in an English translation by Christopher Middleton in 1969; the same translator's selection from the short prose pieces, *The Walk*, appeared in 1957. From 1905 to 1913 Walser lived as a writer in Berlin, drawn there by his brother Karl, an eminent book illustrator and stage designer for Max Reinhardt. He continued to write after his return to Switzerland, and also produced four miniature plays, but he found it increasingly hard to make a living. In 1920 he worked briefly in Berne as an archivist, but soon gave up the job. In 1929 he entered a psychiatric clinic and was moved to the asylum at Herisau in 1933. He gave up writing and was almost forgotten when he died on a walk on Christmas Day, 1956. Much of his work is lost or indecipherable; but two posthumous editions of his works appeared in the course of the 'fifties and 'sixties. Kafka was among the admirers of Walser's prose. His collected works are available in Switzerland and West Germany.

MY FIFTIETH BIRTHDAY

I was born in April in a small town
With charming surroundings, where I
Went to school; vicar and schoolmaster
Were partly satisfied with me. In due course
I nicely got into a bank to learn the trade,
After which I saw cities like Basle, Stuttgart
And Zurich. Here I made the acquaintance
Of a most kind and amiable woman
Who resided now in town, now in the country,
According to which seemed expedient to her,
And who drew my attention to
Heinrich Heine, whom most probably I did not
Fully appreciate until much later.
The woman's name was one that only I
Could divulge: but why should I do so
When discretion makes me happy? Of positions
In businesses I held a good many.

< 29 >

Zu sagen: doch weswegen sollt' ich solches tun,
Da mich Diskretion beglückt? Stellungen
In Handelshäusern hatt' ich manche inne.
Lebhaft verliess ich aus durchaus ureignem
Drang einen Platz, um einen neuen
Zu erschwingen und versehen; nebenbei
Schrieb ich im Industriequartier Gedichte,
Die später im Verlag Bruno Cassirer
Womöglich etwas zu pompös erschienen.
So gegen sieben Jahre lebte ich
Dann in Berlin als ems' ger Prosaist
Und kehrte, als die Herren Verleger keinen
Vorschuss mehr gewähren wollten,
In die Schweiz zurück, die viele um der schönen
Berg' willen lieben, um hier unverdrossen
Fernerhin dichterisch bemüht zu bleiben.
Nun zähl ich immerhin schon fünfzig Jährchen,
Sagen mir heute ein'ge graue Härchen.

< 30 >

With alacrity, out of an impulse entirely
My own, I left one of these to be able to afford
And fill a new one; on the side
I wrote poems in the industrial sector
That later appeared, perhaps too lavishly,
In the publishing firm Bruno Cassirer.
For about seven years I then lived
In Berlin as a hardworking prose writer
And, when those gentlemen the publishers were
No longer willing to grant an advance, returned
To Switzerland, which many people love
For its beautiful mountains, there
To persist unaggrieved in poetic efforts.
Now, to judge by a few gray hairs,
I have reached the age of fifty years.

1928

< 31 >

EDUARD SAENGER:

Geboren 1880 in Berlin. Er verbrachte einen Teil seiner frühen Kindheit in Des Moines, Iowa, wohin seine Mutter ihn nach dem Tod des Vaters mitnahm. Nach ihrer Rückkehr nach Deutschland gab sie ihn in ein Waisenhaus. Er ging in Berlin zu Schule, studierte die Klassiker und Philosophie, schrieb seine Doktorarbeit über *Hamlet* und verfasste Übersetzungen von Shakespeare-Sonnetten. Im Ersten Weltkrieg diente er bei der Artillerie. 1935 emigrierte er nach England, wo er vorwiegend als Sprachlehrer lebte. Seine späteren Gedichte, die alle in englischer Sprache geschrieben sind, wurden posthum unter dem Titel *Die fremden Jahre* (1959) veröffentlicht. Sänger starb 1948 in London. Seine frühen Gedichte, die 1913 und 1922 veröffentlicht worden waren, wurden nicht wieder gedruckt. Er veröffentlichte auch einen Band mit Essays, Übersetzungen von Catull, Äsop, Empedokles und Gedichten der griechischen Anthologie.

SCHWÄNE IN KEW GARDENS

Es rieselt, nebelt, überkühlt
die grüne Senkung;
Schwäne an Seerand
heben den schwarzen Hals,
läuten
einen Zauber über sich,
süssklaren Ton, wie leise
von Gläsern angestimmt beim Wein.—
Denk nicht an Sterben!

PARK IN LONDON

Noch bläht die braune Erde Frost,
doch Vögel spielen sommerlich
im Holz der Rosen.

Ein Teich im Eirund wiegt
die möwenweisse Kinderflotte
welt-um. Da kippt ein Schiff!
Mit dünnen Beinen plätschernd hilft
ein kleiner Gott.

< 32 >

EDUARD SAENGER:

Born in Berlin in 1880. Part of his early childhood was spent in Des Moines, Iowa, where his mother took him after the death of his father. On her return to Germany she placed him in an orphanage. He went to school in Berlin, then studied classics and philosophy, writing his doctorate thesis on *Hamlet* and going on to translate Shakespeare's sonnets. In the First World War he served in the artillery. In 1935 he emigrated to England, where he lived mainly as a language teacher. His later poems, all written in England, were published posthumously as *Die fremden Jahre* (1959). Saenger died in London in 1948. His early poems, published in 1913 and 1922, have not been reprinted. He also published a book of essays, translations of Catullus, Aesop, Empedocles, and poems from the Greek Anthology.

SWANS IN KEW GARDENS

A drizzle falls, a mist, and cools
the green embankment;
swans at the lake's edge
raise their black necks,
peal out
a magic on themselves,
a sweet clear sound, as though
intoned by glasses over wine.—
Don't think of dying.

LONDON PARK

Still the brown earth swells with frost,
but summer-like birds play
in the rosewood.

A pond in its oval rocks
the gull-white children's fleet
around the world. A boat capsizes.
Splashing in on thin legs a small god
comes to the rescue.

Missed benches spend themselves,
newly thawed, on bright grass,
grow cold under old women.

< 33 >

Versäumte Bänke spenden sich,
jung aufgetaut, am hellen Gras,
erkalten unter alten Frauen.
Die Mauerkatze gründet sich
als Monument und glotzt ins Gelbe.

< 34 >

The wall cat founds herself
as a monument, gapes into yellowness.

[Between 1935 and 1948.] 1959

< 35 >

WILHELM LEHMANN:

Geboren 1882 in Puerto Caballo, Venezuela, als Kind deutscher Eltern. Er war Soldat im ersten Weltkrieg und Kriegsgefangener in England (das er 1964 wieder besuchte) und widmete sich englischer Lyrik. In seinen Bemühungen um die Schaffung einer neuen Naturlyrik, die zugleich visionär sein und auf genauesterBeobachtung der Einzelheiten beruhen sollte, war Lehmann eng mit Oskar Loerke verbunden; viele jüngere Lyriker, von Elisabeth Langgässer, Horst Lange und Oda Schäfer zu Günter Eich und Karl Krolow, verdanken diesem Vorläufer viel. Lehmann war auch ein *hervorragender* Romanautor und Kritiker. Sein erster Roman erschien 1917. Sein erster Gedichtband *Antwort des Schweigens*, erschien erst 1935. Seinen gesammelten Gedichten *Überlebender Tag: Gedichte aus den Jahren 1951-1954* folgten *Meine Gedichtbücher (1957), Abschiedslust* (1962), *Gedichte* (1964) und *Sichtbare Zeit* (1967). Er starb 1968. Seine gesammelten Werke wurden 1962 unter dem Titel *Sämtliche Werke* in drei Bänden veröffentlicht.

FEBRUARMOND

Ich seh den Mond des Februar sich lagern
Auf reinen Himmel, türkisblauen.
In wintergelben Gräsern, magern,
Gehn Schafe, ruhen, kauen.

Dem schönsten folgt der Widder, hingerissen.
Die Wolle glänzt, gebadete Koralle.
Ich weiss das Wort, den Mond zu hissen,
Ich bin im Paradiese vor dem Falle.

LONDON (1964)

Jahrhundertespät,
Novemberkühl.
Schallplatten dreht
Chaplinischer Greis
Im Citygewühl.

Die Schallplatte verspritzt
Quäkenden Jazz.
Er knöpft die Hemdbrust
Wie Kinde den Latz.

< 36 >

WILHELM LEHMANN:

Born in 1882 in Puerto Caballo, Venezuela, of German parents. He served in the First World War and was a POW in England (which he revisited in 1964. He was devoted to English poetry). Lehmann was closely associated with Oskar Loerke in initiating a new nature poetry, at once visionary and based on minute observation of particulars; many younger poets, from Elisabeth Langgässer, Horst Lange, and Oda Schäfer to Günter Eich and Karl Krolow owed much to this precedent. Lehmann was a distinguished novelist and critic also. His first novel appeared in 1917. His first book of poems, *Antwort des Schweigens*, did not appear until 1935. His collected poems, *Überlebender Tag: Gedichte aus den Jahren 1951-1954* (1954), were followed by *Meine Gedichtbücher* (1957), *Abschiedslust* (1962), *Gedichte* (1964), and *Sichtbare Zeit* (1967). He died in 1968. His collected works were published in three volumes in 1962 under the title: *Sämtliche Werke*.

FEBRUARY MOON

I see the February moon lie down
On a pure heaven, turquoise-blue.
In winter grasses, yellow-brown,
Sheep ramble, rest and chew.

The loveliest has drawn the ram's desire.
Their fleeces glitter, sea-washed coral.
I know the word to make the moon rise higher,
I am in Paradise before the Fall.

1954: Überlebender Tag

LONDON (1964)

Centuries-late,
November-cool.
Chaplinesque old man
Makes records rotate
In the bustle and din.

The record spurts out
A bleating jazz.
He buttons his shirtfront
As children do bibs.

< 37 >

Er schiebt einen Pram,
Die Schallplatten darin.
Er gräbt nicht mehr
Nach einem Sinn.

Die Melone drückt er
Über dünnes Gesicht.
Den Kopf hält er schief,
London stört nicht.

Aus der wüsten Welt
Lande ich im Zoo:
Pagodeneule
Hält den Kopf auch so.

Aus Südostasien
Hergeweht,
Zweihändehohe
Majestät.

Einsamer Schauer
Nimmt mich hin,
Mir glänzt ein Weg,
Mich streift ein Sinn.

Sie übersieht mich,
La belle Dame sans Merci,
Ich bin der Greis,
Die Göttin sie.

< 38 >

He pushes a pram,
With the records inside.
It's long since he tried
To make sense of his life.

His lean face half-covered
With the bowler, pulled down,
His head held askew,
He confronts the town.

From the wild, waste world
I land in the Zoo:
The pagoda owl
Keeps her head tilted too.

From South-East Asia
Blown over, she:
Two hands in height
Her Majesty.

A lonely shudder
Takes hold of me here,
A path opens up,
A meaning grows clear.

She overlooks me,
La belle dame sans merci;
I am the old man,
The goddess she.

1967: *Sichtbare Zeit*

< 39 >

JOACHIM RINGELNATZ:

Geboren 1883 in Wurzen in Sachsen. Er lief aus der Schule und war jahrlang Seemann. Später arbeitete er u.a. als Zeitungsjunge, Schaufensterdekorateur, Zigarettenverkäufer, Bar-Dichter, Bibliothekar und Touristenführer. Nach dem ersten Weltkrieg, in dem er als Marineoffizier diente, verdiente er seinen Lebensunterhalt als Kabarett-Komödiant überall im deutschsprachigen Europa und rezitierte seine grotesken und satirischen Verse. Seine Lyrik ist mit ihren fast surrealistischen oder fast dadaistischen Effekten, verbunden mit lokalen Anspielungen, schwer zu übersetzen. Er lebte bis 1933 in München, zog dann nach Berlin, wo er 1934 starb. Seine gesammelten Werke wurden 1950 veröffentlicht.

REKLAME

Ich wollte von gar nichts wissen.
Da habe ich eine Reklame erblickt,
Die hat mich in die Augen gezwickt
Und ins Gedächtnis gebeissen.

Sie predigte mir von früh bis spät
Laut öffentlich wie im stillen
Von der vorzüglichen Qualitäät
Gewisser Bettnässer-Pillen.

Ich sagte: "Mag sein! Doch für mich nicht. Nein, nein.
Mein Bett und mein Gewissen sind rein.

Doch sie lief weiter hinter mir her.
Sie folgte mir bis an die Brille.
Sie kam mir aus jedem Journal in die Quer
Und säuselte: "Bettnässer-Pille."

Sie war bald rosa, bald lieblich grün.
Sie sprach in Reimen von Dichtern.
Sie fuhr in der Trambahn und kletterte kühn
Nachts auf die Dächer mit Lichtern.

Und weil sie so zähe und künstlerisch
Blieb, war ich ihr endlich zu Willen.

< 40 >

JOACHIM RINGELNATZ:

Born in 1883 in Wurzen, Saxony. He ran away from school and was a sailor for many years. Later he worked as a newsboy, window-dresser, cigarette vendor, bar-poet, librarian, and tourist guide, among other occupations. After the First World War, in which he served as a naval officer, he earned his living as a cabaret comedian all over German-speaking Europe, reciting his grotesque and satirical verse With its near-surrealist or near-dadaist effects, combined with local allusions, his poetry is hard to translate. He lived in Munich until 1933, then moved to Berlin, where he died in 1934. His collected works were published in 1950.

ADVERTISEMENT

I wanted no thrill, no surprise.
When I saw an advertisement
That clawed into my eyes
And left my memory bent.

Early and late it preached to me
In the street, within my four walls
About the excellent quality
Of certain bed-wetters' pills.

I said: "Maybe. But not for me. That's for sure.
My bed and my conscience are pure."

But it wouldn't leave me alone.
It pursued me up to my spectacles.
In every journal it made soft moan
And murmured: "Bed-wetters' pills."

Now they were pink, now an enchanting green.
They spoke in meter and rhyme.
They rode in the tram and boldly could climb
Rooftops at night, to be seen.

In the end I proved unable
To resist such dogged skills.

< 41 >

Es liegen auf meinem Frühstückstisch
Nun täglich zwei Bettnässer-Pillen.

Die isst meine Frau als "Entfettungsbonbon."
Ich habe die Frau betrogen.
Ein holder Frieden ist in den Salon
Meiner Seele eingezogen.

DON QUIJOTE

Die Winde gehen weiter
Und sind auf einmal wieder da,
Sind wütend, lau oder heiter
Dir wieder nah.

Wie jede Wolke—die gelbe,
Die graue, die vorige—wiederkehrt
Verändert, doch immer dieselbe,
Ist das nicht begrüssenswert?

Ein Schutzmann ist keine Tante.—
Frage die Wolke, frage den Wind:
Warum Bekannte
Nicht immer Freunde sind.

Es gibt so viel Bekanntes
In der Welt.—
Darum hat Cervantes
Den Don Quijote aufgestellt.

< 42 >

Each day on my breakfast table
I place two bed-wetters' pills.

As "slimming tablets" at that session
My duped wife swallows them whole.
A hallowed peace has taken possession
Of the drawingroom of my soul.

1928: Allerdings

LINES INSCRIBED IN A COPY OF *DON QUIXOTE*

The winds go on their way
And then are suddenly back again,
Are furious, mild or gay
And close to you.

How every cloud—the gray,
The yellow, the last one—returns
Changed and yet always the same—
That's good, wouldn't you say?

A policeman isn't your aunt—
Ask the cloud, ask the wind
Why an acquaintance
Isn't always a friend.

So much in this world seems
Familiar, like aunties.
That's why Don Quixote was
Set up by Cervantes.

< 43 >

ERNST STADLER:

Geboren 1883 in Colmar im Elsaß. Er studierte Englisch in Straßburg und München, ging dann als Rhodes-Stipendiat 1908 nach Oxford. 1910 war er wieder in England und schrieb eine Arbeit über Shakespeare. Zwischen 1910 und 1914 hielt er Vorlesungen an der Universität Brüssel. Er wollte gerade Verpflichtungen in Toronto wahrnehmen, als der Kreig ausbrach. Stadler stand mit dem Dichter René Schickele in Verbindung, mit dem er für eine Verbesserung der deutsch-französischen Beziehungen arbeitete und war beeinflußt von dem französischen Lyriker Francis Jammes, den er übersetzte. (Scheinbare Affinitäten zu Walt Whitman gehen vermutlich auf diesen Einfluß zurück, zusammen mit einer Vitalität, die im Deutschland dieser Zeit in der Luft lag). Trotz seiner Bindung zu Frankreich, Belgien und England rückte Stadler ein und fiel im Kampf an der Westfront im Oktober 1914. 1905 hatte er einen Band mit frühen Gedichten veröffentlicht. Seine spätere Sammlung *Der Aufbruch* erschien in seinem Todesjahr. 1955 wurden in zwei Bänden die gesammelten Gedichte, Übersetzungen, Essays und Briefe veröffentlicht.

[handschriftlich: Spontan, aber auch etwas Gebautes]

FÄHRT ÜBER DIE KÖLNER RHEINBRÜCKE BEI NACHT *[handschriftlich: ein innerer Rhythmus]*

Der Schnellzug tastet sich und stösst die Dunkelheit entlang. *[handschriftlich: vermenschlicht]*

Kein Stern will vor. Die ganze Welt ist nur ein enger,
    nachtumschienter Minengang, *[handschriftlich: alles dunkel · düstere Stimmung]*

Darein zuweilen Förderstellen blauen Lichtes jähe Horizonte
    reissen: Feuerkreis

Von Kugellampen, Dächern, Schloten, dampfend,
    strömend . . . nur sekundenweis . . .

Und wieder alles schwarz. Als führen wir ins Eingeweid der
    Nacht zur Schicht. *[handschriftlich: Fahrt ins Innere]*

Nun taumeln Lichter her . . . verirrt, trostlos verein-
    samt . . . mehr . . . und sammeln sich . . . und werden
    dicht. *[handschriftlich: Vermenschlichung]*

[handschriftlich am Rand: Großstadt]

Gerippe grauer Häuserfronten liegen bloss, im Zwielicht
    bleichend, tot—etwas muss kommen . . . oh, ich fühl es
    schwer *[handschriftlich: kann nicht so bleiben · prophetisches Gefühl]*

Im Hirn. Eine Beklemmung singt im Blut. Dann dröhnt der
    Boden plötzlich wie ein Meer:

[handschriftlich am Rand: Aufbruch / Exaltation]

Wir fliegen, aufgehoben, königlich durch nachtentrissne Luft,

[handschriftlich: Begeisterung - Lebensbejahung]

< 44 >

ERNST STADLER:

Born in Colmar, Alsace, in 1883. He studied English at Strasbourg and Munich, then went as a Rhodes Scholar to Oxford in 1908. In 1910 he was again in England, writing a thesis on Shakespeare. He lectured at Brussels University between 1910 and 1914. He was about to take up an appointment in Toronto when the war broke out. Stadler had been associated with the poet René Schickele in working for better German-French relationships, and was himself influenced by the French poet Francis Jammes, whom he translated. (Seeming affinities with Whitman are probably due to this influence, together with a vitalism that was in the air in Germany at this period.) Despite his attachment to France, Belgium, and England, Stadler joined up, and was killed in action on the Western Front in October, 1914. He had published a book of early poems in 1905. His later collection, *Der Aufbruch,* appeared in the year of his death. His collected poems, translations, essays, and letters were published in two volumes in 1955.

ON CROSSING THE RHINE BRIDGE
AT COLOGNE BY NIGHT

The express train gropes and thrusts its way through darkness.
    Not a star is out.
The whole world's nothing but a mine-road the night has railed
    about
In which at times conveyors of blue light tear sudden horizons:
    fiery sphere
Of arc-lamps, roofs and chimneys, steaming, streaming—for
    seconds only clear,
And all is black again. As though we drove into Night's en-
    trails to the seam.
Now lights reel into view . . . astray, disconsolate and lone-
    ly . . . more . . . and gather . . . and densely gleam.
Skeletons of gray housefronts are laid bare, grow pale in the
    twilight, dead—something must happen . . . O heavily
I feel it weigh on my brain. An oppression sings in the blood.
    Then all at once the ground resounds like the sea:
All royally upborne we fly through air from darkness wrested,
    high up above the river. O curve of the million lights,
    mute guard at the sight

< 45 >

hoch übern Strom. O Biegung der Millionen Lichter,
    stumme Wacht,
Vor deren blitzender Parade schwer die Wasser abwärts rollen.
    Endloses Spalier, zum Gruss gestellt bei Nacht!
Wie Fackeln stürmend! Freudiges! Salut von Schiffen über
    blauer See! Bestirntes Fest!
Wimmelnd, mit hellen Augen hingedrängt! Bis wo die Stadt
    mit letzten Häusern ihren Gast entlässt.
Und dann die langen Einsamkeiten. Nackte Ufer. Stille. Nacht.
    Besinnung. Einkehr. Kommunion. Und Glut und Drang
Zum Letzten, Segnenden. Zum Zeugungsfest. Zur Wollust.
    Zum Gebet! Zum Meer. Zum Untergang.

[handwritten left margin: Nach (Extase) Exaltation → Besinnung → Aufbruch]

[handwritten right margin: Nirwana ?? / Niveau ↓ / Gegensatz / expressionistische Sprache]

[handwritten: Auflösung im All des Lebens]

KINDER VOR EINEM
LONDONER ARMENSPEISEHAUS

Ich sah Kinder in langem Zug, paarweis geordnet,
    vor einem Armenspeisehaus stehen.
Sie warteten, wortkarg und müde,
    bis die Reihe an sie käme, zur Abendmahlzeit zu gehen.
Sie waren verdreckt und zerlumpt und drückten sich
    an die Häuserwände.
Kleine Mädchen pressten um blasse Säuglinge
    die versagenden Hände.

Sie standen hungrig und verschüchtert
    zwischen den aufgehenden Lichtern,
Manche trugen dunkle Mäler
    auf den schmächtigen Gesichtern.
Ihr Anzug roch nach Keller, lichtscheuen Stuben,
    Schelten und Darben,
Ihre Körper trugen von Entbehrung
    und früher Arbeitsfrohn die Narben.

Sie warteten: gleich wären die andern fertig,
    dann würde man sie in den grossen Saal treten lassen,
Ihnen Brot und Gemüse vorsetzen und die Abendsuppe
    in den blechernen Tassen.

< 46 >

Of whose flashing parade the waters go roaring down. Endless
    line presenting arms by night!
Surging on like torches! Joyful! Salute of ships over the blue
    sea! Star-jewelled, festive array!
Teeming, bright-eyes urged on! Till where the town with its
    last houses sees its guests away.
And then the long solitudes. Bare banks. And silence. Night.
    Reflection. Self-questioning. Communion. And ardour
    outward-flowing
To the end that blesses. To conception's rite. To pleasure's
    consummation. To prayer. To the sea. To self's undoing.

1913: Die Aktion

CHILDREN IN FRONT OF A LONDON SOUP KITCHEN

I saw children, a long line of them, arranged in pairs, stand in
    front of the building where the poor are fed.
They waited, untalkative, weary, for their turn at the nightly
    spread.
They were dirty and in rags, squeezed up against housefront
    and railing.
Little girls around pale babies cupped hands that were failing.

Hungry, intimidated they stood among lamps being lighted,
Many with delicate faces by marks and dark bruises blighted.
Their clothing smelled of basements, ill-lit rooms, of scolding
    and poverty,
Their bodies were scarred by deprivation and premature
    drudgery.

They waited: soon the others would be through, they'd be ad-
    mitted to the hall,
Served with bread and vegetables, the soup in tin cups and all.
Oh, and then they'd grow sleepy and their twisted limbs would
    be untied
And night and good sleep would bring them to rocking-horses,

< 47 >

Oh, und dann würde Müdigkeit kommen und ihre
   verkrümmten Glieder aufschnüren,
Und Nacht und guter Schlaf sie zu Schaukelpferden
   und Zinnsoldaten
   und in wundersame Puppenstuben führen.

< 48 >

toy soldiers, the rooms of marvelous dolls' houses open wide.

1914: Der Aufbruch

OSKAR LOERKE:

Geboren 1884 in Junhen in Westpreußen. Er zog 1903 nach Berlin, wo er als Lektor für den S. Fischer Verlag arbeitete. Er schrieb Romane, Erzählungen, Essays, Tagebücher, Studien über seine Lieblingskomponisten Bach und Bruckner und sieben Gedichtbände, die zu seinen Lebzeiten veröffentlicht wurden. Seine ausführliche Beschäftigung mit der Natur als einem Speicher zeitloser Archtypen hinderte weder ihn noch seinen Freund Wilhelm Lehmann am Schreiben spezifisch städtischer Lyrik. Loerke war Sekretär der Sektion Literatur der Preußischen Akademie der Künste, trat aber 1933 nach der Machtübernahme der Nazis zurück und zog sich bis zu seinem Tod in Berlin 1941 ins Privatleben zurück. 1958 erschienen seine gesammelten Gedichte und ausgewählte Prosa in zwei Bänden. Seine Tagebücher von 1903 bis 1939 erschienen 1955, ein getrennter Band mit Reisetagebüchern 1960 bis 1939 erschienen 1955, ein getrennter Band sgewählter Gedichte, wurde 1970 veröffentlicht, gefolgt von einem Band Kurzgeschichten, *Chimärenreiter* (1973).

AUS AM RANDE DER GROSSEN STADT

GELEIT

Soll denn die Fremde schon beginnen,
Wo der eiserne Schwung der Maschinen
Nicht schwingt?
Und bleibt das Licht denn ewig drinnen
An seinem glühenden Draht?
Wer will der Glaskugel anbetend dienen?
Wohin das Götzenlicht nicht dringt,
Auch dort grünt Saat.

DRUNTEN

Die Unterwelt wächst in die Ohren.
Am Radio durch Europa geht
Der Zeiger nach einem Trostgebet.
In einem Berg Vergangenheit verloren
Gregorianische Litanei.
Bei gelbem Wachsschein füllt die Stollen
Gepresster Chorklang, Orgelrollen.
Die Lava dröhnt, bald kracht sie frei.

< 50 >

OSKAR LOERKE:

Born in 1884 in Jungen, West Prussia, he moved to Berlin in 1903, where he worked as a reader for the S. Fischer Verlag. He wrote novels, stories, essays, and diaries, and studies of his favorite composers Bach and Bruckner, as well as the seven books of poems published in his lifetime. His preoccupation with nature as a repository of timeless archetypes did not prevent him (or his friend Wilhelm Lehmann) from writing specifically urban poetry. Loerke was Secretary to the literature section of the Prussian Academy of Arts, but he resigned in 1933 after the Nazi take-over, retiring into private life until his death in Berlin in 1941. His collected poems and selected prose appeared in two volumes in 1958. His diaries 1903-1939 appeared in 1955, and a separate volume of travel diaries in 1960. *Die weite Fahrt*, a collection of selected poems, was published in 1970, followed by a volume of short stories: *Chimärenreiter* (1973).

AT THE EDGE OF THE GREAT CITY

ENVOI

Must it be so? Should foreignness begin
Where the iron thrust of machines
Does not thrust?
And does light, then, for ever remain within
Its filament that glows?
Who wants to serve and adore the sphere of glass?
Where the idolatrous light does not pass
There, too, seed grows.

DOWN THERE

The underworld spreads in our ears.
On the radio through all of Europe runs
The pointer, after a solacing prayer.
Lost in a mountain of time past,
Gregorian litany.
By yellow waxlight the galleries fill
With compressed choral song, with organ swell.
The lava roars, soon will crack free.

< 51 >

Und Weihnacht ist? Es war, als sei
Mariä Kind noch nicht geboren.

GENESUNGSHEIM

Was schlug man diesen zum Krüppel?
Er dachte hinter der Stirn:
Da öffnete ihm der Knüppel
Den Schädel, und Hirn war nur Hirn.

Warum haben Jauche-Humpen
Dort jenen die Augen verbrannt?
Sie haben einen Lumpen
Einen Lumpen genannt.

Warum schweigt dieser in Knebel?
Weil sein Gewissen schrie!
Wes Kopf sprang zum Reiche der Nebel?
Dessen Gurgel vor Ekel spie!

BERLINER WINTERABEND

Häuser, trübe Tafeln, beschmiert mit brennender Schrift,
Die zuckend ruft und bettelnd beteuert.
Sterne sind in Wolken auf der Trift,
Der blaue Lein des Sommers ist längst eingescheuert.

Nackte Bäume wie Besen der Arbeitslosen.
Daruber streut der freie Wind.
Ein Hauch von Süden macht das Auge blind:
Weit reicht der Dufthof der Mimosen.

< 52 >

Today is Christmas? It seemed as though
The child of Mary had not yet been born.

CONVALESCENT HOME

Why was this man crippled with blows?
He thought behind his brow:
So the cudgel opened up
His skull, and brain was only brain.

Why did pint-mugs of hogwash
Burn those men's eyes?
Confronted with a knave
They called him a knave.

Why does this one keep silent, gagged?
Because his conscience yelled!
Whose head leapt to realms befogged?
His whose gullet retched with disgust.

WINTER EVENING, BERLIN

Houses, dim boards, daubed with a searing script
That twitching calls out and begging affirms.
Stars are at pasture in clouds,
Summer's blue flax was garnered long ago.

Naked trees like brooms of the unemployed.
Above them tramps the free wind.
A breath from the south makes the eye go blind:
Very far the fragrance range of mimosa extends.

1934: Der Silberdistelwald

< 53 >

GOTTFRIED BENN:

Geboren 1886 in Mansfeld, Preussen. Er studierte Medizin und diente
während des ersten Weltkrieges als Arzt beim deutschen Heer-Seine
erste Gedichtsammlung, *Morgue* (1912) zeigte eine heftige Reaktion
auf seine klinische Erfahrung. Eine noch drastischere Antwort darauf
bildete der Band mit Grzählungen *Gehirne* (1916) und eine
Gedichtsammlung mit dem Titel Titel *Fleisch* (1917)—Werke, die zu
dem, was er "absolute" Lyrik nannte, und zu einem anti-historischen
und anti-realistischen Standpunkt führten. Obwohl man ihn als Expressionisten ansah, blieb er weitab von den humanistischen und vorwiegend linksorientierten Bestrebungen dieser Bewegung. Seine
kurzlebige Unterstützung der Nazi-Bewegung endete ein Jahr nach
ihrem Beginn (1933), und bald fiel er in Ungnade, als er weiterhin das
verfocht, was vom Regime als "entartete Kunst" verdammt worden
war. 1935 entschloß er sich zur Rückkehr ins Medizinische Corps—
ein Schritt, den er als "die aristokratische Form der Emigration" bes-
chrieb. Nach dem Krieg war sein Werk von den Alliierten zwar verboten, drang aber über die Schweiz wieder in den Vordergrund und ließ
Benn als den hervorragendsten und einflußreichsten deutschen Lyriker
des ersten Nachkriegs jahrzehnts hervortreten. Er praktizierte dann
wieder als Arzt in Berlin, wo er 1956 starb. Die endgültige Ausgabe
seiner gesammelten Werke (Gedichte, phantasievolle und kritische
Prosa, Stücke und Dialoge) erschien 1960 in 4 Bänden, herausgegeben
von Dieter Wellershoff. Eine Auswahl in englischer Übersetzung,
Primal Vision, wurde 1958 veröffentlicht.

KARYATIDE

Entrücke dich dem Stein! Zerbirst
die Höhle, die dich knechtet! Rausche
doch in die Flur! Verhöhne die Gesimse—
sieh: Durch den Bart des trunkenen Silen
aus seinem ewig überrauschten
lauten einmaligen durchdröhnten Blut
träuft Wein in seine Scham!

Bespei die Säulensucht: toderschlagene
greisige Hände bebten sie
verhangenen Himmeln zu. Stürze
die Tempel vor die Sehnsucht deines Knies,
in dem der Tanz begehrt!

< 54 >

GOTTFRIED BENN:

Born 1886 in Mansfeld, Prussia. He studied medicine and served as a physician with the German army during the First World War. His first collection of poems, *Morgue* (1912), showed a violent reaction to his clinical experience. An even more drastic response to it, leading to his practice of what he called "absolute" poetry, and an antihistorical antirealistic stance, was the book of stories *Gehirne* (1916), and a collection of poems entitled *Fleisch* (1917). Although regarded as an Expressionist, he remained aloof from the humanistic and predominantly left-wing aspirations of the movement. His short-lived support of the Nazi movement ended one year after it began (1933) and he soon fell into disfavor when he continued to advocate what had been condemned by the regime as "degenerate art." In 1935 he chose to rejoin the Medical Crops, describing that step as "the aristocratic form of emigration." After the war his work was banned by the Allies, but gradually re-emerged via Switzerland, to establish Benn as the most distinguished and influential German poet of the first postwar decade. He returned to practice medicine in Berlin, where he died in 1956. The definitive edition of his collected works, consisting of poems, imaginative and critical prose, plays and dialogues, appeared in four volumes between 1959 and 1960, edited by Dieter Wellershoff. A selection in English translation, *Primal Vision*, was published in 1958.

CARYATID

Leave stone behind, rise higher! Burst
the socket that enslaves you! Rush
into fields and roar! Deride the cornices—
Look at the drunk Silenus: through his beard
from his loud blood for ever drowned in roars,
shivered by alien music and unique,
wine drips into his sex!

Spit on this column mania: done to death
mere senile hands they trembled
toward cloud-covered heavens. Tear down
the temples to the longing of your knee
which prisoned dance desires!

Spread out your limbs, O bloom to death and bleed
your gentle bed away through gaping wounds:

< 55 >

Breite dich hin, zerblühe dich, oh, blute
dein weiches Beet aus grossen Wunden hin:
Sieh, Venus mit den Tauben gürtet
sich Rosen um der Hüften Liebestor—
sieh dieses Sommers letzten blauen Hauch
auf Astermeeren an die fernen
baumbraunen Ufer treiben; tagen
sieh diese letzte Glück-Lügenstunde
unserer Südlichkeit
hochgewölbt.

NACHTCAFÉ

824: Der Frauen Liebe und Leben.
Das Cello trinkt rasch mal. Die Flöte
rülpst tief drei Takte lang: das schöne Abendbrot.
Die Trommel liest den Kriminalroman zu Ende.

Grüne Zähne, Pickel im Gesicht
winkt einer Lidrandentzündung.

Fett im Haar
spricht zu offenem Mund mit Rachenmandel
Glaube Liebe Hoffnung um den Hals.

Junger Kropf ist Sattelnase gut.
Er bezahlt für sie drei Biere.

Bartflechte kauft Nelken,
Doppelkinn zu erweichen.

B-moll: die 35. Sonate.
Zwei Augen brüllen auf:
Spritzt nicht das Blut von Chopin in den Saal,
damit das Pack drauf rumlatscht!
Schluss! He, Gigi!—

< 56 >

Look, Venus with her doves is twining
roses around the love-gate of her hips—
Look how the summer's last and hazy blue
drifts over seas of asters to the far
fall foliage coloured shores: and look:
now dawns the last glad lying hour
of our southernness,
vaulted high.

1916: *Die Weissen Blätter*

NIGHT CAFÉ

824: The Loves and Lives of Women.
The 'cello has a quick drink. The flute
belches three beats long: his tasty evening snack.
The drum reads on to the end of the thriller.

Green teeth, pimples on his face,
waves to conjunctivitis.

Grease in his hair
talks to open mouth with swollen tonsils,
faith hope and charity round his neck.

Young goiter is sweet on saddle-nose.
He stands her three half-pints.

Sycosis buys carnations
to mollify double chin.

B flat minor: Sonata op. 35.
A pair of eyes roars out:
Don't splash the blood of Chopin all over this place
for this lot to slouch about in!
Hey, Gigi! Stop!

< 57 >

Die Tür fliesst hin: ein Weib.
Wüste ausgedörrt. Kanaanitisch braun.
Keusch. Höhlenreich. Ein Duft kommt mit. Kaum Duft.
Es ist nur eine süsse Vorwölbung der Luft
gegen mein Gehirn.

Eine Fettleibigkeit trippelt hinterher.

IKARUS

O Mittag, der mit heissem Heu mein Hirn
zu Wiese, flachem Land und Hirten schwächt,
dass ich hinrinne und, den Arm im Bach,
den Mohn an meine Schläfe ziehe—
o du Weithingewölbter, enthirne doch
stillflügelnd über Fluch und Gram
des Werdens und Geschehns
mein Auge.
Noch durch Geröll der Halde, noch durch Land-aas,
verstaubendes, durch bettelhaft Gezack
der Felsen—überall
das tiefe Mutterblut, die strömende
entstirnte
matte
Getragenheit.

Das Tier lebt Tag um Tag
und hat an seinem Euter kein Erinnern,
der Hang schweigt seine Blume in das Licht
und wird zerstört.

Nur ich, mit Wächter zwischen Blut und Pranke,
ein hirnzerfressenes Aas, mit Flüchen
im Nichts zergellend, bespien mit Worten,
veräfft vom Licht—
o du Weithingewölbter,

< 58 >

The door dissolves: a woman.
Desert dried out. Canaanite brown.
Chaste. Full of caves. A scent comes with her. Hardly scent.
It's only a sweet leaning forward of the air
against my brain.

A paunched obesity waddles after her.

1917: *Fleisch*

ICARUS

I

O noon that with hot hay reduce
my brain to meadow, shepherds and flat land,
so that I flow away, my arm immersed
in the stream's water, and to my brow
draw down the poppies—noon that's vaulted wide,
now mutely winging above the curse and grief
of all that is and will be,
unbrain my eye.
Still through the hillside boulders, still through land-carrion,
turning to dust, through beggarly sharp shapes
of rocks—still everywhere
deep mother-blood, this streaming
deforeheaded
weary
drifting away.

The animal lives only for the day
and in its udder has no memory,
the slope in silence brings its flower to light
and is destroyed.

I only, with a sentry between blood and claw,
mere brain-devoured carrion, shrieking and cursing plunged
into annihilation, bespat with words,
guyed by the light—

< 59 >

träuf meinen Augen eine Stunde
des guten frühen Voraugenlichts—
schmilz hin den Trug der Farben, schwinge
die kotbedrängten Höhlen in das Rauschen
gebäumter Sonnen, Sturz der Sonnen-sonnen,
o aller Sonnen ewiges Gefälle—

II

Das Hirn frisst Staub. Die Füsse fressen Staub.
Wäre das Auge rund und abgeschlossen,
dann bräche durch die Lider süsse Nacht,
Gebüsch und Liebe.
Aus dir, du süsses Tierisches,
aus euern Schatten, Schlaf und Haar,
muss ich mein Hirn besteigen,
alle Windungen,
das letzte Zwiegespräch—

III

So sehr am Strand, so sehr schon in der Barke,
im krokosfarbnen Kleide der Geweihten
und um die Glieder schon den leichten Flaum—
ausrauschst du aus den Falten, Sonne,
allnächtlich Welten in den Raum—
o eine der vergesslich hingesprühten
mit junger Glut die Schläfe mir zerschmelzend,
auftrinkend das entstirnte Blut—

UNTERGRUNDBAHN

Die weichen Schauer. Blütenfrühe. Wie
aus warmen Fellen kommt es aus den Wäldern.
Ein Rot schwärmt auf. Das grosse Blut steigt an.

Durch all den Frühling kommt die fremde Frau.
Der Strumpf am Spann ist da. Doch, wo er endet,

< 60 >

O noon that's vaulted wide,
but for one hour infuse my eyes
with that good light which was before eyes were—
melt down the lie of colours, hurl
these cavities pressed by filth into the roar
of rearing suns, whirl of the sun of suns,
O everlasting fall of all the suns—

II

The brain eats dust. Our feet devour the dust.
If but the eye were round and self-contained
then through the lids sweet night would enter in,
brushwood and love.
From you, the sweetly bestial,
from out your shadows, sleep and hair,
I must bestride my brain,
all loops and turns,
the ultimate duologue—

III

So near the beach, so much embarked already,
dressed in the victim's crocus-coloured garment,
and round your limbs the light and delicate down—
O sun, you rustle forth from out your folds
each night new universes into space—
O, one of these, obliviously scattered here
with its young glow is melting down my temples,
drinks my deforeheaded blood.

[c. 1920]; 1922: Gesammelte Schriften

SUBWAY TRAIN

Lascivious shivers. Early bloom. As if
from warm furred skins it wafted from the woods.
A red swarms up. The great strong blood ascends.

< 61 >

ist weit von mir. Ich schluchze auf der Schwelle:
laues Geblühe, fremde Feuchtigkeiten.

Oh, wie ihr Mund die laue Luft verprasst!
Du Rosenhirn, Meer-Blut, du Götter-Zwielicht,
du Erdenbeet, wie strömen deine Hüften
so kühl den Gang hervor, in dem du gehst!

Dunkel: Nun lebt es unter ihren Kleidern:
nur weisses Tier, gelöst und stummer Duft.

Ein armer Hirnhund, schwer mit Gott behangen.
Ich bin der Stirn so satt. Oh, ein Gerüste
von Blütenkolben löste sanft sie ab
und schwölle mit und schauerte und triefte.

So losgelöst. So müde. Ich will wandern.
Blutlos die Wege. Lieder aus den Gärten.
Schatten und Sintflut. Fernes Glück: ein Sterben
hin in des Meeres erlösend tiefes Blau.

PALAU

"Rot ist der Abend auf der Insel von Palau
und die Schatten sinken—"
singe, auch aus den Kelchen der Frau
lässt es sich trinken,
Totenvögel schrein
und die Totenuhren
pochen, bald wird es sein
Nacht und Lemuren.

Heisse Riffe. Aus Eukalypten geht
Tropik und Palmung,
was sich noch hält und steht,
will auch Zermalmung
bis in das Gliederlos,

< 62 >

Through all of spring the alien woman walks.
The stocking's foot is there. But where it ends
is far from me. I sob upon the threshold:
sultry luxuriance, alien moistures teeming.

O how her mouth squanders the sultry air!
You brain of roses, sea-blood, goddess-twilight,
you bed of earth, how coolly from your hips
your stride flows out, the glide that is your walking.

Dark: underneath her garments now it lives:
white animal only, loosed, and silent scent.

A wretched braindog, laden down with God.
My forehead wearies me. O that a frame
of clustered blooms would gently take its place,
to swell in unison and stream and shudder.

So lax, adrift. So tired. I long to wander.
The ways all bloodless. Songs that blow from gardens.
Shadows and Flood. Far joys: a languid dying
down into ocean's deep redeeming blue.

1922: Gesammelte Schriften

PALAU

"Evening is red on the island of Palau
and the shadows sink—"
sing, from woman's chalices too
it is good to drink,
deathly the little owls cry
and the death-watch ticks out,
very soon it will be
Lemurs and night.

Hot these reefs. From eucalypti there flows
a tropical palm concoction,

< 63 >

bis in die Leere,
tief in den Schöpfungsschoss
dämmernder Meere.

Rot ist der Abend auf der Insel von Palau
und im Schattenschimmer
hebt sich steigend aus Dämmer und Tau:
"niemals und immer,"   → Kreislauf
alle Tode der Welt
sind Fähren und Furten,   → übergang
und von Fremdem umstellt   wir
auch deine Geburten—

Einmal mit Opferfett
auf dem Piniengerüste
tragt sich dein Flammenbett
wie Wein zur Küste,   → Weg zum Meer
Megalithen zuhauf
und die Gräber und Hallen,
Kammer des Thor im Lauf
zu den Asen zerfallen—

Wie die Götter vergehn
und die grossen Cäsaren,
von der Wange des Zeus
emporgefahren—
singe, wandert die Welt   Tod!!
schon in fremdestem Schwunge,
schmeckt uns das Charonsgeld
längst unter der Zunge.

Paarung. Dein Meer belebt
Sepien, Korallen,
was sich noch hält und hebt,
will auch zerfallen,
rot ist der Abend auf der Insel von Palau,
Eukalyptenschimmer

< 64 >

all that still holds and stays
also longs for destruction
down to the limbless stage,
down to the vacuum,
back to the primal age,
dark ocean's womb.

Evening is red on the island of Palau,
in the gleam of these shadows
there issues rising from twilight and dew:
"Never and Always,"
all the deaths of the earth
are fords and ferries,
what to you owes its birth
surrounded with strangeness—

Once with sacrificial
fat on the pinewood floor
your bed of flames would travel
like wine to the shore,
megaliths heaped around
and the graves and the halls,
hammer of Thor that's bound
for the Aesir, crumbled, falls—

As the gods surcease,
the great Caesars decline,
from the cheek of Zeus
once raised up to reign—
sing, already the world
to the strangest rhythm is swung,
Charon's coin if not curled
long tasted under the tongue.

Coupling. Sepias your seas
and coral animate,
all that still holds and sways

< 65 >

hebt in Runen aus Dämmer und Tau:
niemals und immer.

NACHZEICHNUNG

I

O jene Jahre! Der Morgen grünes Licht,
auch die noch nicht gefegten Lusttrottoire—
der Sommer schrie von Ebenen in der Stadt
und sog an einem Horn,
das sich von oben füllte.

Lautlose Stunde. Wässrige Farben
eines hellgrünen Aug's verdünnten Strahls,
Bilder aus diesem Zaubergrün, gläserne Reigen:
Hirten und Weiher, eine Kuppel, Tauben—
gewoben und gesandt, erglänzt, erklungen—,
verwandelbare Wolken eines Glücks!

So standest du vor Tag: die Spring-
brunnen noch ohne Perlen, tatenlos
Gebautes und die Steige; die Häuser
verschlossen, du *erschufst*
den Morgen, jasminene Frühe,
sein Jauchzen, uranfänglich
sein Strahl—noch ohne Ende—o jene Jahre!

Ein Unauslöschliches im Herzen,
Ergänzungen vom Himmel und der Erde;
Zuströmendes aus Schilf und Gärten,
Gewitter abends
tränkten die Dolden ehern,
die barsten dunkel, gespannt von ihren Seimen;
und Meer und Strände,
bewimpelte mit Zelten,
glühenden Sandes trächtig,

< 66 >

also longs to disintegrate,
evening is red on the island of Palau,
eucalyptus glaze
raises in runes from twilight and dew:
Never and Always.

1924: Schutt

RETROSPECTIVE SKETCH

I

O the green light, the mornings of those years,
the pleasure pavements before the sweepers came—
the summer cried of plains within the city
and sucked a horn of plenty
replenished from above.

Hour without sound. Watery colours
of a pale-green eye's diluted ray,
images out of this magical green, dances in glass:
shepherds and ponds, a cupola, pigeons—
woven and vouchsafed, flashed out or intuned—
mutable clouds of a happiness!

So you stood before daybreak: the fountains
still without pearls, constructions
raised without effort, the stairways; the houses
still locked, it was you that *created*
the morning, syringa time of the day,
its jubilation, pristine
its beam—without end as yet—O those years!

A sense of inextinguishable things,
completions of heaven and earth;
encroachments from reeds and gardens,
thunderstorms nightly
watered the umbels to brass
that darkly burst, held taut by their sap;

< 67 >

bräunende Wochen, gerbend alles
zu Fell für Küsse, die niedergingen
achtlos und schnell verflogen
wie Wolkenbrüche!

Darüber hing die Schwere
auch jetzt—doch Trauben
aus ihr,

die Zweige niederziehend und wieder hochlassend,
nur einige Beeren,
wenn du mochtest,
erst—

noch nicht so drängend und überhangen
von kolbengrossen Fruchtfladen,
altem schwerem Traubenfleisch—

O jene Jahre!

II

Dunkle Tage des Frühlings,
nicht weichender Dämmer um Laub;
Fliederblüte gebeugt, kaum hochblickend
narzissenfarben und starken Todesgeruchs,
Glückausfälle,
sieglose Trauer des Unerfüllten.

Und in den Regen hinein,
der auf das Laub fällt,
höre ich ein altes Wälderlied,
von Wäldern, die ich einst durchfuhr
und wiedersah, doch ich ging nicht
in die Halle, wo das Lied erklungen war,
die Tasten schwiegen längst,
die Hände ruhten irgendwo,

< 68 >

and sea and beaches
with their streamers, their tents,
pregnant with glowing sand,
sunburning weeks tanning all
to fur for kisses that descended
heedless and briefly felt
as summer cloudbursts.

Over it all hung the sadness
even then—but grapes
out of it,

dragging the tendrils down and releasing them,
only a berry or two
when you wanted it,
then—
not yet so urgent and overhung
with bunches of fruit as big as clubs,
heavy old grapeflesh—

O those years!

II

Dark days of spring,
halflight clinging to foliage;
lilac blossom that dropped, hardly glancing upward
narcissus-coloured and strongly scented with death,
cessations of gladness,
unavailing gloom of the unfulfilled.

And into the rain
that falls on leaves
I hear an old woodland song
about woods I once drove through
and revisited, but I did not go
to the hall where the song had sounded,

< 69 >

gelöst von jenen Armen, die mich hielten,
zu Tränen rührten,
Hände aus den Oststeppen,
blutig zertretenen längst—
nur noch ihr Wälderlied
in den Regen hinein
an dunklen Tagen des Frühlings
den ewigen Steppen zu.

IDEELLES WEITERLEBEN?

Bald
ein abgesägter, überholter
früh oder auch spät verstorbener Mann,
von dem man spricht wie von einer Sängerin
mit ausgesungenem Sopran
oder vom kleinen Hölty mit seinen paar Versen—
noch weniger: Durchschnitt,
nie geflogen,
keinen Borgward gefahren—
Zehnpfennigstücke für die Tram,
im Höchstfall Umsteiger.

Dabei ging täglich so viel bei dir durch
introvertiert, extrovertiert,
Nahrungssorgen, Ehewidrigkeit, Steuermoral—
mit allem musstest du dich befassen,
ein gerüttelt Mass von Leben in mancherlei Gestalt.

Auf einer Karte aus Antibes,
die ich heute erhielt,
ragt eine Burg in die Méditerranée,
eine fanatische Sache:
südlich, meerisch, schneeig, am Rande hochgebirgig—
Jahrhunderte, dramatisiert,
ragen, ruhen, glänzen, firnen, strotzen
sich in die Aufnahme—

< 70 >

the keyboard had long been still,
the hands were resting somewhere,
detached from those arms that held me,
moved me to tears,
hands out of the Eastern steppes,
long ago bloodily trampled—
only her woodland song
into the rain
in the dark days of spring
toward the undying steppes.

[1937-47]; 1948: *Statische Gedichte*

IDEAL SURVIVAL?

Soon
a sawn-off, out-of-date
man who died early or maybe late,
of whom one speaks as of a singer
whose soprano is worn out
or of poor little Todhunter and his handful of verses—
even less: average,
never flew in a plane,
never drove a Borgward—
pennies paid out on the tram,
a return fare at the most.

Yet daily so much passed through you
introverted, extraverted,
money troubles, marriage vexations, tax morality—
with all these you had to concern yourself,
a full measure of life in many a shape.

On a postcard from Antibes
which I received today
a castle looms over la Méditerranée,
a fanatical thing, that:
southerly, snowy, marine, alpine at the edges—
centuries, dramatized,

< 71 >

Nichts von alledem bei dir,
keine Ingredienzien zu einer Ansichtskarte—
Zehnpfennigstücke für die Tram,
Umsteiger,
und schnell die obenerwähnte Wortprägung:
überholt.

< 72 >

loom, rest, gleam, glaze, swell
into the photograph—
Nothing of all this about you,
no ingredients at all for a picture postcard—
pennies paid out on the tram,
return tickets,
and quickly then the above-named caption:
out of date.

1951

GEORG TRAKL:

Geboren 1887 in Salzburg als Kind protestantischer Eltern. Er blieb in der Schule zurück und entschloß sich zu einer Ausbildung als Apotheker, zunächst von 1905-1908 in Salzburg, dann in Wien. Zwei seiner frühen Stücke wurden in Salzburg aufgeführt. Nach einem Jahr im medizinischen Corps der österreichischen Armee erwog er die Auswanderung nach Borneo. 1912 fand er jedoch einen Gönner und Verleger in Ludwig von Flicker, dem Herausgeber der Zeitschrift *Der Brenner*. Er erhielt auch eine Summe, die der Philosoph Ludwig Wittgenstein gespendet hatte, und teilte sie mit Rilke, der Trakls Lyrik bewunderte. Zwei Sammlungen seiner Gedichte erschienen zu seinen Lebzeiten. Von 1913 bis Kriegsausbruch lebte er vorwiegend Innsbruck, wo Flicker seine Zeitschrift herausgab. Als er dessen Schwester, eine Pianistin, in Berlin besuchte, traf er Else Lasker-Schüler. Seine außergewöhnliche Melancholie trieb ihn zu Drogen und Alkohol. Im August 1914 wurde er als Leutnant im medizinischen Corps nach Galizien beordert; nach der Schlacht von Grodek, auf die sich eins seiner letzten Gedichte bezieht, war Trakl verantwortlich für neunzig Schwerverwundete, denen er kaum helfen konnte, und erlitt einen Nervenzusammenbruch. Er wurde zusammen mit einem anderen Offizier, der an Delirium tremens litt, in eine Beobachtungszelle in Cracow gebracht und starb dort im November 1914 an einer Überdosis Kokain. Trakls Lyrik wurde innerhalb und außerhalb der deutschsprachigen Länder viel gelesen. Verschiedene Auswahlen erschienen in englischer Sprache. 1969 wurde eine kritische Werkausgabe mit Varianten und Lesarten unter dem Titel *Dichtungen und Briefe* veröffentlicht.

DE PROFUNDIS

Es ist ein Stoppelfeld, in das ein schwarzer Regen fällt.
Es ist ein brauner Baum, der einsam dasteht.
Es ist ein Zischelwind, der leere Hütten umkreist—
Wie traurig dieser Abend.

Am Weiler vorbei
Sammelt die sanfte Waise noch spärliche Ähren ein.
Ihre Augen weiden rund und goldig in der Dämmerung
Und ihr Schoss harrt des himmlischen Bräutigams.

Bei der Heimkehr
Fanden die Hirten den süssen Leib
Verwest im Dornenbusch.

< 74 >

GEORG TRAKL:

Born in 1887 in Salzburg, the son of Protestant parents. He was backward at school, and decided to train as a dispensing chemist, first at Salzburg, 1905-1908, then in Vienna. He had two early plays performed in Salzburg. After a year in the medical corps of the Austrian army, he considered emigrating to Borneo, but in 1912 he found a patron and publisher in Ludwig von Ficker, editor of the periodical *Der Brenner*. He also received a sum of money given away by Ludwig Wittgenstein, the philosopher, sharing it with Rilke, who admired Trakl's poetry. Two collections of his poems appeared in his lifetime. From 1913 to the outbreak of war he lived mainly in Innsbruck, where Ficker edited his periodical. He visited his sister, a pianist, in Berlin where he met Else Lasker-Schüler. His extreme melancholia drove him to drugs and drink. In August, 1914, he was posted to Galicia as a lieutenant in the medical corps; after the battle of Grodek, to which one of his last poems refers, Trakl was put in charge of ninety serious casualties whom he could do little to help, and suffered a nervous breakdown. Placed in an observation cell in Cracow together with a fellow officer suffering from delirium tremens, he died there in November, 1914, of an overdose of cocaine. Trakl's poetry has been widely read in and outside the German-speaking countries. Several English selections have been published. A critical edition of his work, with variant readings, was published in 1969 (*Dichtungen und Briefe*).

DE PROFUNDIS

There is a stubble field on which a black rain falls.
There is a tree which, brown, stands lonely here.
There is a hissing wind which haunts deserted huts—
How sad this evening.

Past the village pond
The gentle orphan still gathers scanty ears of corn.
Golden and round her eyes are grazing in the dusk
And her lap awaits the heavenly bridegroom.

Returning home
Shepherds found the sweet body
Decayed in the bramble bush.

A shade I am remote from somber hamlets.
The silence of God

< 75 >

Ein Schatten bin ich ferne finsteren Dörfern.
Gottes Schweigen
Trank ich aus dem Brunnen des Hains.

Auf meine Stirne tritt Kaltes Metall.
Spinnen suchen mein Herz.
Es ist ein Licht, das in meinem Mund erlöscht.

Nachts fand ich mich auf einer Heide,
Starrend von Unrat und Staub der Sterne.
Im Haselgebüsch
Klangen wieder kristallne Engel.

UNTERGANG

An Karl Borromäus Heinrich

Über den weissen Weiher
Sind die wilden Vögel fortgezogen.
Am Abend weht von unseren Sternen ein eisiger Wind.

Über unsere Gräber
Beugt sich die zerbrochene Stirne der Nacht.
Unter Eichen schaukeln wir auf einem silbernen Kahn.

Immer klingen die weissen Mauern der Stadt.
Unter Dornenbogen
O mein Bruder klimmen wir blinde Zeiger gen Mitternacht.

SEBASTIAN IM TRAUM

Mutter trug das Kindlein im weissen Mond,
Im Schatten des Nussbaums, uralten Holunders,
Trunken vom Safte des Mohns, der Klage der Drossel;
Und stille
Neigte in Mitleid sich über jene ein bärtiges Antlitz,

Leise im Dunkel des Fensters; und altes Hausgerät
Der Väter
Lag im Verfall; Liebe und herbstliche Träumerei.

Handwritten annotations:
- Aufzählung von Bildern, Metaphern
- Enjambement, Zeilensprung, "run-on"
- Kälte
- Hell → Vokal, Dunkel
- Alliteration, Assonanz
- Todesbild
- drückt etwas aus, was man nicht anders ausdrücken kann
- Sterne = Schicksal → dunkel
- Gewalt
- Was steht tatsächlich da?
- entfreundliches) Bild des Todes, der Nacht
- Zustand der Unsicherheit
- Schmerz
- Trakls Zustand unter Einfluss von Droge
- Übergang von einem Ufer zum anderen
- Bezug auf die (Menschheit) beschwerlich
- gegen das Ende

< 76 >

① keine logische Verbundenheit der Sätze

I drank from the woodland well.

On my forehead cold metal forms.
Spiders look for my heart.
There is a light that fails in my mouth.

At night I found myself upon a heath,
Thick with garbage and the dust of stars.
In the hazel copse
Crystal angels have sounded once more.

DECLINE

To Karl Borromäus Heinrich

Over the white pond
The wild birds have traveled on.
In the evening an icy wind blows from our stars.

Over our graves
The broken brow of the night inclines.
Under oak trees we sway in a silver boat.

Always the town's white walls resound.
Under arches of thorns,
O my brother, blind minute-hands,
We climb towards midnight.

SEBASTIAN IN DREAM

Mother bore this infant in the white moon,
In the nut tree's shade, in the ancient elder's,
Drunk with the poppy's juice, the thrush's lament;
And mute
With compassion a bearded face bowed down to that woman,

Quiet in the window's darkness; and ancestral heirlooms,
Old household goods,
Lay rotting there; love and autumnal reverie.

< 77 >

Also dunkel der Tag des Jahrs, traurige Kindheit,
Da der Knabe leise zu kühlen Wassern, silbernen
        Fischen hinabstieg
Ruh und Antlitz;
Da er steinern sich vor rasende Rappen warf,
In grauer Nacht sein Stern über ihn kam;

Oder wenn er an der frierenden Hand der Mutter
Abends über Sankt Peters herbstlichen Friedhof ging,
Ein zarter Leichnam stille im Dunkel der Kammer lag
Und jener die kalten Lider über ihn aufhob.

Er aber war ein kleiner Vogel im kahlen Geäst,
Die Glocke klang im Abendnovember,
Des Vaters Stille, da er im Schlaf die dämmernde
        Wendeltreppe hinabstieg.

Frieden der Seele. Einsamer Winterabend,
Die dunklen Gestalten der Hirten am alten Weiher;
Kindlein in der Hütte von Stroh; o wie leise
Sank in schwarzem Fieber das Antlitz hin.
Heilige Nacht.

Oder wenn er an der harten Hand des Vaters
Stille den finstern Kalvarienberg hinanstieg
Und in dämmernden Felsennischen
Die blaue Gestalt des Menschen durch seine Legende ging,
Aus der Wunde unter dem Herzen purpurn das Blut rann.
O wie leise stand in dunkler Seele das Kreuz auf.

Liebe; da in schwarzen Winkeln der Schnee schmolz,
Ein blaues Lüftchen sich heiter im alten Holunder fing,
In dem Schattengewölbe des Nussbaums;
Und dem Knaben leise sein rosiger Engel erschien;
Freude; da in kühlen Zimmern eine Abendsonate erklang,
Im braunen Holzgebälk
Ein blauer Falter aus der silbernen Puppe kroch.

< 78 >

So dark was the day of the year, desolate childhood,
When softly the boy to cool waters, to silver fishes walked
    down,
Calm and countenance;
When stony he cast himself down where black horses raced,
In the gray of the night his star possessed him.

Or holding his mother's icy hand
He walked at nightfall across St. Peter's autumnal churchyard,
While a delicate corpse lay still in the bedroom's gloom
And he raised cold eyelids towards it.

But he was a little bird in leafless boughs,
The churchbell rang in dusking November,
His father's stillness, when asleep he descended the dark of the
    turning stair.

Peace of the soul. A lonely winter evening.
The dark shapes of shepherds by the ancient pond;
Little child in the hut of straw; O how softly
Into black fever his face sank down.
Holy night.

Or holding his father's horny hand
In silence he walked up Calvary Hill
And in dusky rock recesses
The blue shape of Man would pass through His legend,
Blood ran purple from the wound beneath His heart.
O how softly the cross rose up in the dark of his soul.

Love; when in black corners the snow was melting,
Gaily a little blue breeze was caught in the ancient elder,
In the nut tree's vault of shade;
And in silence a rosy angel appeared to that boy;
Gladness; when in cool rooms a sonata sounded at nightfall,
Among dark-brown beams
A blue butterfly crept from its silver chrysalis.

< 79 >

O die Nähe des Todes. In steinerner Mauer
Neigte sich ein gelbes Haupt, schweigend das Kind,
Da in jenem März der Mond verfiel.

Rosige Osterglocke in Grabgewölbe der Nacht
Und die Silberstimmen der Sterne,
Dass in Schauern ein dunkler Wahnsinn
        von der Stirne des Schläfers sank.

O wie stille ein Gang den blauen Fluss hinab
Vergessenes sinnend, da im grünen Geäst
Die Drossel ein Fremdes in den Untergang rief.

Oder wenn er an der knöchernen Hand des Greisen
Abends vor die verfallene Mauer der Stadt ging
Und jener in schwarzem Mantel ein rosiges Kindlein trug,
Im Schatten des Nussbaums der Geist des Bösen erschien.

Tasten über die grünen Stufen des Sommers. O wie leise
Verlief der Garten in der braunen Stille des Herbstes,
Duft und Schwermut des alten Holunders,
Da in Sebastians Schatten die Silberstimme des Engels erstarb.

AN DEN KNABEN ELIS

Elis, wenn die Amsel im schwarzen Wald ruft,
Dieses ist dein Untergang.
Deine Lippen trinken die Kühle des blauen Felsenquells.

Lass, wenn deine Stirne leise blutet
Uralte Legenden
Und dunkle Deutung des Vogelflugs.

Du aber gehst mit weichen Schritten in die Nacht,
Die voll purpurner Trauben hängt,
Und du regst die Arme schöner im Blau.

O the nearness of death. From the stony wall
A yellow head bowed down, silent that child,
Since in that month the moon decayed.

Rose-coloured Easter Bell in the burial vault of the night,
And the silver voices of stars,
So that madness, dark and shuddering, ebbed from the sleeper's
    brow.

O how quiet to ramble along the blue river's bank,
To ponder forgotten things when in leafy boughs
The thrush's call brought strangeness into a world's decline.

Or holding an old man's bony hand
In the evening he walked to the crumbling city walls,
And in his black greatcoat carried a rosy child,
In the nut tree's shade the spirit of evil appeared.

Groping his way over the green steps of summer. O how softly
In autumn's brown stillness the garden decayed,
Scent and sadness of the ancient elder,
When the silver voice of the angel died down in Sebastian's
    shadow.

1913

TO THE BOY ELIS

Elis, when the ouzel calls in the black wood,
This is your own decline.
Your lips drink in the coolness of the blue
Spring in the rocks.

No more, when softly your forehead bleeds,
Primaeval legends
And dark interpretation of the flight of birds.

< 81 >

Ein Dornenbusch tönt,
Wo deine mondenen Augen sind.
O, wie lange bist, Elis, du verstorben.

Dein Leib ist eine Hyazinthe,
In die ein Mönch die wächsernen Finger taucht.
Eine schwarze Höhle ist unser Schweigen,

Daraus bisweilen ein sanftes Tier tritt
Und langsam die schweren Lider senkt.
Auf deine Schläfen tropft schwarzer Tau,

Das letzte Gold verfallener Sterne.

IN HELLBRUNN

[handwritten: eigenwillige Form / zeitlos / melancholisch - Synästhesie]

Wieder folgend der blauen Klage des Abends
Am Hügel hin, am Frühlingsweiher—
Als schwebten darüber die Schatten lange Verstorbener,
Die Schatten der Kirchenfürsten, edler Frauen—
Schon blühen ihre Blumen, die ernsten Veilchen
Im Abendgrund, rauscht des blauen Quells
Kristallne Woge. So geistlich ergrünen
Die Eichen über den vergessenen Pfaden der Toten,
Die goldene Wolke über dem Weiher.

ABENDLAND

Else Lasker-Schüler in Verehrung

I   *[handwritten: Stimmung des Untergangs]*

Mond, als träte ein Totes
Aus blauer Höhle,
Und es fallen der Blüten   *[handwritten: - Herbst]*
Viele über den Felsenpfad.   *[handwritten: - schwieriger Weg]*
Silbern weint ein Krankes
Am Abendweiher,
Auf schwarzem Kahn   *[handwritten: Fluß von Caron]*
Hinüberstarben Liebende.

< 82 >

But you walk with soft footsteps into the night
Which is laden with purple grapes,
And move your arms more beautifully in the blue.

A thorn-bush sounds
Where your lunar eyes are.
O Elis, how long you have been dead.

Your body is a hyacinth
Into which a monk dips his waxen fingers.
Our silence is a black cavern

From which at times a gentle animal
Steps out and slowly lowers heavy lids.
Upon your temples black dew drips,

The last gold of perished stars.

                                        1913

AT HELLBRUNN

Following once again the evening's blue lament
Along the hillside, along the vernal pond—
As if the shades of those long dead, the shades
Of prelates and of noble women hovered over them—
Their flowers are blooming already, the earnest violets
In the evening's depth, the blue wellspring's
Crystal wave purls on. So religiously
Do the oaks grow green over forgotten paths of the dead,
The golden cloud over the pond.

                                        1913

OCCIDENT

For Else Lasker-Schüler

I

Moon, as if a dead thing
Stepped out of a blue cave,

<   83   >

Oder es läuten die Schritte
Elis' durch den Hain
Den hyazinthenen
Wieder verhallend unter Eichen.
O des Knaben Gestalt
Geformt aus kristallenen Tränen,
Nächtigen Schatten.
Zackige Blitze erhellen die Schläfe
Die immerkühle,
Wenn am grünenden Hügel
Frühlingsgewitter ertönt.

II

So leise sind die grünen Wälder
Unserer Heimat,
Die kristallne Woge
Hinsterbend an verfallner Mauer
Und wir haben im Schlaf geweint;
Wandern mit zögernden Schritten
An der dornigen Hecke hin
Singende im Abendsommer
In heiliger Ruh
Des fern verstrahlenden Weinbergs;
Schatten nun im kühlen Schoss
Der Nacht, trauernde Adler.
So leise schliesst ein mondener Strahl
Die purpurnen Male der Schwermut.

III

Ihr grossen Städte
steinern aufgebaut
in der Ebene!
So sprachlos folgt
der Heimatlose
mit dunkler Stirne dem Wind,

< 84 >

And many blossoms fall
Across the rocky path.
Silver a sick thing weeps
By the evening pond,
In a black boat
Lovers crossed over to death.

Or the footsteps of Elis
Ring through the grove
The hyacinthine
To fade again under oaks.
O the shape of that boy
Formed out of crystal tears,
Nocturnal shadows.
Jagged lightning illumines his temples
The ever-cool,
When on the verdant hill
Springtime thunder resounds.

II

So quiet are the green woods
Of our homeland,
The crystal wave
That dies against a perished wall
And we have wept in our sleep;
Wander with hesitant steps
Along the thorny hedge
Singers in the evening summer
In holy peace
Of the vineyards distantly gleaming;
Shadows now in the cool lap
Of night, eagles that mourn.
So quietly does a moonbeam close
The purple wounds of sadness.

< 85 >

kahlen Bäumen am Hügel.
Ihr weithin dämmernden Ströme!
Gewaltig ängstet
schaurige Abendröte
im Sturmgewölk.
Ihr sterbenden Völker!
Bleiche Woge
zerschellend am Strande der Nacht,
fallende Sterne.

DAS HERZ

Das wilde Herz ward weiss am Wald;
O dunkle Angst
Des Todes, so das Gold
In grauer Wolke starb.
Novemberabend.
Am kahlen Tor am Schlachthaus stand
Der armen Frauen Schar;
In jeden Korb
Fiel faules Fleisch und Eingeweid;
Verfluchte Kost!

Des Abends blaue Taube
Brachte nicht Versöhnung.
Dunkler Trompetenruf
Durchfuhr der Ulmen
Nasses Goldlaub,
Eine zerfetzte Fahne
Vom Blute rauchend,
Dass in wilder Schwermut
Hinlauscht ein Mann.
O! ihr ehernen Zeiten
Begraben dort im Abendrot.

Aus Dunklem Hausflur trat
Die goldne Gestalt
Der Jünglingin

< 86 >

III

You mighty cities
stone on stone raised up
in the plain!
So quietly
with darkened forehead
the outcast follows the wind,
bare trees on the hillside.
You rivers distantly fading!
Gruesome sunset red
is breeding fear
in the thunderclouds.
You dying peoples!
Pallid billow
that breaks on the beaches of Night,
stars that are falling.

THE HEART

The wild heart turned white in the wood;
O the dark fear
Of death, when the gold
Died in a gray cloud.
November evening.
By the bare gate of the slaughterhouse there stood
The crowd of poor women.
Into every basket
Rank flesh and entrails fell;
Accursed fare!

The blue dove of nightfall
Brought no atonement.
Dark trumpet call
Rang through the elm trees'
Damp golden leaves,
A tattered banner
Steaming with blood,

< 87 >

Umgeben von bleichen Monden,
Herbstlicher Hofstaat,
Zerknickten schwarze Tannen
Im Nachtsturm,
Die steile Festung.
O Herz
Hinüberschimmernd in schneeige Kühle.

DER SCHLAF

Verflucht ihr dunklen Gifte,
Weisser Schlaf!
Dieser höchst seltsame Garten
Dämmernder Bäume
Erfüllt von Schlangen, Nachtfaltern,
Spinnen, Fledermäusen.
Fremdling! Dein verlorner Schatten
Im Abendrot,
Ein finsterer Korsar
Im salzigen Meer der Trübsal.
Aufflattern weisse Vögel am Nachtsaum
Über stürzenden Städten
Von Stahl.

KLAGE

Schlaf und Tod, die düstern Adler
Umrauschen nachtlang dieses Haupt:
Des Menschen goldnes Bildnis
Verschlänge die eisige Woge
Der Ewigkeit. An schaurigen Riffen
Zerschellt der purpurne Leib.
Und es klagt die dunkle Stimme
Über dem Meer.
Schwester stürmischer Schwermut
Sieh, ein ängstlicher Kahn versinkt
Unter Sternen,
Dem schweigenden Antlitz der Nacht.

< 88 >

So that wild in his sadness
A man gives heed.
O brazen ages
Buried there in the sunset red.

From the house's dark hall there stepped
The golden shape
Of the maiden-youth
Surrounded with pale moons
Of autumnal courtliness,
Black pine trees snapped
In the night gale,
The steep-walled fortress.
O heart
Glistening away into snowy coolness.

1914

SLEEP

Accursed you dark poisons,
White sleep!
This, the rarest of gardens
Of trees wrapped in twilight,
Filled with serpents, nocturnal moths,
Spiders and bats.
Stranger, your lost shadow
In the sunset's red,
A gloomy corsair
On the salt sea of sadness.
White birds on the hem of the night fly off
Over collapsing cities
Of steel.

1914

LAMENT

Sleep and death, the dark eagles
Around this head swoop all night long:

< 89 >

GRODEK *- in Galizien / heute Polen*

Am Abend tönen die herbstlichen Wälder
Von tödlichen Waffen, die goldnen Ebenen
Und blauen Seen, darüber die Sonne
Düstrer hinrollt; umfängt die Nacht
Sterbende Krieger, die wilde Klage
Ihrer zerbrochenen Münder.
Doch stille sammelt im Weidengrund
Rotes Gewölk, darin ein zürnender Gott wohnt,
Das vergossne Blut sich, mondne Kühle;
Alle Strassen münden in schwarze Verwesung.
Unter goldnem Gezweig der Nacht und Sternen
Es schwankt der Schwester Schatten durch den schweigenden
    Hain,
Zu grüssen die Geister der Helden, die blutenden Häupter;
Und leise tönen im Rohr die dunklen Flöten des Herbstes.
O stolzere Trauer! ihr ehernen Altäre,
Die heisse Flamme des Geistes nährt heute ein gewaltiger
    Schmerz.
Die ungebornen Enkel.

< 90 >

Eternity's icy wave
Would swallow the golden image
Of man; against horrible reefs
His purple body is shattered.
And the dark voice laments
Over the sea.
Sister of stormy sadness,
Look, a timorous boat goes down
Under stars,
The silent face of the night.

1914

GRODEK

At nightfall the autumn woods cry out
With deadly weapons and the golden plains,
The deep blue lakes, above which more darkly
Rolls the sun; the night embraces
Dying warriors, the wild lament
Of their broken mouths.
But quietly there in the pastureland
Red clouds in which an angry god resides,
The shed blood gathers, lunar coolness.
All the roads lead to blackest carrion.
Under golden twigs of the night and stars
The sister's shade now sways through the silent copse
To greet the ghosts of the heroes, the bleeding heads;
And softly the dark flutes of autumn sound in the reeds.
O prouder grief! You brazen altars,
Today a great pain feeds the hot flame of the spirit,
The grandsons yet unborn.

1914

< 91 >

JAKOB VAN HODDIS:

Geboren 1887 in Berlin. Er stand in Verbindung mit Hugo Ball, Emmy Hennings und Ludwig Meidner, der Portraits der meisten expressionistischen Lyriker zeichnete. Sein Gedicht *Weltende*, das 1911 in der Zeitschrift *Die Aktion* veröffentlicht wurde, war mit seinem ironischen Nebeneinander von Trivialem und Katastrophalem der Prototyp einer bestimmten Art expressionistischer Gedichte. 1914 erlitt Hoddis einen Nervenzusammenbruch, von dem er sich nicht wieder erholte. Er lebte sieben Jahre lang in einem thüringischen Dorf, schrieb weiterhin, aber die Manuskripte aus dieser Zeit wurden zerstört, als er 1922 den Ort verließ. 1942 wurde er im Rahmen des "Euthanasie"-Programms der Nazis gegen Schwachsinnige verhaftet und getötet. Seine gesammelten Werke wurden 1958 unter dem Titel *Weltende: Gesammelte Dichtungen* veröffentlicht.

[handschriftlich: metaphernreiche Sprache]

MORGENS

Ein starker Wind sprang empor.
Öffnet des eisernen Himmels blutende Tore.
Schlägt an die Türme.
Hellklingend laut geschmeidig über die eherne Ebene der Stadt.

[handschriftlich: Vision]

Die Morgensonne russig. Auf Dämmen donnern Züge.
Durch Wolken pflügen goldne Engelpflüge.
Starker Wind über der bleichen Stadt.
Dampfer und Kräne erwachen am schmutzig fliessenden Strom.

Verdrossen klopfen die Glocken am verwitterten Dom.
Viele Weiber siehst du und Mädchen zur Arbeit gehn.
Im bleichen Licht. Wild von der Nacht. Ihre Röcke wehn.

[handschriftlich: Assonanz]

Glieder zur Liebe geschaffen.
Hin zur Maschine und mürrischen Mühn.
Sieh in das zärtliche Licht.
In der Bäume zärtliches Grün.
Horch! Die Spatzen schrein.
Und draussen auf wilderen Feldern
Singen Lerchen.

[handschriftlich: expressionistische Schwere]

[handschriftlich: negative Beschreibung der Stadt – Großstadtleben]
[handschriftlich: Gegensatz: Stadt ⟷ Natur]

< 92 >

JAKOB VAN HODDIS:

He was born in 1887 in Berlin, and was associated with Hugo Ball, Emmy Hennings, and Ludwig Meidner, who drew portraits of most of the Expressionist poets. His poem, *Weltende*, published in the periodical *Die Aktion* in 1911, was the prototype of one kind of Expressionist poem, with its ironic juxtaposition of trivial and catastrophic events. In 1914 Hoddis suffered a mental breakdown from which he never recovered. He lived for seven years in a village in Thuringia, still writing, but his manuscripts of that period were destroyed when he left in 1922. In 1942 he was arrested and put to death under the Nazi program of "euthanasia" for the mentally defective. His collected works were published in 1958 under the title: *Weltende: Gesammelte Dichtungen*.

IN THE MORNING

A strong wind sprang up.
Opens the blood-red gates of the iron sky.
Beats against the towers.
Brightly ringing blows lithe over the city's brazen plain.

The morning sun sooty. On embankments thunder trains.
Through clouds plough golden angel ploughs.
Strong wind over the pale city.
Steamers and cranes awake by the murkily flowing river.

Morosely bells clap on the weather-beaten cathedral.
Many women you see and girls going to work.
In the pale light. Wild from the night. Their skirts flap.

Limbs made for love.
To the machine and grudging drudgery.
Look into the tender light,
Into the trees' tender green.
Listen! The sparrows shriek.
And outside in the wilder fields
Larks are singing.

1911: Die Aktion

WELTENDE

Dem Bürger fliegt vom spitzen Kopf der Hut.
In allen Lüften hallt es wie Geschrei.
Dachdecker stürzen ab und gehn entzwei,
Und an den Küsten—liest man—steigt die Flut.

Der Sturm ist da, die wilden Meere hupfen
An Land, um dicke Dämme zu erdrücken.
Die meisten Menschen haben einen Schnupfen.
Die Eisenbahnen fallen von den Brücken.

[handschriftliche Notizen:]

umarmender Reim

Kreuzreim

innere Vision

Kein Schutz mehr

Gefahr

man ist schwach – Hilflosigkeit

fast wie ein Spielzeug

Statussymbol vom Bürger
Bild vom Bürger wird entlarvt
zerstört

ungeordnet

gewöhnliche / ungewöhnliche Sprache
Mitteilung

Mensch dargestellt wie eine Puppe

Was der Mensch erbaut, wird zerstört – übertragene Bedeutung – alle

Ernst und Unernst nebeneinander

Angriff auf die bürgerliche Welt und

auf das, worauf der Mensch stolz ist

es kommt etwas, dessen sich das Bürgertum nicht gewachsen ist

die Natur ist größer als der Mensch

< 94 >

END OF THE WORLD

From pointed pates hats fly into the blue,
All winds resound as though with muffled cries.
Steeplejacks fall from roofs and break in two,
And on the coasts—we read—flood waters rise.

The storm has come, the seas run wild and skip
Landwards, to squash fat ladies there.
Most people have a cold, their noses drip.
Trains tumble from the bridges everywhere.

1911: *Die Aktion*

< 95 >

KURT SCHWITTERS:

Geboren 1887 in Hannover. Der Maler und Lyriker Schwitters ist international bekannt vor allem durch seine Collagen, in die Bus-Fahrscheine und anderer Alltagskram eingearbeitet ist. 1918 wollte sich Schwitters dem Berliner Dada-Club anschließen, wurde jedoch von Hülsenbeck abgewiesen, weil er zu unpolitisch sei. Er begann seine eigene Bewegung "Merz". Der Name selbst ist schon ein typisches Collage-Stück, das er zufällig dem Namen einer Hannoveraner Bank entnommen hatte. Er war ein Vorkämpfer der Lautgedichte und der später so genannten "konkreten" Poesie visueller Art, die aus dem Aufsplittern und Verändern von Buchstaben Wörter aufbaute. 1935 emigrierte er nach England, wo er im Lake District eine Werkstatt eröffnete. Er schrieb verschiedene Gedichte in englischer Sprache und übersetzte auch sein Gedicht *Anna Blume*, das später von seinem Sohn Ernst überarbeitet wurde. Diese Übersetzung wurde nicht in die Anthologie aufgenommen. 1948 starb Schwitters in England. Sein gesammeltes literarisches Werk ist noch nicht vollständig erschienen; der Band I des *Literarischen Werks* wurde 1973 veröffentlicht und enthält seine Lyrik.

AN ANNA BLUME

O, du Geliebte meiner siebenundzwanzig Sinne,
    ich liebe dir!—
Du deiner dich dir, ich dir, du mir.—Wir?

Das gehört (beiläufig) nicht hierher.

Wer bist du, ungezähltes Frauenzimmer?
    Du bist—bist du?—Die
Leute sagen, du wärest—lass sie sagen,
    sie sie wissen nicht, wie der
Kirchturm steht.
Du trägst den Hut auf deinen Füssen und wanderst auf die
  Hände,
auf den Händen wanderst du.

Hallo deine roten Kleider, in weisse Falten zersägt. Rot
  liebe ich
Anna Blume, rot liebe ich dir!—Du deiner dich dir, ich
  dir, du
mir.—Wir?

< 96 >

KURT SCHWITTERS:

Born in Hanover in 1887, this painter and poet is best known internationally for his collages incorporating bus tickets and other odds and ends. In 1918 Schwitters tried to join the Berlin Dada Club, but was rejected by Huelsenbeck for being too unpolitical. He started his own movement, "Merz." The name itself is a typical piece of collage, having been picked up at random from the name of a Hanover bank. He was a pioneer of sound poetry and of what later became "concrete" poetry of the visual kind, practicing the splitting and permutation of letters making up words. In 1935 he emigrated to England, where he set up a workshop in the Lake District. He wrote several poems in English, also did an English version of his poem *Anna Blume*, later adapted by his son Ernst. This translation has not been adopted for this anthology. Schwitters died in England in 1948. His collected literary works have not yet appeared in their complete form; volume I of *Das Literarische Werk* was published in 1973 and contains his lyric poetry.

TO ANNA BLOOM

O thou beloved of my twenty-seven senses, I
love thou!—Thee thine thou, me thou, thee I.
—We?
That (by the way) is out of place here.
Who are you, uncounted woman? You are—
are you?—People say you are—let
them say, they don't know what's what.
You wear your hat on your feet and wander
on to your hands, on your hands you wander.
Hallo, your red dresses, sawn up into white pleats.
Red I love Anna Bloom, red I love thou!—Thee
thine thou, me thee, thee I.—We?
The right place for that (by the way) is the cold fire.
Red bloom, red Anna Bloom, what do people say?
Quiz question 1. Anna Bloom has bats in her belfry.
2. Anna Bloom is red.
3. What colour are the bats?
Blue is the colour of your yellow hair.
Red is the chirping of your green bat.
You simple girl in your everyday dress, you dear
green animal, I love thou!—Thee thine thou, me thou, thee
    I—we?

< 97 >

Das gehört (beiläufig) in die kalte Glut.

Rote Blume, rote Anna Blume, wie sagen die Leute?

Preisfrage: 1. Anna Blume hat ein Vogel.
2. Anna Blume ist rot.
3. Welche Farbe hat der Vogel?
Blau ist die Farbe deines gelben Haares.
Rot ist das Girren deines grünen Vogels.

Du schlichtes Mädchen im Alltagskleid, du liebes grünes
 Tier, ich
liebe dir!—Du deiner dich dir, ich dir, du mir.—Wir?
Das gehört (beiläufig) in die Glutenkiste.

Anna Blume! Anne, a-n-n-a ich träufle deinen Namen.
 Dein
Name tropft wie weiches Rindertalg.

Weisst du es Anna, weisst du es schon?

Man kann dich auch von hinten lesen, und du, du
 Herrlichste von
allen, du bist von hinten wie von vorne: "a-n-n-a."
Rindertalg träufelt streicheln über meinen Rücken.
Anna Blume, du tropfes Tier, ich liebe dir!

< 98 >

The right place for that (by the way) is the grate.
Anna Bloom! Anna, a-n-n-a, I drip your
name. Your name drips like soft beef tallow.
Did you know that, Anna, did you know it already?
One can read you back to front, too, and you, you,
loveliest of all, you're the same from either end! "a-n-n-a."
Beef tallow drips caressing over my back.
Anna Bloom, you drippy animal, I love thou.

1919

< 99 >

HANS ARP:

(oder JEAN). Geboren 1887 in Straßburg. Obwohl vorwiegend als Bildhauer tätig, schrieb er sein Leben lang Gedichte in Deutsch und Französisch. Während des ersten Weltkrieges nahm er zusammen mit Ball, Hülsenbeck und Tsara an der Dada-Bewegung teil. Er lebte hauptsächlich in der Schweiz, wo er 1966 starb. Seine deutschsprachigen Gedichte sind erschienen in *Gesammelte Gedichte I* (1963) und *Gesammelte Gedichte II* (1974); der dritte Band steht noch aus. Eine Auswahl in Englisch erschien in *Three Painter-Poets*, Penguin Books, 1974, und in *Arp on Arp* (Gedichte, Aufsätze, Erinnerungen), 1972. Seine *Gesammelten Französischen Schriften* erschienen 1974.

OPUS NULL

1

Ich bin der grôsse Derdiedas
das rigorose Regiment
der Ozonstengel prima Qua
der anonyme Einprozent.

Das P. P. Tit. und auch die Po
Posaune ohne Mund und Loch
das grosse Herkulesgeschirr
der linke Fuss vom rechten Koch.

Ich bin der lange Lebenslang
der zwölfte Sinn im Eierstock
der insgesamte Augustin
im lichten Zelluloserock.

2

Er zieht aus seinem schwarzen Sarg
um Sarg um Sarg um Sarg hervor.
Er weint mit seinem Vorderteil
und wickelt sich in Trauerflor.

Halb Zauberer halb Dirigent
taktiert er ohne Alpenstock
sein grünes Ziffernblatt am Hut
und fällt von seinem Kutscherbock.

HANS ARP:

Born 1887 in Strasbourg. Though primarily a sculptor, he wrote poems in German and French throughout his working life. During the First World War he was associated with Ball, Huelsenbeck, and Tzara in the Dada movement. Lived mainly in Switzerland, where he died in 1966. His German poems have been collected in *Gesummelte Gedichte I* (1963) and *Gesammelte Gedichte II* (1974), with a third volume still to come. A selection in English has appeared in *Three Painter-Poets*, Penguin Books, 1974, as well as in *Arp on Arp* (poems, essays, memories), 1972. His *Collected French Writings* appeared in 1974.

From OPUS NIL

1

I am the mighty He-she-it
the great unbending regiment
the ozone stalk called prima Qua
and the anonymous One per cent.

The P.P.Tit. and also Tro
trombone without a mouth or hole
the famous outfit Hercules
left ankle of the right-hand cook.

I am the lanky Wholelifelong
twelfth sense within the ovary
the entire Augustine top to toes
in radiant frock of cellulose.

2

From his black coffin he pulls out
coffin on coffin like a tape.
He blubbers with his forward end
and wraps himself in mourning crêpe.

Half conjuror and half conductor
without an alpenstock beats time
a grass-green dial on his hat
and tumbles from his coachman's seat.

< 101 >

Dabei stösst er den Ghettofisch
von der möblierten Staffelei.
Sein langer Würfelstrumpf zerreisst
zweimal entzwei dreimal entdrei.

3

Er sitzt mit sich in einem Kreis.
Der Kreis sitzt mit dem eignen Leib.
Ein Sack mit einem Kamm der steht
dient ihm als Sofa und als Weib.

Der eigne Leib der eigne Sack.
Der Vonvon und die linke Haut.
Und tick und tack und tipp und topp
der eigne Leib fällt aus der Braut.

Er schwingt als Pfund aus seinem Stein
die eigne Braut im eignen Sack.
Der eigne Leib im eignen Kreis
fällt nackt als Sofa aus dem Frack.

4

Mit seiner Dampfmaschine treibt
er Hut um Hut aus seinem Hut
und stellt sie auf in Ringelreihn
wie man es mit Soldaten tut.

Dann grüsst er sie mit seinem Hut
der dreimal grüsst mit einem du.
Das traute sie vom Kakasie
ersetzt er durch das Kakadu.

Er sieht sie nicht und grüsst die doch
er sie mit sich und läuft um sich.
Die Hüte inbegriffen sind
und deckt den Deckel ab vom Ich.

< 102 >

So doing knocks the ghetto fish
from off its finished easel frame.
His long square stocking tears in two
twice tears in two and thrice in three.
3
Sits in a circle with himself.
In its own flesh the circle sits.
A sack that holds an upright comb
serves him as sofa and as wife.

His very flesh his very sack.
The ofof and his left-hand skin
and tip and tap and tick and tock
out of his bride his body slips.

As pound found in his stone he swings
his very own bride in his sack.
In its own circle his own flesh
slips nude a sofa from his frock.
4
With his steam engine now he drives
hat after hat from out his hat
and in small rounds disposes them
as one would soldiers—just like that.

Then every hat he fills with blood
anoints himself with banner fat
says cockatoo to cockathree
and with his rifle goes to bed.

In bed he dreams of hat and blood
and of a reddish allthesame.
Around him there's a whirl a surge
moved by an evil melody.

[1919]; 1924: Der Pyramidenrock

SEKUNDENZEIGER

dass ich als ich
ein und zwei ist
dass ich als ich
drei und vier ist
dass ich als ich
wieviel zeigt sie
dass ich als ich
tickt und tackt sie
dass ich als ich
fünf und sechs ist
dass ich als ich
sieben acht ist
dass ich als ich
wenn sie steht sie
dass ich als ich
wenn sie geht sie
dass ich als ich
neun und zehn ist
dass ich als ich
elf und zwölf ist.

Aus: DER GORDISCHE SCHLÜSSEL

als ihm der boden unter den füssen fortgenommen
wurde heftete er sich mit seinen blicken an die decke
und sparte seine schuhe
so hing er regungslos wie ein scharadensack
und frönte dem abc des herren-und damenlosen leibes
es drängte ihn nicht einen befiederten schabrackenhiatus zu
    wichsen
er strebte weder danach ein held des tages noch ein held der
    nacht zu werden
auch die sumpfmedaillen lagunenschnüre gallenschärpen lockten
    ihn nicht

< 104 >

SECOND HAND

That I when I
it's one and two
that I when I
it's three and four
That I when I
what time does it say
that I when I
it ticks and tocks
that I when I
it's five and six
that I when I
it's five and six
that I when I
it's seven eight
that I when I
when it it stops
that I when I
when it it goes
that I when I
it's nine and ten
that I when I
it's eleven and twelve

From THE GORDIAN KEY

when the ground was taken from under his feet
he attached himself to the ceiling with his eyes and saved his
    shoes
hanging motionless there like a charade sack
and serving the abc of the masterless and mistressless body
he was not impelled to wax a plumed comparison hiatus
he did not aspire to become either a hero of the day or a hero
    of the night
nor was he attracted by the bog-medals
 lagoon-laces gall-sashes

<   105   >

er liess die vulkane theodor junior und theodor senior nach her-
    zenslust rauchen
die männer ihren mann stehen
und die frauen ihre frau liegen
auf seinem ruf salve läge fingerdick staub
hätten nicht ein hieratisches quasimodogeniti
und die flicken in seinen blicken
ihn ge zwungen wie eine schlichte lordschaft
sein von jeder patrizischen felonie und matrizischen eugenie
    reines leben zu überblicken
dabei löste er seine blicke wie ein werk des unbebrillten
    augenblickes von der decke los
vergass also sich mit den blicken and der decke festzuhalten
und fiel da ihm der boden unter den füssen fortgenomen war
    wie ein konfettikreuz in den gescheuerten
abgrund des nichts

Aus: DAS TAGESGERIPPE

wo sind die blätter
die glocken welken
es läutet nicht mehr in der erde
wo wir einst schritten
ist das licht zerrissen
die spuren der flügel führen ins leere
wo sind die lippen
wo sind die augen
grauenvoll zerschlug sich ihr herz zwischen den häuptern
der letzte atemzug fällt aus dem körper wie ein stein
wo wir einst sprachen flieht das blut aus dem feuer
und der gestaltlose kranz dreht sich im schwarzen grund
unsichtbar für immer ist die schöne erde
die flügel schweben nie mehr um uns

< 106 >

he allowed the volcanoes theodore junior and theodore senior
    to smoke to their heart's delight
men to stand up like men
and women lie down like women
on his cry salve dust would have lain thick as a finger
had not a hieratic quasimodogeniti
and the patches in his eyes' despatches
forced him like a plain lordship
to survey his life pure of all patrician felony and
    matrician eugenics
doing so he detached his eyes like a work of the unspectacled
    moment from the ceiling
that is forgot to hold on to the ceiling with his eyes
and since the ground had been taken from under his feet fell
    like a confetti cross into the well-scrubbed abyss
of nothingness

                    1925/1927

From: THE DAY'S SKELETON

where are the leaves
the bells wilt
no ringing is heard in the earth
where once we walked
the light is torn
the wakes of wings lead into the void
where are the lips
where are the eyes
their heart between heads was horribly dashed to pieces
the last breath drops from the body like a stone
where once we talked our blood flees from the fire
and the shapeless wreath turns in the blackness below
for ever invisible is our beautiful earth
never again will the wings hover around us

               1930: *'Transition'*

DAS LIED DES ROTEN

hoch oben
hoch hoch oben
singt der rote ein lied.
rote feurige federn wachsen dem roten
und die zeit vergeht.
ich träume und schreib.
nun fallen mir die maler und bildhauer ein
die ich vor zwanzig jahren
im café odeon sitzen sah.
klumpig und düster sitzen sie da
dem unangenehmen prozess der verinnerlichung
hingegeben
und ringen und knurren mit sich.
schon verschwinden diese herrschaften wieder
und rauchende eier liegen an ihren stellen.
wenn ich nicht acht gebe
entsteht nun ein gedicht.
trinken und singen fällt mir ein.
wir trinken und singen
und die zeit vergeht.
es singt und weht
und wandert im licht.
eines tages rascheln wir wie welke blätter fort
zerfallen zu staub
und werden wieder funken und sterne
und singen und trinken
und wandern selig in feurigen mänteln.

Aus: HÄUSER

In einem Hause
hatten alle Bewohner den gleichen Traum.
Sie träumten
dass sie täglich kleiner und kleiner würden
und schliesslich stürben.
Vorsorglich zimmerten sie sich daraufhin
ihre Särge zu Särglein um

< 108 >

THE RED MAN'S SONG

high up
high high up
the red man sings a song
red fiery feathers grow on the red man
and time passes.
I dream and write.
now I recall the painters and sculptors
whom twenty years ago
I saw sit in the café odéon.
lumpy and gloomy they sit there
immersed in the disagreeable business of interiorization
wrestling and growling with themselves.
already those gentlemen vanish again
and smoking eggs lie where they sat.
if I don't watch out
I shall write a poem now.
drinking and singing come back to me.
we drink and we sing
and time passes.
it sings and wafts
and walks in the light.
one day we all rustle off like dead leaves
crumble to dust
and turn again into sparks and stars
and sing and drink
and blissfully walk in our fiery mantles.

[1939]

From HOUSES

In a certain house
all the occupants had the same dream
They dreamed
that each day they grew smaller and smaller
and finally died.
Providently therefore they set to work
converting their coffins to coffinettes

< 109 >

und trugen sie stets mit sich
unter dem Arm.
Sie taten recht daran.
Obwohl zuerst das Kleinerwerden
nicht der Rede wert war
und zudem unregelmässig vor sich ging
ja sogar einmal mehrere Monate stockte
übertraf es plötzlich jede Erwartung.
Eines schönen Tages
erwachten die Bewohner des Hauses
in dem alle den gleichen Traum geträumt hatten
klein wie Puppen
und passten tadellos in ihre Särglein.

DAS RAD

Unaufhörlich sinnt er darüber nach
wie es wäre wenn er sich bedrucken
und zu einem Buche binden liesse
da er doch von einem tadellosen Bogen Papier
nicht zu unterscheiden ist.
An Stelle eines Herzens
trägt er ein Wasserzeichen.
Er grüsst nie
und will auch nie gegrüsst werden
weder ohne noch mit Zylinderhut.
Es fällt ihm auch nie ein
einen Dolch zu ergreifen und stechen zu wollen
obwohl viele Kenner kommen
und den schönen weissen Bogen Papier bewundern.
Viele viele Kenner kommen jeden Tag
um den schönen weissen Bogen gegen das Licht zu halten
und sobald sie das Wasserzeichen entdecken
wie aus einem Munde zu schreien:
das Wasserzeichen das Wasserzeichen das Rad!
Hat je ein Bogen ein solch schönes klares Rad besessen.
So bald die Kenner das Wasserzeichen entdecken

< 110 >

and always carried them around
under their arms.
They did the right thing.
Although at first their growing smaller
was not worth talking about
and also happened sporadically
even stopping once for several months
it suddenly exceeded every expectation
One fine day
the occupants of the house in which
all had dreamed the same dream woke up
small as dolls
and fitted perfectly into their coffinettes.

1956: *Häuser*

THE WHEEL

Perpetually he considers the pros and cons
of having himself covered with print
and bound up into a book
since after all he is indistinguishable
from a flawless sheet of paper.
In place of a heart
he wears a watermark
He never greets passersby
and never wants to be greeted
whether with or without a top hat.
Nor does it ever occur to him
to seize a dagger and feel like stabbing
though many experts come
and admire the lovely sheet of paper.
Many many experts come each day
to hold the lovely white sheet of paper up to the light
and as soon as they discover the watermark
to shriek as though with a single voice:
the watermark the watermark the wheel!
As soon as the experts discover the watermark
they nearly have kittens

< 111 >

geraten sie aus dem Häuschen
und biegen sich sofort
wie man Wörter biegt.
Ein und derselbe Kenner biegt sich als Einzahliger
als Einzahliger und Mehrzahliger
in Gegenwart Vergangenheit und Zukunft.
Die Bewunderer sind furchtlos.
Sie kennen nur noch biegen oder brechen
und das Rad.

< 112 >

and immediately inflect
as words are inflected.
One and the same expert inflects as a singular person
as a singular person and as a plural person
in the present past and future.
The admirers are fearless.
All they can think of now is inflect or break
and the wheel.

1963

GEORG HEYM:

Geboren 1887 in Hirschberg in Schlesien. Er studierte Jura in Berlin und war einer der Initiatoren des Expressionismus in Verbindung mit dem "Neuen Club" und der Zeitschrift *Die Aktion*. Er schrieb ein großes Korpus von Lyrik, erzählender Prosa und Stücken in seinem sehr kurzen Leben—er ertrank, als er versuchte, einen Freund auf dünnem Eis zu retten. Seine Lyrik vereint, beeinflußt von literarischen Vorläufern wie z.B. Baudelaire, Eindrücke der Großstadt mit den apokalyptischen Vorstellungen, die für den Früh-Expressionismus typisch sind, und deren Visionen von Zerfall und Niedergang noch nicht an politische Aktivität geknüpft sind. Einige seiner bekanntesten Gedichte, wie die Beschwörungen oder "Prophezeihungen" Alles-verheerenden Krieges, erwiesen sich als nicht übersetzbar, vor allem deshalb, weil Heym nicht zur Entwicklung neuer Versformen kam, die seiner Vision angemessen gewesen wären, zumindest nicht durchgängig. Ausgewählte Gedichte und Erzählungen wurden erstmals 1922 unter dem Titel *Dichtungen* veröffentlicht, obwohl er einen Gedichtband zu Lebzeiten publizierte und den Erzählband *Der Dieb* vorbereitete. Seine gesammelten Werke erschienen in drei Bänden zwischen 1960 und 1964 (*Dichtungen und Schriften*).

DEINE WIMPERN, DIE LANGEN . . .

An Hildegard K.

Deine Wimpern, die langen,
Deiner Augen dunkele Wasser,
Lass mich tauchen darein,
Lass mich zur Tiefe gehn.

Steigt der Bergmann zum Schacht
Und schwankt seine trübe Lampe
Über der Erze Tor,
Hoch an der Schattenwand,

Sieh, ich steige hinab,
In deinem Schoss zu vergessen,
Fern, was von oben dröhnt,
Helle und Qual und Tag.

An den Feldern verwächst,
Wo der Wind steht, trunken vom Korn,

< 114 >

GEORG HEYM:

Born in 1887 in Hirschberg, Silesia. He studied law in Berlin, and was one of the initiators of the Expressionist movement, connected with the "Neuer Club" and the periodical *Die Aktion*. During his very short working life—he was drowned in 1912 in Berlin while trying to rescue a friend on thin ice—he produced a large body of poetry, narrative prose, and drama. His verse combines impressions of the urban scene—influenced by literary precedents such as Baudelaire—with an apocalyptic imagination characteristic of early expressionism, when visions of decay and decline had not yet been linked to political activism. Some of his best-known poems, such as his evocations or "prophecies" of cataclysmic war, have proved untranslatable, mainly because Heym had not gotten as far as evolving new verse forms appropriate to his vision, at least not consistently. His selected poems and stories were first published in 1922, as *Dichtungen*, though he published one book of poems in his lifetime and prepared the book of stories, *Der Dieb*. His collected works appeared in three volumes between 1960 and 1964 (*Dichtungen und Schriften*).

YOUR EYELASHES, LONG . . .

To Hildegard K.

Your eyelashes, long,
Your eyes' dark waters,
Let me submerge in them,
Let me go down in them deep.

The miner descends to the pit,
Waving his lamp's dim light
Over the gate of ores,
High up the shadowy wall,

Look, I am going down,
In your lap to forget,
Far from what blares from above,
Brightness and anguish and day.

At the fields' edges twists,
Where the wind halts, drunk with corn,

< 115 >

Hoher Dorn, hoch und krank
Gegen das Himmelsblau.

Gib mir die Hand,
Wir wollen einander verwachsen,
Einem Wind Beute,
Einsamer Vögel Flug,

Hören im Sommer
Die Orgel der matten Gewitter,
Baden in Herbsteslicht,
Am Ufer des blauen Tags.

Manchmal wollen wir stehn
Am Rand des dunkelen Brunnens,
Tief in die Stille zu sehn,
Unsere Liebe zu suchen.

Oder wir treten hinaus
Vom Schatten der goldenen Wälder,
Groß in ein Abendrot,
Das dir berührt sanft die Stirn.

Göttliche Trauer,
Schweige der ewigen Liebe.
Hebe den Krug herauf,
Trinke den Schlaf.

Einmal am Ende zu stehen,
Wo Meer in gelblichen Flecken
Leise schwimmt schon herein
Zu der September Bucht.

Oben zu ruhn
Im Hause der durstigen Blumen,
Über die Felsen hinab
Singt und zittert der Wind.

Tall thornbush, tall and sick
Against the sky's blue.

Give me your hand,
Let us intergrow,
Prey for a wind,
Lonely birds' flight,

In summer hear
The organ of feeble thunderstorms,
Bathe in the autumn light,
On the blue day's bank.

At times we will stand
At the dark well's rim,
Deeply to look into stillness,
To look for our love.

Or else we'll emerge
From the golden wood's gloom,
Into the red of a sunset
That gently touches your brow.

Religious sadness,
Silence of lasting love.
Raise the jug to your lips,
Drink from it sleep.

One day to reach the end,
Where sea with yellowish foam
Softly gushes into
The September bay.

To rest above
In the house of thirsty flowers,
Down over the rocks
Shivers and sings the wind.

< 117 >

Doch von der Pappel,
Die ragt im Ewigen Blauen,
Fällt schon ein braunes Blatt,
Ruht auf dem Nacken dir aus.

Bindewort - drückt etwas Spontanes aus

UND DIE HÖRNER DES SOMMERS VERSTUMMTEN

Ausdruck eines inneren Gefühls - visionär -

Und die Hörner des Sommers verstummten im Tode der Fluren,
In das Dunkel flog Wolke auf Wolke dahin.
Aber am Rande schrumpften die Wälder verloren,
Wie Gefolge der Särge in Trauer vermummt.

Füllhorn, Jagdhörner
das Nichts, die schwarze Zukunft
düstere Stimmung

Viele Metaphern

Todesbild

verwendet Herbststimmung als Bild

unreiner Reim
Gott tot

Laut sang der Sturm im Schrecken der bleichenden Felder,
Er fuhr in die Pappeln und bog einen weissen Turm.
Und wie der Kehricht des Windes lag in der Leere
Drunten ein Dorf, aus grauen Dächern gehäuft.

Kraft des Windes - nichts kann dem Sturm widerstehen
gespenstisch
Unwichtigkeit eines Dorfes - Tod, Verlorenheit

Aber hinaus bis unten am Grauen des Himmels
Waren aus Korn des Herbstes Zelte gebaut,
Unzählige Städte, doch leer und vergessen.
Und niemand ging in den Gassen herum.

> Vision

Und es sang der Schatten der Nacht. Nur die Raben noch irrten
Unter den drückenden Wolken im Regen hin,
Einsam im Wind, wie im Dunkel der Schläfen
Schwarze Gedanken in trostloser Stunde fliehn.

schwarz-krächzen
> unrein

Anhäufung von Todesbildern

NACHMITTAG

Die Pappeln im Herbst
Am Rand des Weges
Schütteln sich frierend.
Ein paar Kinder

Durch Genitivkonstruktionen verbindet Heym Sachen, die nicht zusammen hören

< 118 >

But from the poplar tree
That looms into heaven's blue
Already a brown leaf falls
To rest on your neck.

July, 1911

AND THE HORNS OF SUMMER FELL SILENT . . .

And the horns of summer fell silent in the death of the
    meadows,
Into the darkness cloud upon cloud floated off.
But remotely the bordering forests were shrinking,
Muffled in morning like men that follow a hearse.

Loud sang the gale in the terror of fields that were fading;
It drove into poplars to shape a white tower between boughs.
And like the sweepings of wind there lay in the waste land
Below, a village, drab roofs in a huddle of gray.

But on and on, as far as the pallid horizon
The tents of autumn extended their fabric of corn,
The numberless cities, but empty, forgotten.
And no one was walking about in the streets.

And the shade of the night sang. Only the ravens still drifted
Here and there under leaden clouds in the rain,
Alone in the wind, as down in the dark of our foreheads
Black thoughts revolve and recede in disconsolate hours.

August, 1911

AFTERNOON

The autumn poplars
On the roadside
Tremble with cold.
A couple of children
And a few women

Und ein paar Frauen,
Mit Reisig beladen,
Kommen vom Walde
Auf leerer Strasse.

Ein harter Wind
Jagt die Blätter,
Immer,
Und jeder Stoss
Treibt Hunderte los
Braun und rot,
Die zu Boden fallen,
Am erloschenen Himmel
Wie Vögel tot.

DIE NACHT - düstere Großstadtstimmung

Herbstesregen rauscht
Traurig im Dunkel
Über die grauen Flächen hinunter.
Ein paar Bäume verloren.
Alle Dinge sind ferne
Fort in die Nacht geschoben.

Und drohend erhoben
Häusergruppe gross
Im Himmel oben
Hoch in des Dunkels Schoss
Wie ein schwarzer Vorhang gewirkt,
Der ein altes Geheimnis verbirgt.

Ein Zug dröhnt unten über die Schienen.
Rauch flattert über die niedrigen Zäune.
Und die neuen Strassen im Regen
Liegen stumm und ohne Bewegen
Von Laternen bewacht
Im ziehenden Nebel
Wie von gelben Augen der Nacht.

< 120 >

Carrying sticks
Come from the wood
Down an empty road.

A harsh wind
Chases the leaves,
Always,
And every thrust
Makes hundreds drift
Brown and red,
To fall at last
From a sky gone out
Like birds, dead.

September, 1911

THE NIGHT (From AUTUMNAL TETRALOGY)

Autumn rain sadly
Over gray surfaces
Splashes down in the dark.
A few trees, abandoned.
All things have been pushed
Far off into night.

And threateningly raised
A great mass of houses
Looms up to the sky
Into the lap of gloom
Wrought like a black curtain
That hides an ancient secret.

A train rumbles over the rails below,
Smoke flutters over the palings.
And the new streets in the rain
Lie mute and motionless,
Guarded by lamps alight
In the drifting fog
As by yellow eyes of the night.

< 121 >

Und der Regen rauscht
Und der Wind bauscht
Die ärmlichen Bäume.
Die Blätter schwirren,
Und oben im Finstern
Schreien die Vögel
Die nestlos irren.

Die Liebenden stehen
Unter den Türen
Wortlos und stumm,
Geben sich kalte Hände
Auseinanderzugehen,
Und noch einmal sehen
Sie im Dunkel sich um.

Von Liebe keine Spur, ist tot

Die Bettler kriechen
In ihre Löcher
Auf allen vieren.
Und Feuer brennen
Und knistern im Keller.
Ihre alten Stirnen sind rot
Wo die Zunge des Feuers loht.
Sie sitzen rundum
Mit hohen Rücken
Und dickem Rumpf
Und schüren die Flammen
Mit ihren Krücken
Und strecken ins Feuer
Den hölzernen Stumpf.

Schwelle des Todes

Hinter den Bauzäunen winseln
Leise die Hunde und schlagen
Manchmal mit mattem Gebell
Noch an im Traum.
Irgendwo in dem Dunkel
Ist ein Gewein und Klagen

< 122 >

And the rain splashes
And the wind lashes
The sparse trees.
The leaves whir
And up in the gloom
Shriek the birds
That restless roam.

Lovers stand
In doorways
Without a word,
Hold out a cold hand
In token of parting
And one more time
Look back in the dark.

Beggars creep
Into their holes
On all fours.
And fires burn,
Crackling, in cellars.
Their old foreheads are red
Where the fire's tongue leaps.
They sit around it
With tall backs,
Thick necks, heavy rumps,
And fan the flames
With their crutches,
Then into them hold
The wooden stumps.

Behind area fences dogs
Softly whimper and at times
With feeble barking knock
On dream's very door.
Somewhere, too, in the gloom
There's a weeping, a moan

< 123 >

Wie von Kindern allein
Im verlassenen Raum.

Nur ein Loch ist noch hell
Oben in einem der Böden,
Hoch wo der Regen streift
Und die Nacht mit dem Mantel schleift
Über die Dächer fort,
Die den Schlummer scheucht
Von dem Strohsack traurig und feucht,
Wo ein Kranker sitzt
In dem Winkel gestützt,
Und ein kleines Licht
Hält er in magre Faust
Wenn der Wind in die Kammer braust
Und das Licht flackert und weht
Da im Sturm es vergeht.

Lebenslicht

An einem Bette gross
In den langen Vorhang gehüllt
Steht der Mord, uralt
Dunkel und grenzenlos,
Eine schwarze Gestalt
Schwankend im Dunkel tief.

Und das blutige Haupt
Des Gemordeten bleicht
Traurig und sonderbar,
Da über den Himmel schleicht
Der Mond breitmaulig und schief
In dem herbstlichen Jahr.

abstoßend

< 124 >

As of children alone
In a deserted room.

Only one hole still is bright
Up in one of the attics,
High up where the rain creeps
And night with her cloak sweeps
Over the rooftops.
Driving sleep away
From the palliasse, moist and gray,
Where a sick man sits
Propped up against the wall,
His lean fist holding tight
A candle's little light
When the wind enters the room,
The light flickers and waves
Till a gale puts it out.

By a large bed,
Wrapped in a long curtain,
Lurks Murder, ancient as time,
Murky and limitless,
A black shape
Swaying deep in shadow.
And the bloody head
Of the murdered grows pale,
Uncannily clear
As crooked and widemouthed the moon
Slinks across the sky
In the fall of the year.

September, 1911

< 125 >

ALFRED LICHTENSTEIN:

Geboren 1889 in Berlin. Er studierte dort bis 1913 Jura. In diesem Jahr trat er zu einjährigem Militärdienst in ein bayrisches Regiment ein, das bei Kriegsausbruch an die belgische Grenze kommandiert wurde. Er starb im Kampf bei Vermandovillers im September 1914. 1913 hatte er einen kleinen Gedichtband *Die Dämmerung* veröffentlicht. Seine gesammelten Gedichte und Erzählungen erschienen 1919 in zwei Bänden. Zusammen mit Hoddis erfand Lichtenstein den eher ironischen als rhetorischen Typ expressionistischer Gedichte. In einer frühen Sequenz ironisierte er sich selbst in der Person Kuno Kohn; und selbst seine wenigen Kriegsgedichte sind voll Geringschätzung seiner selbst, bitter und lustig. Hätte er länger gelebt, wäre seine Entwicklung wahrscheinlich eher in Richtung *Neue Sachlichkeit* gelaufen als in die des spätexpressionistischen Schwulsts. Seine *Gesammelte Prosa* erschien 1966.

RÜCKKEHR DES DORFJUNGEN

In meiner Jugend war die Welt ein kleiner Teich
Grossmutterchen und rotes Dach, Gebrüll
Von Ochsen und ein Busch aus Bäumen.
Und ringsumher die grosse grüne Wiese.

Wie schön war dieses In-die-Weite-Träumen.
Dies Garnichtssein als helle Luft und Wind
Und Vogelruf und Feenmärchenbuch.
Fern pfiff die fabelhafte Eisenschlange—

DIE GUMMISCHUHE

Der Dicke dachte:
Am Abend geh ich gern in Gummischuhen,
Auch wenn die Strassen fromm und flecklos sind.
In Gummischuhen bin ich nie ganz nüchtern . . .

Ich halte in der Hand die Zigarette.
Auf schmalen Rhythmen tänzelt meine Seele.
Und alle Zentner meines Leibes tänzeln.

[handschriftliche Randnotizen:]
Expressionistisch nur in der letzten Zeile
Geborgenheit
das ländliche Leben
er sieht nicht weiter
Ahnung von der realen Welt
"fabelhaft" – unbekannt
Sehnsucht nach unschuldiger Kindheit, letzte Ahnung von ... birgt Ahnung der Mechanisierung

ALFRED LICHTENSTEIN:

Born in 1889 in Berlin, and studied law there until 1913. In that year he joined a Bavarian regiment for a year's military service, moving to Belgium at the outbreak of war. He was killed in action at Vermandovillers in September, 1914. He had published a small book of poems, *Die Dämmerung*, in 1913. His collected poems and stories appeared in two volumes in 1919. Together with Van Hoddis, Lichtenstein invented the ironic, rather than the rhetorical, type of Expressionist poem. In an early sequence he ironized himself under the persona Kuno Kohn; and even his few war poems are self-deprecating, bitter and funny. Had he lived, his development is likely to have been in the direction of *Neue Sachlichkeit* rather than of late Expressionist bombast. His *Gesammelte Prosa* appeared in 1966.

RETURN OF THE VILLAGE LAD

When I was young the world was a little pond
Grandmother and red roof, the lowing
Of oxen and a bush made up of trees.
And all around was the great green meadow.

Lovely it was, this dreaming-into-the-distance,
This being nothing at all but air and wind
And bird-call and fairy-tale book.
Far off the fabulous iron serpent whistled—

1913

THE GALOSHES

The fat man thought:
At night I like to walk in my galoshes,
Even through pious and immaculate streets.
I'm not quite sober when I wear galoshes . . .

I hold my cigarette in one gloved hand.
On tightrope rhythms then my soul goes tripping.
And all the hundredweights of my body dance.

1913

<   127   >

DER LACKSCHUH

Der Dichter dachte:
Ach was, ich hab den Plunder satt!

Die Dirnen, das Theater und den Stadtmond,
Die Oberhemden, Strassen und Gerüche,
Die Nächte und die Kutscher und die Fenster,
Das Lachen, die Laternen und die Morde—
Den ganzen Dreck hab ich nun wirklich satt,
Beim Teufel!
Mag werden, was da will . . . mir ist es gleich:
Der Lackschuh drückt mich. Und ich zieh ihn aus—

Die Leute mögen sich verwundert wenden.
Nur schade ists um meinen seidnen Strumpf . . .

Gefühl verbunden mit dem Kater nach den Festen —
verkleidet ? aber mehr

ASCHERMITTWOCH

Gestern noch ging ich gepudert und süchtig
In der vielbunten tönenden Welt.
Heute ist alles schon lange ersoffen.

- die Welt ist nicht mehr bunt

Hier ist ein Ding.
Dort ist ein Ding.
Etwas sieht so aus.
Etwas sieht anders aus.
Wie leicht pustet einer die ganze
Blühende Erde aus.

nicht nur der Kater, die Welt ist auch so
- alles ist relativ

Der Himmel ist kalt und blau.
Oder der Mond ist gelb und platt.
Ein Wald hat viele einzelne Bäume.

fern- bietet keinen Schutz mehr
berührt ihn nicht
nicht mehr golden

Ist nichts mehr zum Weinen.
Ist nichts mehr zum Schreien.
Wo bin ich—

keine innere Beteiligung mehr
Frage ?
Man kann sich schwer für etwas engagieren

kein "sanftes Gesetz" mehr
Kein Trost mehr

Ansatz zu Verzweiflung existentiellen Problemen - r Schluß ist offen Kein Frage-zeichen
abwertende Einstellung gegenüber der Natur . bietet keine Hilfe
Vergleich mit der Romantik

< 128 >

THE PATENT LEATHER SHOE

The poet thought:
Enough. I'm sick of the whole lot!

The whores, the theatre and the city moon,
The streets, the laundered shirtfronts and the smells,'
The nights, the coachmen and the curtained windows,
The laughter and the streetlamps and the murders—
To hell with it!
Happen what may . . . it's all the same to me:
This black shoe pinches me. I'll take it off—

Let people turn their heads for all I care.
A pity, though, about my new silk sock.

                                    1913

ASH WEDNESDAY

Only yesterday powdered and lustful I walked
In this various and resonant world.
Today how long ago the lot was drowned.

Here is a thing.
There is a thing.
Something looks like this.
Something else looks different.
How easily one can blow out
The whole blossoming earth.

The sky is cold and blue.
Or the moon is yellow and flat.
A wood contains many single trees.

Nothing now worth weeping for.
Nothing now worth screaming for.
Where am I—

                                    1913

<   129   >

DER MORGEN

. . . Und alle Strassen liegen glatt und glänzend da.
Nur selten hastet über sie ein fester Mann.
Ein fesches Mädchen haut sich heftig mit Papa.
Ein Bäcker sieht sich mal den schönen Himmel an.

Die tote Sonne hängt an Häusern, breit und dick.
Vier fette Weiber quietschen spitz vor einer Bar.
Ein Droschkenkutscher fällt und bricht sich das Genick.
Und alles ist langweilig hell, gesund und klar.

Ein Herr mit weisen Augen schwebt verrückt, voll Nacht,
Ein siecher Gott . . . in diesem Bild, das er vergass,
Vielleicht nicht merkte—Murmelt manches. Stirbt. Und lacht.
Träumt von Gehirnschlag, Paralyse, Knochenfrass.

<   130   >

MORNING

And all the streets lie snug there, clean and regular.
Only at times some brawny fellow hurries by.
A very smart young girl fights fiercely with Papa.
A baker, for a change, looks at the lovely sky.

The dead sun hangs on houses, broad as it is thick.
Four bulging women shrilly squeak outside a bar.
The driver of a cab falls down and breaks his neck.
And all is boringly bright, salubrious and clear.

A wise-eyed gentleman floats madly, full of night,
An ailing god . . . within this scene, which he forgot
Or failed to notice—Mutters something. Dies. And laughs.
Dreams of a cerebral stroke, paralysis, bone-rot.

1913

< 131 >

FRANZ WERFEL:

Geboren 1890 in Prag. Von 1912 bis 1914 war er Verlagslektor. Der Verleger war Kurt Wolff, der Kafka, Trakl, Benn, Heym und viele andere der meist jungen Autoren dieser Zeit veröffentlichte. Damals war Werfel vor allem als Lyriker bakannt, bevor er später international als Romanautor und Stückeschreiber berühmt wurde. Nach dem ersten Weltkrieg lebte er in Berlin, dann in Wien. Er heiratete Alma, die Witwe Gustav Mahlers. 1938 emigrierte er nach Frankreich, 1940 weiter nach Amerika und starb 1945 in Kalifornien. Als produktiver Lyriker, Autor von Romanen, Kurzgeschichten und als Dramatiker galt Werfel in den zwanziger Jahren vor allem als der herausragende expressionistische Lyriker, aber das rhetorische Pathos seiner Verse hielt sich nicht. Werfel selbst griff es in seinen späteren Jahren an und entwickelte einen nüchterneren Stil für seine letzten Gedichte. Die gesammelten Gedichte erschienen 1946 in Los Angeles unter dem Titel *Gedichte aus den Jahren 1908-1945*. Im Jahr zuvor (1945) war ein Band ausgewählter Gedichte in der Übersetzung (*Poems by Franz Werfel*) in Princetown erschienen. Eine weitere Sammelausgabe seiner Gedichte erschien 1967 unter dem Titel *Das Lyrische Werk von Franz Werfel*.

GESANG

Einmal einmal—
Wir waren rein.
Sassen klein auf einem Feldstein
Mit vielen lieben alten Fraun.
Wir waren ein Indenhimmelschaun,
Ein kleiner Wind im Wind
Vor einem Friedhof, wo die Toten leicht sind.
Sahen auf ein halbzerstürztes Tor,
Hummel tönte durch Hagedorn,
Ein Grillen-Abend trat gross ins Ohr.
Ein Mädchen flocht einen weissen Kranz,
Da fühlten wir Tod und einen süssen Schmerz,
Unsere Augen wurden ganz blau—
Wir waren auf der Erde und in Gottes Herz.
Unsre Stimme sang da ohne Geschlecht,
Unser Leib war rein und recht.
Schlaf trug uns durch grünen Gang—
Wir ruhten auf Liebe, heiligem Geflecht,
Die Zeit war wie Jenseits wandelnd und lang.

< 132 >

FRANZ WERFEL:

Born in 1890 in Prague. He was a reader for a publisher from 1912 to 1914. The publisher was Kurt Wolff, who published Kafka, Trakl, Benn, Heym, and many of the mostly young writers of this period. At this time Werfel was best known as a poet, before becoming internationally famous as a novelist and playwright. After the First World War he lived in Berlin, then Vienna. He married Alma, the widow of Gustav Mahler. In 1938 he emigrated to France, moving on to America in 1940, and he died in California in 1945. A prolific poet, novelist, short story writer, and dramatist, Werfel was regarded in the 'twenties as the outstanding Expressionist poet, but the rhetorical pathos of his verse has not worn well. Werfel himself turned against it in later years, evolving a more sober manner for his last poems. His collected poems, *Gedichte aus den Jahren 1908-1945* appeared in Los Angeles in 1946. A book of selected poems in translation had appeared in Princeton the previous year (*Poems by Franz Werfel*, 1945). Another collected edition of his poems, *Das Lyrische Werk von Franz Werfel*, appeared in 1967.

SONG

Once once—
We were pure.
Sat small on a boundary stone
With many dear old women.
We were a gazing-up at the sky,
A little wind in the wind
In front of a churchyard where the dead have no weight.
Looked at a half-dismembered gate,
Bumble-bee hummed though the hawthorn tree,
A nightful of crickets grew vast to the ear.
A girl was winding a daisy-chain
And we felt our death, felt a sweet pain,
Our eyes turned utterly blue—
We were on earth and within God's heart.
Sexless our voices broke into song,
Our bodies were pure and right.
Sleep carried us through a passage all green—
We rested on love, a holy weft,
Our time was outside us, shifting and long.

Before 1920: *Menscheitsdämmerung*

< 133 >

JOHANNES R. BECHER:

Geboren 1891 in München. Sein erster Gedichtband erschien 1911, ein Roman folgte. Er wurde einer der berühmtesten und produktivsten späteren Expressionisten mit seiner rhetorischen Lyrik politisch-religiösen Protestierens oder Mahnens. 1919 trat er der Kommunistischen Partei bei. Von 1935 bis 1945 lebte er in Moskau. Nach dem Krieg wurde er Präsident des Kulturbunds der Deutschen Demokratischen Republik, später Kulturminister (1954-1958). Seine späte Lyrik zeigt eine bewußte Abkehr von expressionistischer "Subjektivität" and syntaktischen und metaphorischen Freiheiten hin zu älteren und verläßlicheren Methoden. 1953 wurde ihm der Lenin-Friedenspreis verliehen. Seine verschiedenen öffentlichen Funktionen schlossen u.a. das Verfassen des Texts für die Nationalhymne der DDR ein, zusammen mit Hanns Eisler. Becher starb 1958. Seine frühen Lyrikbände umfassen u.a. die Titel *Um Gott* (1921) and *Verklärung: Hymne* (1922). Eine Auswahl früher und später Gedichte wurde 1961 unter dem Titel *Verfall und Triumph* mit Illustrationen von Frans Masereel veröffentlicht. Eine frühere *Auswahl in sechs Bänden* erschien 1952. Sein autobiographischer Roman *Abschied* (1945) erschien unter dem Titel *Farewell* 1970 in englischer Übersetzung. Neuere Einzelauswahlen seiner Lyrik umfassen *Schritt der Jahrhundertmitte* (1960), *Lyrik, Prosa, Dokumente. Eine Auswahl* (1965). *Laßt eure Verse teilnehmen am Sportfest* (1970), *Gedichte für ein Volk* (1973), *An Europa und an Alle!* (1973). Seine *Gesammelten Werke in 14 Bänden* erschienen 1966.

DIE NEUE SYNTAX

Die adjektiv-bengalischen-Schmetterlinge
Sie kreisen tönend um des Substantivs erhabenen Quaderbau.
Ein Brückenpartizip muss schwingen! schwingen!
Derweil das kühne Verb sich klirrend Aeroplan
     in Höhen schraubt.

Artikeltanz zückt nett die Pendelbeinchen.
In Kicherrhythmen schaukelt ein Parkett.
Da aber springt metallisch tönend eine reine
Strophe heraus aus dem Trapez. Die Kett

Der Strassenbogenlampen ineinander splittern.
Trotz jener buntesten Dame heiligem Vokativ.
Ein junger Dichter sich Subjekte kittet.
Bohrt des Objekts Tunnel . . . Imperativ

< 134 >

JOHANNES R. BECHER:

Born 1891 in Munich. His first book of poems appeared in 1911, followed by a novel. He became one of the most prominent and prolific of the later Expressionists, writing a rhetorical poetry of political and religious protest or exhortation, and joined the Communist Party in 1919. From 1935 to 1945 he lived in Moscow. After the war he became President of the Kulturbund in East Germany, then Minister of Culture (1954-1958). His later verse shows a calculated retreat from expressionist "subjectivity," syntactic and metaphorical freedom, to older and more reliable modes of arousing stock responses. In 1953 he was awarded the Lenin Peace Prize. His many public functions included the writing of the words for the National Anthem of the GDR together with Hanns Eisler. He died in 1958. His early books of poems include, among others, *Um Gott* (1921) and *Verklärung: Hymne* (1922). A selection from his early and late poems was published in 1961 as *Verfall und Triumph* with illustrations by Frans Masereel. An earlier selection in six volumes appeared in 1952 (*Auswahl in sechs Bänden*). His autobiographical novel, *Abschied* (1945), appeared in English translation under the title *Farewell* in 1970. More recent individual collections of his poetry include *Schritt der Jahrhundertmitte* (1960), *Lyrik, Prosa, Dokumente. Eine Auswahl* (1965), *Lasst eure Verse teilnehmen am Sportfest* (1970), *Gedichte für ein Volk* (1973), *An Europa* and *An Alle!* (1973). His *Gesammelte Werke in 14 Bänden* appeared in 1966.

THE NEW SYNTAX

The Bengal butterfly adjectives,
They circle humming around the lofty freestone structure of
    nouns
A bridge participle shall rock and give! give!
While the bold verb a whirring aeroplane whirls up from the
    ground.

Article dance nicely twitches little pendulum legs.
In titter rhythms a floor swings up and down.
But then metallically ringing a pure
Stanza leaps out of the trapeze. The chain

Of street arclights splinter one into the other.
Despite that most colourful lady's holy vocative.
A young poet for himself puts subjects together.
Drills the object's tunnel . . . The imperative

< 135 >

Schnellt Steil empor. Phantastische Sätzelandschaft
    überzüngelnd
Bläst sieben Hydratuben. Das Gewölke fällt.
Und Blaues fliesst. Geharnischte Berge dringen.
So blühen auf wir in dem Glanz mailichter Überwelt.

< 136 >

Steeply shoots up. Flame-licking over a fantastic landscape
Of sentences. Blows seven hydra tubas. Clouds down are
    hurled.
And blueness flows. Mountains in armour surge up.
So we burst into flower in the gleam of a May-time super-
    world.

1916: An Europa

YVAN GOLL:

Geboren 1891 in St. Die in den Vogesen. Er schrieb in deutscher, französischer und auch in englischer Sprach. Er studierte in Staßburg und Berlin. Während des ersten Weltkrieges gründete er in der Schweiz den Rhein Verlag, der die erste deutsche Übersetzung von Joyces *Ulysses* veröffentlichte. Er war ein produktiver Kyriker, Prosaschriftsteller und Dramatiker des Spätexpressionismus. Zwischen den beiden Weltkriegen lebte er in Frankreich, der Schweiz und Deutschland. Er stand in Verbindung mit dem französischen Surrealismus, Picasso und Chagall. 1939 emigrierte er in die USA, zusammen mit seiner Frau Claire. Er gab in New York die Zeitschrift *Hémisphères* heraus und schrieb die Sequenz *Jean Sans Terre*. Dieses Gedicht erschien, zusammen mit anderen späten Gedichten, in französisch, 1958 in englischer Übersetzung. Goll kehrte 1947 nach Paris zurück und starb 1950 an Leukämie. Seine letzten Gedichte, Visionen der Krankheit und der Gewißheit des Todes, sind in dem Band *Traumkraut* (1951) gesammelt. Seine Witwe gab die gesammelten Gedichte heraus: *Dichtungen* erschien 1960. Seither sind mehrere andere Sammlungen seiner lyrischen Arbeiten erschienen: *Die Antirose* (1967), *Der Eiffelturm* (1973) und *Die Unterwelt* (1973).

ELECTRIC

Auf die Leiter des Eiffelturms steigt der Blaue Maschinist
Den Mond
Schutzmarke für Parfüms
Und der der Friseure Schild herabzuhägen—
Aber die Welt strahlt weiter
Kupferne Ströme rauschen die Berge herab
Rhone
Montblanc
Mars
Elektrische Wellen fliessen durch blonde Nacht
Disken über uns
Das Lachen der Bahnhöfe
Das Perlenhalsband der Boulevards
Und still an eine Parklinde gelehnt
Mademoiselle Nature
Meine Braut

< 138 >

YVAN GOLL:

Born in 1891 in St. Die in the Vosges, he wrote both in German and French (and, for a time, also in English). He studied at Strasbourg and Berlin. In Switzerland, during the First World War, he founded the Rhein Verlag, which published the first German translation of Joyce's *Ulysses*. He was prolific as a poet, prose writer, and dramatist during the late Expressionist phase, and he lived in France, Switzerland, and Germany between the wars. Associated with French surrealism, with Picasso and with Chagall. He emigrated to the U.S. in 1939 with his wife Claire. In New York he edited the magazine *Hémisphères*, and wrote the sequence *Jean Sans Terre*. This, and other of his later poems in French, have appeared in English translation (1958). Goll returned to Paris in 1947, and died of leukemia in 1950. His last poems, visions induced by his illness and the certainty of death, were collected in the volume *Traumkraut* (1951). His collected poems, edited by his widow, appeared in 1960 as *Dichtungen*. Other collections of his poetry have appeared since then: *Die Antirose* (1967), *Der Eiffelturm* (1973), and *Die Unterwelt* (1973).

ELECTRIC

Up the Eiffel Tower's ladder climbs the Blue Machinist
To hang out
The moon
Trademark of perfumes
And the signs of hairdressers—
But the world's radiance extends
Copper torrents splash down mountainsides
Rhône
Montblanc
Mars
Electric waves flow through the blond night
Discs above us
The laughter of railway stations
The pearl necklaces of the boulevards
And quiet, leaning against a lime tree in the park
Mademoiselle Nature
My fiancée

1922: *Der Sturm*

< 139 >

BLUTHUND

Bluthund vor meinem Herzen
Wachend über mein Feuer
Der du dich nährst von bitteren Nieren
In der Vorstadt meines Elends

Leck mit der nassen Flamme deiner Zunge
Das Salz meines Schweisses
Den Zucker meines Todes

Bluthund in meinem Fleisch
Fang die Träume die mir entfliegen
Bell die weissen Geister an
Bring zurück zu ihrem Pferch
Alle meine Gazellen

Und zerbeiss die Knöchel meines flüchtigen Engels

DER SALZSEE

Der Mond leckt wie ein Wintertier das Salz deiner Hände,
Doch schäumt dein Haar violett wie ein Fliederbusch,
In dem das erfahrene Käuzchen ruft.

Da steht für uns erbaut die gesuchte Traumstadt,
In der die Strassen alle schwarz und weiss sind.
Du gehst im Glitzerschnee der Verheissung,
Mir sind gelegt die Schienen der dunklen Vernunft.

Die Häuser sind mit Kreide gegen den Himmel gezeichnet
Und ihre Türen bleigegossen;
Nur oben unter Giebeln wachsen gelbe Kerzen
Wie Nägel zu zahllosen Särgen.

Doch bald gelangen wir hinaus zum Salzsee.
Da lauern uns die langgeschnäbelten Eisvögel auf,
Die ich die ganze Nacht mit nackten Händen bekämpfe,
Bevor uns ihre warmen Daunen zum Lager dienen

< 140 >

BLOODHOUND

Bloodhound in front of my heart
Watching over my fire
You that feed on bitter kidneys
In the suburb of my misery

With the wet flame of your tongue lick
The salt of my sweat
The sugar of my death

Bloodhound in my flesh
Catch the dreams that fly off from me
Bark at the white ghosts
Bring back to their pen
All my gazelles

And savage the ankles of my fleeting angel

THE SALT LAKE

The moon like a winter animal licks the salt of my hands,
Yet your hair foams violet like a lilac bush.
In which experienced the little owl calls.

There, built for us, stands the dream city we look for,
All of whose streets are black and white.
You walk in the glittering snow of promise,
For me the rails of dark reason have been laid.

The houses are marked with chalk toward the sky
And the doors are of cast lead;
Only under the gables above yellow candles grow
Like nails for countless coffins.

But soon we have made our way out to the salt lake.
There the long-beaked icebirds lie in wait for us,
They that I fight all night long with my bare hands,
Before their warm down serves us for our couch.

< 141 >

DER REGENPALAST

Ich hab die einen Regenpalast erbaut
Aus Alabastersäulen und Bergkristall
    Dass du in tausend Spiegeln
    Immer schöner dich für mich wandelst
Die Wasserpalme nährt uns mit grauem Most
Aus hohen Krügen trinken wir silbernen Wein
    Welch ein perlmutternes Konzert!
    Trunkne Libelle im Regenurwald!

Im Käfig der Lianen ersehnst du mich
Die Zauberbienen saugen das Regenblut
    Aus deinen blauen Augenkelchen
    Singende Reiher sind deine Wächter

Aus Regenfenstern blicken wir wie die Zeit
Mit Regenfahnen über das Meer hinweht
    Und mit dem Schlachtheer fremder Stürme
    Elend in alten Morästen endet

Mit Regendiamanten bekleid ich dich
Heimlicher Maharadscha des Regenreichs
    Des Wert und Recht gewogen wird
    Nach den gesegneten Regenjahren

Du aber strickst mir verstohlen im Perlensaal
Durchwirkt von Hanf und Träne ein Regentuch
    Ein Leichentuch breit für uns beide
    Bis in die Ewigkeit warm und haltbar

DER STAUBBAUM

Ein Staubbaum wächst
Ein Staubwald überall wo wir gegangen
Und diese Staubhand weh! rühr sie nicht an!

< 142 >

THE RAIN PALACE

I have built for you a rain palace
Of alabaster columns and rock crystal
    So that a thousand mirrors shall tell me
    How ever more beautifully for me you change

The water palm feeds us with a gray cider
From tall jugs we drink a silver wine
    What a concert of mother-of-pearl!
    Drunken dragonfly in the rain jungle!

In the liana cage you crave for me
The magical bees drink the rain blood
    Out of your azure eye-calyxes
    Singing herons are your guards

Through rain windows we look at time
Wafting with rain banners across the sea
    And with the army of alien storms
    Wretchedly ending in ancient swamps

With rain diamonds I clothe you
Secret maharajah of the rain kingdom
    Whose worth and right are weighed
    By the prosperous rain years

But stealthily in the pearl room you knit for me
Threaded with hemp and tears a rain cloth
    A cerecloth wide enough for us two
    Warm and strong enough to last for ever

THE DUST TREE

A dust tree grows
A dust wood everywhere we walked
And this dust hand, oh, do not touch it.

< 143 >

Rings um uns steigen Türme des Vergessens
Türme die nach innen fallen
Aber noch bestrahlt von deinem orangenen Licht!
Ein Staubvogel fliegt auf

Die Sage unsrer Liebe lass ich in Quarz verwahren
Das Gold unsrer Träume in einer Wüste vergraben
Der Staubwald wird immer dunkler
Weh! Rühr diese Staubrose nicht an!

< 144 >

Around us towers of oblivion rise
Towers that collapse inwards
But still lit by your orange beams.
A dust bird flies off.

I'll have the legend of our love preserved in quartz
The gold of our dreams buried in a desert
The dust wood grows darker and darker
Oh, do not touch this dust rose!

1951: Traumkraut

< 145 >

NELLY SACHS:

Geboren 1891 in Berlin. Obwohl sie schon in ihrer Jugendzeit Gedichte schrieb, wurde sie erst nach dem letzten Krieg durch ihre Gedichte und ihre Stücke in Versform über die Vernichtung der Juden bekannt. 1940 wurde ihr befohlen, bei einem Arbeitslager vorzusprechen; sie wurde jedoch im letzten Augenblick durch das Eingreifen der schwedischen Schriftstellerin Selma Lagerloef gerettet, die sie nach Schweden brachte. In ihren frühen Jahren war sie nicht mit Themen wie Religion oder Juden beschäftigt, sondern schrieb Puppenspiele und wollte Balletttänzerin werden. Sie verbrachte die späteren Jahre ihres Lebens in Stockholm. Ihr erster Gedichtband, *Sternverdunkelung* (1949), wurde in Ost-Berlin veröffentlicht, der nächste in Amsterdam. Die folgenden Sammlungen erschienen in West-Deutschland, wo sie viele Ehrungen erhielt. 1966 wurde ihr der Nobel-Preis für Literatur verliehen. Ihre Gedichte und Stücke wurden unter den folgenden Titeln gesammelt: *Fahrt ins Staublose* (1961), *Zeichen im Sand* (1962), *Glühende Rätsel* (1968) und *Suche nach Lebenden* (1971), gefolgt von einem Band der letzten Gedichte *Teile dich Nacht* (1971). Sie starb 1970 in Stockholm. Große Teile ihres Werks sind in England und den USA erschienen. *O the Chimneys* ist eine Sammlung ausgewählter Gedichte, die auch *Eli* (1967), ein Stück in Versform, enthält.

IN DER BLAUEN FERNE

In der blauen Ferne,
wo die rote Apfelbaumallee wandert
mit himmelbesteigenden Wurzelfüßen,
wird die Sehnsucht destilliert
für Alle die im Tale leben.

Die Sonne, am Wegesrand liegend
mit Zauberstäben,
gebietet Halt den Reisenden.

Die bleiben stehn
im gläsernen Albtraum,
während die Grille fein kratzt
am Unsichtbaren

und der Stein seinen Staub
tanzend in Musik verwandelt.

< 146 >

NELLY SACHS:

Born in Berlin in 1891. Although she wrote poems in her youth, she became known only after the last war with poems and verse plays about the destruction of the Jews. In 1940 she was ordered to report to a labor camp, but was saved at the last moment by the intervention of the Swedish writer Selma Lagerlöf, who got her to Sweden. In her early years she was not preoccupied with religious or Jewish themes, but wrote puppet plays and wanted to be a ballet dancer. Her later years were spent in Stockholm. Her first book of poems, *Sternverdunkelung* (1949), was published in East Berlin, her next in Amsterdam. Her subsequent collections appeared in West Germany, where she received many honors. She received the Nobel Prize for literature in 1966. Her poems and plays were collected in 1961 (*Fahrt ins Staublose*), 1962 *Zeichen im Sand*), 1968 (*Glühende Rätsel*) and 1971 (*Suche nach Lebenden*), followed by a volume of last poems, *Teile dich Nacht* (1971). She died in 1970 in Stockholm. Large selections from her work have appeared in England and in the U.S. *O the Chimneys* is a collection of selected poems including the verse play, *Eli* (1967).

IN THE BLUE DISTANCE

In the blue distance
where the red avenue of apple trees roams
with root-feet that climb the sky
longing is distilled
for all those who live in the valley.

The sun, lying beside the path
with magic wands,
orders travelers to stop.

They halt
in a glassy nightmare
while the cricket lightly scratches
at invisible doors.

And dancing the stone transmutes
its dust into music.

1957: Und niemand weiss weiter

< 147 >

WEISSE SCHLANGE

Weisse Schlange
Polarkreis
Flügel im Granit
rosa Wehmut im Eisblock
Sperrzonen um das Geheimnis
Herzklopfenmeilen aus Entfernung
Windketten hängend am Heimweh
flammende Granate aus Zorn—

Und die Schnecke
mit dem tickenden Gepäck der Gottzeit.

DER SCHLAFWANDLER

Der Schlafwandler
kreisend auf seinem Stern
an der weissen Feder des Morgens
erwacht—
der Blutfleck darauf erinnerte ihn—
lässt den Mond
erschrocken fallen—
die Schneebeere zerbricht
am schwarzen Achat der Nacht—
traumbesudelt—

Kein reines Weiss auf Erden—

LINIE WIE

Linie wie
lebendiges Haar
gezogen
todnachtgedunkelt
von dir
zu mir.

<   148   >

WHITE SERPENT

White serpent
polar circle
wings in the granite
rose-colored sadness in blocks of ice
frontier zones around the secret
heart-throbbing miles of distance
wind-chains hanging from homesickness
flaming grenade of anger—

And the snail
with the ticking luggage of God's time.

THE SLEEPWALKER

The sleepwalker
circling upon his star
is awakened by
the white feather of morning—
the bloodstain on it reminds him—
startled, he drops
the moon—
the snowberry breaks
against the black agate of night
sullied with dream—

No spotless white on this earth—

LINE LIKE

Line like
living hair
drawn
deathnightobscured
from you
to me.

< 149 >

Gegängelt
ausserhalb
bin ich hinübergeneigt
durstend
das Ende der Fernen zu küssen.

Der Abend
wirft das Sprungbrett
der Nach über das Rot
verlängert deine Landzunge
und ich setze meinen Fuss zagend
auf die zitternde Saite
des schon begonnenen Todes

Aber so ist die Liebe—

< 150 >

Reined in
outside
I bend
thirstily
to kiss the end of all distances.

Evening
throws the springboard
of night over the redness
lengthens your promontory
and hesitant I place my foot
on the trembling string
of my death already begun.

But such is love—

1959: *Feucht und Verwandlung*

< 151 >

GERTRUD KOLMAR:

Geboren 1894 in Berlin. Sie hatte gerade mit der Veröffentlichung ihrer *reifen* Arbeiten begonnen, als die Nazis an die Macht kamen, obwohl ein frühes Buch von ihr schon 1917 erschienen war. Von ihrer Ausbildung her war sie Fremdsprachenlehrerin und arbeitete als Übersetzerin während des ersten Weltkrieges in Kriegsgefangenenlagern. In den zwanziger und frühen dreißiger Jahren lebte sie bei ihren Eltern und sorgte für ihre Mutter, die 1930 starb. Während dieser Zeit reiste sie und unterrichtete taubstumme Kinder. 1934 erschien ihre Gedichtsequenz *Preußische Wappen*; ihre Sammlung *Die Frau und die Tiere* wurde als 'jüdisches' Buch in einem der jüdischen Verlage zur Publikation zugelassen, die zur Wahrung des Scheins weiterarbeiten durften, aber das Buch wurde eingestampft, bevor es in den Verkauf kam. 1943 wurde sie verhaftet; Zeit und Ort ihres Todes sind unbekannt. Ihre besten Gedichte erschienen posthum: die erste Auswahl 1947; 1955 und 1960 folgten größere Sammlungen: *Das lyrische Werk von Gertrud Kolmar*. Ein kleiner Verlag in London veröffentlichte 1975 einige ihrer späten Gedichte in englischer Übersetzung. *Dark Soliloquy*, eine grosse Auswahl, erschien 1975 in New York.

AUS DEM DUNKEL

Aus dem Dunkel komme ich, eine Frau.
Ich trage ein Kind und weiss nicht mehr, wessen;
Einmal had ichs gewusst.
Aber nun ist kein Mann mehr für mich . . .
Alle sind hinter mir eingesunken wie Rinnsaal,
Das die Erde trank.
Ich gehe weiter und weiter.
Denn ich will vor Tag ins Gebirge, und die Gestirne
    schwinden schon.

Aus dem Dunkel komme ich.
Durch finstere Gassen schritt ich einsam,
Da jäh vorstürzendes Licht mit Krallen die sanfte Schwärze
    zerriss,
Der Pardel die Hirschkuh,
Und weit aufgestossene Tür hässliches Kreischen, wüstes
    Gejohle, tierisches Brüllen spie.
Trunkene wälzten sich . . .
Ich schüttelte das am Wege vom Saum meines Kleides.

< 152 >

GERTRUD KOLMAR:

Born in 1894 in Berlin, she had only begun to publish her mature work when the Nazis came to power, although an early book had appeared in 1917. By professional training she was a teacher of foreign languages, and worked as an interpreter in a POW camp during the First World War, but in the 'twenties and early 'thirties she lived with her parents, looking after her mother, who died in 1930. During this period she traveled and taught deaf-mute children. Her sequence of poems *Preussische Wappen* appeared in 1934; her collection *Die Frau und die Tiere* was allowed to be "published" as a "Jewish" book in 1938 by one of the Jewish firms kept on as a showcase, but the book was pulped before it could be distributed. In 1943 she was arrested; the time and place of her death are not known. Her best poems appeared posthumously: a first selection in 1947, followed by larger collections in 1955 and 1960 (*Das lyrische Werk von Gertrud Kolmar*). An English translation of some of her later poems was published by a small press in London; a larger selection, *Dark Soliloquy,* in the U.S. in 1975.

OUT OF THE DARKNESS

Out of the darkness I come, a woman.
I am with child and have forgotten, whose;
Once I did know it.
But now there remains no man for me . . .
All went down behind me like rills of water
Drunk by the earth.
I move on and on.
For I want to reach the mountains before day, and the stars are
    already fading.

Out of the darkness I come.
Through gloomy streets I walked lonely,
When light that came gushing forth tore the gentle blackness
    with its talons,
The leopard the hind,
And a door pushed wide open spewed ugly shrieking, wild yel-
    ling, bestial roars.
Drunkards rolled on the ground . . .
On my way I shook it all from the hem of my dress.

< 153 >

Und ich wanderte über den verödeten Markt.
Blätter schwammen in Lachen, die den Mond spiegelten.
Magere, gierige Hunde berochen Abfälle auf den Steinen.
Früchte faulten zertreten,
Und ein Greis in Lumpen quälte noch immer sein armes
    Saitenspiel
Und sang mit dünner, misstönig klagender Stimme
Ungehört
Und diese Früchte waren einst in Sonne und Tau gereift,
Träumend noch vom Duft und Glück der liebenden Blüte,
Doch der wimmernde Bettler
Vergass das längst und kannte nichts anderes mehr als Hunger
    und Durst.

Vor dem Schlosse des Mächtigen stand ich still,
Und da ich die unterste Stufe trat,
Zerbarst der fleischrote Porphyr knackend an meiner Sohle.—
Ich wendete mich
Und schaute empor zu dem kahlen Fenster, der späten Kerze
    des Denkenden,
Der sann und sann und nie seiner Frage Erlösung fand,
Und zu dem verhüllten Lämpchen des Kranken, der doch nicht
    lernte,
Wie er sterben sollte.
Unter dem Brückenbogen
Zankten zwei scheussliche Gerippe sich um Gold.
Ich hob meine Armut als grauen Schild vor mein Antlitz
Und zog ungefährdet vorbei.

Im Fernen redet der Fluss mit seinen Ufern.

Nun strauchle ich den steinigen, widerstrebenden Pfad hinan.
Felsgeröll, Stachelsträucher verwunden die blinden, tastenden
    Hände:
Eine Höhle wartet,
Die im tiefsten Geklüft den erzgrünen Raben herbergt, der
    keinen Namen hat.

And I ambled over the deserted marketplace.
Leaves floated in puddles that mirrored the moon.
Lean, hungry dogs sniffed at refuse on the stones.
Trodden fruit rotted,
And an old man in rags still tortured his poor stringed instru-
     ment
And sang with a thin, discordantly plaintive voice
Unheard.
And these fruits had once ripened in sunshine and dew
Still dreaming of the fragrance and joy of the loving blossom,
But the whining beggar
Had long forgotten that and knew no more now than his hunger
     and thirst.

In front of the mighty man's palace I stopped,
And when I trod the lowest step
The flesh-red porphyry burst with a crack under my sole.—
I turned about
And looked up to the uncurtained window, the late candle of
     the thinking man,
Who pondered and pondered and never found an answer to his
     question
And to the little shaded lamp of the sick man who had not yet
     learnt
How he was to die.
Under the arch of the bridge
Two repulsive skeletons were quarreling over gold.
I raised my poverty as a gray shield to my face
And walked by unendangered.
Far away the river is conversing with its banks.

Now I stagger up the stony recalcitrant path.
Scree, thron bushes wound my blind, groping hands:
A cave awaits me
That in its deepest crevice harbours the green raven without a
     name.
There I shall enter,

<   155   >

Da werde ich eingehn,
Unter dem Schutz der grossen schattenden Schwinge mich
    niederkauern und ruhn.
Verdämmernd dem stummen wachsenden Wort meines Kindes
    lauschen
Und schlafen, die Stirn gen Osten geneigt,
Bis Sonnenaufgang.

DAS OPFER

Ihre purpurnen Schuhe kennen den Weg, und die Spange um
    ihren Knöchel weiss ihn.
So wandelt sie ohne Willen, gebunden, im Traum.
So wandeln die heissen dunkelnden Augen durch Reihen
    steinerner Flügelkatzen und schwerer bemalter Säulen
    zum Vorhof des Tempels,
Da ein nackter Greis in schmutzigem Lendentuche auf winziger
    Pauke hämmert und endlos sein näselnder Singsang fleht.
Die Aussätzige, von wirren Haaren verhangen, reckt stöhnend
    den Arm.
Unfruchtbare seufzen Gebete.
Ein Jüngling steht hoch und steil, unbeweglich, mit breitem
    bronzenen Schwert,
Und ein Wahnsinniger krümmt mit leisem verzückten Lachen
    sich über rosengranitener Schwelle.
Wie sie vorüberstrebt, hascht die Kranke, Verdeckte nach
    ihrem Kleide, den amarantfarbenen Säumen;
Sie aber zieht, die Wolke, an unerreichbaren Abendhimmeln
    dahin.

Dreimal fragt ihre pochende Hand die kupferne Tür, die ihr
    dreimal erwidert.
Ein Priester öffnet.
Sein Bart rinnt, blauer Fluss, über die linnene Bleiche des Un-
    tergewandes, den Safran des Mantels.
Auf seiner hohen schwarzen Haube spreizt ein silberner Vogel
    sich.

Under the shelter of the great overshadowing wing I shall
   crouch down and rest.
Fading away shall listen to the dumb growing words of my
   child
And sleep, my brow inclined to the East,
Until sunrise.

THE VICTIM

Her purple shoes know the way, and the clasp around her ankle
   knows it.
So she moves on without volition, fettered, in a dream.
So the hot, darkling eyes move on through rows of stone cats
   with wings and heavy painted columns to the forecourt of
   the temple,
Where a naked old man in a dirty loincloth beats a tiny kettle-
   drum and endlessly his nasal singsong beseeches.
The leprous woman, her face covered with tangled hair, extends an arm, groaning.
Infertile women sigh prayers.
A youth stands, tall and upright, immovable, with a broad
   sword of bronze,
And a madman contorts himself with softly frenzied laughter
   over the rose-granite threshold.

As she makes her way past, the sick, covered woman snatches
   at her dress, the amaranth-coloured hem;
But she, the cloud, drifts on along inaccessible evening skies.

Thrice her knocking hand questions the copper door, which an-
   swers her thrice.
A priest opens it.
His beard, blue stream, flows over the linen paleness of his un-
   dergarment, the saffron of his cloak.
On his tall black hood a silver bird preens itself.
He pours milk into red clay dishes, milk of the wax-white cow
   with gilt horns.

< 157 >

Er giesst Milch in rote Tonschalen, Milch der wachsweissen
    Kuh mit vergoldeten Hörnern,
Trank den heiligen Schlangen,
Die ihre glatten, getuschten Leiber am Boden des düsternden
    Raumes knäueln und wälzen.
Und eine grösste chrysolithäugige hebt sich und lauscht und
    wiegt den Bauch zu unhörbarem Liede.
Die Frau verneigt sich ihr, schirmt mit dem Finger das Auge
    und küsst der Natter die Stirn.—
Sie schweigt
Und tritt hinaus in den leeren inneren Hof;
Nur perlmutterne Tauben picken Weizenkörner vom
    lauchgrünen Nephrit.
Sie ängsten nicht.
Zwischen bunt beladenen Wänden hält streng und schmal eine
    Ebenholzpforte sich,
Und dreimal rührt die Frau mit elfenbeinernem Stabe das
    Schloss, das ihr Antwort weigert.
Sie bleibt und wartet.

Dort wird sie eingehn.
Unter dem Bilde des Abgotts mit goldenen Krötenschenkeln,
Im Rauche glimmenden Sandelholzes,
Beim Strahlen zuckenden Feuers
Wird der Fremde nahn,
Wird langsam schreiten und seine rechte Hand auf ihre Mitte
    legen als ein Zeichen.
Er wird sie hinführen in den sengenden Kreis
Und ihre Brüste schauen
Und schweigend stark aus glühen Umarmungen Wollust
    schmelzen.
Sie töten . . .
So ist es ihr vorbestimmt und sie weiss es.

Sie zaudert nicht. Kein Beben zwingt ihre Glieder; sie blickt
    nicht um,

Drink for the holy serpents
That wind and knot their smooth, tinted bodies on the floor of
the darkening hall.
And a large one, chysolite-eyed, rises and listens and sways its
belly to an inaudible song.
The woman bows to it, shields her eyes with one finger and
kisses the adder's forehead.—
She keeps silent
And walks out into the empty inner courtyard;
Only nacreous pigeons peck wheat grain from the leak-coloured
nephrite.
They do not frighten her.
Between many-coloured wall hangings an ebony door maintains
a narrow severity.
And thrice the woman touches its lock with an ivory wand, but
receives no answer.
She stands and waits.

There she will enter
Under the statue of the idol with golden toad thighs,
In the smoke of glimmering sandalwood,
In the radiance of flickering fire
The stranger will approach,
Will slowly stride and lay his right hand on her middle as a
sign.
He will lead her into the searing circle
And look upon her breasts
And silently strong melt lust from glowing embraces.
Kill her . . .
So it is predestined, and she knows it.
She does not hesitate. No trembling overpowers her limbs; she
does not look around her,
Knows neither fortune nor misfortune.
She filled herself utterly with burning darkness, with dimly ef-
fulgent humility that serves the monster's commandments,
and she will die for the golden idol.—

<   159   >

Kennt weder Glück noch Unglück.

Sie füllte sich ganz mit brennender Finsternis, mit dumpf
erglänzender Demut, die dem Gebote des Scheusals dienen, dem goldenen Götzen sterben will.—

Doch in ihrem Herzen ist Gott.

Auf ihrem ernsten und schönen Antlitz haftet sein Siegel.

Das aber weiss sie nicht.

Yet in her heart is God.
To her grave and beautiful face a seal attaches.
But that she does not know.

[c. 1940]; 1955: *Das Lyrische Werk*

< 161 >

BERTOLT BRECHT:

Geboren 1898 in Augsburg. Er studierte Medizin in München und arbeitete während des Ersten Weltkrieges als Lazarettgehilfe, bevor er Dramatiker wurde. Vor 1933 lebte er in München und Berlin; dann floh er über Prag und Wien nach Zürich, weiter nach Dänemark, dann nach Finnland und schließlich nach Amerika, wo er in Kalifornien und New York lebte. 1947 kehrte er nach Europa zurück—zuerst in die Schweiz, dann nach Ost-Berlin, wo der das Deutsche Theater übernahm und das Berliner Ensemble gründete. 1950 wurde er österreichischer Staatsbürger, blieb aber bis zu seinem Tod 1956 in Ost-Berlin. Zu seinen Lebzeiten veröffentlichte er nur wenige Gedichtsammlungen, obwohl er kontinuierlich Lyrik schrieb. Eine neunbändige Sammlung seiner Gedichte erschien nach seinem Tod. Eine Auswahl von Gedichten, die nach seiner Rückkehr nach Deutschland entstanden, ist in der Anthologie *East German Poetry* greifbar. In beiden Teilen Deutschlands wirkte während der fünfziger und sechziger Jahre seine Lyrik fruchtbar. Brechts gesammelte Werke erschienen 1967 in zwanzig Bänden in West-Deutschland. Eine grosse Auswahl von Gedichten *Poems 1913-1956* wird 1976 in London und New York erscheinen.

VOM ARMEN B. B. — Alltagsleben

Ich, Bertolt Brecht, bin aus den schwarzen Wäldern.
Meine Mutter trug mich in die Städte hinein
Als ich in ihrem Leibe lag. Und die Kälte der Wälder
Wird in mir bis zu meinem Absterben sein.

In der Asphaltstadt bin ich daheim. Von allem Anfang
Versehen mit jedem Sterbsakrament:
Mit Zeitungen. Und Tabak. Und Branntwein. — Wichtig für ihn
Mißtrauisch und faul und zufrieden am End.

Ich bin zu den Leuten freundlich. Ich setze
Einen steifen Hut auf nach ihrem Brauch.
Ich sage: es sind ganz besonders riechende Tiere
Und ich sage: es macht nichts, ich bin es auch.

In meine leeren Schaukelstühle vormittags
Setze ich mir mitunter ein paar Frauen
Unc ich betrachte sie sorglos und sage ihnen:
In mir habt ihr einen, auf den könnt ihr nicht bauen.

< 162 >

BERTOLT BRECHT:

Born in Augsburg in 1898. He studied medicine in Munich and worked as a medical orderly during the First World War before becoming a dramatist. He lived in Munich and Berlin before 1933, when he fled to Zurich via Prague and Vienna, moving on to Denmark, then Finland, and finally to America, where he lived in California and in New York. He returned to Europe in 1947, at first to Switzerland and then to East Berlin, where he took over the Deutsches Theater and founded the Berliner Ensemble. In 1950 he became an Austrian citizen, but remained in East Berlin until his death in 1956. He published only a few collections of poems in his lifetime, but never ceased to write them. A nine-volume collection of his poems appeared after his death. A selection from his poems written after his return to Germany is available in the anthology *East German Poetry*. In both Germanys his poetry has proved of seminal importance in the 'fifties and 'sixties. Brecht's collected works, in twenty volumes, were published in West Germany in 1967. Some of his poetry has appeared in translation in the USA, and the large selection, *Poems 1913-1956* was published in London in 1976.

OF POOR B.B.

I, Bertolt Brecht, came out of the black forests.
My mother moved me into the cities while I lay
Inside her body. And the chill of the forests
Will be inside me till my dying day.

In the asphalt cities I'm at home, From the very start
Provided with every unction and sacrament:
With newspapers. And tobacco. And brandy.
To the end mistrustful, lazy, and content.

I'm polite and friendly to people. I put on
A stiff hat because that's what they do.
I say: they're animals with a quite peculiar smell,
And I say: Does it matter? I am too.

Sometimes in the morning on my empty rocking chair
I'll sit a woman or two, and with an untroubled eye
Look at them steadily and say to them:
Here you have someone on whom you can't rely.

< 163 >

Gegen Abend versammle ich um mich Männer
Wir reden uns da mit "Gentlemen" an
Sie haben ihre Füsse auf meinen Tischen
Und sagen: es wird besser mit uns. Und ich frage nicht: wann?

Gegen Morgen in der grauen Frühe pissen die Tannen
Und ihr Ungeziefer, die Vögel, fängt an zu schrein.
Um die Stunde trinke ich mein Glas in der Stadt aus und schmeisse
Den Tabakstummel weg und schlafe beunruhigt ein.

Wir sind gesessen, ein leichtes Geschlechte
In Häusern, die für unzerstörbar galten
So haben wir gebaut die langen Gehäuse des Eilands Manhattan
Und die dünnen Antennen, die das Atlantische Mee-
  runterhalten.

Von diesen Städten wird bleiben: der durch sie hindurchging,
  der Wind!
Fröhlich machet das Haus den Esser: er leert es.
Wir wissen, dass wir Vorläufige sind
Und nach uns wird kommen: nichts Nennenswertes.

Bei den Erdbeben, die kommen werden, werde ich hoffentlich
Meine Virginia nicht ausgehen lassen durch Bitterkeit
Ich, Bertolt Brecht, in die Asphaltstädte verschlagen
Aus den schwarzen Wäldern in meiner Mutter in früher Zeit.

VON DEN RESTEN ÄLTERER ZEITEN

Immer noch steht zum Beispiel der Mond
Über den Neubauten die Nächte her
Unter den Dingen aus Kupfer
Ist er
Der Unbrauchbarste. Schon
Erzählt die Mutter von Tieren
Die Wägen zogen, Pferde geheissen.
Freilich in den Gesprächen der Kontinente

< 164 >

Toward evening it's men I gather round me
And then we address one another as "gentlemen."
They're resting their feet on my table tops
And say: Things will get better for us. And I don't ask: When?

In the gray light before morning the pine trees piss
And their vermin, the birds, raise their twitter and cheep.
At that hour I drain my glass in town, then throw
The cigar butt away and worriedly go to sleep.

We have sat, an easy generation
In houses thought to be indestructible
(Thus we built those tall boxes on the island of Manhattan
And those thin antennae that amuse the Atlantic swell.)

Of those cities will remain: what passed through them, the
        wind!
The house makes glad the consumer: he clears it out.
We know that we're only tenants, provisional ones,
And after us there will come: nothing worth talking about.

In the earthquakes to come, I very much hope,
I shall keep my Virginia alight, embittered or no,
I, Bertolt Brecht, carried off to the asphalt cities
From the black forests inside my mother long ago.

                                                    1922

ON THE REMAINS OF PAST AGES

Still for instance the moon
Hangs above the new buildings at night
Of the things made of copper
It is
The most useless. Already
Mothers tell stories of animals
That drew carts—called horses.
True, in the conversation of continents
These no longer occur, nor their names:

<   165   >

Kommen sie nicht mehr vor mit ihren Namen:
An den grossen neuen Antennen
Ist von alter Zeit
Nichts mehr bekannt.

VON ALLEN WERKEN

Von allen Werken die liebsten
Sind mir die gebrauchten.
Die Kupfergefässe mit den Beulen und den abgeplatteten Rän-
    dern
Die Messer und Gabeln, deren Holzgriffe
Abgegriffen sind von vielen Händen: solche Formen
Schienen mir die edelsten. So auch die Steinfliesen um alte
    Häuser
Welche niedergetreten sind von vielen Füssen, abgeschliffen
Und zwischen denen Grasbüschel wachsen, das
Sind glückliche Werke.

Eingegangen in den Gebrauch der vielen
Oftmals verändert, verbessern sie ihre Gestalt und werden köstlich
Weil oftmals gekostet.
Selbst die Bruchstücke von Plastiken
Mit ihren abgehauenen Händen liebe ich. Auch sie
Lebten mir. Wenn auch fallen gelassen, wurden sie doch getra-
    gen.
Wenn auch überrannt, standen sie doch nicht zu hoch.
Die halbzerfallenen Bauwerke
Haben wieder das Aussehen von nicht vollendeten
Gross geplanten: ihre schönen Masse
Sind schon zu ahnen; sie bedürfen aber
Noch unseres Verständnisses. Andrerseits
Haben sie schon gedient, ja, sind schon überwunden. Dies alles
Beglückt mich.

< 166 >

The great aerials
Know nothing now
Of a past age.

1925

OF ALL WORKS

Of all works I prefer
Those used and worn.
Copper vessels with dents and with flattened rims
Knives and forks whose wooden handles
Many hands have grooved: such shapes
Seemed the noblest to me. So too the flagstones around
Old houses, trodden by many feet and ground down,
With clumps of grass in the cracks, these too
Are happy works.

Absorbed into the use of the many
Frequently changed, they improve their appearance, growing
    enjoyable
Because often enjoyed.
Even the remnants of broken sculptures
With lopped-off hands I love. They also
Lived with me. If they were dropped at least they must have
    been carried.
If men knocked them over they cannot have stood too high up.
Buildings half dilapidated
Revert to the look of buildings not yet completed
Generously designed: their fine proportions
Can already be guessed; yet they still make demands
On our understanding. At the same time
They have served already, indeed have been left behind. All
    this
Makes me glad.

1932

< 167 >

FAHREND IN EINEM BEQUEMEN WAGEN

Fahrend in einem bequemen Wagen
Auf einer regnerischen Landstrasse
Sahen wir einen zerlumpten Menschen bei Nachtanbruch
Der uns winkte, ihn mitzunehmen, sich tief verbeugend.
Wir hatten ein Dach und wir hatten Platz und wir fuhren
    vorüber
Und wir hörten mich sagen, mit einer grämlichen Stimme: Nein
Wir können niemand mitnehmen.
Wir waren schon weit voraus, einen Tagesmarsch vielleicht
Als ich plötzlich erschrak über diese meine Stimme
Dies mein Verhalten und diese
Ganze Welt.

AN DIE NACHGEBORENEN

I

Wirklich, ich lebe in finsteren Zeiten!
Das arglose Wort ist töricht. Eine glatte Stirn
Deutet auf Unempfindlichkeit hin. Der Lachende
Hat die furchtbare Nachricht
Nur noch nicht empfangen.

Was sind das für Zeiten, wo
Ein Gespräch über Bäume fast ein Verbrechen ist,
Weil es ein Schweigen über so viele Untaten einschliesst!
Der dort ruhig über die Strasse geht,
Ist wohl nicht mehr erreichbar für seine Freunde,
Die in Not sind?

Es ist wahr: ich verdiene noch meinen Unterhalt.
Aber glaubt mir: das ist nur ein Zufall. Nichts
Von dem, was ich tue, berechtigt mich dazu, mich sattzuessen.
Zufällig bin ich verschont. (Wenn mein Glück aussetzt,
Bin ich verloren.)

< 168 >

TRAVELING IN A COMFORTABLE CAR

Traveling in a comfortable car
Down a rainy road in the country
We saw a ragged fellow at nightfall
Signal to us for a ride, with a low bow.
We had a roof and we had room and we drove on
And we heard me say, in a peevish voice: No
We can't take anyone with us.
We had gone on a long way, perhaps a day's march
When suddenly I was shocked by this voice of mine
This behaviour of mine and this
Whole world.

1937

TO POSTERITY

I

Truly, the age I live in is bleak.
The guileless word is foolish. A smooth brow
Denotes insensitiveness. The laughing man
Has only not yet received
The dreadful news.

What times are these when a conversation
About trees is almost a crime.
Because it includes a silence about so many misdeeds!
That one there calmly crossing the street,
Hasn't he ceased to be at home to
His friends in need?

True enough: I still earn my living.
But, believe me, it's only luck.
Nothing I do gives me the right to eat my fill.
It happens that I've been spared. (When my luck gives out
I shall be lost.)

< 169 >

einfache Sprache

Man sagt mir: Iss und trink du! Sei froh, dass du hast!
Aber wie kann ich essen und trinken, wenn
Ich es dem Hungernden entreisse, was ich esse, und
Mein Glas Wasser einem Verdurstenden fehlt?
Und doch esse und trinke ich.

Ich wäre gerne auch weise. *Bibel*
In den alten Büchern steht, was weise ist:
Sich aus dem Streit der Welt halten und die kurze Zeit
Ohne Furcht verbringen
Auch ohne Gewalt auskommen,
Zitat aus der Bibel Böses mit Gutem vergelten,
Seine Wünsche nicht erfüllen, sondern vergessen,
Gilt für weise.
Alles das kann ich nicht:
Wirklich, ich lebe in finsteren Zeiten!

II

In die Städte kam ich zur Zeit der Unordnung,
Als da Hunger herrschte.
Unter die Menschen kam ich zur Zeit des Aufruhrs,
Und ich empörte mich mit ihnen.
So verging meine Zeit
Die auf Erden mir gegeben war.

Mein Essen ass ich zwischen den Schlachten.
Schlafen legte ich mich unter die Mörder.
Der Liebe pflegte ich achtlos
Und die Natur sah ich ohne Geduld.
So verging meine Zeit
Die auf Erden mir gegeben war.

Die Strassen führten in den Sumpf zu meiner Zeit.
Die Sprache verriet mich dem Schlächter. → *Hitler*
Ich vemochte nur wenig. Aber die Herrschenden
Sassen ohne mich sicherer, das hoffte ich. → *will Gefahr sein – er ist darum freut er sich*

< 170 >

They tell me: Eat and drink. Be glad that you can!
But how can I eat and drink, when
From the hungry man I snatch what I eat, and
My glass of water deprives the man dying of thirst?
And yet I eat and drink.

And I'd also like to be wise.
In the old books you read what is wise:
To keep out of the strife of the world and spend
Your brief span without fear.
And to refrain from violence
Render good for evil
Not fulfil one's desires, but forget
Is accounted wise.
All these are beyond me:
Truly, the age I live in is bleak.

II

I came into the cities at the time of disorder
When hunger was rife.
I mixed with men at the time of rebellion
And revolted as they did.
So passed the time
Granted to me on earth.

I ate my meals between battles.
I lay down to sleep between the murderers.
Love I pursued unheeding
And on nature looked without patience.
So passed the time
Granted to me on earth.

The streets led into morasses in my time.
Speech betrayed me to the butcher.
There was little I could do. Yet the rulers
Sat more secure but for me, that was my hope.

<   171   >

So verging meine Zeit
Die auf Erden mir gegeben war.

Die Kräfte waren gering. Das Ziel
Lag in grosser Ferne.
Es war deutlich sichtbar, wenn auch für mich
Kaum zu erreichen.
So verging meine Zeit
Die auf Erden mir gegeben war.

III

Ihr, die ihr auftauchen werdet aus der Flut
In der wir untergegangen sind,
Gedenkt
Wenn ihr von unseren Schwächen sprecht
Auch der finsteren Zeit
Der ihr entronnen seid.

Gingen wir doch, öfter als die Schuhe die Länder wechselnd
Durch die Kriege der Klassen, verzweifelt
Wenn da nur Unrecht war und keine Empörung.

Dabei wissen wir doch:
Auch der Hass gegen die Niedrigkeit
Verzerrt die Züge.
Auch der Zorn über das Unrecht
Macht die Stimme heiser. Ach, wir
Die wir den Boden bereiten wollten für Freundlichkeit,
Konnten selber nicht freundlich sein.

Ihr aber, wenn es soweit sein wird
Dass der Mensch dem Menschen ein Helfer ist
Gedenkt unsrer
Mit Nachsicht.

< 172 >

So passed the time
Granted to me on earth.

My resources were not great. The goal
Lay far ahead.
It was clearly visible, if for me
Scarcely attainable.
So passed the time
Granted to me on earth.

III

You that will emerge from the deluge
In which we drowned,
When you speak of our shortcomings
Remember too
The bleak age
Which you have escaped.

For, changing countries more often than shoes, we walked
Through the wars of the classes, despairing
When there was injustice only and no rebellion.

And yet we know well:
Even hatred of vileness
Distorts a man's features.
Even anger at injustice
Makes hoarse his voice. Ah, we
Who desired to prepare the soil for kindness
Could not ourselves be kind.

But you, when the times permit
Men to be the helpers of men
Remember us
With indulgence.

1938

< 173 >

✗ LEGENDE VON DER ENTSTEHUNG DES BUCHES TAOTEKING AUF DEM WEG DES LAOTSE IN DIE EMIGRATION

1

Als er Siebzig war und war gebrechlich
Drängte es den Lehrer doch nach Ruh
Denn die Güte war im Lande wieder einmal schwächlich
Und die Bosheit nahm an Kräften wieder einmal zu.
Und er gürtete den Schuh.

2

Und er packte ein, was er so brauchte:
Wenig. Doch es wurde dies und das.
So die Pfeife, die er immer abends rauchte
Und das Büchlein, das er immer las.
Weissbrot nach dem Augenmass.

3

Freute sich des Tals noch einmal und vergass es
Als er ins Gebirg den Weg einschlug.
Und sein Ochse freute sich des frischen Grases
Kauend, während er den Alten trug.
Denn dem ging es schnell genug.

4

Doch am vierten Tag im Felsgesteine
Hat ein Zöllner ihm den Weg verwehrt:
"Kostbarkeiten zu verzollen?"—"Keine."
Und der Knabe, der den Ochsen führte, sprach: "Er hat
    gelehrt."
Und so war auch das erklärt.

< 174 >

LEGEND OF THE ORIGIN OF
THE BOOK TAO TE CHING
ON LAO TZU'S WAY INTO EXILE

1

When he was seventy and growing frail
The teacher after all felt the need for peace,
For once again in the country kindness did not prevail
And malice once again was on the increase.
So he tied his shoelace.

2

And he packed every necessary thing.
Not much. But this and that into his bundle sped.
So the pipe that he smoked every evening,
And the slender book that he always read.
Also a ration of white bread.

3

Was glad once more of the valley, and put it out of mind
When toward the mountains he began to track.
And his ox was glad of all the new grass it could find,
Chewing, as it carried the old man on its back.
For he was not the hurrying kind.

4

But before the fourth day's rocky traveling was done,
A customs man interposed his authority.
"Please declare your valuables!"—"None."
And the boy who led the ox said: "A teacher, you see."
This met the contingency.

< 175 >

5

Doch der Mann in einer heitren Regung
Fragte noch: "Hat er was rausgekriegt?"
Sprach der Knabe: "Dass das weiche Wasser in Bewegung
Mit der Zeit den mächtigen Stein besiegt.
Du verstehst, das Harte unterliegt." *der ständige Widerstand*
                                          man braucht nur Zeit √ evolutionär

6

Dass er nicht das letzte Tageslicht verlöre
Trieb der Knabe nun den Ochsen an
Und die drei verschwanden schon um eine schwarze Föhre
Da kam plötzlich Fahrt in unsern Mann
Und er schrie: "He, du! Halt an!

7

Was ist das mit diesem Wasser, Alter?"
Hielt der Alte: "Intressiert es dich?"
Sprach der Mann: "Ich bin nur Zollverwalter
Doch wer wen besiegt, das intressiert auch mich.
Wenn du's weisst, dann sprich!

8

Schreib mir's auf! Diktier es diesem Kinde!
So was nimmt man doch nicht mit sich fort.
Da gibt's doch Papier bei uns und Tinte
Und ein Nachtmahl gibt es auch: ich wohne dort.
Nun, ist das ein Wort?"

9

Über seine Schulter sah der Alte
Auf den Mann: Flickjoppe. Keine Schuh.
Und die Stirne eine einzige Falte.

< 176 >

5

But the man, cheerful, and struck by a sudden notion,
Went on to ask: "Who discovered something, you'd say?"
The boy replied: "That yielding water in motion
Gets the better in the end of granite and porphyry.
You get me: the hard thing gives way."

6

To lose no more time in the failing light
The boy drove on the ox, and the three had passed
Behind a black Scotch fir, and were out of sight
When our man, jerked into action at last,
Yelled out: "Hey there, stop! Not so fast!

7

What's this about water, old man, that's so special?"
The old man stopped: "Does it interest you?"
Said the other: "I'm only a customs official,
But who gets the better of whom, that interests me too.
If you know and can tell me, do!

8

Write it down for me. Dictate it to this boy.
You don't take things like that with you. Have a care.
Of paper and ink we've a copious supply.
And there's a bite for you too: I live in there.
Well, do you call that fair?"

9

Over his shoulder the old sage now
Glanced at the man. Patched coat. Never owned a shoe.
One deep wrinkle his brow.

< 177 >

Ach, kein Sieger trat da auf ihn zu.
Und er murmelte: "Auch du?"

10

Eine höfliche Bitte abzuschlagen
War der Alte, wie es schien, zu alt.
Denn er sagte laut: "Die etwas fragen
Die verdienen Antwort." Sprach der Knabe: "Es wird auch
schon kalt."
"Gut, ein kleiner Aufenthalt."

11

Und von seinem Ochsen stieg der Weise
Sieben Tage schrieben sie zu zweit.
Und der Zöllner brachte Essen (und er fluchte nur noch leise
Mit den Schmugglern in der ganzen Zeit).
Und dann war's soweit.

12

Und dem Zöllner händigte der Knabe
Eines Morgens einundachtzig Sprüche ein.
Und mit Dank für eine kleine Reisegabe
Bogen sie um jene Föhre ins Gestein.
Sagt jetzt: kann man höflicher sein? *Brecht an den Leser*

13

Aber rühmen wir nicht nur den Weisen
Dessen Name auf dem Buche prangt!
Denn man muss dem Weisen seine Weisheit erst entreissen.
Darum sei der Zöllner auch bedankt:
Er hat sie ihm abverlangt.

Man muß fragen, wenn man etwas lernen will
e Dialektik.

< 178 >

Oh, this was no victor. So much he knew.
And he murmured: "You too?"

10

To reject a courteous suggestion
The old man, it seemed, was too old.
For he said aloud: "Those who ask a question
Deserve an answer." Said the boy: "And it's turning cold."
"We'll stay, then. Hold!"

11

And the sage dismounted, having made his choice.
For seven days the two of them wrote on.
The customs man brought them food (and all that time lowered
      his voice
When he swore at the smugglers and those on the run).
Then the work was done.

12

And one morning the boy could present to
The customs man eighty-one maxims completed,
And, thanking him for his gift of a small memento,
To the rocky track, round that fir, they retreated.
Rare politeness, you'll grant. Can you beat it?

13

But not to that wise man alone our praise is due
Whose name adorns the book Tao Te Ching.
For the wise man's wisdom must be dragged out of him too.
So the customs man also deserves our thanks for the thing:
He did the eliciting.

1938

<   179   >

Thesc - Antithese - Synthese
↳ wird dem Leser überlassen

✗ DIE MASKE DES BÖSEN

An meiner Wand hängt ein japanisches Holzwerk
Maske eines bösen Dämons, bemalt mit Goldlack.
Mitfühlend sehe ich
Die geschwollenen Stirnadern, andeutend
Wie anstrengend es ist, böse zu sein.

ÜBERALL FREUNDE

Die finnischen Arbeiter
Gaben ihm Betten und einen Schreibtisch
Die Schriftsteller der Sowjetunion brachten ihn aufs Schiff
Und ein jüdischer Wäscher in Los Angeles
Schickte ihm einen Anzug: der Feind der Schlächter
Fand Freunde.

VOM SPRENGEN DES GARTENS

O Sprengen des Gartens, das Grün zu ermutigen!
Wässern der durstigen Bäume! Gib mehr als genug. Und
Vergiss nicht das Strauchwerk, auch
Das beerenlose nicht, das ermattete
Geizige! Und übersieh mir nicht
Zwischen den Blumen das Unkraut, das auch
Durst hat. Noch giesse nur
Den frischen Rasen oder den versengten nur:
Auch den nackten Boden erfrische du.

< 180 >

THE MASK OF EVIL

On my wall hangs a Japanese carving
Mask of an evil demon, lacquered in gold.
Sympathetic I see
The swollen veins on the forehead, implying
How strenuous it is to be evil.

1942

FRIENDS EVERYWHERE

Finnish working men
Gave him beds and a desk
Writers of the Soviet Union saw him on to the boat
And a Jewish laundryman in Los Angeles
Sent him a suit: the enemy of the Butchers
Found friends.

1942

ON WATERING THE GARDEN

O the spraying of gardens, to encourage green!
Watering of thirsty trees! Give them more than enough and
Do not forget the shrubs,
Even those without berries or those
Exhausted, grown mean. And don't overlook
The weeds between the flowers—these too
Are thirsty. Nor water only
The fresh parts of the lawn, or only the scorched:
Even the naked soil take care to refresh.

1943

<   181   >

ERICH KÄSTNER:

Geboren 1899 in Dresden. Er wurde international berühmt durch seine Kinderbücher, z.B. *Emil und die Detektive*. Er studierte an den Universitäten Leipzig, Rostock und Berlin. Als Romanautor und Lyriker vertrat er die sogenannte "Neue Sachlichkeit," eine Reaktion auf expressionistische Subjektivität. Andere Schriftsteller, die in den zwanziger und dreißiger Jahren eine ähnliche Richtung zeigten, waren Brecht, Tucholsky und Zuckmayer, die alle eine sozial engagierte Lyrik schrieben. Obwohl seine lyrischen Arbeiten weniger gelesen wurden als seine Prosa, gewannen seine Gedichtsammlungen, wie z.B. die *Lyrische Hausapotheke* (1935) eine Popularität, die noch größer gewesen wäre, wenn sein Werk nicht von den Nazis verboten worden wäre; das Buch erschien in der Schweiz. Andere Gedichtbände: *Bei Durchsicht meiner Bücher . . . eine Auswahl aus vier Versbänden* (1946), *Die kleine Freiheit; Chansons und Prosa 1949-1952* (1952), *Der Gegenwart ins Gästebuch* (1958). Ein Großteil von Kästners Prosa wurde in englischer Übersetzung veröffentlicht. 1963 wurde eine Gedichtauswahl *Let's Face It* veröffentlicht. 1965 erschienen seine *Gesammelte Schriften* in 7 Bänden, gefolgt von einer Auswahl aus seinen Werken *Wer nicht hören will, muß lesen* (1971). Kästner starb 1974 in München.

DIE HUMMERMARSEILLAISE

Das Leben ist doch bloss zum Sterben da.
O we . . . o welche Lust, Soldat zu sein!
Wer sich im Schlaf noch niemals lächeln sah,
dem leuchtet . . . hupp . . . dem leuchtet das nicht ein.

Ich möchte manchmal—immer möcht ich nicht—
ich möchte manchmal in die Kissen lachen.
Der Güter höchstes Übel ist die Pflicht.
Und kann man nichts dage . . . dagegen machen.

Da ist noch ei . . . noch eins, was ich erwäge:
Mit Vitriol einmal den Mund zu spülen.
Treib Sport, mein Volk! Trei . . . treibe Körperpflege!
Denn wer nicht hören will, muss . . . will, muss fühlen.

Oft bin ich Menschen weiblichen Geschlechts
als Hei . . . als Heiliger erschienen.

< 182 >

ERICH KÄSTNER:

Born in Dresden in 1899, he became internationally famous with his children's books, such as *Emil und die Detektiven*. He studied at the universities of Leipzig, Rostock, and Berlin. As a novelist and poet he represented the trend known as "die nuee Sachlichkeit" (the new matter-of-factness), a trend in reaction against Expressionist subjectivity. Other writers who showed this trend in the 'twenties and 'thirties were Brecht, Tucholsky, and Zuckmayer, all of whom wrote a poetry of social comment. Though less widely read than his prose, Kästner's collections of poems, such as his *Lyrische Hausapotheke* (1935), attained a popularity that would have been even greater if his work had not been banned in Germany under the Nazis; the book appeared in Switzerland. His other books of poems include: *Bei Durchsicht meiner Bücher . . . eine Auswahl aus vier Versbänden* (1946), *Die kleine Freiheit; Chansons und Prosa 1949-1952* (1952), *Der Gegenwart ins Gästebuch* (1958). Many of Kästner's prose books have been published in English translation. A selection of poems, *Let's Face It*, was published in England in 1963. His *Gesammelte Schriften* in seven volumes appeared in 1965, and was followed by a selection from his works: *Wer nicht hören will, muss lesen* (1971). Kästner died in Munich in 1974.

THE LOBSTER MARSEILLAISE

The only point of living is to die.
To be a so—a soldier—oh, what bliss!
Only a chap who's seen his own self lie
In bed and smile would get the point of this.

Some of the time—not all the time—I itch
To tell my pillows, laughing as I shout it:
Du—duties are the bane of being rich.
And there is nothing one can do about it.

One more . . . one more thing, come to think of it:
To rinse one's mouth with vitriol one day.
Sport, games, my people! Keep your bodies fit!
Those who don't want to . . . why, we'll make them play.

Often I've seemed—and acted—like a saint
To persons of the female sex, I swear:

<   183   >

Ich gab das letzte her, nach links und rechts.
Sogar das Lager teilte ich mit ihnen.

Zehntausend Liter Leuchtgas will ich kaufen
und . . . und als Vorrat in den Keller tun.
Ich werde wieder öfter Rollschuh laufen.
Im Au . . . im Auto fahren wird kommun.

Ich liebe es, das Atmen zu vermeiden.
Es lohnt nicht . . . hupp . . . auch weiss man nicht, wozu.
Ich frag' mich oft, warum sie uns beneiden.
Denn Geld macht arm. Und lässt uns nicht in Ruh.

Ich möchte es einmal nicht eilig haben.
Und morgen nicht zur Bö . . . zur Börse gehn.
Ich möchte wie ganz . . . wie ganz kleine Knaben
ganz ohne Geld vor einem Laden stehn . . .

Ich will mein Kapital den Armen geben.
So . . . so bin ich. Das ist doch edel. Wie?
In Flo . . . Florenz möcht' ich von Renten leben.
Es lebe Franz von . . . Franz von Assisi! Hupp!

GEFÄHRLICHES LOKAL

Mir träumte neulich, dass mein Stammcafé
auf einer Insel unter Palmen stünde.
Persönlich kenne ich bloss Warnemünde.
Doch Träume reisen gern nach Übersee.

Ich sass am Fenster und versank in Schweigen.
Wo sonst die Linie 56 hält
war eine Art von Urwald aufgestellt.
Und Orang Utans hingen in den Zweigen.

Sie waren sicher noch nicht lange da.
So leicht verändern sich die Metermasse!

< 184 >

I gave up all I had without constraint,
Gave up my very couch for them to share.

I'll buy a thousand drums of lamp oil too
And put it in the cellar as a store.
Go roller-skating as I used to do.
Driving is not distinguished any more.

I like to hold my breath . . . stop breathing . . . thus!
A mug's game, breathing . . . hip . . . and not much fun.
I ask myself, why do they envy us.
Money makes poor. And keeps you on the run.

Not to be rushed! For once be free again,
And not go to the stock exchange tomorrow!
Window-shop like a boy and rack my brain
For just one penny I could cadge or borrow . . .

I'll give away my capital—and be blessed.
That's what *I*'m like. Generous. Noble. Eh?
Retire to Florence, live on interest.
Three cheers for Fr—ancis of Assisi! Hip.

1928: Herz auf der Taille

DANGEROUS ESTABLISHMENT

My favorite café—so I dreamed recently—
stood amidst palm trees in an island port.
Now, Margate is *my* holiday resort;
but dreams are rather apt to cross the sea.

I settled near the window, ill at ease:
where once the number 2 bus used to stop
they'd set a sort of pristine jungle up
and apes—orangutans—hung on the trees.

I'm sure they'd not been there so very long:
you can't just change dimensions, yards and feet.

<   185   >

Bevor ich kam, war's noch die Prager Strasse.
Man setzt sich hin, schon ist es Sumatra.

Erst wollte ich den Oberkellner fragen.
Dann dachte ich, es hätte keinen Zweck.
Was soll ein Kellner namens Urbanek,
selbst wenn er wollte, weiter dazu sagen?

Dann ging die Tür. Das war der Doktor Uhl.
Und hinter ihm erschien ein schwarzer Panther,
der setzte sich, als sei er ein Bekannter,
an meinem Tisch auf einen leeren Stuhl.

Ich fragte ihn betreten, ob er rauche.
Er sah mich an. Und sagte keinen Ton.
Dann kam der Wirt in eigener Person
und kitzelte den seltnen Gast am Bauche.

Der Ober brachte Erbspüree mit Speck.
Er hatte grosse Angst und ging auf Zehen.
Der Panther liess das gute Essen stehen
und frass den Kellner. Armer Urbanek!

Von oben drang der Klang der Billardbälle.
Der schwarze Panther war noch beim Diner.
Ich sass bestürzt in meinem Stammcafé.
Und sah nur Wald. Und keine Haltestelle.

Weil man mich dann zum Telephone rief
(ein Kunde wollte mich geschäftlich sprechen),
war ich genötigt, plötzlich aufzubrechen.
Als ich zurückkam, sah ich, dass ich schlief . . .

< 186 >

Before I came it was still Bishop's Street;
you pick a place, and now it's Belitong.

At first I felt like asking the head waiter.
But then I thought this wasn't any good.
What sort of comment should a man called Slater
make on this business, even if he could?

Now the door opened. It was Dr. Clare.
And, close behind him, a black panther who
sat down as any Tom or Dick might do—
and at my table, on a vacant chair.

I asked him softly if he'd care to smoke.
He did not stir, but stared at me defiant.
Now the proprietor approached this client,
solemnly tickled him, but never spoke.

The waiter brought us scrambled egg on toast.
He walked on tip-toe and seemed liverish.
The panther did not touch this wholesome dish
but ate poor Slater. Peace be with his ghost!

From up above came sounds of ball and cue.
The panther dined. He saw no need to hurry.
What could I do but sit there, watch and worry,
with jungle all around, no number 2?

Because they called me to the phone (old Deeping,
my senior clerk, to tell me he was sick),
I was obliged to make my exit quick.
When I came back I saw that I was sleeping . . .

1930: *Ein Mann gibt Auskunft*

< 187 >

PETER HUCHEL:

Geboren 1903 in Berlin. In der Landschaft um die Stadt verbrachte er auch den größten Teil seiner Kindheit. Er studierte Philosophie und Literatur in Berlin, Freiburg und Wien, verbrachte mehrere Jahre als Arbeiter in Frankreich und lebte dann als Schriftsteller. 1932 wurde ihm ein Preis für seine erste Gedichtsammlung verliehen, aber er zog das Manuskript zurück, als die Nazis an die Macht kamen. Während des Krieges war er Soldat; 1945 kehrte er aus russischer Gefangenschaft heim und ließ sich als künstlerischer Leiter von Radio Ost-Berlin in Ost-Berlin nieder. Von 1949 bis 1962 gab er die *hervorragende* Literaturzeitschrift *Sinn und Form* heraus, wurde aber wegen seiner Editionspolitik angegriffen; man entzog ihm die Herausgeberschaft und verbot die Veröffentlichung seiner Werke in Ost-Deutschland. Neun Jahre lang lebte er zurückgezogen und in Ungnade bei Potsdam. 1971 erlaubte man ihm die Ausreise nach Italien, dann nach West-Deutschland, wo er jetzt lebt. Obwohl er eine Zeitlang mit Brecht in Verbindung stand, zeigt seine Lyrik eher ein ethisches als ein strikt politisches Engagement. Er steht Günter Eich und Johannes Bobrowski nahe. Sein erster Gedichtband erschien erst 1948 unter dem Titel *Gedichte* in beiden Teilen Deutschlands. Spätere Sammlungen: *Chausseen, Chausseen* (1963) und *Gezählte Tage* (1972) und nur in Westdeutschland veröffentlicht. Eine. Sammlung *Ausgewählte Gedichte* erschien 1973, und seine *Selected Poems*, eine Auswahl aus den beiden späteren Bänden, erschien 1974 in England.

JAN-FELIX CAERDAL

Für Günter Eich

Am Ende der Öde
sah ich die grosse Eskorte,
das Banner zerfetzt, die Trommel durchlöchert,
die Sänfte,
von acht zerlumpten Knechten getragen,
war leer.

Einem Toten,
die Arme zerbrachen wie trockene Äste,
gelang im Sturz der Stirnaufschlag.

Ich, der Bretone,

<   188   >

PETER HUCHEL:

Born in Berlin in 1903, he spent most of his childhood in the country around Berlin. He studied philosophy and literature in Berlin, Freiburg, and Veinna, spent several years in France as a laborer, then lived as á writer. He received a prize for his first collection of poems in 1932, but withdrew the manuscript when the Nazis came to power. He served in the army during the war, returned from imprisonment in Russia in 1945, and settled in East Berlin as artistic director of East Berlin Radio. From 1949 to 1962 he edited the distinguished literary periodical *Sinn und Form*, but was attacked for his editorial policy, deprived of his editorship and forbidden to publish his work in East Germany. For nine years he lived in retirement and disgrace near Potsdam. In 1971 he was allowed to leave for Italy, then West Germany, where he now lives. Although he was associated with Brecht at one period, his poetry shows an ethical rather than a narrowly political commitment. His affinities are with Günter Eich and Johannes Bobrowski. His first book of poems did not appear until 1948, in East and West Germany, under the title *Gedichte*. His later collections are *Chausseen. Chausseen* (1963) and *Gezählte Tage* (1972), both published in West Germany only. A collection of *Ausgewählte Gedichte* appeared in 1973, and his *Selected Poems*, taken from the two later volumes, appeared in England in 1974.

JAN-FELIX CAERDAL

For Günter Eich

At the waste's end
I saw the great convoy,
their banner torn, their drum pierced,
the litter,
carried by eight servants in rags,
was empty.

A dead man,
his arms snapped like dry sticks,
succeeded in touching the ground with his brow as he fell.

I, the Breton,

mit meerdurchsickerten Schuhen
und einem Hemd aus Nebel
über dem Sonnengeflecht,

ich, der Nachzügler,
der einst
Geschmeide wie Ähren auflas,
im Licht der Messe versank,

ging nun voran
mit leeren Händen
und einer Rinne Salz im Gesicht.

DAS GRAB DES ODYSSEUS

Niemand wird finden
das Grab des Odysseus,
kein Spatenstich
den krustigen Helm
im Dunst versteinerter Knochen.

Such nicht die Höhle,
wo unter die Erde hinab
ein wehender Russ, ein Schatten nur,
vom Pech der Fackel versehrt,
zu seinen toten Gefährten ging,
die Hände hebend waffenlos,
bespritzt mit dem Blut geschlachteter Schafe.

Mein ist alles, sagte der Staub,
das Grab der Sonne hinter der Wüste,
die Riffe voller Wassergetöse,
der endlose Mittag, der immer noch warnt
den Seeräubersohn aus Ithaka,
das Steuerruder, schartig vom Salz,
die Karten und Schiffkataloge
des alten Homer.

<   190   >

my shoes soaked in sea water,
in a shirt of fog over my diaphragm,

I, the straggler
who once
gathered up jewels like ears of corn,
sank in the light of the Mass,

now walked in the van
with empty hands
and a furrow of salt in my face.

1973

THE GRAVE OF ODYSSEUS

No one will find
the grave of Odysseus,
no stab of spade
the encrusted helmet
in the haze of petrified bones.

Do not look for the cave
where down below the earth
a wafting soot, a mere shadow,
damaged by pitch from torches
went to his dead companions,
raising weaponless hands,
splattered with blood of slaughtered sheep.

All is mine, said the dust,
the sun's grave behind the desert,
the reefs full of the sea's roar,
unending noon that still warns
the pirate's boy from Ithaca,
the rudder jagged with salt,
the maritime charts and lists
of ancient Homer.

<   191   >

DER AMMONITER

Für Axel Vieregg

Überdrüssig der Götter und ihrer Feuer
lebte ich ohne Gesetz
in der Senke des Tales Hinnom.
Mich verliessen die alten Begleiter,
das Gleichgewicht von Erde und Himmel,
nur der Widder, die Moderhinke
schleifend über die Sterne, blieb mir treu.
Unter seinem Gehörn aus Stein,
das rauchlos glänzte, schlief ich nachts,
brannte Urnen jeden Tag,
die ich abends vor der Sonne
am Felsen zerschlug.
Nicht sah ich in den Zedern
die Katzendämmerung, den Aufflug des Vogels,
die Herrlichkeit des Wassers,
das über meine Arme rann,
wenn ich im Bottich schlämmte den Ton.
Der Geruch des Todes machte mich blind.

UNTERWEGS

Die streifende Rotte
vereister Blätter
fällte der Tag
mit Drähten über der Feuergrube.

Neben dem Karren
im Schutz der Plache
die Zigeunerin,
zu ihren Füssen
eingewickelt das schlafende Kind.
Sie hebt aus dem Schafspelz
einen jungen Hund an die Brust,
ihn säugend,
säugt sie den hungrigen Wind im Schnee.

< 192 >

THE AMMONITE

For Axel Vieregg

Tired of the gods and of their fires,
I lived without laws
in the dip of the valley of Hinnon.
My old companions left me,
the balance of earth and sky,
only the ram, trailing its footrot limp
across the stars, remained loyal.
Under its horns of stone
that shone without smoke, I slept by night,
every day baked urns
that I shattered against the rock
in face of the setting sun.
In the cedars I did not see
the cats' twilight, the rising of birds,
the splendour of water
flowing over my arms
when in my bucket I mixed the clay.
The smell of death made me blind.

ON THE WAY

Day felled
the roaming troop
of ice-covered leaves
with wires above the fire pit.

Beside her wagon,
sheltered by its cover,
the Gipsy woman,
her swaddled infant
asleep at her feet.
From the sheepskin she raises
a puppy to her breast;
suckling it,
she suckles the hungry wind in the snow.

< 193 >

Ferne Tochter
der asiatischen Göttin,
die Feuersteinsichel
hast du verloren
am Rand der höllischen Sümpfe.
Du hörst das Gebell in der Nacht,
das der Radspur folgt von Lager zu Lager.

ÖSTLICHER FLUSS

Such nicht die Steine
im Wasser über dem Schlamm,
der Kahn ist fort,
der Fluss
nicht mehr mit Netzen
und Reusen bestückt.
Der Sonnendocht,
die Sumpfdotterblume verglomm im Regen.

Nur die Weide gibt noch Rechenschaft,
in ihren Wurzeln
sind die Geheimnisse
der Landstreicher verborgen,
die kümmerlichen Schätze,
der rostige Angelhaken,
die Büchse ohne Boden
zum Aufbewahren längst
vergessener Gespräche.

An den Zweigen
die leeren Nester der Beutelmeisen,
die vogelleichten Schuhe.
Keiner streift sie
den Kindern über die Füsse.

<   194   >

Distant daughter
of the Asiatic goddess,
you've lost your flint sickle
on the edge of the hellish marshes.
By night you hear the barking
that follows the wheel tracks from camp to camp.

EASTERN RIVER

Do not look for the stones
in water above the mud,
the boat is gone.
No longer with nets and baskets
the river is dotted.
The sun wick,
the marsh marigold flickered out in rain.

Only the willow still bears witness,
in its roots
the secrets of tramps lie hidden,
their paltry treasures,
a rusty fishhook,
a bottle full of sand,
a tin with no bottom,
in which to preserve
conversations long forgotten.

On the boughs,
empty nests of the penduline titmice,
shoes light as birds.
No one slips them
over children's feet.

March, 1974

<   195   >

BEGEGNUNG

Für Michael Hamburger

Schleiereule,
Tochter des Schnees,
dem Nachtwind unterworfen,

doch Wurzel fassend
mit den Krallen
im modrig grindigen Gemäuer,

Schnabelgesicht
mit runden Augen,
herzstarre Maske
aus Federn weissen Feuers,
das weder Zeit noch Raum berührt,

kalt weht die Nacht
ans alte Gehöft,
im Verhof fahles Gelichter,
Schlitten, Gepäck, verschneite Laternen,

in den Töpfen Tod,
in den Krügen Gift,
das Testament an den Balken genagelt.

Das Verborgene unter
den Klauen der Felsen,
die Öffnung in die Nacht,
die Todesangst
wie stechendes Salz ins Fleisch gelegt.

Lasst uns niederfahren
in der Sprache der Engel
zu den zerbrochenen Ziegeln Babels.

< 196 >

MEETING

For Michael Hamburger

Barn owl
daughter of snow,
subject to the night wind,

yet taking root
with her talons
in the rotten scab of walls,

beak face
with round eyes,
heart-rigid mask
of feathers a white fire
that touches neither time nor space.

Coldly the wind blows
against the old homestead,
in the yard pale folk,
sledges, baggage, lamps covered with snow,

in the pots death,
in the pitchers poison,
the last will nailed to a post.

The hidden thing
under the rocks' claws,
the opening into night,
the terror of death
thrust into flesh like stinging salt.

Let us go down
in the language of angels
to the broken bricks of Babel.

                          1974

<   197   >

PFEILSPITZE DES ADA

Bewohner der kahlen Berge,
Nachzügler, Zelte, flatternd und finster,
unduldsam der Tod,
als stürze er von der Sonne hinab
in gleissende Ziegelscherben.

Sandkauend, in Stössen
und Wirbeln der Wind,
der heiss durch die Disteln fegt.
Eselfarben die Mauer,
lehmrissig,
der Mann, der sich nähert,
geht ohne Schatten.

Einst fliege ich auf
zu den Gazellen des Lichts,
sagt eine Stimme.

BLICK AUS DEM WINTERFENSTER

Kopfweiden, schneeumtanzt,
Besen, die den Nebel fegen.
Holz und Unglück
wachsen über Nacht.
Mein Messgerät
die Fieberkurve.

Wer geht dort ohne Licht
und ohne Mund,
schleift übers Eis
das Tellereisen?

Die Wahrsager des Waldes,
die Füchse mit schlechtem Gebiss
sitzen abseits im Dunkel
und starren ins Feuer.

ADA'S ARROWHEAD

Inhabitants of the bare mountains,
stragglers, tents, flapping and gloomy,
death intolerant
as though it came hurtling down from the sun
into gleaming brick shards.

Chewing sand, in bursts
and whirls the wind
that sweeps hot through the thistles.
The well donkey-coloured,
with cracks in the clay,
the man approaching
walks without a shadow.

One day I shall fly up
to the gazelles of light,
says a voice.

VIEW FROM THE WINTER WINDOW

Pollarded willows, the snow dancing around them,
brooms that sweep the mind.
Wood and misfortune
shoot up overnight.
My gauge
is the temperature chart.

Who goes there without a light,
without a mouth,
sliding a steel trap
across the ice?

The soothsayers of the forest,
the foxes with bad teeth
sit in the dark, apart,
staring into the fire.

< 199 >

MARIE LUISE KASCHNITZ:

Geboren 1901 in Karlsruhe. Die sie prägenden Jahre verbrachte sie in Süddeutschland, Italien und Ostpreußen. Nach dem Krieg wurde sie als Lyrikerin, Autorin von Romanen und Kurzgeschichten und als Biographin bekannt. Sie starb 1974 in Süddeutschland. 1965 veröffentlichte sie einen Band ausgewählter Gedichte, der den größten Teil ihres Werks bis zu diesem Zeitpunkt umfaßt: *Überallnie* (Gedichte 1928-1965). *Engelsbrücke*, ein autobiographisches Werk, erschien 1955; zehn Jahre danach *Das Tagebuch des Schriftstellers* (1965). Ihre Erzählungen umfassen *Lange Schatten* (1960; eine englische Fassung erschien 1966 unter dem Titel *Long Shadows*), *Ferngespräche* (1966), *Vogel Rock. Unheimliche Geschichten* (1969), *Steht noch dahin* (1970) und *Eisbären* (1972). Sie veröffentlichte auch einige Hörspiele: *Catarina Cornaro und die Reise des Herrn Admet* (1966), *Gespräche im All* (1971). Ihre späteren Gedichtbände umfassen die Titel: *Kein Zauberspruch* (1972) und die Auswahl *Gedichte* herausgegeben von Peter Huchel.

NUR DIE AUGEN

Tauft mich wieder
Womit?
Mit dem nächstbesten Wasser
Dem immer heiligen.
Legt mir die Hand auf
Gebt mir den nächstbesten Namen
Einen geschlechtslosen
Frühwind- und Tannennamen
Für das letzte Stück Wegs.
Verwandelt mich immerhin
Nur meine Augen lasst mir
Diese von jeher offen
Von jeher tauglich.

AUFERSTEHUNG

Manchmal stehen wir auf
Stehen wie zur Auferstehung auf
Mitten am Tage
Mit unserem lebendigen Haar
Mit unserer atmenden Haut.

< 200 >

MARIE LUISE KASCHNITZ:

Born in Karlsruhe in 1901, she spent her formative years in South Germany, Italy, and East Prussia. She became known after the war as a poet, novelist, short story writer, and biographer. She died in South Germany in 1974. In 1965 she published a volume of selected poems containing most of her work up to that time: *Überallnie* (poems 1928-1965). An autobiographical work, *Engelsbrücke*, appeared in 1955, followed a decade later by *Das Tagebuch des Schriftstellers* (1965). Her stories include *Lange Schatten* (1960, an English version appeared in 1966 under the title: *Long Shadows*), *Ferngespräche* (1966), *Vogel Rock. Unheimliche Geschichten* (1969), *Steht noch dahin* (1970), and *Eisbären* (1972). She also published some radio plays: *Catarina Cornaro und die Reise des Herrn Admet* (1966), *Gespräche im All* (1971). Her later books include *Kein Zauberspruch* (1972) and the selection *Gedichte* (1975), edited by Peter Huchel.

ONLY THE EYES

Re-christen me
With what?
With any water to hand
With the always holy.
Lay a blessing on me
Give me the first name to hand
A sexless name
Morning breeze, pine name
For the last stretch of my way.
Transform me anyhow
Only leave me my eyes
That have always been open
Always reliable.

                    1958/1961

RESURRECTION

Sometimes we get up
Get up as for a resurrection
In broad daylight
With our living hair
With our breathing skin.

<   201   >

Nur das Gewohnte ist um uns.
Keine Fata Morgana von Palmen
Mit weidenden Löwen
Und sanften Wölfen.

Die Weckuhren hören nicht auf zu ticken
Ihre Leuchtzeiger löschen nicht aus.

Und dennoch leicht
Und dennoch unverwundbar
Geordnet in geheimnisvolle Ordnung
Vorweggenommen in ein Haus aus Licht.

DEMUT

Mir aufgelauert entdeckt
Die Blüten Falschgeld
Die ich unter die Leute bringe
Und die falschen Papiere
Mit denen ich reise
Und das falsche Zeugnis
Das ich ablege ehe
Der Morgen kräht
Und das falsche Spiel
Das ich treibe
Mit wem
Mit mir

Rotwelsch entziffert
Letzthin
Im Jahr der ruhigen Sonne
Blutsenkung erhöht
Und gewusst
Es ist Zeit für Demut.

Only the usual things are around us.
No mirage of palm trees
With grazing lions
And gentle wolves.

The alarm clocks don't cease to tick
Their phosphorescent hands are not extinguished.

And yet weightlessly
And yet invulnerably
Ordered into mysterious order
Admitted early into a house of light.

1958/1961: Dein Schweigen, meine Stimme

HUMILITY

Ambushed myself discovered
The counterfeit blossoms
I circulate
And the forged documents
With which I travel
And the false witness
I bear before
Morning crows
And the loaded dice
With which I play
With whom
With me

Thieves' lingo deciphered
Lately
In the year of the calm sun
Blood pressure going down
And knew
It's time for humility.

1962/1965: Überallnie

JESSE THOOR:

Geboren 1905 in Berlin. Seine Eltern waren österreichische Arbeiter. Er kehrte in seiner Kindheit nach Österreich zurück, als der Vater keine Arbeit als Zimmermann finden konnte; später zog die Familie jedoch wieder nach Berlin. Wenn Thoor nicht trampte, arbeitete er in einer Vielzahl von Gewerben—in einer Werkzeugfabrik, als Zahntechniker, als Seemann und als blinder Passagier, der die Seeleute unterhielt. Nach dem Tod seiner Mutter lebte er bei seiner Tante in Wien. Da er Kommunist war, mußte er von Wien in die Tschechoslowakei fliehen, von da nach England, wobei er dank der Protektion des Prinzen Hubertus von Löwenstein auf das letzte Flugzeug kam. Der Prinz besorgte ihm auch eine Unterstützung. Während er in der Tschechoslowakei war, brach er mit der Partei, wurde in England als Nazi-Spion denunziert und gefangengenommen. Seine spätere Lyrik war religiös und visionär, ohne die dialektale Direktheit und Kraft seiner früheren, an Villon erinnernden Sonnette zu verlieren. In seinen letzten Lebensjahren in London arbeitete er als Silber- und Goldschmied unter starker geistiger Anspannung und in Armut, da er sich weigerte, für eine Firma zu arbeiten, viele seiner Kunstwerke weggab und mit seinen Schriften kein Geld verdienen wollte. Er starb 1952 an einer Herzthrombose, als er mit Freunden bei Lienz in Österreich war. Zu seinen Lebzeiten wurde ein Band Sonnette veröffentlicht. Seine Gedichte wurden 1956 und, nocheinmal mit ausgewählten Erzählungen und weiteren Gedichten, 1965 gesammelt. Eine kleinere Auswahl erschien zu seinem siebzigsten Geburtstag 1975 (*Gedichte*).

Aus: REDEN UND RUFE (1944-1949)

Meine Freunde, hört:—unser Nachbar ist krank!—Ach, unser
    Nachbar!
Der ein Träumer war zur Nacht . . . und wachsam bis in den
    Schlaf hinein.
Und der erzählt hat die Geschichten von der Torheit der
    Gerechten.
Und dass einer umgeht in uns, der auch meine Stimme ver-
    nommen hat.

Denn noch immer brennen die hellen Wundermale der Verwir-
    rung in mir.
Und fallen die Tränen fort . . . wachsen Rosen . . . und lauter
    Anmut hervor.

<   204   >

JESSE THOOR

Born in Berlin in 1905, of working-class Austrian parents, and returned to Austria in his childhood when his father could find no work as a carpenter, but they subsequently moved back to Berlin again. Thoor worked at a variety of trades—in a tool factory, as a dental technician, as a sailor and stowaway entertainer of sailors—when not tramping. After the death of his mother he lived with his aunt in Vienna. As a Communist he had to flee from Vienna to Czechoslovakia, then to England, leaving by the last plane out, thanks to the patronage of Prince Hubertus von Loewenstein, who also obtained a grant for him. He broke with the Party while in Czechoslovakia, and in England he was denounced as a Nazi spy, and imprisoned. His later verse was religious and visionary, while retaining the vernacular directness and forcefulness of his earlier Villonesque sonnets. In his last years in London he worked as a goldsmith and silversmith, under great mental stress and in poverty, since he refused to work for a firm, gave away many of his artifacts, and refused to earn money with his writings. He died of a coronary thrombosis in 1952 while staying with friends near Lienz, Austria. He published a book of sonnets in his lifetime. His poems were collected in 1956 and again, with selected stories and additional poems, in 1965. A smaller selection appeared on his seventieth birthday in 1975 (Gedichte).

From SPEECHES AND INVOCATIONS

Listen, my friends:—our neighbor is ill!—Oh, our neighbor!
Who was a dreamer by night and watchful even in sleep.
And who told us the stories about the follies of the just.
And that one walks about within us, who has heard my voice
   also.

For still the bright stigmata of confusion smart in me.
And the tears fall away . . . roses grow . . . and all manner of
   grace.
And the songs of homecoming, and the solemn hymns of wisdom.
And the discourse of transformation and of glad community.

< 205 >

Und die Lieder der Heimkehr, und die hohen Gesänge der Vernunft.
Und die Gespräche der Verwandlung und der fröhlichen Gemeinschaft.

Ach, ihr Leute . . . entschuldigt meine Worte, achtet nicht meiner Reden.
Ihr Gebete von Madrid . . . und ihr Kathedralen an den raschen Flüssen.
Das polnische Kreuz . . . das wie die Sonne zwischen meinen Augen kreist.

Ach, Unbegreiflicher . . . der du bist—und wie aus der Mitte der Zeit.
Und wie die Zuversicht . . . und wie die Mitteilung der Ermunterung.
Und dass wieder der Grund wie Gold sei, rufen die Diener des Trostes.

Aus: REDEN UND RUFE (1944-49)

Herr Herr . . . sie haben meinen Verstand zerstochen, dass ich schreibe:
Sie haben meinen Verstand zerstochen, die Elenden!
Herr . . . die der Mord freigelassen hat!—Lausige Knechte, die der neuen Obrigkeit ihre Dienstbarkeit beweisen, dass ich schreibe:

Rattenzüngiger Dreck, der über den Ruinen tanzt.
Der du den Verdacht des Wahnsinns in mein Gemüt niedergelegt hast.
Verwischt die Spuren der Einfalt und der Frömmigkeit, zerbrochen
den Hammer, der das Gold hämmert in meiner Hand, dass ich schreibe:

< 206 >

Ah, you people, excuse my words, do not heed my speeches.
You prayers of Madrid . . . and you cathedrals by the fast-
flowing rivers.
The Polish Cross . . . that revolves like a sun between my
eyes.

Ah, incomprehensible one . . . that you are—and as though
from the middle of time.
And like confidence . . . and like the communication of cheer.
And that the ground is like gold once more, exclaim the servants of comfort.

1956

From SPEECHES AND INVOCATIONS

Lord Lord . . . they have stabbed my reason, so that I write:
They have stabbed my reason, the wretched ones!
Lord . . . those whom murder let loose! Lousy lackeys who
show their servility to the new masters, so that I write:

Filth with the tongues of rats that dances over the ruins.
That have put the suspicion of madness into my mind.
Erased the traces of innocence and devotion, broken
the hammer that beats the gold in my hand, so that I write:

I have awaited my death with impatience . . . day after day.
That I weep without cause, that I speak without anguish.
I who wander about . . . embarrassed—or silly—so that I
write:

I was pushed over the rim of endurance . . . three times
hanged.
Burnt like dry sticks . . . ground into powder like sun-parched

< 207 >

Meinen Tod habe ich erwartet mit Ungeduld . . . und tagelang.
Das ich weine ohne Ursache, dass ich rede ohne Schmerz.
Der ich einhergehe . . . verlegen—oder läppisch—dass ich
   schreibe:

Gestossen wurde ich über den Rand des Ertragens . . . gehenkt
   dreimal.
Verbrannt wie Reisig . . . zerrieben wie trockene Erde . . .
Was soll bestehn—wenn nichts als Speichel allein uns verbindet?

<   208   >

clay . . .
What shall remain—when nothing but spittle holds us all together?

1956

WOLFGANG WEYRAUCH:

Geboren 1907 in Königsberg. Er begann 1929 zu schreiben; zuvor war er Schauspieler. Im Zweiten Weltkrieg diente er in der Armee und wurde in Russland gefangengenommen. Nach seiner Rückkehr arbeitete er als Verlagslektor in Hamburg. Heute lebt er bei München. Seine vielen Veröffentlichungen umfassen Erzählungen, Hörspiele, und Essays *(Dialog über neue deutsche Lyrik,* 1965). Gedichtbände: *Von des Glücks Barmherzigkeit* (1946), *Lerche und Sperber* (1948), *An die Wand geschrieben* (1950), *Gesang um nicht zu sterben* (1956), und *Die Spur: neue Gedichte* (1963). Sein Buch *Mit dem Kopf durch die Wand: Geschichten, Gedichte, Essays und ein Hörspiel* erschien 1972.

EVEREST AUS TRÄNEN

Ich sehne mich nach Dir,
araberhäutige.
Aber unsere Ebene schrumpfte
unter den Heuschrecken.
Unsere Lerchen versteinerten im Flug.
Unser Lied wurde eine Lautlosigkeit.
Ein Everest aus Tränen
schwärzte unsere Himmel.
Ich sehne mich nach Dir,
dotterhaarige.
Du aber sprangst in das Delta.
wo die Rochen warten.

ROTER STAUB

Ich ging in meinen Wald, ich war allein,
ging bis zur Mitte, bis zu meinem Stein,
den ich dorthin gewälzt hatte,
wo der Wald so stumm wie die Stummheit ist.

Dann baute ich aus Ast und Blatt ein Nest,
auch verwandte ich vertrocknete Boviste,
zusammengeschrumpfte Salamanderhüllen,
und kroch hinein, war fort, fort war die Pest
der Sekunden, Millimeter,
die Lepra der Summe der Zahlen, Buchstaben.

< 210 >

WOLFGANG WEYRAUCH

Born in 1907 in Königsberg. He began to write in 1929 after working as an actor. In the Second World War he served in the army and was taken prisoner in Russia. After his return he worked as a publisher's reader in Hamburg. He now lives near Munich. His many publications include stories, radio plays, and essays (*Dialog über neue deutsche Lyrik*, 1965). His books of poems are: *Von des Glücks Barmherzigkeit* (1946), *Lerche und Sperber* (1948), *An die Wand geschrieben* (1950), *Gesang um nicht zu sterben* (1956), and *Die Spur: neue Gedichte* (1963). His *Mit dem Kopf durch die Wand: Geschichten, Gedichte, Essays und ein Hörspiel*, appeared in 1972.

EVEREST OF TEARS

I long for you,
Arabian-skinned.
But our lowland shriveled
under the locust's attack.
Our larks turned to stone as they flew.
Our songs became a silence.
An Everest of tears
blackened our sky.
I long for you,
yolk-yellow-haired.
But you leapt into the delta
where the rayfish wait.

1956

RED DUST

I went into the woods, I was alone,
went to the center, as far as my stone
which I had rolled to that place
where the wood is mute as muteness.

Then out of branch and leaf I built a nest,
also using desiccated puffballs,
shriveled skins of salamanders,
and crawled inside, was gone, gone was the pest
of seconds and of millimeters,
the leprosy of the sum of numbers, letters.

< 211 >

Ich atmete nicht mehr, war blind und taub,
merkte, wie ich sofort einunddasselbe
mit Mistkäfer und Sumpfanfang wurde;
ich lächelte. Dann war ich roter Staub.

EZRA POUND

Ezra Pound,
in der Mitte der italienischen Stadt,
in einem Käfig, ausgestellt,
stinkenden Stein unter sich,
stinkende Pferdedecke über sich,
frierend, weil Winter ist,
bebend, vor Gleichgültigkeit
über die amerikanischen Soldaten,
die ihn beschimpfen, bespucken,
durch das Gitter nach ihm treten,
betrachtend den Tausendfüssler
aus Stiefel, Pistole, Uniform,
US-Tausendfüssler, UdSSR-Tausendfüssler,
NS-Tausendfüssler, Nasser-Tausendfüssler,
Tausendfüssler ohne Ursache, Wirkung,
ohne Voraussetzung, Erkenntnis,
Irrtum, Verwerfung des Irrtums,
stinkend, frierend, bebend,
denkend: wohl Euch,
dass ich kein Gedicht mache,
denn schreibe ich ein Gedicht,
und einer stört mich dabei,
töte ich ihn,
aber ich mache kein Gedicht,
ich kann kein Gedicht machen,
denn ich überlege mir,
ob ich mich geirrt habe,
im Gehege des Tausendfüsslers,
im Gehäuse der Anfechtung.

< 212 >

I ceased to breathe, grew deaf and blind,
noticed how immediately I became
one with dung-beetles, bogland, one and the same;
I smiled. And then I was red dust.

1956

EZRA POUND

Ezra Pound,
in the middle of the Italian town
in a cage, exhibited,
stinking stone underneath him,
stinking horse blanket above him,
freezing, because it's winter,
shivering, with indifference
toward the American soldiers
who jeer at him, spit at him,
kick at him through the bars.
Ezra Pound,
observing the millipede
of boot, pistol, uniform,
U.S. millipede, U.S.S.R. millipede,
Nazi millipede, Nasser millipede,
millipedes without cause, effect,
without premiss, knowledge,
error, rejection of error,
Ezra Pound,
stinking, freezing, shivering,
thinking:
count yourselves lucky
that I'm not writing a poem,
for if I write a poem
and someone interferes
I kill him,
but I am not writing a poem,
cannot write a poem

< 213 >

because I'm asking myself
whether I was wrong,
in the millipede's enclosure,
in the shell of my trial, impugnment.

1963: *Die Spur*

< 215 >

WALTER BAUER:

Geboren 1904 in Merseburg. Arbeitete eine Zeitland als Lehrer. Nach dem Publikationsverbot ab 1933 diente er als Gefreiter im Krieg. 1952 emigrierte er nach Kanada, wo er an der Toronto University Deutsch unterrichtete. Er veröffentlichte Romane, Erzählungen, Essays Biographien und Hörspiele. Eine Auswahl seines Lyrik- und Prosa-Werks von 1928 an erschien 1964: *Der Weg zählt, nicht die Herberge.* Ein späterer Gedichtband ist *Fragment vom Hahnenschrei* (1966). Ein Band ausgewählter Gedichte mit englischer Übersetzung, *The Prince of Morning*, wurde 1968 in Kanada veröffentlicht.

Aus DEUTSCHER TAG

II

Wir werden
Unserer Tage nicht mehr
Froh werden.
Aber vielleicht werden wir
Der Nacht froh und vielleicht
Des ersten Saumes
Von Morgenlicht.
Nicht heute.
Nicht morgen.
Nicht nächstes Jahr.
Irgendwann.

III

Im Lande lebend,
Hört man die Schreie
So deutlich nicht.

Auf einem anderen
Kontinente lebend,
Zerreissen sie mir
Das Gehör.
Da ist keine Ausflucht.

< 216 >

WALTER BAUER:

Born 1904 in Merseburg. Worked for a time as a schoolmaster. Forbidden to publish after 1933, he served as a private soldier in the war. In 1952 he emigrated to Canada where he taught German at Toronto University. Has published novels, stories, essays, and biographies as well as radio plays. A selection from his work since 1928, including verse and prose, appeared in 1964 as *Der Weg zählt, nicht die Herberge*. A later book of poems is *Fragment vom Hahnenschrei* (1966). A book of his selected poems with English translations, *The Price of Morning*, was published in Canada in 1968.

From GERMAN DAY

II

We shall never again
Be glad of our days.
But perhaps
We shall be glad of our nights, and perhaps
Of the first hem
Of morning light.
Not today
Not tomorrow.
Not next year.
Some time.

III

Those who live in our country
Do not hear the screams
So clearly.

They rip my hearing
Where I live,
On another
Continent.
There I cannot
Escape them.

< 217 >

IV

Ich beneide
Die Vergesslichen
Ich beneide
Die Unschuldigen.
Ich beneide sogar jene,
Jene, die beteuern,
Sie seien unschuldig.
Wie ruhig sie schlafen.

VI

Sie haben vergessen,
Ein anderes Wappentier
Zu wählen.
Die Adler sind tot.
Aber den Menschen
Gibt es noch.
Daran haben sie
Nicht gedacht.
Sie haben vergessen,
Eine andere Hymne zu wählen.
Sie singen alle das alte Lied
Und fühlen sich wohl.
Wie wohl sie sich fühlen.
Indes: Nicht alle.
Ich schreie: Nicht alle.
Indes: wieviel Hoffnung
Liegt auf
Jenem Rest?

< 218 >

IV

I envy
Forgetful people.
I envy
The innocent.
I even envy those
Who insist
That they are innocent.
How calmly they sleep.

VI

They forgot
To choose
A new heraldic animal.

The eagles are dead.
But man
Still exists.
They didn't think
Of that.
They forgot
To choose
A new anthem.
They sing the old song
And feel happy about it.
How happy they feel.
And yet: not all of them.
I shout: not all.
And yet: how much hope
Attaches to
Those few?

1964: *Der Weg zählt, nicht die Herberge*

<   219   >

GÜNTER EICH:

Geboren 1907 in Lebus an der Oder. Er wuchs in Brandenburg auf. Er studierte Jura und Sinologie, bevor er als Schriftsteller in Berlin, Dresden und Paris lebte. 1929 schrieb er sein erstes Hörspiel, ein Genre, in dem er sich nach dem Krieg besonders auszeichnen sollte. Sein erster Gedichtband erschien 1930, sein zweiter erst nach Kriegsende. Während des Krieges war er Soldat. Er wurde berühmt durch seine Gedichte, die er als Kriegsgefangener schrieb. Er war mit Ilse Aichinger verheiratet, lebte vorwiegend in Bayern und starb 1972. Gedichtsammlungen nach dem Krieg: *Abgelegene Gehöfte* (1948), *Untergrundbahn* (1949), *Botschaften des Regens* (1955), *Zu den Akten* (1964) und *Anlässe und Steingärten* (1966). Seine gesammelten Werke, einschließlich der posthumen Arbeiten, erschienen 1973 in vier Bänden. Die Sammlungen seiner Hörspiele umfassen *Träume* (1953), *Stimmen* (1958), *In anderen Sprachen* (1964), *Festianus, Märtyrer* (1966) und *Fünfzehn Hörspiele* (1973). In seinen letzten Lebensjahren schrieb er kurze Prosastücke, die er *Maulwürfe* nannte (1970); 1972 erschienen seine *Gesammelten Maulwürfe*. Eine kleine Auswahl seiner Gedichte mit englischer Übersetzung erschien in den USA. Zwei seiner Hörspiele wurden in England in dem Buch *Journeys* (1968) veröffentlicht.

INVENTUR

[handwritten: — Stil ist linear]

Dies ist meine Mütze,
dies ist mein Mantel,
hier mein Rasierzeug
im Beutel aus Leinen.

[handwritten: bedeutet für ihn das Leben]

Konservenbüchse:
Mein Teller, mein Becher,
ich hab in das Weissblech
den Namen geritzt.

[handwritten: Das ist im nicht deshalb keine Verse, ist tischen — Er ist nicht rhetorisch — Soldatenleben Kriegsgefangenenlager roman tisch roman — kalt und bündig nicht verschönernd nicht rhetorisch]

Geritzt hier mit diesem
kostbaren Nagel,
den vor begehrlichen
Augen ich berg.

Im Brotbeutel sind
ein Paar wollene Socken
und einiges, was ich

GÜNTER EICH:

Born in Lebus on the Oder in 1907, Eich grew up in Brandenburg. He studied law and Chinese before living as a writer in Berlin, Dresden, and Paris. In 1929 he wrote his first radio play, a genre in which he came to excel after the war. His first book of poems appeared in 1930, his second not until after the end of the war, in which he served as a soldier. He became famous by poems written as a prisoner of war. Married to Ilse Aichinger, he lived mainly in Bavaria and died in 1972. His postwar collections of poems were *Abgelegene Gehöfte* (1948), *Untergrundbahn* (1949), *Botschaften des Regens* (1955), *Zu den Akten* (1964) and *Anlässe und Steingärten* (1966). His collected works, including posthumous work, appeared in four volumes in 1973. His collections of radio plays include *Träume* (1953), *Stimmen* (1958), *In anderen Sprachen* (1964), *Festianus, Märtyrer* (1966), and *Fünfzehn Hörspiele* (1973). In his last years he wrote brief prose pieces which he called *Maulwürfe* (Moles) (1970); his *Gesammelte Maulwürfe* appeared in 1972. A small selection of his poems with English versions appeared in the U.S. Two of his radio plays were published in England in the book *Journeys* (1968).

INVENTORY

This is my cap,
this is my greatcoat,
and here's my shaving kit
in its linen bag.

A can of meat:
my plate, my mug,
into its tin
I've scratched my name.

Scratched it with this
invaluable nail
which I keep hidden
from covetous eyes.

My bread bag holds
two woollen socks
and a couple of things
I show to no one,

< 221 >

niemand verrate,
so dient es als Kissen
nachts meinem Kopf.
Die Pappe hier liegt
zwischen mir und der Erde.

Die Bleistiftmine *- das geistige überleben*
lieb ich am meisten:
Tags schreibt sie mir Verse,
die nachts ich erdacht.

Dies ist mein Notizbuch,
dies meine Zeltbahn,
dies ist mein Handtuch,
dies ist mein Zwirn.

Durch das Schöpferische setzt er sich über seine Lage hinweg - schreibt dieses Gedicht

TAUBEN

Taubenflug über die Äcker hin,—
ein Flügelschlag, der schneller ist als die Schönheit.
Sie holt ihn nicht ein, sondern bleibt mir
als Unbehagen zurück im Herzen.

Als wäre auch Taubengelächter vernehmbar
vor den Schlägen, den grün gestrichenen Zwerghäusern,
und ich beginne nachzudenken,
ob der Flug ihnen wichtig ist,
welchen Rang die Blicke zum Erdboden haben
und wie sie das Aufpicken des Korns einordnen
und das Erkennen des Habichts.

Ich rate mir selbst, mich vor den Tauben zu fürchten.
Du bist nicht ihr Herr, sage ich, wenn du Futter streust,
wenn du Nachrichten an ihre Federn heftest,
wenn du Zierformen züchtest, neue Farben,
neue Schöpfe, Gefieder am Fuss.
Vertrau deiner Macht nicht,
so wirst du auch nicht verwundert sein,
wenn du erfährst, dass du unwichtig bist,

< 222 >

like that it serves me
as a pillow at night.
Between me and the earth
I lay this cardboard.

This pencil lead
is what I love most:
by day it writes verses
I thought up in the night.

This is my notebook
and this is my groundsheet,
this is my towel,
this is my thread.

1948: *Abgelegene Gehöfte*

PIGEONS

Flight of pigeons over the ploughed fields—
a wingbeat more swift than beauty
that cannot catch up with such speed
but remains in my heart as discomfort.

As if the laughter of pigeons too could be heard
in front of the dovecotes, dwarf dwellings painted green,
and I begin to consider
whether flight is important to them,
what rank they accord to the earthward glance
and how they value the pecking of grain,
how the recognition of hawks.

I advise myself to be afraid of pigeons.
You are not the master, I say, when you throw them food,
when you fasten messages to their legs,
when you breed curious variants, new colors,
new crests, or tufts of feathers above the feet.
Put no trust in your power,
then you'll not be astonished
when you discover how little you count,

< 223 >

dass neben deinesgleichen heimliche Königreiche bestehen,
Sprachen ohne Laut, die nicht erforscht werden,
Herrschaften ohne Macht und unangreifbar,
dass die Entscheidungen geschehen im Taubenflug.

BOTSCHAFTEN DES REGENS

Nachrichten, die für mich bestimmt sind,
weitergetrommelt von Regen zu Regen,
von Schiefer- zu Ziegeldach,
eingeschleppt wie eine Krankheit,
Schmuggelgut, dem überbracht,
der es nicht haben will—

Jenseits der Wand schallt das Fensterblech,
rasselnde Buchstaben, die sich zusammenfügen,
und der Regen redet
in der Sprache, von welcher ich glaubte,
niemand kenne sie ausser mir—

Bestürzt vernehme ich
die Botschaften der Verzweiflung,
die Botschaften der Armut
und die Botschaften des Vorwurfs.
Es kränkt mich, dass sie an mich gerichtet sind,
denn ich fühle mich ohne Schuld.

Ich spreche es laut aus,
dass ich den Regen nicht fürchte und seine Anklagen
und den nicht, der sie mir zuschickte,
dass ich zu guter Stunde
hinausgehen und ihm antworten will.

ZU SPÄT FÜR BESCHEIDENHEIT

Wir hatten das Haus bestellt
und die Fenster verhängt,

that beside your kind there are hidden kingdoms,
languages without sounds that cannot be studied,
dominions without power and unassailable;
that decisions are made by the pigeons' flight.

1955

MESSAGES OF THE RAIN

News intended for me,
drummed out from rain to rain,
from slate roof to tiled roof,
introduced like an illness,
contraband, delivered to him
who has no wish to receive it.

Beyond the wall my metal window-sill clamors,
pattering letters link up
and the rain speaks
in that language which once I believed
none but I could decipher—

Disconcerted now I hear
the messages of despair,
the messages of poverty
and the messages of reproach.
It hurts me to think they're addressed to me,
feeling guiltless of any offense.

And I say out loud
that I do not fear the rain or its accusations,
nor him who sent them to me;
and that all in good time
I will go out and give him my answer.

1955

TOO LATE FOR MODESTY

We had set the house in order
and curtained the windows,

<   225   >

hatten Vorräte genug in den Kellern,
Kohlen und Öl,
und zwischen Hautfalten
den Tod in Ampullen verborgen.

Durch den Türspalt sehn wir die Welt:
Einen geköpften Hahn,
der über den Hof rennt.

Er hat unsere Hoffnungen zertreten.
Wir hängen die Bettücher auf die Balkone
und ergeben uns.

BESTELLUNG

Füng Gänge,
sag es den hölzernen Mädchen,
für den Pfennig unter der Zunge,
und die Teller gewärmt.

Ihr habt uns hingehalten
mit Fasanen und Stör,
Burgunder und Bouillabaisse.
Tragt endlich die Speise auf,
die es nicht gibt,
und entkorkt die Wunder!

Dann wollen wir gern
die Mäuler öffnen
und was wir schuldig sind
zahlen.

SCHIFFAHRT DER GÄRTEN

Ausruhend auf einem Ast
verlernte die Amsel das Fliegen:
Eine Bö in der Takelage
von Tannen und Lichtmasten,
eine Rose irrtümlich,

< 226 >

had provisions enough in the cellars,
coal and oil,
and between wrinkles had hidden
death in medicine bottles.

Through a chink in the door we see the world:
A beheaded cock
running across the yard.

He has trampled our hopes.
We hang up our sheets on the balconies
and give in.

ORDER

Five courses,
tell them, the wooden girls,
for the penny beneath the tongue,
and the plates warmed up.

You tried to keep us happy
with pheasant and sturgeon,
champagne and bouillabaisse.
Enough of that. Now serve
the dish that doesn't exist
and uncork the miracles.

Gladly then
we'll open our gobs
and pay
the bill that's due.

GARDENS AFLOAT

Resting on a bough
the blackbird forgot how to fly.
A gust in the rigging
of pines and lamp masts,
a rose by mistake

< 227 >

als die Schlüssel klirrten.

Die Amselaugen
erraten, wer öffnen wird:
Eiserne Treppen aufwärts
auf ein grasiges Deck,
Stimmen gehen genug
durch die Korridore.

TIMETABLE

Diese Flugzeuge
zwischen Boston und Düsseldorf.
Entscheidungen aussprechen
ist Sache der Nilpferde.
Ich ziehe vor,
Salatblätter auf ein
Sandwich zu legen und
unrecht zu behalten.

SPÄTER

Erfahrungen abdrehen
und ungehemmt
zählen bis
93, auch weiter.

Jedenfalls
für die Silvesternacht
1999
bin ich verabredet.
Weiter im Gebirge, auf
einem Kanapee,
freue mich, man hat
wenig Abwechslung.

< 228 >

when the keys clinked.

Those blackbird eyes
guess who will open:
Iron steps going up
to a grassy deck,
voices enough
pass through the corridors.

1964: *Zu den Akten*

TIMETABLE

Those aeroplanes
between Boston and Düsseldorf.
It's up to hippopotamuses
to pronounce decisions.
I prefer
to lay lettuce leaves
on a sandwich and
remain in the wrong.

1966: *Anlässe und Steingärten*

LATER

Turn off experiences
and without inhibition
count up to
93, or farther.

Anyway,
for New Year's Eve
1999
I have a date.
Farther up the mountains, on
a couch,
I'm pleased, one has
so few diversions.

1972: *Nach Seumes Papieren*

<   229   >

FRANZ BAERMANN STEINER:

Geboren 1909 in Prag als Sohn orthodox jüdischer Eltern. Er studierte
Soziologie, Orientalistik und Anthropologie in Prag. Nach einjährigen
Arabistikstudien in Palästina promovierte er 1935, setzte aber seine
Studien in Wien, London und Oxford fort, wo er auch nach dem Aus-
bruch des Krieges blieb. Seine Eltern starben beide 1942 in Ver-
nichtungslagern. Eines seiner längsten und besten Gedichte, *Gebet im
Garten*, ist eine Meditation über ihren Tod. Steiner erlitt kurz nach
dem Krieg einen Zusammenbruch, arbeitete aber intensiv an seiner
Lyrik, seinen Vorlesungen und Forschungen in Anthropologie weiter.
Er erlebte die Publikation keines seiner Gedichtbände mehr, obwohl
einer von einem Verleger angenommen wurde, der dann in Konkurs
ging. Seine ungewöhnliche Bildung bereicherte seine Gedichte: er
schrieb Variationen über die Überlieferungen der Indianer, der Es-
kimos, Siberiens und Afrikas und wertete jüdische und christliche
mystische Schriften aus. Steiner starb 1952 in Oxford an Herzthrombose. Zwei Gedichtsammlungen erschienen posthum: *Unruhe ohne Uhr*
(1954) und *Eroberungen* (1964), ebenso einige seiner anthropologi-
schen Schriften in englischer Sprache. Ein großer Teil seines Werks ist
nach wie vor unveröffentlicht.

SCHWEIGSAM IN DER SONNE

Rief nicht die stimme: wo weilst du? wo weilst du?
Ach, unter menschen verweile ich.
Es sind ihrer viele und um fast jeden ein haus.
Lieder vernahm ich oft, worte vergingen,
Ich bin unterwegs.

Rief nicht die stimme: der abend! der abend!
Ja, es wird abend werden, wie abende sind:
Über die roten hügel giessen die schatten sich aus
Und die flöte des hirten
Bereut das reifen der zeit.

Vormittags war ich im Viehmarkt und hörte die sprache der
      schafe,
Männer mit messern liefen feilschend umher.
Neben mir zählte einer sein geld. ein streifen
Von seinem kopftuch wehte mir über die stirn,
Als ich emporsah.

<   230   >

FRANZ BAERMANN STEINER:

Born in Prague in 1909 as the son of Orthodox Jewish parents. He studied sociology, oriental languages, and anthropology at Prague. After a year in Palestine devoted to Arabic studies he obtained his doctorate in 1935, but continued his studies in Vienna, London, and Oxford, where he remained after the outbreak of war. Both his parents died in extermination camps in 1942. One of his longest and finest poems, *Gebet im Garten*, is a meditation on their death. Steiner suffered a breakdown soon after the war, but continued to work intensively on his poetry and his lecturing and research in anthropology. He did not live to see a book of his poems published, although one was accepted by a publisher who went bankrupt. His unusual erudition contributed to his poems: he wrote variations on American Indian, Eskimo, Siberian, and African lore, as well as drawing on Jewish and Christian mystical writings. Steiner died at Oxford of coronary thrombosis in 1952. Two collections of his poems appeared posthumously: *Unruhe ohne Uhr* (1954) and *Eroberungen* (1964), as did some of his anthropological writings in English. Much of his work remains unpublished.

TACITURN IN THE SUN

Did not the voice call: where are you? where are you?
Oh, among human beings I linger.
There are many of them, and most have a house around them.
Songs I have often heard, words came and went,
I am on my way.

Did not the voice call: evening! evening!
Yes, it will be evening, as evenings are:
Over the reddening hills the shadows pour out,
And the flute of the shepherd
Repents the ripening of time.

Before noon I was at the cattle-market, heard the language of
    sheep,
Bargaining, men with knives ran about.
Near me someone counted his money. A strip
Of his headcloth, windblown, passed over my forehead
As I looked up.
Birds were circling up there.

< 231 >

Vögel kreisten da droben.
Langsam, vor sonne, ward mein gesicht schwer und golden,
Einer zählte sein geld.
Mählich, vor sonne, verstummten die schafe.

Rief nicht die stimme: der abend! der abend!
Rief nicht die stimme: wo weilst du? wo weilst du?

Viele tore hat die heilige stadt.
In der nacht liegt sie einsam
Auf weiten, schweigenden bergen.

8. MAI 1945

Hastig ist der vogelflug. weh, was jemals sich heben wollte,
Hat der steine gewicht,
Die unter der erde dauern, verkittet mit leibern und jahren der
    liebe.

Gürger begruben ihren ruchlos verzärtelten krieg.
Mohnblumen blühen aus bier.
Girlanden schnüren die leiber fiebernder häuser.

Die nassen fahnen tropfen in schwüle festluft.
Hinter dem trommelwirbel
Zickzackt ein eisläufer über gefrorenen blutsee.

KAFKA IN ENGLAND

Weder via Belsen, noch als dienstmädchen
Kam der fremde, keineswegs ein flüchtling.
Dennoch wars ein trauriger fall:
Die nationalität war strittig,
Die religion umlispelte peinlichkeit.

"Haben sie Kafka gelesen?" fragt Mrs. Brittle beim frühstück,
"er ist recht unausweichlich und ziemlich fundamental!"
"haben sie Kafka gelesen?" fragt Mr. Tooslick beim tee.

<   232   >

Slowly, with sunshine, my face grew heavy and golden,
Someone counted his money.
One by one, with sunshine, the sheep fell silent.

Did not the voice call: evening! evening!
Did not the voice call: where are you? where are you?

Many gates has the holy city.
In the night it lies lonely
On silent, far-spreading mountains.

[November, 1930]; 1950: *Sinn und Form*

8th MAY 1945

Hasty is the flight of birds. Woe, all that was ever ready to
    soar
Has the weight of stones
That endure under the earth, cemented with the bodies and
    years of love.

People have buried their wickedly pampered war.
Poppies bloom out of beer.
Paper-chains lace up the bodies of feverish houses.

The wet flags drip into sultry, festive air.
Behind the roll of drums
A skater zigzags over a frozen lake of blood.

[1945, 2nd version 1947]

KAFKA IN ENGLAND

Neither via Belsen, nor as a maid of all work
The stranger came, by no means a refugee.
And yet the case was a sad one:
His nationality was in doubt,
His religion occasioned lisping embarrassment.

"Have you read Kafka?" asks Mrs. Brittle at breakfast.

< 233 >

"man versteht dann die welt viel besser—
Doch freilich ist nichts real."
Miss Diggs sagt: "aber wirklich?
Ist das nicht reaktionär?"
Nur der kleine Geoffrey Piltzman
Träumt: "wer?

Ich meine, wer daran verdient,
Sie müssen doch tot sein,
Ich mein die leute in Prag—nun, wer auch immer . . ."
Doch aus dem tor bricht trotzdem der schimmer . . .

DIE MUSE DES VERSTUMMTEN

Es wollt ein knabe in die wüstenei, ein mann nach haus;
Und gingen beide doch, und spurlos fast,
An mir vorbei: o hungrige, gedrängte zeit.
Wie mussten sie mich lieben,
Die meinen Schmerz so feingesiebt,
So dicht gesät.

Der stillen sängerin genug besungnes haar,
Der ich auf meinen knien gelauscht,
Nun ringelt sich mir um den kleinen finger:
Fühlst du den goldreif, süss im schneegestöber?

<   234   >

"He's rather inescapable and quite fundamental, I feel."
"Have you read Kafka?" asks Mr. Tooslick at tea,
"Then you'll understand the world much better—
Though nothing in him is real."
Miss Diggs says: "Is that so?
I thought that was reactionary. Don't you?"
Only little Geoffrey Piltzmann
Dreams: "Who?

"I mean, who does well out of this,
They must be dead, after all,
I mean those people in Prague—well, no matter what
    name . . ."
Yet the brightness shines through the gateway all the same.

[1946, 2nd version 1952]

THE MUSE OF THE SILENCED MAN

For the desert a boy made, a man for home;
And both of them, and almost without a trace
Went past me: O hungry, contracted age.
How they must have loved me
Who so finely sifted my pain,
So densely sowed it.

The sufficiently hymned hair of the silent singer
To whom on my knees I listened,
Now round my little finger it curls:
Do you feel the gold ring, sweet in the flurrying snow?

[February, 1947]; 1948: *Literarische Revue*

ERNST MEISTER:

Geboren 1911 in Hagen in Westfalen, wo er heute noch lebt. Er studierte Theologie, Philosphie und Deutsch und diente im Krieg als Soldat, vorwiegend in Italien, Zwanzig Jahre lang war er in der Fabrik seines Vaters beschäftigt. Seit 1961 lebt er als Schriftsteller. Er begann schon vor dem Krieg zu schreiben und zu veröffentlichen, veröffentlichte aber nicht während des Dritten Reichs und trat 1952—nach erneuten Studien in Heidelberg—als Lyriker wieder in den Vordergrund. Als reiner und leidenschaftlicher Lyriker hielt er sich fernab von Literaturbetrieb jeglicher Art und hatte deswegen unter Nichtbeachtung zu leiden. Außer Gedichten schrieb er Hörspiele und ein Stück. Gedichtbände: *Ausstellung* (1932), *Unterm schwarzen Schafspelz* (1955), *Dem Spiegelkabinett gegenüber* (1954), *Der Südwind sagte zu mir* (1955), *Fermate* (1957), *Pithyusa* (1958), *Zahlen und Figuren* (1958), *Lichtes Labyrinth* (1959), *Die Formel und die Stätte* (1960), *Flut und Stein* (1962), *Gedicht* (1964), *Zeichen um Zeichen* (1968), *Es kam die Nachricht* (1970) und *Sage vom Ganzen den Satz* (1972). Zwei seiner Gedichtbände sind in französischer Übersetzung erschienen.

ES WAR DA EIN ANDERES HAUS

Es war da
Ein anderes Haus.
Doch bevor ich eintrat,
Behangen mit aasigem Elend,
Rief ich es an:
Du wirst nicht schallen,
Haus, von obsiegendem Lachen
Über den Mann "ganz aus Wasser,"
Deine Schellen nicht tönen
Über den Mann "ganz aus Lehm."

Und als ich eintrat, war
In der Tat kein Gelächter
Noch Hohn der Schellen; es war
Still.

Aber die Stille
War gefuchst auf Alarm; sie setzte
Die erzne, die sich windende dunkle

< 236 >

ERNST MEISTER:

Born in Hagen, Westphalia, in 1911, where he still lives today. He studied theology, philosophy, and German, and served as a soldier in the war, mainly in Italy. For twenty years he was employed in his father's factory. Since 1961 he has lived as a writer. He began to write and publish before the war, but published nothing during the Third Reich, re-emerging as a poet in 1952, after renewed studies at Heidelberg. A pure and dedicated poet, he has kept aloof from literary business of all kinds, and has suffered neglect in consequence. Apart from poems, he has written radio plays and one stage play. His books of poems are: *Ausstellung* (1932), *Unterm schwarzen Schafspelz* (1955), *Dem Spiegelkabinett gegenüber* (1954), *Der Südwind sagte zu mir* (1955), *Fermate* (1957), *Pithyusa* (1958), *Zahlen und Figuren* (1958), *Lichtes Labyrinth* (1959), *Die Formel und die Stätte* (1960), *Flut und Stein* (1962), *Gedichte* (collected poems, 1964), *Zeichen um Zeichen* (1968), *Es kam die Nachricht* (1970), and *Sage vom Ganzen den Satz* (1972). Two books of his poems have appeared in French translation.

IN THAT PLACE WAS ANOTHER HOUSE

In that place was
Another house.
But before I entered it,
Wrapped in carious misery,
I called out to it:
You will not roar,
House, with triumphant laughter
At the man "all made of water"
Nor sound your bells
At the man "all made of clay."

And when I entered there
Was indeed no laughter
Nor mockery of the bells; it was
Silent.

But the silence
Was set for alarm; it climbed
The iron winding dark
Stairs, and at once, as though

< 237 >

Treppe hinauf, und sofort, als
Wären sie beim Genick genommen,
Eilten die Stockwerkbewohner,
Viele Versucher ohne Augen,
Auf Pfoten die Treppe hinunter,
Mich zu umringen.

And meine Ohren hängten sie sich
Mit einem Geflüster:
Des Nichtses Wimpern,
Zeig sie, Lynkeus, uns!—

Sagt, nachdem ich
Zeugnis abgelegt
Von diesem Wachtraum:

Ist denn wirklich,
Unbezweifelbar (und wie,
Ihr irrtet?) ich sage:
Wirklich, unbezweifelbar (und wie,
Ihr irrtet?) das Haus erbaut,
Um dessentwillen ich
Wie Gilgamesch nicht ächzen will,
Das Haus, darin mitnichten
Die Schellen hängen, das böse
Lachen lauert? Ich sage:
Wirklich, unbezweifelbar (und wie,
Ihr irrtet?)

Hab ich nicht Liebe?

WINTERLICH

I

Hier, wo die blutige
Wildspur endet,
der Jäger in Stricken liegt

< 238 >

They had been seized by the neck,
The tenants of all the floors,
Many tempters without eyes,
Hurried downstairs on their paws
To surround me.

On my ears they hung
With a whispering:
The eyelashes of Nothingness,
Show them to us, Lynkeus—

Tell me, after I
Have testified
To this waking dream:
Was that house really
Indubitably (and what,
You were mistaken?) I say:
Really, indubitably (and what,
You were mistaken?) built,
For whose sake
Like Gilgamesh I would not moan,
The house in which neither
Do the bells hang, nor does the evil
Laughter lurk. I say:
Really, indubitably (and what,
You were mistaken?)

Do I not have charity?

1956: *Fermate*

WINTERLY

I

Here, where the bloodstained
game track ends
the huntsman lies bound

<   239   >

und sein Hund Schnee frisst,
ein schwarzer Hund,
sind meine Augen sehend
von Kristallen der Luft.

II

Schnee im Mund
läutert
das Liebeswort.
Im Froste glimmen
Augen des Sanddorns.

Da ist
wie von blauem
Erz,
Sterne enthalten es,
Geschmack
auf der Zunge—

Torheit
kaum noch gewährend.

III

Stunde, in deren Winter
ihr standet, Todesgedanken, .
bereifte Pappeln,

das Blut
glitzernd war, so
dass mit einem Mal

Gewieher erscholl
zweier Rappen
und wir rannten und reisten

<   240   >

and his dog eats snow,
a black dog,
my eyes have the power to see
crystals of the air.

II

Snow in the mouth
purifies
the word of love.
In the frost glimmer
eyes
of the sea-buckthorn.

There, as of
blue ore,
stars contain it,
is a taste
on the tongue—

scarcely affording
folly.

III

Hour in whose winter
you stood, thoughts of death
hoar-covered poplars,

the blood
glittered, so
that all at once

neighing rang out
of the black horses
and we ran and roamed

<   241   >

auf blanker Seele
mit Schlitten und Zügel
ziemlich weit.

IV

Schnee fällt.
Die vielen Wimpern
während Augen oben,
die weissen Wimpern,
die sich lösen, fallen.

Das Jung- und Alte,
schlafend Wache,
Reine,—ach,
das unerbittlich
Winterliche,
den Leib betauend . . .

Der Kinder Münder
fangen Flocken sich.

STÄDTE

Städte, glänzende
in der Torheit,
die sich sonnen,

Darin Tiere
in Fibeln lesen
Gebrauch ihres Tods,

darin Mütter
den Kindern sprechen
von der Sonne

und summen.

on blank souls
with sleigh and reins
quite far.

IV

Snow is falling.
The many lashes
of lasting eyes above,
the white eyelashes
that detach themselves, fall.

The young and old,
sleeping on guard,
the pure,—ah,
the inexorably
winterly,
moistening bodies with dew . . .

The mouths of children
catch themselves flakes.

1960: *Die Formel und die Stätte*

CITIES

Cities, brilliant
in folly,
that bask,

where animals
read up in primers
the use of their death,

where mothers
speak to their children
of the sun

and hum.

< 243 >

EIN KIND

Blickt auf die Schale
voll Zeit,
sieht nippen
den grauen grossmächtigen
Schmetterling,

ein Kind,
und geht,
schwarze Schafe zu hüten
im Finstern.

IRDISCH

Am Rande des Tellers
sitzen die Könige
tot.

Sagt mir ein Märchen!

Sie schweigen.

Sagt mir Gewalt!

Sie schweigen.

Sagt mir,
wer mich regiert!

Sie schweigen.

Der Teller dreht sich.

AM ENDE SAGT . . .

Am Ende sagt
von zweien
der eine noch:

< 244 >

A CHILD

Looks at the bowl
full of time,
sees the gray
great-power butterfly
sip,

a child,
and goes
to guard black sheep
in the dark.

TERRESTRIAL

On the plate's rim
sit the kings
dead.

Tell me a fairy tale!

They are silent.

Tell me power!

They are silent.

Tell me
who governs me!

The plate revolves.

1962: *flut und stein*

IN THE END . . .

In the end
out of two
one says:
I have settled you down

< 245 >

Ich hab
dich eingelebt
in die Verlassenheit.
Am Ende sagt
von zweien
der andere noch:
Sieh, alles Nahe
ist so weit,
so weit.

< 246 >

in forsakenness.
In the end
out of two
the other says:
Look, all that's near
is so far,
so far away.

1970: Es kam die Nachricht

RUDOLF HAGELSTANGE:

Geboren 1912 in Nordhausen im Harz. Gegen Kriegsende wurde er durch seine Sonnettsequenz *Venezianisches Credo* bekannt, die als moralische Anklage gegen den Nazismus im Untergrund von Hand zu Hand gegeben wurde, während er beim Heer war. Ein anderes Werk, das große Aufmerksamkeit erregte, ist das erzählende Gedicht *Ballade vom Verschütteten Leben* (1953). In späteren Jahren wurde er auch als Prosaschriftsteller, Roman- und Reisebuchautor bekannt. Er lebte vorwiegend in Unteruhldingen am Bodensee und im Odenwald. Gedichtbände: *Venezianisches Credo* (1946, Privatdruck 1945), *Strom der Zeit* (1948), *Zwischen Stern und Staub* (1953), *Ballade vom verschütteten Leben* (1953), *Corazon* (1963) und *Gast der Elemente, Zyklen und Nachdichtungen 1944-1972* (1972). Seine Romane: *Altherrensommer* (1969) und *Der General und das Kind* (1974). Seine kürzeren Prosastücke umfassen *Der Krak in Prag: ein Frühlingsmärchen* (1969), *Alleingang. 6 Schicksale* (1970), *Es war im Wal zu Askalon* (1971) und *Venus im Mars; Liebesgeschichten* (1972).

ARAN

Aus dem Chaos gebrochen,
der erste Wurf von der Hand
des schaffenden Gottes:
Aran.

Wurzellos stehst du
auf geschichtetem Fels.
Wirf deinen Namen über den Absturz
vierhundert Fuss in die Tiefe!
Meer—ist ein Name für Namenloses,
ein bitterer Schluck aus der Flut
unseres Ungenügens. Du möchtest
den kleinen Vogel Hoffnung
auf die Schwinge des Adlers setzen,
die, hoch oben, reglos sich spannt?—
Du bist nicht mehr
als der flüchtige Schatten der Möwe
über die salzgefurchte
westwärts gewendete Stirne der Insel . . .

< 248 >

RUDOLF HAGELSTANGE:

Born in Nordhausen (Harz) in 1912. Toward the end of the war he became known with his sonnet sequence *Venezianisches Credo*, which, as a moral indictment of Nazism, was privately circulated while he was serving in the army. Another work that received much attention is the narrative poem *Ballade vom Verschütteten Leben* (1953). In later years he became more prominent as a prose writer, novelist, and author of travel books. He has lived mainly at Unteruhldingen, Lake Constance, and in the Odenwald. His books of poems are: *Venezianisches Credo* (1946, privately printed in 1945), *Strom der Zeit* (1948), *Zwischen Stern und Staub* (1953), *Ballade vom Verschütteten Leben* (1953), *Corazon* (1963), and *Gast der Elemente, Zyklen und Nachdichtungen 1944-1972* (1972). His novels include *Altherrensommer* (1969) and *Der General und das Kind* (1974). His shorter prose pieces include: *Der Krak in Prag: ein Frühlingsmärchen* (1969), *Alleingang. 6 Schicksale* (1970), *Es war im Wal zu Askalon* (1971), and *Venus im Mars; Liebesgeschichten* (1972).

ARAN

Quarried from chaos,
the first rough image carved
by the Creator's hand:
Aran.

Rootless you stand
on the many-layered rock.
Cast your name over the sheer drop,
four hundred feet to fall!
Sea—is the name for the nameless,
a bitter draught from the flood
of our insufficiency. So you'd like
to set the small bird hope
upon the eagle's pinions
stretching motionless high above?—
You are no more
than the passing seagull's shadow
above the salt-furrowed
western brow of the island . . .

< 249 >

Hassen und Lieben, Schuld und Ruhm—
eine Handvoll Staub,
für eine Stunde im Lichte geduldet.

Denke an Aufbruch . . .

TINTENFISCH

Der reglose Tintenfisch
regte sich,
als ich ihn aufhob am Strande:
ein Knäul von eklen Egeln,
an eine dunkle Qualle gesetzt.

Mit zwei Hölzern
(dreimal entglitt er mir)
trug ich ihn in das knietiefe Becken am Fels.
Und dort, im Wasser,
wurden die Egel zu Schlangen.
Achtfach warf sich sein Wille
dahin und dorthin, gelassen
ausholend und wieder verhaltend,
tastend und fahren lassend,
langend halb und verzichtend,
spielend, rudernd, wandernd—es stäubte
unter dem atlmenden Muskel des Rumpfes
im Wasser wehend der Sand.
Dann ruhte er, das Oktett von Schlangen
zum Stirnschmuck der Gorgo ordnend.
Ich sah: er war schön.

Wenig später entdeckte ihn der kurzbeinige Fischer
und zerschmetterte ihn am Stein.

<   250   >

Hatred and love, guilt and fame—
a handful of dust
held for an hour in the tolerant light.

Think of departure . . .

1953

OCTOPUS

The motionless octopus
moved
when I picked him up on the beach:
a bundle of nauseous leeches
fixed to a darker jellyfish.

With two sticks
(three times he slipped out of them)
I carried him to the knee-deep rockpool.
And there, in the water,
the leeches turned into snakes.
Eight-fold a will projected thcm
this way and that way, quietly
stretching and then withholding,
fingering, letting go,
half holding on, half releasing,
playing, wandering, paddling—the sand
under his torso's breathing muscle
whirled in the water.
Then he rested, arranging
his octet of snakes as Gorgon's diadem.
I saw he was beautiful.

Soon after, the short-legged fishermen spotted him
and smashed him against a rock.

1963: Corazon

<   251   >

HILDE DOMIN:

Geboren 1912 in Köln. Sie studierte Jura, dann Soziologie und Politikwissenschaft an deutschen und italienischen Universitäten. Von 1932 bis 1939 lebte sie in Italien und in England. Von 1940 bis 1952 lebte sie in der Dominikanischen Republik, dann in den USA, und kehrte 1954 nach Deutschland zurück. In Spanien arbeitet sie als Übersetzerin aus dem Spanischen und als Literaturkritikerin. Ihre Gedichtbände: *Nur eine Rose als Stütze* (1959), *Zückkehr der Schiffe* (1962), *Hier* (1964), *Höhlenbilder* (1968) und *Ich Will Dich* (1970). Sie gab die Anthologie *Doppelinterpretationen* (1966) heraus und schrieb ein Buch über moderne Lyrik, *Wozu Lyrik Heute* (1968). Ihr Roman *Das zweite Paradies* erschien ebenfalls 1968. 1974 erschien *Von der Natur nicht vorgesehen* (autobiographische Stücke).

MAKABRER WETTLAUF

Du sprachst vom Schiffe-Verbrennen
—da waren meine schon Asche—,
du träumtest vom Anker-Lichten
—da war ich auf hoher See—,
von Heimat im Neuen Land
—da war ich schon begraben
in der fremden Erde,
und ein Baum mit seltsamem Namen,
ein Baum wie alle Bäume,
wuchs aus mir,
wie aus allen Toten,
gleichgültig, wo.

EXIL

Der sterbende Mund
müht sich
um das richtig gesprochene
Wort
einer fremden
Sprache.

< 252 >

HILDE DOMIN:

Born in Cologne in 1912. She studied law, then sociology and politics in German and Italian universities. From 1932 to 1939 she lived in Italy, then in England. From 1940 to 1952 she lived in the Dominican Republic, then in the U.S., returning to Germany in 1954. She has also lived in Spain, where she worked as a translator from the Spanish and as a literary critic. Her books of poems are: *Nur eine Rose als Stütze* (1959), *Rückkehr der Schiffe* (1962), *Hier* (1964), *Höhlenbilder* (1968), and *Ich will Dich* (1970). She edited the anthology *Doppelinterpretationen* (1966) and wrote a book on modern poetry, *Wozu Lyrik Heute?* (1968). Her novel, *Das zweite Paradies*, appeared in 1968. *Von der Natur nicht vorgesehen* (autobiographical pieces) appeared in 1974.

SINISTER RACE

You spoke of burning boats
—when mine were already ashes.—
You dreamed of weighing anchor
—when I was out in mid-ocean—
of a home in the New World
-—when I was already buried
in this foreign soil,
and a tree with a curious name,
a tree like any tree,
grew out of me
as out of anyone dead,
no matter where.

1959: Nur eine Rose als Stütze

EXILE

The dying mouth
twists with the effort
to correctly pronounce
the word
in a foreign
language.

1964: Hier

< 253 >

MAX HÖLZER:

Geboren 1915 in Graz, Österreich. Er lebte *jahrelang* als Rechtsanwalt. Von 1950 bis 1952 gab er die *Surrealistischen Publikationen* haraus und war als Übersetzer französischer surrealistischer Schriften tätig. Zur Zeit lebt er in Frankfurt. Seine Gedichtbände: *Entstehung eines Sternbilds* (1958), *Der Doppelgänger* (1959), *Nigredo* (1962) und *Gesicht ohne Gesicht* (1968). Eine englische Ausgabe von einigen seiner Gedichte wurde 1968 unter dem Titel *Amfortiade and other Poems* veröffentlicht.

VON DORT

Die Sonne jener Nacht
ist ein saugender Brunnen
gebohrt in den Zenit
durch das schwarze Tuch
in das Nicht-mehr-zu-Atmende
ein Brunnen viele Sonnen leer
ein Brunnen viele Sonnen dunkel
ein Brunnen viele Sonnen schweigend

WAS WIR MIT AUGEN NICHT MEHR SEHEN

Was wir mit Augen nicht mehr sehen
ist gestorben
Welche Luft die nicht verweht
trägt im Schoss
unsere Umarmungen

Im Spiegel
ist niemand
oder sind andere

Wie hätten wir nicht glauben sollen
als wir
einmal noch
zurückkamen
da stünde ein Wald

Was hatten wir vergessen

< 254 >

MAX HÖLZER:

Born in 1915 in Graz, Austria. He has lived for many years as a lawyer. From 1950 to 1952 he edited the *Surrealistische Publikationen*, and has been active as a translator of French surrealist writings. He presently lives in Frankfurt. His books of poems are: *Entstehung eines Sternbilds* (1958), *Der Doppelgänger* (1959), *Nigredo* (1962), and *Gesicht ohne Gesicht* (1968). An English translation of some of his poems was published in 1968: *Amfortiade and other Poems*.

FROM THERE

The sun of that night
is a sucking well
bored into the zenith
through the black cloth
into the no-more-to-be-breathed
a well empty of many suns
a well dark of many suns
a well silent of many suns

WHAT WE CAN NO LONGER SEE . . .

What we can no longer see with our own eyes
has died
What air that does not blow away
carries within it
our embraces

In the mirror
there is no one
or there are others

We should not have believed
when we
returned
just once
that a wood grew there

What had we forgotten

< 255 >

Aug in Auge
sahn wir die anderen
die wir waren
im Spiegel der uns ganz vergessen

Mit unseren Umarmungen
gingen auch wir
dahin
Unser Gedächtnis ist nicht so wirklich
wie das Gedächtnis
einer Photographie

Was wir mit Augen nicht mehr sehen
ist tot
Mit der Erinnerung
sterben nur noch
wir selbst.

< 256 >

Eye to eye
we saw the others
that we were
in the mirror that has quite forgotten us

With our embraces
we too passed
away
Our memory is not as real
as the memory
of a photograph

What we can no longer see with our eyes
is dead
In remembering
it is only ourselves
who die

                              1962: *Nigredo*

KARL KROLOW:

Geboren 1915 in Hannover. Er studierte Deutsch, Romanistik, Philosophie und Kunstgeschichte in Göttingen und Breslau. Seit 1956 lebt er als Schriftsteller in Darmstadt woer Präsident der Deutschen Akademie für Sprache und Literatur war. Seine frühen Gedichte zeigen den Einfluß französischer und spanischer Lyrik. Seine vielen Gedichtbände umfassen u.a.: *Gedichte* (1948), *Die Zeichen der Welt* (1952), *Fremde Körper* (1959), *Unsichtbare Hände* (1962), *Eine Landschaft für mich* (1965), *Poetisches Tagebuch* (1966), *Alltägliche Gedichte* (1968), *Nichts weiter als Leben* (1970), *Bürgerliche Gedichte* (1970) und *Zeitvergehen* (1972). Seine *Gesammelten Gedichte* erschienen 1956, gefolgt von einem zweiten Band (1975). Er veröffentlichte auch *phantasievolle und kritische Prosa* und Übersetzungen aus dem Französischen und Spanischen. Ein Gedichtband mit englischen Übersetzungen erschien in London und den USA unter dem Titel *Foreign Bodies* (1969).

LIEBESGEDICHT

Mit halber Stimme rede ich zu dir:
Wirst du mich hören hinter dem bitteren Kräutergesicht
Des Mondes, der zerfällt?
Unter der himmlischen Schönheit der Luft,
Wenn es Tag wird,
Die Frühe ein rötlicher Fisch ist mit bebender Flosse?

Du bist schön.
Ich sage es den Feldern voll grüner Pastinaken.
Kühl und trocken ist deine Haut. Ich sage es
Zwischen den Häuserwürfeln dieser Stadt, in der ich lebe.
Dein Blick—sanft und sicher wie der eines Vogels.
Ich sage es dem schwingenden Wind.
Dein Nacken—hörst du—ist aus Luft,
Die wie eine Taube durch die Maschen des blauen Laubes
　　schlüpft.

Du hebst dein Gesicht.
An der Ziegelmauer erscheint es noch einmal als Schatten.
Schön bist du. Du bist schön.
Wasserkühl war mein Schlaf an deiner Seite.
Mit halber Stimme rede ich zu dir.
Und die Nacht zerbricht wie Soda, schwarz und blau.

< 258 >

KARL KROLOW:

Born in Hanover in 1915; studied German, romance languages, philosophy, and history of art at Göttingen and Breslau. Since 1956 he has lived as a writer in Darmstadt, when he was President of the German Academy for Language and Literature. His early poems show the influence of French and Spanish poetry. His many books of poems include: *Gedichte* (1948), *Die Zeichen der Welt* (1952), *Fremde Körper* (1959), *Unsichtbare Hände* (1962), *Eine Landschaft für mich* (1965), *Poetisches Tagebuch* (1966), *Alltägliche Gedichte* (1968), *Nichts weiter als Leben* (1970), *Bürgerliche Gedichte* (1970), and *Zeitvergehen* (1972). His collected poems, *Gesammelte Gedichte*, appeared in 1965, followed by a second volume in 1975. He has also published imaginative and critical prose, and translations from the French and Spanish. A book of his poems with English versions has appeared in London and in the U.S., under the title *Foreign Bodies* (1969).

LOVE POEM

With half my voice I speak to you:
Will you hear me behind the bitter herb face
Of the moon that is crumbling?
Under the heavenly beauty of the air
When dawn breaks,
Morning a red-hued fish with a quivering fin?

You are beautiful.
I say it to the fields full of green parsnips.
Cool and dry is your skin. I say it
Between the house cubes of this town in which I live.
Your glance—gentle and sure as a bird's.
I say it to the veering wind.
Your neck—do you hear—is of air
That slips like a dove through the blue leaves' meshes.

You raise your face.
On the brick wall it appears once more as a shadow.
Yes, you are beautiful.
Cool as water was my sleep at your side.
With half my voice I speak to you.
And the night breaks like soda, blue and black.

1955: *Deutsche Lyrik der Gegenwart*

<   259   >

ERINNERUNG AN PREUSSEN

Preussen, so tot wie
jedes Reiterstandbild,
weiss von Taubenkalk.

Deine Augen: kalt und blau
wie die Geschichte
auf brandenburgisch.

Sand fiel durch sie
schon vorgestern.
Die Mörser und Minister
begrub er, Könige,
Kinderspielzeug
aus Blei und Zinn.

Dein präparierter Adler
für den Stubenzoo.

Die ausgestopfte Zeit
der Gloria stirbt immer noch:—
Kinder lesen
im Märchenbuche deiner Macht.

ZEIT

Zeit: etwas
das die Taschen
feucht von Blut macht.

Es regnet Leben
aus offenen Körpern.

Die Tage und
ihr stilles Geschäft
mit Menschen, die verloren
gehen.

<   260   >

REMEMBERING PRUSSIA

Prussia, as dead as
any equestrian statue
whitened by pigeons.

Your eyes: cold and blue
as history written
in Brandenburgian.

The day before yesterday
sand was falling through it.
Sand buried the mortars
and ministers, kings,
children's toys
of lead or tin.

Your preserved eagle
for the drawing-room zoo.

The stuffed era
of glory is dying still:—
children turn the pages of
the fairy-tale book of your power.

1963: *Gesammelte Gedichte*

TIME

Time: something
that makes your pockets
moist with blood.

It makes life drizzle
out of open bodies.

Days and
their quiet business
with people who will
be lost.

< 261 >

Ein Monat malt
dem nächsten sein Bild
in den Sand,
ohne Verwandtschaft
mit dem, was kommt.

Kein schönes Wetter
verändert ein Karzinom.

Die geordneten Papiere
verbrennen Jahr um Jahr.

DIE LIEBE

I

Die am Fenster stehend stirbt,
Sehnsucht, Atemlos
lebt die Liebe
im steifen Schnee oder jetzt
mit den künstlichen Blumen
im Arm,
die Wünsche nach oben
gekehrt,
den Kleidern entwachsen.

Ihre Spielsachen kommen
mit auf die Reise.
Ungekämmt, eine Puppe im Wind,
vergeht sie langsam
in der Luft, die ihr
die Luft nimmt—

bei geschlossenen Augen
ohne Gewicht.

< 262 >

One month paints
its image on sand
for the next,
unrelated to what's
to come.

No fine weather
alters a cancer.

Your papers put in good order
year by year burn.

[1965]; 1968: *Alltägliche Gedichte*

LOVE

I

That standing at the window dies,
longing. Breathless
love lives
in stiff snow or now
carrying those artificial flowers,
desires up-turned,
clothes outgrown.

Love's toys are taken
on the journey.
Unkempt, a doll in the wind,
slowly it perishes
in the air that
deprives it of air—

eyes closed,
without weight.

< 263 >

II

Es ist still im Haus.
Die stille Oberfläche des Gefühls.

Etymologische Rosen
blühen sprachlos
für die Augenblicke,
in denen ein Körper
nich mehr Körper ist.

< 264 >

II

The house is quiet.
The quiet surface of feeling.

Etymological roses
flower speechless
for those moments
in which a body
is no longer a body.
[1966]; 1968: *Alltägliche Gedichte*

< 265 >

CHRISTINE LAVANT:

Geboren 1915 in Großedling bei St. Stefan in Kärnten als neuntes Kind eines Bergmanns. Sie *verdiente ihren Lebensunterhalt durch Stricken, litt aber in späteren Jahren unter extremer körperlicher Entkräftung und war fast blind.* Alle ihre Gedichte sind religiöse Aufschreie und Meditationen. Sie schrieb Erzählungen, ein *hervorragendes* Hörspiel und Gedichte. Obwohl sie weitgehend Autodidakt war, überwand sie diese Benachteiligung, die noch eine Lappalie war, gemessen an den anderen Schwierigkeiten, mit denen sie in ihrem Werk rang. Sie war nicht nur oft der Verzweiflung, sondern auch dem Wahnsinn nahe. Nachdem sie den größten Teil ihres Lebens im heimischen Tal verbracht hatte, dem Lavanttal, von dem sie auch ihr Pseudonym nahm, starb sie 1973 in Wolfsberg. Im Alter von 24 heiratete sie den sechzigjährigen Maler Habernig, für den sie im Alter sorgte. Ihre Gedichtbände: *Die vollendete Liebe* (1942), *Die Bettlerschale* (1956), *Spindel im Mond* (1959), *Der Sonnenvogel* (1961), *Wirf ab den Lehm* (1962), *Der Pfauenschrei* (1962), *Hälfte des Herzens* (1967). Sie veröffentlichte außerdem fünf Bände mit Erzählungen, den letzten mit dem Titel *Nell* (1968).

KAUF UNS EIN KÖRNCHEN . . .

Kauf uns ein Körnchen Wirklichkeit!
Wir könnten doch endlich auch Schwarzbrot essen
statt eingezuckerte Engel.

Ich mag nicht mehr hungrig schlafen gehn,
ich mag nimmer meinem murrenden Magen
zur Strafe die Engel versalzen.

Schaff her einen doppelten Branntweinkrug,
wir müssen uns endlich richtig betrinken
und Du zu uns sagen von Mund zu Mund,
nicht ewig vom Weihwasser taumeln.

Ich mag nicht mehr durstig schlafen gehen,
ich mag auch die fluchende Kehle nimmer
mit Essig ans Beten gewöhnen.

FRAGT NICHT . . .

Fragt Nicht, was die Nacht durchschneidet,

< 266 >

CHRISTINE LAVANT:

Born in 1915 in Grossedling, near St. Stefan in Carinthia, as the ninth child of a miner. She earned her living by knitting, though in later years she suffered extreme physical disability, including near-blindness. All her poems are religious outcries and meditations. She wrote short stories and a distinguished radio play, as well as poems. Though largely self-educated, she overcame that disadvantage, which was trifling compared to others that she grappled with in her work. She was often close not only to despair but to madness. After spending most of her life in her native valley, the Lavanttal, from which she took her name, she died in 1973 at Wolfsberg. At the age of twenty-four she married the sixty-year-old painter Habernig, whom she looked after in his extreme old age. Her books of poems are: *Die vollendete Liebe* (1942), *Die Bettlerschale* (1956), *Spindel im Mond* (1959), *Der Sonnenvogel* (1961), *Wirf ab den Lehm* (1962), *Der Pfauenschrei* (1962), *Hälfte des Herzens* (1967). She also published five books of stories, the last of which was *Nell* (1968).

BUY US A LITTLE GRAIN . . .

Buy us a little grain of reality!
At last we could eat coarse bread
instead of iced angels.

I don't want to go to bed hungry again
I don't want to go on drowning the angels in salt
as a punishment for my rebellious guts.

Bring in a double-sized jug of brandy
we must get really drunk at last
and say you to each other from mouth to mouth
not stagger about forever on holy water.

I don't want to go to bed again thirsty
nor ever again with vinegar will I accustom
my cursing throat to prayer.

1962: Der Pfauenschrei

DO NOT ASK . . .

Do not ask what rips the night
for that night is only mine,

< 267 >

denn es ist ja meine Nacht
und mein grosser Pfauenschrei
und ganz innen drin die Zunge
mit der Botschaft nur für mich.
Selbst wenn morgen dann die Sonne
ganz erschöpft und fast verwachsen
mit der Fegefeuerknospe
rasten will, wird sie vertrieben—
denn es ist ja meine Knospe
auf dem Rücken meines Steines
und für meine nächste Nacht.

< 268 >

mine the peacock's mighty scream
and, deep down inside, the tongue
with the message that's for me.
If by tomorrow the sun,
quite exhausted, almost twined
with the purgatory bud,
wants to rest, it's driven out—
for that bud is only mine
on the back of my own stone
and reserved for my next night.

1962: Der Pfauenschrei

< 269 >

CHRISTINE BUSTA:

Geboren 1915 in Wien. Für den größten Teil ihres Lebens blieb Wien ihre Heimat, wo sie als Bibliothekarin arbeitet. Ihre Gedichtbände: *Jahr um Jahr* (1950), *Der Regenbaum* (1951), *Lampe und Delphin* (1955), *Die Scheune der Vögel* (1958), und *Unterwegs zu älteren Feuern* (1965). Sie schrieb auch Kinderbücher.

SCHNEE IM ADVENT

Leiser wird nichts verkündigt:
        so reden Liebende nachts,
die fern voneinander schlafen,
        und finden am Morgen die fremde
Erde wieder als Nest
        voll von himmlischem Flaum.

EPITAPH

Nichts kann stillen!
Wirf Erde in meinen Mund,
und ich singe dir Gras . . .

ZU ÄLTEREN FEUERN

Nimm Abschied von Halm und Holz,
von der kindlichen Haut der Flamme.
Wir sind unterwegs zu älteren
Feuern aus Stein und Erz.

Kältere Tode warten,
nicht Blutopfer, Atemopfer.
Und nur das Herzgeborgne
schifft sich mit uns noch ein.

Flügellos meldet die Taube
Unbetretbares, Fremdes.
Die verlassene Erde
ist schon Mythe und Stern.

< 270 >

CHRISTINE BUSTA:

Born in Vienna in 1915, she has continued to live there for most of her life, except for travels in many parts of Europe. She works as a librarian. Her books of poems are *Jahr um Jahr* (1950), *Der Regenbaum* (1951), *Lampe und Delphin* (1955), *Die Scheune der Vögel* (1958), and *Unterwegs zu älteren Feuern* (1965). She has also written books for children.

SNOW AT ADVENT

Nothing's announced more softly:
   so lovers converse in the night,
who sleep remote from each other
   and waking at daybreak discover
the strange earth changed to a nest
   full of celestial down.

        [1955] 1958: *Die Scheune der Vögel*

EPITAPH

Nothing can still or staunch.
Throw earth into my mouth
and I'll sing you grass.

1965: *Unterwegs zu älteren Feuern*

TO OLDER FIRES

Take leave of stalk and bough,
of the childish skin of flames.
We are on our way to the older
fires of rock and ore.

Colder deaths await us,
immolation of breath, not blood.
And what the heart holds only
can embark with us now.

Wingless the dove reports
land out of bounds, and alien.
The earth we have left behind
already is myth and star.

        1965: *Unterwegs zu älteren Feuern*

< 271 >

HANS WERNER COHN:

Geboren 1916 in Breslau. Er studierte dort Medizin. Vor Ausbruch des Krieges emigrierte er nach England und lebt in Kew, Surrey als Psychotherapeu. Während des Krieges arbeitete er als Lazarettgehilfe. Sein erster Gedichtband erschien 1950 in England, gefolgt von *Gedichte* (1964) in West-Deutschland. Seither veröffentlichte er wenig Lyrik, aber 1974 erschien seine Studie über Else Lasker-Schüler. Eine Sammlung späterer Gedichte liegt zur Veröffentlichung bereit.

DAS LOCH

Im Boden seines Zimmers ist ein Loch.
Er lebt am Rande dieses Loches: isst
schläft liebt und hasst am Rande dieses Loches.

Manchmal erscheint das Loch ihm klein. Er sieht
es kaum. Es ist genügend Platz
am Rande dieses Loches.

Manchmal erscheint das Loch sehr gross. Er kniet
am engen Rande seines Loches: starrt
in seine Tiefe stundenlang.

Manchmal ergreift er Bücher Platten Bilder
und Worte: wirft sie in das Loch
um es zu füllen.
Das Loch verschlingt die Bücher Platten Bilder
und Worte. Es bleibt ungefüllt.

Einmal zog er auch in ein anderes Zimmer
und fand im Boden dort das gleiche Loch.

SCHLAF

Schlaf: Rückzug
auf dunklen Gängen

bis du dir plötzlich
aus dem Spiegel des Traumes

< 272 >

HANS WERNER COHN:

Born in 1916 in Breslau, where he studied medicine. He emigrated to England before the war, and lives in Kew, Surrey, working as a psychotherapist. He worked as a medical orderly during the war. His first book of poems appeared in England in 1950, followed by *Gedichte* (1964) in West Germany. Since then he has published little poetry, but his study of Else Lasker-Schüler appeared in 1974. A collection of his later poems awaits publication.

THE HOLE

In the floor of his room there's a hole.
He lives on the edge of the hole: eats
sleeps loves and hates on the edge of the hole.

Sometimes the hole seems small to him. He kneels
on the short edge of his hole: stares
into its depth for hours.

Sometimes he seizes books records pictures
and words: throws them into the hole
to fill it.
The hole swallows the books records pictures
and words. It remains unfilled.

Once, too, he moved into another room
and found in the floor the same hole there.

1964: Gedichte

SLEEP

Sleep: retreat
into dark corridors

till suddenly out
of dream's mirror you run
into yourself

and the collision wakes you.

< 273 >

entgegenläufst
und erwachst von dem Anprall.

FALL

Eines Morgens
fiel sein Gesicht aus dem Spiegel
in seine Hände:

er liess es fallen.

<   274   >

FALL

One morning
his face fell out of the mirror
into his hands:

he let it fall.

1970/1972

< 275 >

RAINER BRAMBACH:

Geboren 1917 in Basel, wo er noch heute lebt und vorwiegend als Gärtner, Torfstecher und Landarbeiter taetig war. Als Lyriker wurde er 1956 bekannt. Seine Gedichtbände umfassen *Tagwerk* (1959), *Marco Polos Koffer* (mit Gedichten von ihm und Jürg Federspiel) (1968), und eine spätere Sammlung, *Ich fand keinen Namen dafür* (1969). Seine gesammelte Prosa erschien 1961 unter dem Titel *Wahrnehmungen*, gefolgt von einem Band später Prosa, der 1972 erschien (*Für sechs Tassen Kaffee und andere Geschichten*). 1974 veröffentlichte er mit Frank Geerk zusammen *Kneipenlieder*.

DER BAUM

Seit ich weit draussen
Das Haus in der Siedlung bewohne,
Wächst aus dem Keller ein Baum
Durch Diele und Mansarden.
Laub hängt fahnengleich
Zu allen Fenstern hinaus,

Der Wipfel wiegt sich
Über dem moosgrauen Dach.

Ich hause unbesorgt nah dem Gezweig.
Im Hof fault der Spaltklotz,
Auf dem Speicher rostet die Säge.
Nachbarn freilich rufen sich zu:
Sein Haus ist wie unsere Häuser,
Was ist der Narr fröhlich—
Hört, er singt in der Frühe, redet
Und lacht wenn es dämmert!

Der Baum wächst.

GRANIT

Über Granit gebeugt—aus südlichen Brüchen.
Während dein Hammer fällt
steigt dir ein Milchglashimmel ins Auge
während dein Meissel die Rinne gräbt

< 276 >

RAINER BRAMBACH:

He was born in Basle in 1917, where he still lives and where he has worked mainly as a gardener, peat-cutter, and farm laborer, becoming known as a poet in 1956. His books of poems include *Tagwerk* (1959), *Marco Polos Koffer* (containing poems by him and Juerg Federspiel) (1968), and a later collection, *Ich fand keinen Namen dafür* (1969). His collected prose appeared in 1961 under the title *Wahrnehmungen*, and was followed by later prose appearing in 1972 (*Für sechs Tassen Kaffee und andere Geschichten*). In 1974 he published *Kneipenlieder* together with Frank Geerk.

THE TREE

Since I've been living far out
In that house on the estate
From the cellar a tree has been growing
Through the hall and attic.
Leafage hangs like flags
Out of all the windows.

The crest waves
Over the moss-gray roof.

I live unperturbed near its branches.
In the yard my chopping-block rots,
In the shed my saw rusts.
Neighbours, true, call out to one another:
His house is like our houses,
What has the fool got to be cheerful about—
Listen, he sings first thing in the morning,
Talks and laughs in the dusk!

The tree keeps growing.

1956: *Junge Lyrik*

GRANITE

Bent over granite—from southern quarries
While your hammer falls
a sky of milk-white glass ascends to your eyes

< 277 >

schmeckst du den Staub versteinerter Wälder.

Über Granit gebeugt—
O Ginster und Aloe schiefergrau verschwommen
während dein Knie sich
an die ausgetrockneten Ebenen presst
—aus südlichen Brüchen
während dein schweissnasser Rücken gestreift wird
vom kühlen Hauch nördlichen Sommers.

< 278 >

while your chisel incises the groove
you taste the dust of petrified forests.

Bent over granite—
O broom and aloe hazy, slate-gray
while your knee
leans against the dried-out plains—
from southern quarries
while your back moist with sweat is strafed
by the cool breath of a northern summer.

1959: Tagwerk

JOHANNES BOBROWSKI:

Geboren 1917 in Tilsit. Er wuchs an der deutschlitauischen Grenze auf, bevor er mit 11 Jahren nach Königsberg zog. 1937 begann er mit dem Studium der Kunstgeschichte in Königsberg, wurde aber bald darauf zum Arbeitsdienst und dann zum Heer eingezogen. Von 1945 bis 1949 war er Kriegsgefangener in Rußland. Nach seiner Rückkehr ließ er sich in Ost-Berlin nieder, wo er für einen an die Lutherische Kirche angeschlossenen Verlag arbeitete. Sein reifes und charakteristisches Werk erschien erst in seinen letzten Lebensjahren, als er in West- und Ost-Deutschland als Lyriker von Rang anerkannt wurde. Er starb 1965. Seine Gedichtbände: *Sarmatische Zeit* (1962), *Schattenland Ströme* (1962), *Wetterzeichen* (1966) und *Im Windgesträuch* (1970). Er veröffentlichte auch zwei Romane, und drei Sammlungen von Erzählungen. Ein Großteil seines Werks erschien in englischer Übersetzung; den Anfang bildete *Shadow Land* (1966). Die Sammlung *From the River* erschien 1975 in London.

OSTEN

Alle meine Träume
gehn über Ebenen, ziehn
unbetretenen Wäldern
windhell entgegen, kalten
einsamen Strömen, darüber
fernher Rufe schallen
bärtiger Schiffer—

Dort sind alle Gesänge
ohne End, im geringsten
Ding steht Gefahr, vieldeutig,—
nicht zu halten mit dem und
jenem Namen: Gefilde,
Moore, eine Schlucht; wie Verhängnis
schlägt sie hinab, bleibt, gemieden,—
dort um die niederen Hügel
fliehn die Pfade davon.

Worte gelten nicht.
Aber ein Streicheln, Grüsse,

< 280 >

JOHANNES BOBROWSKI:

Born in Tilsit in 1917, he grew up on the German-Lithuanian border before moving to Königsberg at the age of eleven. In 1937 he began to study history of art at Königsberg, but was soon called up for labor service, then for military service. From 1945 to 1949 he was a prisoner of war in Russia. On his return he settled in East Berlin, where he worked for a publishing house affiliated with the Lutheran Church. His mature and characteristic work appeared only in the last few years of his life, when he was recognized as a major poet both in West and in East Germany. He died in 1965. His books of poems are: *Sarmatische Zeit* (1962), *Schattenland Ströme* (1962), *Wetterzeichen* (1966) and *Im Windgesträuch* (1970). He also published two novels and three collections of stories. Most of his work has appeared in English translation, beginning with *Shadow Land* in 1966; the collection *From the Rivers* was published in 1975 in London.

EAST

All my dreams
move across the plains, travel
windbright toward
untrodden forests, cold
lonely rivers, over which ring out
from afar the calls
of bearded boatmen—

There all songs are
without end, in the humblest
thing lies danger, ambiguous,—
not to be held with this or
that name: meadows,
moors, a ravine; like doom
it strikes down, strays, avoided,—
there, around the low hills
tracks run, fleeing.

Words do not count.
But a caress, greetings,
lightning flash under darkening eyelid

< 281 >

Blitz unterm dunkelnden Lid
und in der Brust jenes Ziehn;
noch als Umarmungen stärker.

Händler kommen von weit. Die
unter uns wohnen, sind Fremde.
Unsicher gehn sie, fragend,
ziellosen Strassen nach, hängen
Fähren und Brücken immer
an, als wär dort Gewisses—

Wir aber kennen uns leicht.
Unsre Gespräche steigen
alle aus gleichem Grunde.
Und im Erwarten ewig
wohnt uns das Herz.

PFERDE

Auf das Fell gelegt
deine Hand, den Quell
spür, über den Leib
das Zucken, Blut, eine Welle
läuft auf dich zu.

Als die Steppen waren:
die Schütte Sommer immer,
aber die Zeit aus Wind,
gross mit den Himmeln, Lüfte
durstig, gesunken trockenen
Munds auf den See—
als die Steppen waren:
unter dem Wirbel der Sterne,
ihrem räderrasselnden
Lärm, und die Stille
zerschlug ihn, Nacht und lichtlose
Frühe, kalt—
als die Steppen waren:

< 282 >

and in the breast that spasm;
stronger even than embraces.

Traders come from far places. Those
who live among us are strangers.
Unsure they walk, asking,
roads that lead nowhere, always
linger at ferries and bridges
as though there lay certainty—

But we with ease know each other.
Our conversations all
rise from the same ground.
And in expectation forever
our hearts live.

                                    1953

HORSES

Your hand laid
on the skin, feel
the source, over the body
the twitching, blood, a wave
rolls toward you.

When the steppes were there:
the granary summer always,
but time made of wind,
great with the skies, breezes
thirsty, collapsed with dry
mouths onto the lake—
when the steppes were there:
under the vortex of stars,
their wheel-rattling
noise, and the silence
smashed it, night and lightless
dawn, cold—
when the steppes were there:

<   283   >

keine Heimstatt, die Wälder
hoben sich rauh, wir zogen
vor ihnen her—

damals bist du gekommen,
Pferd, Gefangener, dunkel
im Aufgang der Schönheit, der Wildnis
Traum,—das Zucken, die Welle
Blut überlief dich,
dem in die Hand, der dich rief,
der aus der Höhle trat, Jäger,
hinter ihm die gefiederten
Wände, der Feuerschein. Rauch
löschte dein Bild aus.

TRAKL

Stirn.
Der braune Balken.
Dielenbretter. Die Schritte
zum Fenster.
Das Grün grosser Blätter. Zeichen,
geschrieben über den Tisch.

Die splitternde Schwelle. Und
verlassen. Langsam
hinter dem Fremdling her
unter Flügeln der Dohlen
in Gras und Staub
die Strasse ohne Namen.

MOBILE VON CALDER

Weisses Metall
in der Luft
gehalten von Nebeln
weiss
eine Bewegung
wir geben ihr Flügel

< 284 >

no homestead, the forests
roughly rose, we kept
ahead of them—

at that time you came,
horse, prisoner, dark
in beauty's rising, dream
of the wilderness,—the twitching, the wave of
blood ran over you,
into the hand of him who called you,
who stepped from the cave, huntsman,
behind him the feathered
walls, the fire's gleam. Smoke
extinguished your image.

                                    1960

TRAKL

Brow.
The brown beam.
Floorboards. The steps
to the window.
The green of large leaves. Signs,
written over the table.

The splintering threshold. And
deserted. Slowly
pursuing the stranger
under the jackdaws' wings
in grass and dust
the road with no name.

                        1958/1964

MOBILE BY CALDER

White metal
in the air
held up by mists
white

<   285   >

Dein Mund
hat sich geöffnet als eine Rose
an deiner Schläfe
blättert Laub

STEH. SPRICH. DIE STIMME

Steh. Sprich. Die Stimme
nicht, die singende
nicht. Die andere, die das Gras
niederlegt. Das Insekt
schliesst seine Flügel zusammen
mitten im Flug,

wirbelt, ein Blatt. Die andre
Stimme: Wollflies, Gehörn,
Klauen. Der Rost
geht auf dem Sand, der Fels
bricht aus dem Grund.

Redende Stimme. Wo Angst
eingegraben war, fliegen
Blätter, geädert
mit splitternden Fäden, Eis
fliegt, eine Hand
fängt es im Flug.

Unwirsch Liebe, verwischt
mit der Hand: die Zeichnung,
die den Regen nicht übersteht,
Regen wird, fliegend,
aufschlägt
gegen den Wind.

Jona komm
Wir reden und reden
Sag Ninive
Sag morgen morgen morgen

< 286 >

a motion
we give it wings

Your mouth
has opened as a rose
on your temples
leafage curls

1964

STAND. SPEAK. THE VOICE

Stand. Speak. Not
the voice, not the
singing voice. The other that
flattens the grass. The insect
folds its wings
in mid-flight,

whirls, a leaf. The other
voice: fleece, horns,
talons. Rust
moves over sand, the rock
breaks from the ground.

Talking voice. Where fear
lay buried, leaves
fly, veined
with splitting threads, ice
flies, a hand
catches it in flight.

Harsh love, blurred
with the hand: the drawing
that does not outlast rain,
becomes rain, flying,
collides with the wind.

JONAH COME

<   287   >

ENTFREMDUNG

Zeit
geht umher
in Kleidern
aus Glück
und Unglück.

Der im Unglück
spricht mit der Klapperstimme
der Störche, die Störche
meiden ihn: sein Gefieder
schwarz, seine Bäume Schatten,
da ist Nacht, seine Wege
gehn in der Luft.

< 288 >

WE TALK AND TALK
SAY NINIVEH
SAY TOMORROW TOMORROW TOMORROW

[1964]; 1970: *Im Windgesträuch*

ESTRANGEMENT

Time
moves about
dressed
in fortune
or misfortune.

He in misfortune
speaks with the rattling voice
of storks, the storks
avoid him: his plumage
black, his trees shadows,
here is night, his ways
pass through air.

[1965]; 1966: *Wetterzeichen*

< 289 >

MICHAEL GUTTENBRUNNER:

Geboren 1919 in Althofen in Kärnten. Er arbeitete als Bauunternehmer und Stallknecht. 1935 verbüßte er eine sechsmonatige Gefängnisstrafe wegen politischer Vergehen. Nachdem er sich eine Zeitlang als Zeichner ausbildete, wurde er 1938 festgenommen und 4 Monate von der Gestapo festgehalten. Seit 1940 war er beim Heer, wurde dreimal verwundet, vor ein Kriegsgericht gestellt und zum Tode verurteilt. Von 1947 bis 1948 arbeitete er für die Kulturabteilung der Kärntener Lokalregierung. In späteren Jahren lebte er als Schriftsteller in Wien. Er ist sich seiner Arbeiter- und Bauern-Herkunft bewußt; sein Werk setzt eine spezifisch österreichische Tradition des Mundartverses fort, wie sie in früherer Zeit von Theodor Kramer gepflegt wurde. Er veröffentlichte Prosa und Lyrik. Gedichtbände: *Schwarze Ruten* (1947), *Ungereimte Gedichte* (1956), *Die lange Zeit* (1965) und *Der Abstieg* (1975).

DER STRICK
HÄNGT VON OBEN NACH UNTEN

Als die tausend Jahre begannen,
ward jedermann Gelegenheit gegeben
zu sehen, wie der Fisch gesalzen
und zum Trocknen in die Luft gehängt wird.
Wenn die letzte Strophe des Urteils verklang,
ward dem Besiegten
der Strick um den Hals gelegt
und der Boden unter den Füssen fortgezogen.
Der Strick kommt von oben wie der Befehl,
er hängt von oben nach unten wie der Mensch.
Vor tausend Jahren und einem Tag
bin ich als Stückgut zur See gefahren.
Ich Fleischkonserve ruhte kühlgelagert
im Bauch eines 10000-Tonnen-Dampfers.
Das Schiff hiess Delos.
In der Ägäis spielten Delphine.

VORBEIMARSCHIEREND

Das schönste Singen, das ich je gehört,
kam aus den Kehlen russischer Soldaten,
verhungernder—sie konnten kaum mehr stehn.

< 290 >

MICHAEL GUTTENBRUNNER:

Born in Althofen, Carinthia, in 1919. He worked as a builder and as a groom. In 1935 he served a six-month prison sentence for political offenses. After a period of training as a graphic artist, he was arrested in 1938 and held for four months by the Gestapo. From 1940 he served in the army, and was wounded three times, court-martialed and condemned to death. From 1947 to 1948 he worked for the cultural section of the Carinthian local government. In later years he lived in Vienna as a writer. He is conscious of his working-class and peasant background, and his work continues a peculiarly Austrian tradition of vernacular verse, as practiced at an earlier period by Theodor Kramer. He has published prose as well as verse. His collections of poems are: *Schwarze Ruten* (1947), *Opferholz* (1954), *Ungereimte Gedichte* (1956), *Die lange Zeit* (1965) and *Der Abstieg* (1975).

WHEN THE THOUSAND YEARS BEGAN . . .

When the thousand years began
everyone was given the opportunity
to see how the fish is salted
and hung up to dry in the air.
When the last words of the sentence died away
the defeated man
had a rope laid round his neck
and the ground pulled from under his feet.
The rope, like the order, comes from above,
it hangs down from above like the man.
A thousand years ago and a day
I went to sea as flotsam.
Tinned meat I rested in cold storage
in the belly of a 10,000-ton steamer.
The ship's name was Delos.
In the Aegean dolphins played.

                    1959: *Ungereimte Gedichte*

MARCHING PAST

The finest singing I have ever heard
came from the throats of Russian soldiers,
close to starvation—they could hardly stand.
"Sing. If you sing you shall have some grub!"

<   291   >

"Singt! Wenn ihr singt, dann kriegt ihr was zu fressen!"
So sangen sie. Ich, dort vorbeimarschierend,
hörte noch lange sterbenden Gesang.

< 292 >

So they began to sing. I, marching past there,
long after that could hear it, dying song.

1965: Die lange Zeit

WOLFDIETRICH SCHNURRE:

Geboren 1920 in Frankfurt. Er verbrachte den größten Teil seines Lebens in Berlin. Sechseinhalb Jahre diente er als Soldat. Er ist vor allem bekannt als Prosaschriftsteller und als Autor von Romanen, Kurzgeschichten und Essays. Er war einer der Mitgründer der Gruppe 47, einer einflußreichen Vereinigung antifaschistischer und antimilitaristischer Schriftsteller, bei deren Treffen Autoren vorlasen und ihre Arbeiten kritisieren ließen. Seine Gedichtsammlungen umfassen die Titel *Kassiber* (1956), *Abendländler* (satirische Gedichte, 1957), und *Kassiber: neue Gedichte* (1964). Die Sammlungen seiner Kurzgeschichten umfassen die Titel: *Meine Oasen: Meine fünf Schicksalbücher* (1971), *Der Meerschweinchendieb: eine Bildgeschichte* (1972) und *Die Weihnachtsmannaffäre* (1974).

STROPHE

Als der Falke
der Taube
die Fänge ins Fleisch schlug,
sank eine Feder
der Welt auf den Mund.
Reglos hing sie
an den dörrenden Lippen
und harrte des Atems.
Er kam nicht; es
war der Abendwind,
der sie fortnahm.

DENUNZIATION

Mond,
Milchspinne der Frauen,
Lästerer;
Mond:
Wir klagen dich an.
Du hast Spionage getrieben,
das Weiss deiner Hände, es lügt.
So weiss ist Nebel, so weiss ist Linnen;
Chlor, das auf Erschossene rieselt,
Schnee, der die Erfrorenen wärmt.
So weiss ist Nebel, no weiss ist Linnen;
Nebel, der ins Pesttal sich senkt,

< 294 >

WOLFDIETRICH SCHNURRE:

Born in Frankfurt in 1920, but has spent most of his life in Berlin. He served for six and a half years as a soldier. He is best known as a prose writer, novelist, short story writer and essayist. He was one of the co-founders of the Gruppe 47, the influential association of antifascist and antimilitarist writers at whose meetings writers read and received criticism of their works. His collections of poems include *Kassiber* (1956), *Abendländler* (satirical poems, 1957), and *Kassiber: neue Gedichte* (1964). His short story collections include: *Meine Oasen: Meine fünf Schicksalbücher* (1971), *Der Meerschweinchendieb: eine Bildgeschichte* (1972), and *Die Weihnachtsmannaffäre* (1974).

STROPHE

When the hawk
struck his talons
into the dove's flesh,
a feather drifted
onto the mouth of the world.
Unmoving it clung
to those wilting lips
and waited for them to breathe.
No breath came; it
was the evening breeze
that bore the feather away.

1956

DENUNCIATION

Moon,
milk spider of the women,
blasphemer;
moon,
we accuse you.
You have practised espionage,
the whiteness of your hands deceives:
the whiteness of chlorine, whiteness of snow;
chlorine that drizzles on those shot dead,
snow that warms those frozen to death;
the whiteness of mist, the whiteness of linen;
mist that settles on the plague-filled valley,
linen that cools the murdered.

<   295   >

Linnen, das die Ermordeten kühlt.

Mond,
Heuschreckenmünze der Männer,
Verhöhner;
Mond:
Du hast Spionage getrieben.
Dein Auftraggeber ist uns bekannt;
er wohnt jenseits der Liebe.

HAUCH AUF DER SCHERBE

Nicht mit dem Donner,
nicht unterm Faustschlag
des Winds weht es heran:
sanft,
auf Kolibrischwingen,
mild wie das Gift
im Dolchzahn der Viper
wird es sich zeigen,
als goldener Ausschlag
erscheint es
auf Papierdrachenfetzen,
auf brüchigen Fellen,
auf Schläfen, verdorrt
zu Fledermauspergament:
das zarte Entsetzen.

GEHENKTER PARTISAN

Archangelskaja, VII.42

Ein Sensenschatten
schlug die Sonnenblumenfelder.
Das Samenantlitz,
weiss noch unter gelber
Jugend bienensüssem Staube,
knickte mit der Laubmonstranz
ins Stengelhaar, und klaffend

< 296 >

Moon,
locust coin of the men,
scoffer;
moon,
you have practised espionage.
Your employer is known to us;
he lives on the far side of love.

1956

BREATH ON A PIECE OF BROKEN GLASS

Not with the thunder,
not under the clenched blow
of the wind does it approach:
gently,
on hummingbird wings,
mild as the venom
in the viper's dagger tooth
it will reveal itself,
as a golden rash
it appears
on scraps of paper kites,
on mangy pelts,
on temples withered
to batskin parchment:
the delicate horror.

1956

HANGED PARTISAN

Archangel, vii, 42

The shadow of a scythe
struck the sunflower fields.
The face of seeds,
still white beneath the bee-sweet
pollen of yellow youth,
fell with its leafy pyx on to
the stalk's fine hair, and gaping

<   297   >

bot der Schaft des Silberhalses
dem Himmel seine Wunde dar.

O, federleichtes Mark
gebrochnen Julitags,
vor dessen Blau
der eimerlose Brunnenbalken
knarrend auf die Lerche weist,
die, Glut im Munde, über
russgeschwärzten Katen kreist.

TOTER SOLDAT

Nun noch den Asseln pfeifen unterm Stein,
dass sie die Panzer rasseln lassen,
und im Turm aus Sand
der Feuerkäferschütze am MG.
Den Krieg begann die Maus,
ihr Grau ist nur geliehn,
darunter geht sie nackt
und flechsig, blau und bloss.
Gefordert ward das Fell,
die Ohren blieben dran:
Jetzt schweigt das Gras,
und eingemummt in Stille
stemmt der Pilz die bleiche Schulter
unters Laub, das blasig birst.
Der kahle Eichenoffizier hat ausgedient,
im hohlen Stammbaum steigt der Staub
zu roten Schwaden auf.
Das Moos verblutet ungestillt.
Geschient ist worden, was zerbrach;
doch das Geheilte west,
und nur was beinlos ist und ohne Hand,
das darf noch hoffen, dass es lebt:
Der Wurm wird siegen,
und der Arm verliert.

<   298   >

the stem of the silvery neck
offered its wound to heaven.

O marrow light as a feather
of a broken day in July
against whose blue
the well's bucketless beam,
creaking, points to the lark
that circles, with fire in its throat,
above cottages black with soot.

DEAD SOLDIER

Now whistle to the woodlice under the stone,
so that they'll make their armour rattle
and in the tower of sand
the firebug marksman at his brengun post.
This war was started by the mouse,
its gray is only borrowed,
beneath it the mouse goes naked
and sinewy, blue and bare.
Its pelt was requisitioned,
the ears were not cut off:
Now grass keeps mum
and masked, wrapped up in silence
the fungus pushes a pale shoulder
at leafmould which, bubbly, bursts.
The bald oak officer has been discharged,
dust rises in the hollow family tree,
thickens to reddish clouds.
The moss, unnourished, bleeds to death.
Splinters were fixed to broken bones;
but what was healed decays,
and only what is legless, handless now
still dares to hope that it's alive:
the worm will win,
and the arm is losing.

1964: Kassiber: neue Gedichte

< 299 >

PAUL CELAN· ·

Geboren 1920 in Czernovitz, Rumänien, als Kind deutschsprachiger Juden. 1938 ging er nach Frankreich, um dort Medizin zu studieren, kehrte aber nach Czernovitz zurück, um Romanistik zu studieren. Nach der russischen Besetzung 1941 übernahmen deutsche und rumänischen Arbeitslager, und kehrte dann mit den Besatzern russischen Besatzern nach Czernovitz zurück., Er nahm seine Studien bis 1945 wieder auf, zog dann nach Bukarest, wo er als Übersetzer und Verlagslektor arbeitete. Nachdem er sich kurz in Wien niedergelassen hatte und einen ersten Gedichtband, der später wieder zurückgezogen wurde, veröffentlicht hatte, ließ er sich 1948 in Paris nieder, wo er bis zu seinem Tod durch Selbstmord im ahre 1970 lebte. Neben seiner Arbeit als Dozent für Deutsch an der Ecole Normale Supérieure übersetzte er Lyrik aus dem Französischen, Russischen und Englischen. Mit der Veröffentlichung von *Mohn und Gedächtnis* (1952) in West-Deutschland, besonders mit dem Gedicht *Todesfuge,* das er aus seiner früheren Sammlung übernommen hatte, gelang ihm der Durchbruch als Lyriker. Zu seinen Lebzeiten folgten fünf weitere Sammlungen, posthum wurden nocheinmal zwei veröffentlicht. *Atemwende* (1967), *Ausgewählte Gedichte* (1970), *Lichtzwang* (1970) und *Schneeport* (1971). Eine Ausgabe seiner gesammelten Werke wird vorbereitet. Auswahlen der Gedichte Celans in englischer Übersetzung sind in England und Amerika erschienen. Eine zweibändige Sammlung, *Gedichte,* erschien 1975, und eine kritische Ausgabe ist in Vorbereitung.

MIT WECHSELNDEM SCHLÜSSEL — *das dichterische Wort will die Wirklichkeit bewältigen*

Mit wechselndem Schlüssel
schliesst du das Haus auf, darin
der Schnee des Verschwiegenen treibt.
Je nach dem Blut, das dir quillt
aus Auge oder Mund oder Ohr,
wechselt dein Schlüssel.

das Schwierige das ausgedrückt werden soll

Wechselt dein Schlüssel, wechselt das Wort,
das treiben darf mit den Flocken.
Je nach dem Wind, der dich fortstösst,
ballt um das Wort sich der Schnee.

TENEBRAE ⟹ *Todesnacht - Latein - hängt mit dem Tod Christi zusammen*

Nah sind wir, Herr,
nahe und greifbar.

< 300 >

PAUL CELAN:

Born in Czernowitz, Romania, of German-speaking Jewish parents in 1920. He went o France in 1938 to study medicine, but returned to Czernowitz to study romance languages and literatures. In 1941, after a Russian occupation, German and Romanian forces took over, and the Jews were herded into a ghetto. In 1942 his parents were deported to an extermination camp. Paul Celan escaped arrest, but remained in a Romanian labor camp until February, 1944, when he returned to Czernowitz under a second Russian occupation. He resumed his studies until 1945 when he moved to Bucharest, working as a translator and publisher's reader. In 1948, after settling briefly in Vienna and publishing a first book of poems which was later withdrawn, he settled in Paris, where he lived until his death by suicide in 1970. Besides his work as a lecturer in German at the Ecole Normale Supérieure, he translated poetry from the French, Russian, and English. He won immediate recognition as a poet with the publication of *Mohn und Gedächtn* (1952) in West Germany, especially with the poem *Todesfuge*, which was taken over from his earlier collection. Five more collections followed in his lifetime, with two more published posthumously. A two-volume collection, *Gedichte*, was published in 1975, and a critical edition is in preparation. Two selections from Celan's poems in English translation have appeared in England and America respectively.

WITH A VARIABLE KEY

With a variable key
you unlock the house in which
drifts the snow of that left unspoken.
Always what key you choose
depends on the blood that spurts
from your eye or your mouth or your ear.

You vary the key, you vary the word
that is free to drift with the flakes.
What snowball will form round the word
depends on the wind that rebuffs you.

1955: Von Schwelle zu Schwelle

TENEBRAE
We are near, Lord,
near and at hand.

< 301 >

Gegriffen schon, Herr,
ineinander verkrallt, als wär
der Leib eines jeden von uns
dein Leib, Herr.

Bete, Herr,
bete zu uns,
wir sind nah.

Windschief gingen wir hin,
gingen wir hin, uns zu bücken
nach Mulde und Maar.

Zur Tränke gingen wir, Herr.

Es war Blut, es war,
was du vergossen, Herr.

Es glänzte.

Es warf uns dein Bild in die Augen, Herr.
Augen und Mund stehn so offen und leer, Herr.

Wir haben getrunken, Herr.
Das Blut und das Bild, das im Blut war, Herr.

Bete, Herr.
Wir sind nah.

ALLERSEELEN

Was hab ich
getan?
Die Nacht besamt, als könnt es
noch andere geben, nächtiger als
diese.

< 302 >

Handled already, Lord,
clawed and clawing as though
the body of each of us were
your body, Lord.

Pray, Lord,
pray to us,
we are near.

Wind-awry we went there,
went there to bend
over hollow and ditch.

To be watered we went there, Lord.

It was blood, it was
what you shed, Lord.

It gleamed.

It cast your image into our eyes, Lord.
Our eyes and our mouths are open and empty, Lord.
We have drunk, Lord.
The blood and the image that was in the blood, Lord.

Pray, Lord.
We are near.

1959: Sprachgitter

ALL SOULS

What did I
do?
Seminated the night, as though
there could be others, more nocturnal than
this one.

<   303   >

Vogelflug, Steinflug, tausend
beschriebene Bahnen. Blicke,
geraubt und gepflückt. Das Meer,
gekostet, vertrunken, verträumt. Eine Stunde,
seelenverfinstert. Die nächste, ein Herbstlicht,
dargebracht einem blinden
Gefühl, das des Wegs kam. Andere, viele,
ortlos und schwer aus sich selbst: erblickt und umgangen.
Findlinge, Sterne,
schwarz und voll Sprache: benannt
nach zerschwiegenem Schwur.

Und einmal (wann? auch dies ist vergessen):
den Widerhaken gefühlt,
wo der Puls den Gegentakt wagte.

PSALM

Niemand knetet uns wieder aus Erde und Lehm,
niemand bespricht unsern Staub.
Niemand.

Gelobt seist du, Niemand.
Dir zulieb wollen
wir blühn.
Dir
entgegen.

Ein Nichts
waren wir, sind wir, werden
wir bleiben, blühend:
die Nichts-, die
Niemandsrose.

Mit
dem Griffel seelenhell,

<   304   >

Bird flight, stone flight, a thousand
described routes. Glances,
purloined and plucked. The sea,
tasted, drunk away, dreamed away. An hour
soul-eclipsed. The next, an autumn light,
offered up to a blind
feeling which came that way. Others, many,
with no place but their own heavy centers: glimpsed and
    avoided.

Foundlings, stars,
black, full of language: named
after an oath which silence annulled.

And once (when? that too is forgotten):
felt the barb
where my pulse dared the counter-beat.

                                    1959: *Sprachgitter*

PSALM

No one moulds us again out of earth and clay,
no one conjures our dust.
No one.

Praised be your name, no one.
For your sake
we shall flower.
Toward
you.

A nothing
we were, are, shall
remain, flowering;
the nothing-, the
no one's rose.

< 305 >

dem Staubfaden himmelswüst,
der Krone rot
vom Purpurwort, das wir sangen
über, o über
dem Dorn.

RADIX, MATRIX

Wie man zum Stein spricht, wie
du,
mir vom Abgrund her, von
einer Heimat her Ver-
schwisterte, Zu-
geschleuderte, du,
du mir vorzeiten,
du mir im Nichts einer Nacht,
du in der Aber-Nacht Be-
gegenete, du
Aber-Du—:

Damals, da ich nicht da war,
damals, da du
den Acker abschrittst, allein:

Wer
wer wars, jenes
Geschlecht, jenes gemordete, jenes
schwarz in den Himmel stehende:
Rute und Hode—?

(Wurzel.
Wurzel Abrahams, Wurzel Jesse. Niemandes
Wurzel—o
unser.)

Ja,
wie man zum Stein spricht, wie
du

<   306   >

With our pistil soul-bright
with our stamen heaven-ravaged
our corolla red
with the crimson word which we sang
over, O over
the thorn.

1963: *Die Niemandsrose*

RADIX, MATRIX

As one speaks to stone, like
you,
from the chasm, from
a home become a
sister to me, hurled
toward me, you,
you that long ago
you in the nothingness of a night,
you in the multi-night en-
countered, you—:

At that time, when I was not there,
at that time when you
paced the ploughed field, alone:

Who,
who was it, that
lineage, the murdered, that looms
black into the sky:
rod and bulb—?

(Root.
Abraham's root. Jesse's root. No one's
root—O
ours.)

Yes,
as one speaks to stone, as

< 307 >

mit meinen Händen dorthin
und ins Nichts greifst, so
ist, was hier ist:

auch dieser
Fruchtboden klafft,
dieses
Hinab
ist die eine der wild-
blühenden Kronen.

FADENSONNEN

Fadensonnen
über der grauschwarzen Ödnis.
ein baum—
hoher Gedanke
greift sich den Lichtton: es sind
noch Lieder zu singen jenseits
der Menschen.

WEGGEBEIZT

Weggebeizt vom
Strahlenwind deiner Sprache
das bunte Gerede des An-
erlebten—das hundert-
züngige Mein-
gedicht, das Genicht.

Aus-
gewirbelt,
frei
der Weg durch den menschen-
gestaltigen Schnee,
den Büsserschnee, zu
den gastlichen
Gletscherstuben und—tischen.

<   308   >

you
with your hands grope into there,
and into nothing, such
is what is here:

this fertile
soil too gapes,
this
going down
is one of the
crests growing wild.

1963: *Die Niemandsrose*

THREAD SUNS

Thread suns
above gray-black wilderness.
A tree-
high thought
tunes into light's pitch: there are
still songs to be sung on the other side
of mankind.

ETCHED AWAY FROM . . .

Etched away from
the ray-shot wind of your language
the garish talk of rubbed-
off experience—the hundred—
tongued my—
poem, the noem.

Whirled
clear,
free
your way through the human-
shaped snow,
the penitents' snow, to

< 309 >

Tief
in der Zeitenschrunde,
beim
Wabeneis
wartet, ein Atemkristall,
dein unumstössliches
Zeugnis.

SCHALTJAHRHUNDERTE

Schaltjahrhunderte, Schalt-
sekunden, Schalt-
geburten, novembernd, Schalt-
tode,

in Wabentrögen gespeichert,
bits
on chips,
das Menoragedicht aus Berlin,

(Unasyliert, un-
archiviert, un-
umfürsorgt? Am
Leben?),

Lesestationen im Spätwort,

Sparflammenpunkte
am Himmel,

Kammlinien unter Beschuss,

Gefühle, frost-
gespindelt,

Kaltstart—
mit Hämoglobin.

< 310 >

the hospitable
glacier rooms and tables.

Deep in time's crevasse
by the alveolate ice
waits, a crystal of breath,
your irreversible
witness.

1967: Atemwende

LEAP-CENTURIES

Leap-centuries, leap-
seconds, leap-
births, novembering, leap-
deaths,

stacked in honeycomb troughs,
"bits
on chips,"

the menora poem from Berlin

(Unasylumed, un-
archived, un-
welfare-attended? A-
live?),

reading stations in the late word,

saving flame points
in the sky,

comb lines under fire,

feelings, frost-
mandrelled,

< 311 >

MAPESBURY ROAD

Die dir zugewinkte
Stille von hinterm
Schritt einer Schwarzen.

Ihr zur Seite
die
magnolienstündige Halbuhr
vor einem Rot,
das auch anderswo Sinn sucht—
oder auch nirgends.

Der volle
Zeithof um
einen Steckschuss, daneben, hirnig.

Die scharfgehimmelten höfigen
Schlucke Mitluft.

Vertag dich nicht, du.

< 312 >

cold start
with haemoglobin.

1970: *Lichtzwang*

MAPESBURY ROAD

The stillness waved
at you from behind
a black woman's gait.

At her side
the
magnolia-houred halfclock
in front of a red
that elsewhere too looks for meaning—
or nowhere perhaps.

the full
time-yard around
a lodged bullet, next to it, cerebrous.

The sharply heavened courtyardy
gulps of co-air.

Don't adjourn yourself, you.

1971: *Schneepart*

< 313 >

ILSE AICHINGER:

Geboren 1921 in Wien. Bekannt vor allem durch ihre Prosaarbeiten: *Die größere Hoffnung* (Roman), 1948; *Der Gefesselte (Erzählungen)*, *1953*. *Teile* dieser Sammlung wurden 1952 unter dem Titel: *Rede unter dem Galgen* veröffentlicht. *Zu keiner Stunde* (Dialoge), 1957; *Wo ich wohne* (Erzählungen, Dialoge, Gedichte), 1963; *Eliza, Eliza* (Erzählungen), 1965; und *Nachricht von Tag* (Erzählungen), 1970. Sie schrieb auch Hörspiele, darunter u.a. *Auckland* (4 Hörspiele), 1969. 1971 erschienen gesammelte *Dialoge, Erzählungen, Gedichte*, und eine englischsprachige Übersetzung *The Bound Man and other Stories*. Ilse Aichinger war mit dem verstorbenen Günter Eich verheiratet.

WINTERANTWORT

Die Welt ist aus dem Stoff,
der Betrachtung verlangt:
keine Augen mehr,
um die weissen Wiesen zu sehen,
keine Ohren, um im Geäst
das Schwirren der Vögel zu hören.
Grossmutter, wo sind deine Lippen hin,
um die Gräser zu schmecken,
und wer riecht uns den Himmel zu Ende,
wessen Wangen reiben sich heute
noch wund an den Mauern im Dorf?
Ist es nicht ein finsterer Wald,
in den wir gerieten?
Nein, Grossmutter, er ist nicht finster,
ich weiss es, ich wohnte lang
bei den Kindern am Rande,
und es ist auch kein Wald.

BRIEFWECHSEL

Wenn die Post nachts käme
und der Mond schöbe die Kränkungen
unter die Tür:
Sie erschienen wie Engel
in ihren weissen Gewändern
und stünden still im Flur.

< 314 >

ILSE AICHINGER:

Born 1921 in Vienna. Best known for her prose works: *Die grössere Hoffnung* (novel), 1948; *Der Gefesselte* (stories), 1953, published in 1952 under the title: *Rede unter dem Galgen*. *Zu keiner Stunde* (dialogues), 1957; *Wo ich wohne* (stories, dialogues, poems), 1963; *Eliza, Eliza* (stories), 1965; and *Nachricht von Tag* (stories), 1970. She has also written radio plays, among them *Auckland* (4 radio plays), 1969. Collected *Dialoge, Erzählungen, Gedichte* appeared in 1971, as did an English-language version of *The Bound Man and Other Stories*. Married to Günter Eich, who died in 1972.

WINTER ANSWER

The world is of the stuff
that calls for perception:
no eyes left
to see the white meadows,
no ears to hear
the whirring of birds in the boughs.
Grandmother, what's become of your lips,
to savour the grasses,
and who will smell the sky for us all the way,
whose cheeks today
still rub themselves sore on walls in the village?
Is it not a gloomy wood
into which we have all strayed?
No, grandmother, it isn't gloomy,
I know, for a long time I've lived
with the children on the edge,
and neither is it a wood.

CORRESPONDENCE

If the post came at night
and the moon pushed those insults
under the door:
They would appear like angels
in their white array
and would stand still in the hall.

1963: *Wo ich wohne*

<   315   >

HELMUT HEISSENBÜTTEL:

Geboren 1921 in Wilhelmshaven. 1941 wurde er als Soldat schwer verwundet. In späteren Jahren studierte er Architekur, Kunstgeschichte und deutsche Literatu; er schloß seine Studien nach dem Krieg in Hamburg ab. Nach seiner Verlagstätigkeit dort zog er nach Stuttgart, wo er seit 1959 als Rundfunkredakteur arbeitet. Seine frühen Sammlungen *Kombinationen* und *Topographien* erforschen die Brüche des Bewußtseins. In einem Teil seiner Arbeiten steht er der konkreten Poesie nahe, aber er führte seine semantischen Experimente bewußter und philosphischer durch als die Praktiker der reinen Sprachspiele. Er nutzte die zu Beginn des Jahrhunderts geleistete Arbeit, u.a. der Dadaisten und Gertrude Steins. Seine ''Texte''—in Prosa und Lyrik—erschienen in einer Reihe von sechs ''Textbüchern'', die nun in einem Band gesammelt vorliegen: *Das Textbuch* (1970). Außerdem veröffentlichte er einen Roman *D'Alemberts Ende* (1970) und wichtige kritische und theoretische Essays *Über Literatur* (1966), *Was ist das Konkrete an einem Gedicht?* (1969), *Briefwechsel über Literatur* (mit Heinrich Vormweg) (1969), und *Zur Tradition der Moderne* (1972). Jüngst erschieneneBande umfassen: *Die Freuden des Alterns* (1971), *Gelegenheitsgedichte und Klappentexte* (1973) und *Das Durchhauen des Kohlhaupts* (1974).

ZUSPRUCH

die vorhandene Fläche wird allmählich weiss werden
die ausweglosen dreidimensionalen Ecken werden zusam-
     menklappen
fester wird das Gesicht seine Vergesslichkeit um die Schultern
     ziehen
tränenverzerrte Lippen werden aufstehn und weggehn
das was wir glücklich sein nannten
die flache Schale des Beunruhigenden wird sich lautlos abheben
     wie Rauch
der Wind der nicht riecht wird seine Hand ausstrecken

HIER RASTEN DIE GROSSEN BLAUEN SCHMETTERLINGE

VIII

hier rasten die grossen blauen Schmetterlinge
Aufspreizungen aus Unhörbarem geschehen
hier landen die grünen Balkons meiner Vorzeit

< 316 >

HELMUT HEISSENBÜTTEL:

Born in Wilhelmshaven in 1921. He was seriously wounded during military service in 1941. In the later war years he studied architecture, history of art, and German, completing his studies at Hamburg after the war. After working for a publishing house in Hamburg he moved to Stuttgart, where he has been a radio producer since 1959. His early collections *Kombinationen* and *Topographien* explored the discontinuities of consciousness. He is close to concrete poetry in part of his work, but his semantic experiments have been conducted more deliberately and more philosophically than those of the practitioners of pure language games. He has made good use of the work done early in the century by the Dadaists and by Gertrude Stein, among others. His "texts"—either in prose or verse—appeared in a series of six "textbooks," now collected in one volume, *Das Textbuch* (1970). He has also published a novel, *D'Alemberts Ende* (1970), and important critical and theoretical essays, *Über Literatur* (1966), *Was ist das Konkrete an einem Gedicht?* (1969), *Briefwechsel über Literatur* (with Heinrich Vormweg) (1969), and *Zur Tradition der Moderne* (1972). His recent publications include: *Die Freuden des Alterns* (1971), *Gelegenscheitsgedichte und Klappentexte* (1973), and *Das Durchhauen des Kohlhaupts* (1974).

WORDS OF COMFORT

the plane that confronts you will gradually turn white
the inescapable three-dimensional corners will stick together
more closely your face will draw forgetfulness round your
    shoulders
lips distorted with weeping will get up and go
what we called being happy
the shallow bowl of anxiety will silently rise like smoke
the wind with no smell will extend its hand

HERE THE LARGE BLUE BUTTERFLIES REST

here the large blue butterflies rest
spreadings out that occurred in the inaudible
here the green balconies of my prehistory land
glossed areas wander slowly through unknown parts of the city
the black poplars bend over one another and fall silent
dead bicycles roll lonely through the forgetful world
empty windows move in wide ranks over the soundless land-
    scape

< 317 >

eingesehene Bezirke wandern langsam durch fremde Stadtteile
die schwarzen Pappeln neigen sich übereinander und
    verstummen
gestorbene Fahrräder rollen langsam durch die
    vergessliche Welt
leere Fenster bewegen sich in breiten Ketten tief über die laut-
    lose Landschaft
was suchen die leeren Fenster?

DIE ZUKUNFT DES SOZIALISMUS

niemand besitzt was
niemand beutet aus
niemand unterdrückt
niemand wird ausgebeutet
niemand wird unterdrückt
niemand gewinnt was
niemand verliert was
niemand ist Herr
niemand ist Sklave
niemand ist Vorgesetzter
niemand ist Untergebener
niemand ist einem was schuldig
niemand tut einem was

niemand besitzt nichts
niemand beutet niemand aus
niemand unterdrückt niemand
niemand wird von niemand ausgebeutet
niemand wird von niemand unterdrückt
niemand gewinnt nichts
niemand verliert nichts
niemand ist Herr von niemand
niemand ist Sklave von niemand
niemand ist niemands Vorgesetzter
niemand ist niemands Untergebener
niemand ist niemand was schuldig

? what do the empty windows look for?

1956: *Topographien*

THE FUTURE OF SOCIALISM

no one owns anything
no one exploits
no one oppresses
no one is exploited
no one is oppressed
no one gains anything
no one loses anything
no one is a master
no one is a slave
no one is a superior
no one is a subordinate
no one owes anyone anything
no one does anything to anyone

no one owns nothing
no one exploits no one
no one oppresses no one
no one is exploited by no one
no one is oppressed by no one
no one gains nothing
no one loses nothing
no one is no one's master
no one is no one's slave
no one is no one's superior
no one is no one's subordinate
no one owes no one anything
no one does anything to no one

all own everything
all exploit all
all oppress all
all are exploited by all
all are oppressed by all

< 319 >

niemand tut niemand was

alle besitzen alles
alle beuten alle aus
alle unterdrücken alle
alle werden von allen ausgebeutet
alle werden von allen unterdrückt
alle gewinnen alles
alle verlieren alles
alle sind Herr von allen
alle sind Sklave von allen
alle sind Vorgesetzter von allen
alle sind Untergebener von allen
alle sind allen alles schuldig
alle tun allen alles

alle besitzen nichts
alle beuten niemand aus
alle unterdrücken niemand
alle werden von niemand ausgebeutet
alle werden von niemand unterdrückt
alle gewinnen nichts
alle verlieren nichts
alle sind Herr von niemand
alle sind Sklave von niemand
alle sind niemands Vorgesetzter
alle sind niemands Untergebener
alle sind niemand nichts schuldig
alle tun niemand nichts

SO WHAT

die Ehrlichen haben sich als korrupt erwiesen
die Biedermänner haben sich als Angeber erwiesen
die Vitalität erweist sich als Impotenz
Keuschheit erweist sich als triebübersteuert
die Nüchternen haben sich als süchtig erwiesen

< 320 >

all gain everything
all lose everything
all are everyone's masters
all are everyone's slaves
all are everyone's superiors
all are everyone's subordinates
all owe everyone everything
all do anything to everyone

all own nothing
all exploit no one
all oppress no one
all are exploited by no one
all are oppressed by no one
all gain nothing
all lose nothing
all are no one's masters
all are no one's slaves
all are no one's superiors
all are no one's subordinates
all owe no one nothing
all do nothing to no one

SO WHAT

the honest people have proved to be corrupt
the decent people have proved to be bogus
vitality proves to be impotence
chastity proves to be oversexed
the sober people have proved to be addicts
the responsible people have proved to be irresponsible
magnanimity proves to be pettiness
discipline proves to be confusion
love of truth has proved to be riddled with lies
fearlessness proves to be cowardice
justice to be cruelty
the life-affirmers prove to be a shifty lot

< 321 >

die Verantwortung besassen erwiesen sich als verantwor-
tungsscheu
Grossmut erweist sich als Kleinlichkeit
Disziplin erweist sich als Konfusion
Wahrheitsliebe hat sich als verlogen erwiesen
Furchtlosigkeit erweist sich als Feigheit
Gerechtigkeit als Grausamkeit
die das Leben bejahen erweisen sich als lichtscheues Gesindel

die korrupt sind sind die einzig Ehrlichen
die Angeber allein sind Biedermänner
die Impotenz allein ist vital
Triebübersteuerung ist die einzige Art von Keuschheit
Süchtigkeit allein ist nüchtern
die Verantwortungsscheuen sind die einzigen die Verantwortung besitzen
die Kleinlichen sind die einzig Grossmütigen
Konfusion allein ist diszipliniert
die Lüge ist die einzige Wahrheit
die grausam sind allein sind gerecht
das lichtscheue Gesindel ist das einzige das das Leben bejaht

wer ehrlich ist ist korrupt
wer einen Biedermann vorstellen will gibt an
wer als vital gelten will sorgt für Impotenz
wer als keusch gelten will übersteuert seine Triebe
wer nüchtern ist ist süchtig
wer Verantwortung tragen will ist verantwortungsscheu
wer als grossmütig gelten will sollte kleinlich sein
wer auf Disziplin hält ist konfus
wer die Wahrheit sagt lügt
wer keine Furcht hat ist ein Feigling
wer gerecht sein will ist grausam
wer das Leben bejaht gehört zum lichtscheuen Gesindel

ehrlich korrupt oder korrupt ehrlich

< 322 >

the corrupt people prove to be the only honest ones
the bogus only are decent people
impotence only is vital
being oversexed is the only kind of chastity
only addiction is sober
only irresponsible people have a sense of responsibility
the petty are the only magnanimous people
confusion alone is disciplined
lies are the only truth
only cowards are fearless
only those who are cruel are just
only those who are a shifty lot are life-affirmers

whoever is honest is corrupt
whoever pretends to be decent is bogus
whoever wants to seem vital produces impotence
whoever wants to seem chaste becomes oversexed
whoever is sober is an addict
whoever wants to take on responsibility is irresponsible
whoever wants to seem magnanimous ought to be petty
whoever believes in discipline is confused
whoever tells the truth is a liar
whoever is fearless is a coward
whoever wants to be just is cruel
whoever affirms life is a shifty lot

honestly corrupt or corruptly honest
decent bogusness or bogus decency
vital impotence or impotent vitality
oversexed chastity or chaste oversexedness
addicted through sobriety or soberly addicted
responsible irresponsibility or irresponsible responsibility
magnanimously petty or petty magnanimity
disciplined confusion or confused discipline
true lie or truth riddled with lies
fearlessly cowardly or cowardly fearlessness

<   323   >

biedere Angabe oder angeberische Biederkeit
vitale Impotenz oder impotente Vitalität
triebübersteuernde Keuschheit oder keusche Triebübersteuerung
süchtig vor Nüchternheit oder nüchtern süchtig
verantwortungsbewusste Verantwortungsscheu oder verantwor-
    tungs- scheues Verantwortungsbewusstsein

grossmütig kleinlich oder kleinliche Grossmut
disziplinierte Konfusion oder konfuse Disziplin
wahre Lügen oder verlogene Wahrheit
furchtlos feige oder feige Furchtlosigkeit
gerechte Grausamkeit oder grausam gerecht
lichtscheue Lebensbejahung oder lebensbejahend lichtscheu

so what

just cruelty or cruelly just
a shifty lot's affirmation of life or life-affirmingly shifty

so what   1965: *Textbuch 5*

< 325 >

HANS CARL ARTMANN:

Geboren 1921 in St. Achaz am Walde, Österreich. Er war das *enfant terrible* der zeitgenössischen österreichischen Lyrik und schon zu Lebzeiten—zum Teil dank seines Maskenkults und eines bewußten Eklektizismus—eine legendäre Figur. Er wurde mit seinen Dialektgedichten *Med anna schwoazzn dintn* (1958) berühmt. Interessierte sich für keltische, persische und spanische Literatur. Seine verschiedenen Lyrik- und Prosa-Veröffentlichungen erschienen wie zufällig, meist von anderen gesammelt oder veröffentlicht; z.B.: *The Best of H. C. Artmann* (1970). Vorausgegangen waren *Ein lilienweisser Brief aus Lincolnshire: Gedichte aus 21 Jahren* (1969), und *Frankenstein in Sussex: Fleiß und Industrie* (1969). Es folgten *Das im Walde verlorene Totem* (Prosa gedichte) (1949-1953), 1970, und *H. C. Artmann: Selections from the 'Persian Quatrains'* (1970). Seine neueste Gedichtsammlung trägt den Titel *Ompuel* (1974).

DER GRAF . . .

der graf mit dem einglas ass von den kuchen
er hatte ein nordlicht verkauft er war reich

eine lange reihe ford neunzehndreissig hielt
vor der villa die puppen kamen es donnert stark

eine um die andre kam zu dem grafen gesichter
wie milch und porzellan es donnert im winter

den grafen reute der verkauf des nordlichts
er war reich die puppen erschienen zum tee

es donnerte stark der graf mit dem einglas
liess kuchen servieren man trank dazu tee

der graf vertrieb sich die zeit mit den puppen
er war reich es donnert im winter noch kuchen

meine puppen sagte der graf mit dem einglas
sind wie milchporzellan es donnerte stark

das nordlicht kam in die hand eines führers
der kommandierte es rasch und direkt an die front

< 326 >

HANS CARL ARTMANN:

Born 1921 at St. Achaz am Walde, Austria. The *enfant terrible* of contemporary Austrian poetry, and a legendary figure in his lifetime, due in part to his cult of masks and a deliberate eclecticism. He became famous with his dialect poems *Med anna schwoazzn dintn* (1958). Interested in Celtic, Persian, and Spanish literature. His many publications in verse and prose have appeared as though fortuitously, often collected or edited by others; e.g.: *The Best of H. C. Artmann* (1970). This was preceded by *Ein lilienweisser Brief aus Lincolnshire: Gedichte aus 21 Jahren* (1969); *Frankenstein in Sussex: Fleiss und Industrie* (1969); and followed by *Das im Walde verlorene Totem* (prose poems), (1949-1953), 1970; *H. C. Artmann: Selectons from the "Persian Quatrains"* (1970). His latest publication of poems is called *Ompül* (1974).

THE COUNT . . .

the count with the monocle ate of the cakes
he had sold a northern light he was rich

a long row of nineteenthirty fords stopped
in front of the villa the dolls came there was loud thunder

one after the other went up to the count faces
like milk and china there's thunder in winter

the count regretted the sale of the northern light
he was rich the dolls came to tea

there was loud thunder the count with the monocle
had cakes served they were eaten for tea

the count passed the time with those dolls
he was rich there's thunder in winter more cakes

my dolls said the count with the monocle
are like milky china there was loud thunder

the northern light got into the hands of a leader
who quickly and straight sent it out to the front

< 327 >

es donnerte stark die puppen erzitterten sehr
sie meinten zu sterben sie tranken viel tee

das nordlicht erschien vor dem feind es war
bald von kugeln durchlöchert es donnerte stark

es donnert im winter dem grafen entglitt oft
das einglas es fiel zwischen kuchen und tee

es reute ihn sehr das nordlicht verschachert
zu haben das trieb nun durchlöchert im wind

der graf war sehr reich und es donnerte stark
die puppen die sagten adieu sie gingen hinaus

ein ford um den andren verschwand sie traten so
zart die pedale die puppen der graf war sehr reich

es reute ihn sehr das nordlicht durchlöchert
zu sehen er trank etwas tee es donnerte stark

ICH BIN EIN POLARES GESTIRN . . .

ich bin ein polares gestirn ich koste hundert dollars
eine eisbärin hat mich geboren winternachts glitzernd

ich kaufe meine pelze in den besten läden alaskas
ich sage guten frost beim einkauf sie geben ihn mir

mein licht macht sprünge an den wänden der atomuboote
glitzernd zeigt sich mein name in nautischen girlanden

kapitäne verehren mich als präsident präsidenten lieben
mich wie ihre besten kapitäne winternachts glitzere ich

sie tragen mich wic einen glasmond was wären sie alle
ohne mich ich beherrsche sie wie die sprungdeckel von uhren

< 328 >

there was loud thunder the dolls trembled greatly
they thought they would die they drank many cups of tea

the northern light appeared to the enemy soon
it was riddled with bullet-holes there was loud thunder

there's thunder in winter the count often dropped
his monocle it fell between cakes and tea

he sorely regretted his sale of the northern light
which full of holes was drifting now in the wind

the count was very rich there was loud thunder
the dolls they said goodbye and they left

one ford after another vanished they stepped on the pedals
so delicately those dolls the count was very sick

he sorely regretted to see the northern light
all riddled he drank some tea there was loud thunder

[1962]; 1966: *verbarium*

I AM A POLAR PLANET . . .

i am a polar planet i cost a hundred dollars
a polar bear gave birth to me glittering one winter night

i buy my furs in the best shops of alaska
i say good frost to the shopgirl she gives it to me

my light makes cracks in the walls of atomic submarines
glittering my name is displayed in nautical streamers

captains honour me as their president presidents love me
as they love their very best captains winter nights i glitter

they carry me like a glass moon what would become of them
all

< 329 >

ich sehe allen in die augen meinetwegen gibt es viele
blaue augen aus der flaschengrünen see tauche ich oft auf

es donnert in den eisbergen ich knackte mit den fingern
drei eskimomädchen liegen wartend in meinem seehundbett

einer meiner namen ist seehund die mädchen gehen nackt
im schnee sie erneuern ihre schönheit in meinem glitzern

ich kaufe ihnen häute in den besten läden von ganz alaska
ich bin auch ein sehr nördlicher totempfahl winternachts

wenn ich mit meinem glitzern zu bett gehe so werfe ich
die drei eskimomädchen auf den boden sie kreischen sanft

sie kommen wieder zurück sie kratzen mein glitzern stark
ich liebe mein glitzern aber die eskimomädchen mag ich auch

ich hänge ihnen viele kinder an schönste robben und bären
seehunde und alke alle meine namen fülle ich in ihren bauch

meine seehundhütte ist sehr anständig gebaut sehr fest auch
über dem eingang steht ein lichter schnabel vor vogelhaus

ich bin ein glitzernder seehund und ein eisbär und ein alk
eine robbe ein kapitän und ein walrossfänger bin ich auch

< 330 >

without me i master them as they do the lids of their watches

i look them all in the eyes because of me there are
many blue eyes out of the bottlegreen sea i often emerge

thunder booms in the icebergs i snap my fingers
three eskimo girls lie waiting in my sea-lion's bed

one of my names is sea-lion the girls walk naked in
the snow in my glitter they renew their beauty

i buy them skins in the best shops anywhere in alaska
and i'm also a very northerly totem pole winter nights

when i go to bed with my glitter i throw
the three eskimo girls on the floor they utter low shrieks

they come back again they scratch my glitter quite fiercely
i love my glitter but also like the eskimo girls

i give them a lot of children beautiful seals and bears
sea-lions and auks i fill their bellies with all my names

my sea-lion hut is well-built very decent and solid
over the entrance a shining beak is mounted my birdhouse

i am a glittering sea-lion an auk and a polar bear
a seal a captain and a walrus trapper as well

[1962]; 1966: *verbarium*

< 331 >

ERICH FRIED:

Geboren 1921 in Wien. Er emigrierte nach der Ermordung seines Vaters durch die Gestapo 1938 nach England. Dort arbeitete er als Chemiker, Glasbläser, Bibliothekar und in verschiedenen anderen Verlegenheitsjobs, bevor er sich ausschließlich dem Schreiben widmete. Von 1952 bis 1968 arbeitete er bei der Deutschen Welle der BBC. Seine vielen Übersetzungen aus dem Englischen umfassen die großen Shakespeare-Stücke und Schriftsteller des 20. Jahrhunderts, wie z.B. Dylan Thomas, T. S. Eliot, e.e. cummings und Sylvia Plath. Seine ersten Gedichtbände *Deutschland* und *Österreich* wurden in England veröffentlicht. Spätere Gedichtbände: *Gedichte* (1958), *Reich der Steine* (1963), *Warngedichte* (1964), *Überlegungen* (1964) *Vietnam* (1966), *Anfechtungen* (1967), *Die Beine der größeren Lügen* (1969), *Unter Nebenfeinden* (1970), *Aufforderung zur Unruhe* (1972), *Die Freiheit den Mund aufzumachen* (1972) und *Gegengift* (1974). Außerdem veröffentlichte er einen Roman, einen Band mit Erzählungen und Hörspiele. Er schreibt kritische und polemische Essays für viele deutsche Zeitschriften. Englische Übersetzungen einiger seiner Gedichte sind in Buchform erschienen: *On Pain of Seeing* (1969).

DIE MASSNAHMEN

Die Faulen werden geschlachtet
die Welt wird fleissig

Die Hässlichen werden geschlachtet
die Welt wird schön

Die Narren werden geschlachetet
die Welt wird weise

Die Kranken werden geschlachtet
die Welt wird gesund

Die Traurigen werden geschlachtet
die Welt wird lustig

Die Alten werden geschlachtet
die Welt wird jung

< 332 >

ERICH FRIED:

Born in Vienna in 1921, he emigrated to England in 1938 after his father had been murdered by the Gestapo. In England he worked as a chemist, glass blower, librarian, and in other odd jobs before becoming a full-time writer. From 1952 to 1968 he worked in the German Service of the BBC. His many translations from the English include the major plays of Shakespeare, as well as twentieth-century poets such as Dylan Thomas, T. S. Eliot, e.e. cummings, and Sylvia Plath. His first books of poems, *Deutschland* and *Österreich*, were published in England. His later books of poems include: *Gedichte* (1958), *Reich der Steine* (1963), *Warngedichte* (1964), *Überlegungen* (1964), *und Vietnam und* (1966), *Anfechtungen* (1967), *Die Beine der grösseren Lügen* (1969), *Unter Nebenfeinden* (1970), *Aufforderung zur Unruhe* (1972), *Die Freiheit den Mund aufzumachen* (1972), and *Gegengift* (1974). He has also published a novel, a book of stories, and radio plays. He contributes critical and polemical essays to many German periodicals. English translations of some of his poems have appeared in book form: *On Pain of Seeing* (1969).

THE MEASURES TAKEN

The lazy are slaughtered
the world grows industrious

The ugly are slaughtered
the world grows beautiful

The foolish are slaughtered
the world grows wise

The sick are slaughtered
the world grows healthy

The sad are slaughtered
the world grows merry

The old are slaughtered
the world grows young

The enemies are slaughtered
the world grows friendly

< 333 >

Die Feinde werden geschlachtet
die Welt wird freundlich

Die Bösen werden geschlachtet
die Welt wird gut

TRENNUNG

Nun wirst du wieder zu Stein
und im Schlaf
kommt das Moos
und wird wohnen

unter deinen Augen
bei Spuren
von Wasser
und Salz

VERLASSENES ZIMMER

Im Zimmer der Staub
zart auf den Fensterscheiben
der leise Staub
auf dem Tisch
auf dem alten Kissen:
Pfirsichflaum
der streichelt
die streichelnde Hand
der zeigt der Sonne
den Weg durch geschlossene Fenster

Müde sein
und nicht weinen wollen
und nicht
sterben wollen
geweint haben und schon tot sein:
Im leichten Staub
der dem Sonnenlicht seinen Weg zeigt

Beweinung eines Verstorbenen

< 334 >

The wicked are slaughtered
the world grows good

1958: *Gedichte*

SEPARATION

Now you turn to stone again
and in sleep
the moss will come
and will live

beneath your eyes
with traces
of water
and salt

1964: *Warngedichte*

UNOCCUPIED ROOM

The dust in this room
delicate on the windowpanes
the quiet dust
on the table
on the old cushion:
peach skin down
that fondles the fondling hand
that shows the sun
the way through fastened windows

To be tired
and unwilling to weep
and unwilling
to die
to have wept and to be already dead:
In the light dust
that shows sunlight the way
to lie on the cushion
not again

< 335 >

auf dem Kissen liegen
nicht wieder
nein immer
noch immer
und schon für immer
Staub auf Staub unter Staub

Staub auf dem Tisch
auf dem Bett
auf den Fensterscheiben:
Staub im Staub
Sonne im Staub
Staub in der Sonne
Ich Staub im Zimmer der Sonne
ich Staub auf dem Kissen
ich Wieder ich Noch ich Immer
im Zimmer aus Staub

EISERNE RATION

Wenn man das Unrecht
in viele Scheiben zerlegt
wie dünn muss die Scheibe
auf meinem täglichen Brot sein

ANGST UND ZWEIFEL

Zweifle nicht
an dem
der dir sagt
er hat Angst

aber hab Angst
vor dem
der dir sagt
er kennt keinen Zweifel

<   336   >

but always
and still
and already for always
dust on dust amid dust

Dust on the table
on the bed
on the windowpanes:
dust in dust
sun in dust
dust in the sun
I dust in the room of the sun
I dust on the cushion
I Again I Still I Always
in the room of dust
[1959]; new version in *Anfechtungen*, 1967

IRON RATIONS

When injustice
is carved into many slices
how thin must that slice be
that's put on my daily bread?
1966: *und VIETNAM und*

FEAR AND DOUBT

do not doubt
the man
who tells you
he's afraid

but be afraid
of the man
who tells you
he never doubts
1974: *Gegengift*

<   337   >

KUNO RAEBER:

Geboren 1922 in Klingnau in der Schweiz. Er lebt heute in München. Er veröffentlichte ein Reisebuch *Calabria* (1961) und schrieb einen Roman *Alexius unter der Treppe; oder Geständnisse vor einer Katze* (1973). Gedichtbände: *Gesicht im Mittag* (1950), *Die verwandelten Schiffe* (1957), *Gedichte* (1960) und *Flußufer* (1963).

DER MUND

Sacro Bosco in Bomarzo

Ehe das Moos den von Efeu schon überwachsenen Schrei
    schliesst,
tritt hinein in den offenen Steinmund.

Unter der Lampe, die baumelt vom Gaumen,
kaufe der Händlerin eine Karte mit dem Vulkan ab,
dessen Rauch den Horizont überrötet,
und mit dem steinernen Mund, wie er war,
ehe erstmals das Moos den vom Efeu schon überwachsenen
    Schrei schloss:

eine Gartengrotte, wohin der Kavalier seine Dame
zog, weil unter den bunten Laternen die Geigen
peitschten das Blut, das schrie,
bis er mit ihr den steilen
Ohrweg hinanklomm zum Lid, wo Platz war zum Liegen . . .

Ehe Moosschweigen den Schrei schliesst
und der Vulkan vergeblich den Tiefschläfer anruft,
ehe die Asche die Wange pudert,
die doch nicht zum Fest will:
Tritt hinein in den offenen Mund und kaufe die Karte.

< 338 >

KUNO RAEBER:

Born in Klingnau, Switzerland, in 1922, and now lives in Munich. He has published a travel book, *Calabria* (1961), and has written a novel, *Alexius unter der Treppe; oder Geständnisse vor einer Katze* (1973). His books of poems are: *Gesicht im Mittag* (1950), *Die verwandelten Schiffe* (1957), *Gedichte* (1960), and *Flussufer* (1963).

THE MOUTH

(Sacro Bosco at Bomarzo)

Before moss closes the scream already overgrown with ivy
enter the open mouth of stone.

Under the lamp that swings from the palate
let the girl at the counter sell you a postcard of the volcano
whose smoke is reddening the horizon
and with the mouth of stone, as it was
before moss first closed the scream already overgrown with ivy:

a garden, grotto, into which the cavalier dragged
his lady, because under the coloured lamps violins
whipped up the blood that screamed
till together with her he climbed the
steep earway up to the eyelid, where there was room to lie . . .

Before the silence of moss closes the scream
and the volcano in vain calls out to the deep sleeper,
before ash powders the cheek
reluctant still to go to the celebration:
Enter the open mouth and buy the postcard.

1957: Die verwandelten Schiffe

<   339   >

WALTER HÖLLERER:

Geboren 1922 in Sulzbach-Rosenberg in Bayern. Er studierte
Philosophie, Geschichte, Deutsch und Komparatistik, lehrte an ver-
schiedenen Universitäten Literatur, und ist heute Professor an der
Technischen Universität in Berlin. Daneben gab er die Zeitschriften
Akzente und *Sprache im Technischen Zeitalter* heraus, war bei
Rundfunk und Film tätig und organisierte literarische Symposien und
Ausstellungen. Er reiste und lehrte in Amerika. Gedichtbände:
Der andere Gast (1952), *Gedichte* (1964), *Ausserhalb der Saison*
(1967), und *Systeme* (1969). Er veröffentlichte außerdem Stücke und
den Roman *Die Elephantenuhr* (1973); daneben mehrere *vorzügliche*
Bücher über Literaturkritik, u.a. *Theorie der modernen Lyrik,
Dokumente zur Poetik* (als Herausgeber, 1965), und *Zwischen Klassik
und Moderne; Lachen und Weinen in der Dichtung einer* Übergangszeit (1958).

GESICHT DES FISCHERS

Europaspur im Antlitz, Geleitzug von
Triëren, Koggen, Masken des Dionys,
Verwandelte, in dunklen Rillen
Um seine Brauen.

Mehr, als du ahnst, Gesang.
Fernblickend Inseln.
Prall wie am ersten Tag die Segel.

ZWEIERLEI SINGEN

Dass er sang
Um eine Bedrückung
Hinwegzukommen
Hatten sie bald heraus
Und sie sagten es ihm.

Sein Nachdenken
Über die Methode des Singens
Führte ihn so weit,
Dass er sich bedrückt stellte,

< 340 >

WALTER HÖLLERER:

Born in 1922 in Sulzbach-Rosenberg in Bavaria. He studied philosophy, history, German, and comparative literature, has taught literature
at several universities, and is a professor at the Technical University in
Berlin. He has also been active as editor of the periodicals *Akzente* and
Sprache im Technischen Zeitalter, as an anthologist, broadcaster, film
maker, and organizer of literary symposia and exhibitions. He has
traveled and taught in America. His books of poems are: *Der andere
Gast* (1952), *Gedichte* (1964), *Ausserhalb der Saison* (1967), and *Systeme* (1969). He has also published plays and a novel, *Die Elephantenuhr* (1973), and several distinguished volumes of criticism, including *Theorie der modernen Lyrik, Dokumente zur Poetik* (editor, 1965),
and *Zwischen Klassik und Moderne; Lachen und Weinen in der
Dichtung einer Übergangszeit* (1958).

FISHERMAN'S FACE

Europe's trace in his features. Escort of
Triremes, galleons, masks of Dionysus,
Transformed, in dark furrows
Around his eyebrows.

More than you guess of song.
Islands distantly gazing.
Taut as the sails on the first day.

1952: *Der andere Gast*

TWO WAYS OF SINGING

That he sang
To get over
Some kind of distress
They very soon found out,
And they told him so.

His reflections
On how to sing
Brought him to the point
Of pretending to be distressed

<   341   >

Um über einen heimlichen,
Ihn gehörigen
Freudenschrei
Hinwegzukommen.

UNGLÜCK MIT BETTLERN

Ich habe Unglück mit Bettlern.
Einmal einem
Die Milch umgestossen—
Rennt er hinter mir her.
Milch schwimmt auf den Wegen.

Ich stehe sitze knie mit gebasteltem Instrument.
Schuhe der Passanten. Hohe Absätze der Damen

Klappern ums Bettlereck,
Hüpfen durch Bettlermusik:
Ballklänge Rufe vom Skihang Wintersport

So as to get over
A secret
Whoop of joy
Peculiar to him.

1964: *Gedichte*

UNLUCKY WITH BEGGARS

I'm unlucky with beggars.
Once knocked over
One beggar's milk—
Runs after me.
Milk covers the paths.

I stand sit kneel with a homemade instrument.
Shoes of the passers-by. High heels of the ladies

Tap round the beggar's corner,
Hop through beggar's music:
Ball sounds calls from the ski-slope winter sport.

1964: *Gedichte*

< 343 >

FRIEDERIKE MAYRÖCKER:

Geboren 1924 in Wien. Ihre experimentellen Prosa- und Lyrik-Texte verbinden Phantasie mit Collage-Techniken. Obwohl ihr späteres Werk originell und verblüffend ist, erwies sich bis jetzt nur wenig davon als übersetzbar und kann deshalb an dieser Stelle nicht entsprechend vertreten sein. Ihre vielen Veröffentlichungen—zusammen mit den Werken, die sie in Zusammenarbeit mit Ernst Jandl schrieb—reichen von Lyrik über Drama und Dialog zu phantasievoller Prosa. Ihre Gedichtbände umfassen u.a.: *metaphorisch* (1965), *Tod durch Musen* (1966), *Texte* (1966), *Fantom Fan* (1971), *Sägespäne für mein Herzbluten* (1973), *Blaue Erleuchtungen* (1973) und *In langsamen Blitzen* (1974), 1974 erschien *Augen wie Schaljapin bevor er starb;* 1972 veröffentlichte sie ein Theaterstück mit dem Titel *Arie auf tönernen Füßen,* dem eine Sammlung von Erzählungen folgte: *Je ein umwölkter Gipfel* (1973).

SCHIRMHERR MAKELLOSER

Schirmherr makelloser Schlangeschönheit
hoher Beschliesser der unbändigen Meere
Bereiter stetiger Felder

dem grünen Hochwald kämmst du durchs feuchte Fell
Gras-Strähnen tauen um deine Stirn

winters die langen Täuflinge: kristallene Eiszapfen
sammelt deine Faust im Becken der Dorfteiche
und die silberäugigen warmen Schwärme der Vögel
nisten in deinem blassen Geäder

gross bist du und ich fürchte dich sehr
hin sprengst du auf meinen gesattelten Wünschen

< 344 >

FRIEDERIKE MAYRÖCKER:

Born in Vienna in 1924. Her experimental texts in prose and verse combine fantasy with collage techniques. Original and striking though it is, little of her later work has proved translatable until now, and could not be adequately represented here. Her many publications— including works produced in collaboration with Ernst Jandl—extend from poetry to drama, dialogue, and imaginative prose. Her books of poems include: *metaphorisch* (1965), *Tod durch Musen* (1966), *Texte* (1966), *Fantom Fan* (1971), *Sägespäne für mein Herzbluten* (1973), *Blaue Erleuchtungen* (1973), and *In langsamen Blitzen* (1974), though in her case generic classifications are difficult and irrelevant. *Augen wie Schaljapin bevor er starb* appeared in 1974; in 1972 she published a piece for the theater entitled: *Arie auf tönernen Füssen*, which was followed by a collection of stories: *Je ein umwölkter Gipfel* (1973).

PATRON OF FLAWLESS SERPENT BEAUTY

Patron of flawless serpent beauty
exalted keeper of untamable seas
cultivator of the constant fields

you comb the green pelt of the towering forest
wisps of grass thaw around your brow

the long-christened in winter: the crystal icicles
your fist collects in the basins of village ponds
and the silver-eyed warm flocks of birds
nest in your pale arteries

Mighty you are and I fear you greatly
away you gallop on my saddled desires

[1960]; 1974: *In langsamen Blitzen*

EUGEN GOMRINGER:

Geboren 1925 in Bolivien. Er war einer der Väter der "konkreten" Poesie. Von 1954 bis 1958 arbeitete er als Sekretär Max Bills an der Ulmer Hochschule für Gestaltung. Seit 1962 leitet er den Schweizer Werkbund und gibt in Frauenfeld in der Schweiz die Broschürenreihe *konkrete poesie* heraus. Wie die meisten Arbeiten reinster konkreter Poesie ist sein Werk vielfach unübersetzbar, obwohl es vielsprachig und Lesern anderer Sprachgruppen zugänglich ist. Die erste Sammlung dessen, was er "Konstellationen" nennt, erschien 1953; eine erweiterte Sammlung, die den Zeitraum bis 1962 erfaßt, erschien 1963, gefolgt von *Worte sind Schatten: die Konstellationen 1951-1968*, herausgegeben von Helmut Heißenbüttel (1969). Eine Essaysammlung mit dem Titel *Poesie als Mittel der Umweltgestaltung. Referat und Beispiele* wurde 1969 veröffentlicht. 1972 gab er die Anthologie *Konkrete Poesie; deutschsprachige Autoren* heraus.

WORTE

worte sind schatten
schatten werden worte

worte sind spiele
spiele werden worte

sind schatten worte
werden worte spiele

sind spiele worte
werden worte schatten

sind worte schatten
werden spiele worte

sind worte spiele
werden schatten worte

< 346 >

EUGEN GOMRINGER:

He was born in Bolivia in 1925, and became one of the originators of "concrete" poetry. From 1954 to 1958 he worked as secretary to Max Bill at the Ulm Hochschule für Gestaltung. Since 1962 he has directed the Swiss Werkbund and edits the pamphlet series *konkrete poesie* at Frauenfeld, Switzerland. Like most of the purest concrete poetry, his work is often untranslatable, though it is multilingual and accessible to readers of other language groups. His first collection of what he calls "constellations" appeared in 1953; an enlarged collection, covering the years up to 1962, appeared in 1963, followed by *Worte sind Schatten: die Konstellationen 1951-1968*, edited by Helmut Heissenbüttel (1969). A collection of essays entitled *Poesie als Mittel der Umweltgestaltung, Referat und Beispiele* was published in 1969. In 1972 he edited an anthology: *Konkrete Poesie; deutschsprachige Autoren*.

WORDS

words are shadows
shadows become words

words are games
games become words

if shadows are words
words become games

if games are words
words become shadows

if words are shadows
games become words

if words are games
shadows become words

1960: *33 Konstellationen*

< 347 >

ELISABETH BORCHERS:

Geboren 1926 in Homberg. Sie lebte zeitweilig im Elsaß, in Frankreich und Amerika. Zur Zeit arbeitet sie als Lektorin in einem Verlag. Sie schrieb literarische Prosa, Hörspiele, Kinderbücher und Gedichte, und übersetzte aus dem Französischen. Ihre Gedichtbände umfassen *Gedichte* (1961) und *Der Tisch, an dem wir sitzen* (1967). Eine Auswahl ihrer Gedichte mit englischer Übersetzung erschien in der Reihe Unicorn German (1969) in den USA. *Eine glückliche Familie und andere Prosa* erschien 1970, gefolgt von einer Gedichte- und Lieder-Sammlung, die die Autorin unter dem Titel *Das Buch der Liebe* (1974) selbst zusammenstellte.

JEMAND SCHWEIGT

jemand schweigt
und du glaubst er spircht
und du antwortest
und sprichst gut
und entblösst dich
haut um haut die du nicht
geben kannst du der du sprichst
und es wird kalt und kälter

jemand schweigt
und du wartest
auf das schweigen
nach allen enden
und weiter hinaus
und es trägt nicht das wort
und nicht weisst du
wo das licht ist
das helle und dunkle

jemand geht
und du glaubst
er geht gut
und du folgst ihm
und hältst seinen schritt aus
und wirst nicht irre

< 348 >

ELISABETH BORCHERS:

Born at Homberg in 1926, she has lived in Alsace at one time, as well as in France and in America. She presently works as a reader for a publisher. She has written prose fiction, radio plays, and books for children, as well as poems, and has translated from the French. Her books of poems include *Gedichte* (1961) and *Der Tisch, an dem wir sitzen* (1967). A selection of her poems with English translations has appeared in the U.S. in the Unicorn German Series (1969). *Eine glückliche Familie und andere Prosa* appeared in 1970 and was followed by a collection of poems and songs selected by the author herself under the title *Das Buch der Liebe*, 1974.

SOMEONE IS SILENT

someone is silent
and you think he is speaking
and you answer
and speak well
and expose yourself
skin by skin that you can't
give away you that are speaking
and it grows colder and colder

someone is silent
and you wait
for the silence
in all directions
and beyond its limits
and it won't support words
and you don't know
where the light is
the bright and the dark

someone walks
and you think
he walks well
and you follow
and keep up with his pace
and don't grow confused

< 349 >

jemand geht
und du glaubst er geht weich
auf weichen sohlen
und du pflückst das weiche
and lässt das harte stehen
und das eis knirscht
und du sagst ich hör es nicht

< 350 >

someone walks
and you think he walks softly
on soft soles
and you pick the softness
and leave the hardness
and the ice crunches
and you say I don't hear it

1961: Gedichte

< 351 >

ERNST JANDL:

Geboren 1925 in Wien. Jandl studierte Englisch und lehrte diese Sprache jahrelang an der Höheren Schule. Er ist zwar ein führender Repräsentant der konkreten Poesie, besonders als Autor von Lautgedichten, die er mit bewundernswerter Verve und Präzision vorträgt, schreibt aber nach wie vor auch andere Gedichte. Er lebte in England, schrieb Gedichte in englischer Sprache und übersetzte zeitgenössische englische Lyrik. Die Lesungen seiner Lautgedichte *und Schallplatten davon* fanden in vielen europäischen Ländern und in Amerika ein begeistertes Publikum. Wie Helmut Heißenbüttel benutzt er die Verfahrensweisen rein verbaler Lyrik für satirische und kritische Effekte. Allein oder zusammen mit Friederike Mayröcker schrieb er auch eine Anzahl *hervorragender* Hörspiele. Seine vielen Gedichtbände umfassen u.a.: *Andere Augen* (1956), *lange gedichte* (1964), *klare gerührt* (1964), *mai hart lieb zapfen eibe hold* (1965), *Laut und Luise* (1968), *Sprechblasen* (1968), *Der künstliche Baum* (1970), *flöda und der schwan* (1971, mit Zeichnungen des Autors), *Dingfest* (1973) und *wischen möchten* (1974). Neuere Veröffentlichungen: *Übung mit Buben* (1973), *Für alle* (1974), *Serienfuß* (1974), und *Der versteckte Hirte* (1975).

LIED

schlaf gut für mich
bis morgen
schlaf für mich;
schlaf für mich
denn ich möchte dich jetzt.
schlaf gut für mich
bis morgen
schlaf für mich;
schlaf für mich
denn du kannst erst morgen.
schlaf gut für mich
bis morgen
schlaf für mich,
denn ich möchte dich jetzt
und du kannst erst morgen.
schlaf gut für mich
bis morgen

< 352 >

ERNST JANDL:

Born in Vienna in 1925. Jandl studied English and has taught it for many years at a secondary school. A leading representative of the concrete poetry movement, especially as a writer of sound poems which he performs with admirable zest and precision, he has also continued to write poems in other modes. He has lived in England and written poems in English, as well as translating contemporary English poetry. His readings of sound poems have been enjoyed in many European countries and in America, as have his recordings of them. Like Helmut Heissenbüttel, he has used the processes of purely verbal poetry for satirical and critical effects. Alone or together with Friederike Mayröcker, he has also written a number of outstanding radio plays. His many books of poems include: *Andere Augen* (1956), *lange gedichte* (1964), *klare gerührt* (1964), *mai hart lieb zapfen eibe hold* (1965), *Laut und Luise* (1968), *Sprechblasen* (1968), *Der künstliche Baum* (1970), *floeda und der schwan* (1971, with drawings by the author), *Dingfest* (1973), and *wischen möchten* (1974). More recent publications include: *Übung mit Buben* (1973), *Für alle* (1974), *Serienfuss* (1974), and *Der versteckte Hirte* (1975).

SONG

sleep well for me
till tomorrow
sleep for me;
sleep for me
for I want you now.
sleep well for me
till tomorrow
sleep for me;
sleep for me
since you can't till tomorrow.
sleep well for me
till tomorrow
sleep for me,
for I want you now
and you can't till tomorrow.
sleep well for me
till tomorrow

<   353   >

schlaf für mich,
denn du kannst erst morgen
und jetzt ist die liebe.

IM DELIKATESSENLADEN

bitte geben sie mir eine maiwiesenkonserve
etwas höher gelegen aber nicht zu abschüssig
so, dass man darauf noch sitzen kann.

nun, dann vielleicht eine schneehalde, tiefgekühlt
ohne wintersportler. eine fichte schön beschneit
kann dabeisein.

auch nicht. bliebe noch—hasen sehe ich haben sie da hängen.
zwei drei werden genügen. und natürlich einen jäger.
wo hängen denn die jäger?

TASCHEN

schau, meine vielen taschen.
in dieser hab ich ansichtskarten.

in dieser zwei uhren.
meine zeit und deine zeit.

in dieser einen würfel.
23 augen sehen mehr als zwei.

du kannst dir denken
was ich an brillen schleppe.

JEDER SEIN EDISON

im nest der taufologie
behagt es jedem. kautomation

< 354 >

sleep for me,
since you can't till tomorrow
and love is now.

1954

AT THE DELICATESSEN SHOP

please give me a potted may meadow
a slightly higher altitude but not too steep
so that one can still sit on it.

all right, then, maybe a snowy slope, deep-frozen
but no skiers, please. a fir tree beautifully snowed on
can be thrown in.

you haven't? that leaves—I see you have some hares hanging
     there.
two or three should be enough. and a huntsman of course.
where do you hang them? I don't see the huntsmen.

1962

POCKETS

look, all those pockets of mine.
in this one I keep picture postcards

in this one two watches
my time and your time.

in this one a die.
23 eyes see more than two.

you can imagine
how many pairs of glasses I lug around.

[1963]; 1973: *Dingfest*

EVERY MAN HIS OWN EDISON

in the nest of mistology
everybody feels snug. eatomation

< 355 >

verspricht lebenslängliche atzung. kraftologie
ist die einzige wissenschaft. telefant
trägt jeden zu jedem, telekraft
ebenso. lyrkitsch und krankophon
beschäftigen drüsen und ohren. orden aus quarzinom
verleiht der präsident der u.s.w.

promises lifelong fodder. powerology
is the only science. telephant
carries each to each, telepower
likewise. lyrekitsch and sickophone
occupy glands and ears. quarcinoma medals
are awarded by the president of the e.t.c.

1974: wischen möchten

< 357 >

CHRISTA REINIG:

Geboren 1926 in Berlin. Von ihrer Ausbildung her ist sie Floristin. Sie studierte Kunstgeschichte und Christliche Archäologie, arbeitete eine Zeitlang im Museum, verließ Ost-Berlin 1964 und ließ sich in West-Deutschland nieder. Heute lebt sie in München. Obwohl sie bereits ziemlich viel Lyrik und etwas Prosa vor dem Verlassen der DDR geschrieben hatte, war es ihr nicht möglich, dort einen Band zu veröffentlichen. Zwei ihrer Gedichtbände, *Die Steine von Finisterre* (1960) und *Gedichte* (1963) erschienen in West-Deutschland vor ihrer Entscheidung, sich dort niederzulassen. 1969 folgte ihre Sammlung *Schwalbe von Olevano*. Sie veröffentlichte auch eine Sammlung burlesker und nonsense-Lyrik *Schwabinger Marterln* (1969) und *Papantscha Vielerlei* (1971). Daneben schrieb sie Hörspiele *Das Aquarium* (1969), Erzählungen, kurze Prosa-Sketche und Erzählungen für Kinder. In 1975 erschien *Die himmlische und die irdische Geometrie*.

DER MANN DER VORÜBERGING

Er ging vorüber an einem holzgriff daran hingen sechs geknotete
riemen nieder

er ging vorüber am zeitalter der technik

er ging vorüber an einer hürde aus stacheldraht und ein faltiger gnom richtete sich vor ihm auf

er ging vorüber am jahrhundert des kindes
er ging vorüber an zerdroschenen bierflaschen und einem papier
zwischen zwei mülltonnen geklebt
er ging vorüber an dem tag der befreiung
er ging vorüber an einem stiefel und ohne zu grüssen

er ging vorüber an der stunde der bewährung

er stand still an einer ziegelmauer im augenblick der gewehre

er ging vorüber

< 358 >

CHRISTA REINIG:

Born in Berlin in 1926, and trained as a wreathmaker. She studied history of art and Christian archeology, worked for a time in a museum, and left East Berlin in 1964, settling in West Germany. She now lives in Munich. Though she had written a good deal of poetry and some prose before leaving the GDR, she was unable to publish a book there. Two books of her poems, *Die Steine von Finisterre* (1960) and *Gedichte* (1963), appeared in West Germany before her decision to settle there. Her collection *Schwalbe von Olevano* followed in 1969. She has also published a collection of burlesque and nonsense verse, *Schwabinger Marterln* (1969) and *Papantscha Vielerlei* (1971). She has written radio plays, *Das Aquarium* (1969), stories, and brief prose sketches, as well as stories for children. Her latest work is a novel: *Die himmlische und die irdische Geometrie* (1975).

THE MAN WHO PASSED BY

He passed by a wooden handle from which six knotted thongs
    hung down
he passed by the age of technology
he passed by a barrier of barbed wire and a wrinkled gnome
    rose up before him
he passed by the century of the child
he passed by shattered beerbottles and a piece of paper affixed
    between two dustbins
he passed by the day of liberation
he passed by a boot and without saluting
he passed by the hour of fulfilment
he stood still against a brick wall at the moment of rifles
he passed by

1963: Gedichte

MY POSSESSIONS

I have a coat to put in my jacket pocket a pocket coat
I have a radio to put in my jacket pocket a pocket radio
I have a bible to put in my jacket pocket a pocket bible
I have no jacket like that at all with pockets no jacket pocket

< 359 >

MEIN BESITZ

Ich habe einen mantel in die jackentasche zu stecken einen
   taschen-mantel
ich habe ein radio in die jackentasche zu stecken ein taschen-
   radio
ich habe eine bibel in die jackentasche zu stecken eine taschen-
   bibel
ich habe gar keine solche jacke mit taschen gar keine jackentasche

ich habe eine schnapsflasche mit zwölf gläsern für mich und
   alle meine onkels und tanten
ich habe eine kaffeekanne mit vier tassen für mich und meine
   drei besten freundinnen
ich habe ein schachbrett mit schwarzen und weissen steinen für
   mich und einen freund
ich habe gar keine freunde einzuladen
   niemanden

ich habe einen himmel endlos über mir
   darunter mich wiederzufinden
ich habe eine stadt voll strassen endlos
   darin mir zu begegnen
ich habe ein lied endlos und endlos
   darin ein- und auszuatmen
ich habe nicht mehr als ein gras zwischen zwei pflastersteinen
   nicht mehr zu leben

SIGNALE AUS DEM RAUM

Sie schafften es, das Nichts zu überklettern.
Nie werden wir erfahren, wer sie sind.
Wenn sie noch sind.

HERBST

Es war ein Blatt, es schlief in einer Knospe.

< 360 >

I have a whiskey bottle with twelve glasses for me and all my
    uncles and aunts
I have a coffee pot with four cups for me and my three best
    girl friends
I have a chessboard with black and white men for me and a
    boy friend
I have no friends at all to invite
    no one

I have a sky endless above me
    under which to find myself again
I have a city full of streets endless
    in which to meet myself
I have a song endless and endless
    in which to breathe in and out
I have no more than one grassblade between two paving-stones
    only that to live on

1963: Gedichte

SIGNALS FROM OUTER SPACE

They managed to climb up past Nothingness.
And never we shall discover who they are.
If they are, still.

AUTUMN

There was a leaf, it slept within a bud.
There was a falcon's son within a falcon's nest.
There was a bride, dancing in little boots.
There was a star, burning above a sail
And in the cosmos long ago went out.

A crone is ripping weeds from a cold field.
A crone is sweeping a sparrow into the fire.
A crone is turning over a heap of leaves.
There was a star, burned briefly, a long time had gone out,

< 361 >

Es war ein Falkensohn in einem Falkennest.
Es war eine Braut, tanzend in Stiefelchen.
Es war ein Stern, brennt über einem Segel
und ist erloschen längst im All.

Ein altes Weib reisst Kraut aus einem kalten Acker.
Ein altes Weib fegt einen Sperling ins Feuer.
Ein altes Weib krückt um einen Blätterhaufen.
Es war ein Stern, brannt kurz, war lang erloschen,
ein toter Stern hat mich gebeugt.

< 362 >

a star that's dead has bent my back.

1969: *Schwalbe von Olevano*

< 363 >

HEINZ PIONTEK:

Geboren 1925 in Kreuzberg in Oberschlesien. Er lebt seit Kriegsende in Bayern. Er schrieb einen Roman *Die mittleren Jahre* (1967), Erzählungen und kritische Essays und übersetzte Gedichte von Keats. Zur Zeit ist er einer der Herausgeber des internationalen literarischen Jahrbuchs *ensemble*, das von der Bayrischen Akademie der Künste veröffentlicht wird. Gedichtbände: *Die Furt* (1952), *Die Rauchfahne* (1953), *Wassermarken* (1957), *Mit einer Kranichfeder* (1962), *Klartext* (1966) und *Tot oder lebendig* (1971). Seine *Gesammelten Gedichte* erschienen 1975.

MIT 30 JAHREN

Keine sichtbaren Narben,
keine Medaillen,
keine Titel—
aber das Auge scharf, unbezähmbar
wie Zorn und Entzücken,
dicht die Erinnerung
und leicht der Schlaf.

Fahrten, Märsche vor zwanzig.
Nachher genügten vier Wände:
Wir werden nicht
überschaubarer unterwegs!
Oft reichen drei Schritte.
Und immer genügt
weniger als wir vermuten.

Zum Beispiel die Stadt.
Man kann sie umwandern
in einer einzigen Stunde.
Ihre Steige bröckeln,
in den Türmen haust
die blinde Geschichte.
Helle von Silberkörern,
wenn die Flussnebel fallen . . .

Mühsal ist wirklich:
Last und Hitze

< 364 >

HEINZ PIONTEK:

Born in Kreuzberg, Upper Silesia, in 1925. Since the end of the war
he has lived in Bavaria. He has written a novel, *Die mittleren Jahre*
(1967), stories, and critical essays, and has translated poems by Keats.
At present he is one of the editors of the international literary annual
ensemble, published by the Bavarian Academy of Arts. His books of
poems are: *Die Furt* (1952), *Die Rauchfahne* (1953), *Wassermarken*
(1957), *Mit einer Kranichfeder* (1962), *Klartext* (1966), and *Tot oder
lebendig* (1971). His collected poems, *Gesammelte Gedichte*, appeared
in 1975.

AT THIRTY YEARS

no visible scars,
no medals,
no titles—
but the eye sharp, untamable
as rage or as rapture,
memory crowded
and sleep light.

Journeys, marches before the twentieth year.
Later four walls were enough:
to move about
does not make one more palpable!
Often three steps are enough.
And enough is always
less than we think.

The town, for instance.
You can walk all round it
in a single hour.
Its pavements are crumbling,
in its towers lives
blind history.
Brightness of silver grain
when the mist falls . . .

Effort is real:
burdens and heat

< 365 >

und das steinerne Glück.
Wirklich der überwundene Tod—
und alles Vergebliche wird
fest unter den Sohlen.
Mehr wissen wir nicht.

Erwachet früh—
wenn der Morgen
mit halben Farben erscheint
und satt das Holz leuchtet,
das geteert ist—
denn der Wind steht gegen euch!
Doch sputet euch nicht.
Wir leben gezählte Tage.

DIE TOCHTER DES SCHMIEDS

Ich hatte einen Vater,
mächtig wie der Pfosten des Ziehbrunnens
in Kobniza,
mit Augen aus blauem Eisen und Funken im Bart,
der hinkte und konnte in den Legenden lesen.

Er hatte eine Tochter,
schön wie der Fluss in den Wiesen
bei Kobniza.
Winters trug sie die zierlichen Stiefel,
sommers eine Fahne Katun um die Hüften.

Ihm träumte, er lebe als Köhler
und verstünde die Vögel.
Aber Schmied war er auf einem verlotterten Vorwerk
und bückte sich vor dem Vogt.

Und sie, seine Tochter, wäre am liebsten
mit einem zwanzigjährigen Fähnrich geritten,
aber ein Posthalter nahm sie,
kaufte ihr Zwieback und eine Brille.

< 366 >

and stony joy.
Real too is death overcome—
and all that was vain
grows solid under your feet.
That is all we know.

Awaken early—
when the morning
with muted colours appears
and wood has a mellow gleam,
wood that has been tarred—
for the wind is against you!
But do not hurry.
The days of our lives are counted.

1957: *Wassermarken*

THE BLACKSMITH'S DAUGHTER

I had a father
powerful as the post of the well
at Kobnitza,
with eyes of blue iron and sparks in his beard;
he limped and knew what the legends mean.

He had a daughter
lovely as the river in the meadows
near Kobnitza.
In winter she wore her dainty boots,
in summer a sash of cotton around her hips.

He dreamed that he was a charcoal-burner
and understood the language of birds.
But a blacksmith he worked in a tumbledown manor farm
and went in fear of the bailiff.

And she, his daughter, would have liked best
to go out riding with an ensign twenty years old,
but a postmaster made her his wife,

< 367 >

Ein Apfelschimmel schlug meinen Vater lahm.
Mein Vater kam nie in die Wälder.
Er schüttete Kohlengrus auf:
sein Herz war eine ausgeblasene Esse.
Er trank neun Krüge Dünnbier
und starb daran.

Ich lernte, dass man vor seinem Gedächtnis
nie sicher ist.
Ich sehe des Morgens unseren kleinen Horizont,
und unter der Funzel schreib ich Adressen
für die Leute.

IM WASSER

Unter Badenden
bin ich als Schiffbrüchiger
nicht kenntlich.

Wo bleibt meine Zukunft?
Über mir, unter mir
nichts.

Mit letzter Kraft forme ich Worte.
Von meinem Mund
ist nichts abzulesen.

Ein halbtoter Fisch,
der zu schreien versucht,
das sieht lustig aus.

BÄUME

Für Alfred Focke

Ihr ja ihr.

Ruhig auf der dunklen
Erde fussend.

< 368 >

bought her rusks and a pair of spectacles.

My father was lamed by a dapple-gray's kick.
His leg kept him out of the forests.
He stoked the fire with small coal:
his heart was a forge gone out.
He drank nine tankards of thin beer
and died of it.

I learned that one is never safe
from his memory.
In the mornings I see our little horizon
and in feeble lamplight I write addresses
for the customers.

1957

IN THE WATER

Among bathers
I am not recognizable
as a shipwrecked man.

What's become of my future?
Above me, below me
nothing.

The strength I have left goes into forming words.
You can't read anything
on my lips.

A half-dead fish
trying to scream—
that's a funny sight.

< 369 >

Doch verwundbar
wie wir,

die wir uns vorwärts-
kämpfen müssen.

Nützlich oder
einfach schön

und immer etwas
Neues bedeutend.

So wachsen:

In die Höhe,
in die Tiefe

und mit ausgebreiteten Armen.

NICHT MEHR GEWILLT

Ist es wahr,
wir verknöchern?

Dauert der Frieden
schon zu lange?

Unser mit Blutverlusten,
Salz, Nerven erkaufter,
windiger Frieden?

Ja, rechnet nur mit uns
ab, uns
Feiglingen:

geschlagen, gebrannt
wie wir sind—

< 370 >

TREES

For Alfred Focke

You. Yes. You.

Quietly based
on dark earth.

Yet vulnerable
as we are,

who have to fight for
every inch of the way.

Useful or
simply beautiful

and always with
a new meaning.

To grow like that:

upward,
downward

and with
arms outstretched.

NO LONGER WILLING

Is it true
we are ossifying?

Has peace
lasted too long already?

Our windy peace
bought with bloodletting

<   371   >

und nicht mehr gewillt,
die Gewalt

noch einmal
auf unsere Schultern
zu heben.

BILLETDOUX

Komm
denn Glocke und Hahn
probieren schon etwas Klassisches
für drei Stimmen

Komm
denn zwischen den Steinplatten
wird das Hungergras
fett

Komm
ja komm und wring
aus den Segeltüchern
das helle Wasser

Komm
mit einer Mütze
voll Wind
an unsren bolzengraden Steg

Komm
und stell
meine brennende Ungeduld
in den Schatten

<   372   >

salt and nerves?

Yes, by all means call
us to account,
us cowards:

beaten, branded
as we are—

and no longer willing
to heave

violence once again
onto
our shoulders.

BILLET-DOUX

Come
for bell and cock
are rehearsing something classical
for three voices

Come
for between the flagstones
the hunger grass
grows fat

Come
yes, come and wring
from the sails
bright water

come
with a cap
full of wind
to our landing-stage straight as a bolt

<   373   >

< 374 >

Come
and put
my burning impatience
in the shade

1971: *Tot oder lebendig*

< 375 >

INGEBORG BACHMANN:

Geboren 1926 in Klagenfurt, Österreich; gestorben 1973 in Rom. Sie studierte Philosophie in Innsbruck, Graz und Wien; arbeitete eine Zeitlang als Rundfunk, redakteurin, dann als Lyrikerin und Erzählerin. Neben drei Libretti für Hans Werner Henze schrieb sie Hörspiele (*Der gute Gott in Manhattan*, 1958). Ihren Gedichtbänden *Die gestundete Zeit* (1953) und *Anrufung des grossen Bären* (1956) folgten Bände mit Erzählungen und ein Roman, *Malina* (1971). Einige spätere Gedichte erschienen in der Auswahl aus ihren Werken *Gedichte, Erzählungen, Hörspiele, Essays* (1964). Die neuesten Sammlungen von Erzählungen umfassen: *Das dreißigste Jahr* (1961), *Simultan: neue Erzählungen* (1972); und *Undine geht* (1973).

AN DIE SONNE — *Hymne - Lobgesang*

Schöner als der beachtliche Mond und sein geadeltes Licht,
Schöner als die Sterne, die berühmten Orden der Nacht,
Viel schöner als der feurige Auftritt eines Kometen
Und zu weit Schönrem berufen als jedes andre Gestirn,
Weil dein und mein Leben jeden Tag an ihr hängt, ist die
    Sonne.

[handwritten left margin: Steigerung / erweckt / Neugier]

Schöne Sonne, die aufgeht, ihr Werk nicht vergessen hat
Und beendet, am schönsten im Sommer, wenn ein Tag
An den Küsten verdampft und ohne Kraft gespiegelt die Segel
Über dein Aug ziehn, bis du müde wirst und das letzte ver-
    kürzt.

[handwritten: den Schleier nehmen — geht ins Kloster]

Ohne die Sonne nimmt auch die Kunst wieder den Schleier,
Du erscheinst mir nicht mehr, und die See und der Sand,
Von Schatten gepeitscht, fliehen unter mein Lid.

[handwritten left margin: Kunst von der Sonne abhängig]

Schönes Licht, das uns warm hält, bewahrt und wunderbar
    sorgt,
Dass ich wieder sehe und dass ich dich wiederseh!

Nichts Schönres unter der Sonne als unter der Sonne zu
    sein . . . *[handwritten: Lobgesang auf das Leben]*

Nichts Schönres als den Stab im Wasser zu sehn und den
    Vogel oben,

[handwritten: ↳ Grundelement des Lebens]

[handwritten: ↳ Freiheit]

< 376 >

INGEBORG BACHMANN:

Born 1926 in Klagenfurt, Austria, and died in Rome in 1973. Studied philosophy at Innsbruck, Graz, and Vienna, worked for a time as a radio producer, then as a poet and novelist, also writing three libretti for Hans Werner Henze, and radio plays (*Der gute Gott in Manhattan*, 1958). Her books of poems, *Die gestundete Zeit* (1953) and *Anrufung des grossen Bären* (1956) were followed by books of stories and a novel, *Malina* (1971). A few later poems appeared in the selection from her works, *Gedichte, Erzählungen, Hörspiel, Essays* (1964). Her collections of stories are: *Das dreissigste Jahr* (1961); *Simultan: neue Erzählungen* (1972); and *Undine geht* (1973).

TO THE SUN

More beautiful than the remarkable moon and her noble light,
More beautiful than the stars, the famous medals of night,
Much more beautiful than the fiery entrance a comet makes,
And called to a part far more splendid than any other planet's
Because daily your life and my life depend on it, is the sun.

Beautiful sun that rises, his work not forgotten,
And completes it, most beautifully in summer, when a day
Evaporates on the coast, and effortlessly mirrored the sails
Pass through your sight, till you tire and cut short the last.

Without the sun even art takes the veil again,
You cease to appear to me, and the sea and the sand,
Lashed by shadows, take refuge under my eyelids.

Beautiful light, that keeps us warm, preserves us, marvelously
    makes sure
That I see again and that I see you again!

Nothing more beautiful under the sun than to be under the
    sun . . .

Nothing more beautiful than to see the stick in water and the
    bird above,
Pondering his flight, and, below, the fishes in shoals,

Coloured, moulded, brought into the world with a mission of
    light,

< 377 >

Der seinen Flug überlegt, und unten die Fische im Schwarm,

Gefärbt, geformt, in die Welt gekommen mit einer Sendung
    von Licht,
Und den Umkreis zu sehn, das Geviert eines Felds, das
    Tausendeck meines Lands

Und das Kleid, das du angetan hast. Und dein Kleid, glockig
    und blau!
Schönes Blau, in dem die Pfauen spazieren und sich verneigen,
Blau der Fernen, der Zonen des Glücks mit den Wettern für
    mein Gefühl,
Blauer Zufall am Horizont! Und meine begeisterten Augen
Weiten sich wieder und blinken und brennen sich wund.

Schöne Sonne, der vom Staub noch die grösste Bewundrung
    gebührt,
Drum werde ich nicht wegen dem Mond und den Sternen und
    nicht,
Weil die Nacht mit Kometen prahlt und in mir einen Narren
    sucht,
Sondern deinetwegen und bald endlos und wie um nichts sonst
Klage führen über den unabwendbaren Verlust meiner Augen.

Wegen der Sonne, wird sie den Tod betrauern

NEBELLAND

Im Winter ist meine Geliebte
unter den Tieren des Waldes.
Dass ich vor Morgen zurückmuss,
weiss die Füchsin und lacht.
Wie die Wolken erzittern! Und mir
auf den Schneekragen fällt
eine Lage von brüchigem Eis.

Im Winter ist meine Geliebte
ein Baum unter Bäumen und lädt
die glückverlassenen Krähen

< 378 >

And to see the radius, the square of a field, my landscape's
thousand angles

And the dress you have put on. And *your* dress, bell-shaped
and blue!
Beautiful blue, in which peacocks walk and bow,

Blue of far places, the zones of joy with weathers that suit my
mood,
Blue chance on the horizon! And my enchanted eyes
Dilate again and blink and burn themselves sore.

Beautiful sun, to whom dust owes great admiration yet,
Not for the moon, therefore, and not for the stars, and not
Because night shows off with comets, trying to fool me,
But for your sake, and endlessly soon, and for you above all

I shall lament the inevitable loss of my sight.

1956: *Anrufung des grossen Bären*

FOG LAND

In winter my loved one retires
to live with the beasts of the forest.
That I must be back before morning
the vixen knows well, and she laughs.
Now the low clouds quiver! And down
on my upturned collar there falls
a landslide of brittle ice.

In winter my loved one retires,
a tree among trees, and invites
the crows in their desolation
into her beautiful boughs. She knows
that as soon as night falls the wind
lifts her stiff, hoar-frost-embroidered
evening gown, sends me home.

< 379 >

ein in ihr schönes Geäst. Sie weiss,
dass der Wind, wenn es dämmert,
ihr starres, mit Reif besetztes
Abendkleid hebt und mich heimjagt.

Im Winter ist meine Geliebte
unter den Fischen und stumm.
Hörig den Wassern, die der Strich
ihrer Flossen von innen bewegt,
steh ich am Ufer und seh,
bis mich Schollen vertreiben,
wie sie taucht und sich wendet.

Und wieder vom Jagdruf des Vogels
getroffen, der seine Schwingen
über mir streift, stürz ich
auf offenem Feld: sie entfiedert
die Hühner und wirft mir ein weisses
Schlüsselbein zu. Ich nehm's um den Hals
und geh fort durch den bitteren Flaum.

Treulos ist meine Geliebte,
ich weiss, sie schwebt manchmal
auf hohen Schuh'n nach der Stadt,
sie küsst in den Bars mit dem Strohhalm
die Gläser tief auf den Mund,
und es kommen ihr Worte für alle.
Doch diese Sprache verstehe ich nicht.

Nebelland hab ich gesehen,
Nebelherz hab ich gegessen.

ALLE TAGE

Der Krieg wird nicht mehr erklärt,
sondern fortgesetzt. Das Unerhörte
ist alltäglich geworden. Der Held
bleibt den Kämpfern fern. Der Schwache

< 380 >

In winter my loved one retires,
a fish among fishes, and dumb.
Slave to the waters she ripples
with her fins' gentle motion within,
I stand on the bank and look down
till ice floes drive me away,
her dipping and turning hidden.

And stricken again by the blood-cry
of the bird that tautens his wings
over my head, I fall down
on the open field: she is plucking
the hens, and she throws me a whitened
collar bone. This round my neck,
off I go through the bitter down.

My loved one, I know, is unfaithful,
and sometimes she stalks and she hovers
on high-heeled shoes to the city
and deeply in bars with her straw
will kiss the lips of the glasses,
and finds words for each and for all.
But this language is alien to me.

It is fog land I have seen,
It is fog heart I have eaten.

                              1956

EVERY DAY

War is no longer declared
but continued. The unheard-of thing
is the everyday. The hero
keeps away from the fighters. The weak man
has moved up to the battle zones.
The uniform of the day is patience,
its decoration the humble star
of hope worn over the heart.

< 381 >

ist in die Feuerzonen gerückt.
Die Uniform des Tages ist die Geduld,
die Auszeichnung der armselige Stern
der Hoffnung über dem Herzen.

Er wird verliehen,
wenn nichts mehr geschieht,
wenn das Trommelfeuer verstummt,
wenn der Feind unsichtbar geworden ist
und der Schatten ewiger Rüstung
den Himmel bedeckt.

Er wird verliehen
für die Flucht von den Fahnen,
für die Tapferkeit vor dem Freund,
für den Verrat unwürdiger Geheimnisse
und die Nichtachtung
jeglichen Befehls.

DIE GESTUNDETE ZEIT

Es kommen härtere Tage.
Die auf Widerruf gestundete Zeit
wird sichtbar am Horizont.
Bald musst du den Schuh schnüren
und die Hunde zurückjagen in die Marschhöfe.
Denn die Eingeweide der Fische
sind kalt geworden im Wind.
Ärmlich brennt das Licht der Lupinen.
Dein Blick spurt im Nebel:
die auf Widerruf gestundete Zeit
wird sichtbar am Horizont.

Drüben versinkt dir die Geliebte im Sand,
er steigt um ihr wehendes Haar,
er fällt ihr ins Wort,
er befiehlt ihr zu schweigen,

< 382 >

It is awarded
when nothing goes on,
when the drumbeat subsides,
when the enemy has grown invisible
and the shadow of everlasting arms
covers the sky.

It is awarded
for desertion of the flag,
for courage in the face of the friend,
for the betrayal of unworthy secrets
and for the nonobservance
of every order.

1957: Die Gestundete Zeit

THE RESPITE

A harder time is coming.
The end of the respite allowed us
appears on the skyline.
Soon you must tie your shoelace
and drive back the dogs to the marshland farms.
For the fishes' entrails
have grown cold in the wind.
Poorly the light of the lupins burns.
Your gaze gropes in the fog:
the end of the respite allowed us
appears on the skyline.

Over there your loved one sinks in the sand,
it rises toward her blown hair,
it cuts short her speaking,
it commands her to be silent,
it finds that she is mortal
and willing to part
after every embrace.

< 383 >

er findet sie sterblich
und willig dem Abschied
nach jeder Umarmung.

Sieh dich nicht um.
Schnür deinen Schuh.
Jag die Hunde zurück.
Wirf die Fische ins Meer.
Lösch die Lupinen!

Es kommen härtere Tage.

EXIL

Ein Toter bin ich der wandelt
gemeldet nirgends mehr
unbekannt im Reich des Präfekten
überzählig in den goldenen Städten
und im grünenden Land

abgetan lange schon
und mit nichts bedacht

Nur mit Wind mit Zeit und mit Klang

der ich unter Menschen nicht leben kann

Ich mit der deutschen Sprache
dieser Wolke um mich
die ich halte als Haus
treibe durch alle Sprachen

O wie sie sich verfinstert
die dunklen die Regentöne
nur die wenigen fallen

In hellere Zonen trägt dann sie den Toten hinauf

< 384 >

Do not look round.
Tie your shoelace.
Drive back the dogs.
Throw the fishes into the sea.
Put out the lupins!

A harder time is coming.

1957: *Die Gestundete Zeit*

EXILE

A dead man I am who travels
not registered anywhere
unknown in the realm of prefects
redundant in the golden cities
and in the countryside's green

written off long ago
and provided with nothing

Only with wind with time and with sound

who cannot live among human beings

I with the German language
this cloud around me
that I keep as a house
drive through all languages

Oh, how it darkens
those muted those rain tones
only few of them fall

Up into brighter zones it will carry the dead man

1964: *Gedichte, Erzählungen, Hörspiel, Essays*

< 385 >

FRANZ WURM:

Geboren 1926 in Prag. 1939 schickte man ihn ins Cheltenham College nach England; von da aus ging er nach Oxford und wurde englischer Staatsbürger. 1949 bekam er eine Einladung nach Zürich, wo er seither lebt—mit Ausnahme eines Aufenthalts in Prag 1971 und, ein Jahr später, in Israel. Wurm ist einer jener deutsch schreibenden Menschen "außer der Reihe", die die akademische Kategorie der Exil-Literatur ad absudum führen, die—wie man annimmt—1945 zu Ende ging. Aber die Arbeit und die Probleme Wurms und anderer wie er begannen erst dann. Wurm arbeitete als Rundfunkredakteur; jetzt ist er als Physiotherapeut tätig. Sein Gedichtband *Anmeldung* wurde 1959 in Zürich veröffentlicht. Seine Sammlung *Anker und Unruh* (Frankfurt 1964) enthält Lyrik und Prosa. In letzter Zeit veröffentlichte er kleine Sammlungen in London und Prag, letztere mit tscheschischen Übersetzungen. Seine neue Sammlung *Sechs Gedichte* wird 1976 in London erscheinen.

BRÜCKE

Was ist das: ich? Ein Gang
Herüber
Und wieder
Zurück.

Schritte? Schritte.
Und Stillstehn und Drehn
Und
Vergehn.

Vergehn, ich? So. Und gekrümmt.
Die Winde
Beugen sich
Kaum.

VOLL MÜSSEN

Ein Ort mein Ort vertauschbar ersetzbar wer braucht
Orte wer meinen Ort verlass ich ihn keiner
Wird ihn erobern Ort nicht zu nehmen warum dann
Fortgehn voll Müssen ein Ort und ein Ausgang
Keinem zuteil Ort namenlos Winkel
Im Auge des Wachseins Ort nichts und hier

< 386 >

FRANZ WURM:

Born in 1926 in Prague, he emigrated in 1938 to France, then to England, where he went to Cheltenham College and Queen's College, Oxford, becoming a British subject. In 1948 he was invited to Zürich, where he has lived since, with stays in Prague and in Israel. Worked as a radio producer for several years. At present he is a therapist, practicing the applied physiology of behaviour or "functional integration." His collections of poems are *Anmeldung* (1959) and *Anker und Unruh* (1964). He has published translations from the French, and a book of his poems has appeared in Czech translation. His new collection, *Sechs Gedichte*, was published in London in 1976.

BRIDGE

What is that: I? A walk
Across
And back
Again.

Paces? Paces.
And stopping and turning
And
Ceasing to be.

Ceasing to be, I? Yes. And warped.
The winds
Hardly
Bend.

FULL OF MUST

A place my place interchangeable dispensable who needs
Places who my place if I leave it no one
Will conquer it place not to be occupied why then
Go full of must a place and an exit
Allotted to no one place nameless corner
In the eye the place of wakefulness nothing and here
But room armchair bed wall door and the handle
The handle going street meadow wood blade of grass even clay

< 387 >

Aber Zimmer Sessel Bett Wand Tür und die Klinke
Die Klinke Fortgehn Strasse Wiese Wald Halm Lehm sogar

Ist Bin—Bitte um Zeit
Ist Bin—Bitte um Sein
Ist Bin—Bitte um Ich

Tanzend auf der Spitze des Atems

Auf der Spitze
Stehn
Und dann
Springen
Hinein

< 388 >

Is Am—Beg for time
Is Am—Beg to be
Is Am—Beg for I

Dancing on the needle-point of breath

On the point
Balance
And then
Leap
In

1959: Anmeldung

KLAUS DEMUS:

Geboren 1927 in Wien, wo er als Kunsthistoriker und Museumskurator lebt. Seine kosmologische, fast mystische Orientierung setzt seine Lyrik ab von den Hauptströmungen der letzten zwei Jahrzehnte, und seit der Veröffentlichung seines ersten Gedichtbandes, *Das schwere Land* (1958) erregte sein Werk wenig Aufmerksamkeit. Da er keine kurzen Gedichte, sondern längere zusammenhängende Sequenzen schreibt, ist er kaum in Anthologien vertreten. Seine späteren Werke sind *Morgennacht* (1969) und *In der neuen Stille* (1974).

DER BODHIBAUM

Die Wurzel des Baums hat
in der Tiefe klares
strahlendes Wasser erreicht,
so denkt die Krone
lichtgestaltig sie sei
Stern. Es wandert
die Sonne in ihr als in
ihresgleichen, es hängen
die Häuser des Monds
als weisse Kammern
des Tieftraums in ihr.
Im Nebel blüht sie.
Erregungslos selbsterregt
reist sie in sich
durch die Ostern der Seele.

Aus: MORGENNACHT

Steil aufwärts Wald.
Tannen, Geröll. Blad
Schnee. Wolkennah Wildnis.
Kar, Scharte und Grat. Und
blendend der Gletscher.

Ödnis. Im Kreis
die Gipfel, winterlich.
Grau im Sturmlicht düstere
Tiefen. Dann, noch vor Abend,
Nebel. Dämmerung. Allein.

< 390 >

KLAUS DEMUS:

Born in Vienna in 1927, where he lives as an art historian and curator. His cosmological, almost mystical preoccupations set his poetry apart from the main trends in the past two decades, and his work has received little attention since the publication of his first book of poems, *Das schwere Land*, in 1958. Since he does not write short poems, but coherent sequences, he is rarely represented in anthologies. His later volumes are *Morgennacht* (1969) and *In der neuen Stille* (1974).

THE BODHI TREE

The tree's root in
the depth has reached
clear shining water,
so the crest,
light-shaped, thinks
itself a star. In it
the sun roams as in
its own kind, the moon's
houses hang there
as white rooms
of deep dream.
Unimpelled self-impelled
it travels within itself
through the soul's Easter.

> 1958: *Das Schwere Land*

From MORNINGNIGHT

Steeply up, forest.
Firs, scree. Soon
snow. Wilderness close to clouds.
Crevasse, dip and ridge. And
the glacier dazzling.

Waste. In a circle
the peaks, wintry.
Gray in the storm-light murky
Depths. Then, before nightfall,
Mist. Dusk. Alone.

> 1969: *Morgennacht*

< 391 >

Aus: IN DER NEUEN STILLE

—Hier wo der Bach
durch den Nebel glänzt, das
Gottesland mit nahen Bäumen
wie fern beginnt und
seelisches Licht die Träume öffnet . . .
Droben leuchtet der Abend frei. Was
einstrahlt, wie Feuer durchglühts
das Haus der Welt, noch
aufblühend—Hier an des
Nebellands Glanzwassern,
verdämmernd . . .

from IN THE NEW SILENCE

—Here, where the stream
gleams through mist, the
god-land with near trees
begins as though far and
spiritual light opens dreams . . .
Up there evening shines free. What
radiates in, like fire it glows
through the world's house, still
in blossom—here by the
mist-land's gleaming waters,
fading away . . .

1974: In der neuen Stille

GÜNTER GRASS:

Geboren 1927 in Danzig. Während des Krieges war er Flakhelfer und Soldat. Nach einem Krankenhausaufenthalt und einer kurzen Internierung als Kriegsgefangener arbeitete er als Landarbeiter und als Bergmann in einem Kalibergwerk, bevor er 1947 Steinmetzlehrling wurde. Zwischen 1948 und 1953 studierte er Malerei und Bildhauerei in Düsseldorf und Berlin und schrieb daneben Lyrik. 1955 fand seine erste Ausstellung statt; im gleichen Jahr las er auch vor der Gruppe 47 in Berlin. Im Jahr darauf zog er nach Paris, wo er an seinem ersten Roman *Die Blechtrommel* (1959) arbeitete. Sein Stück *Hochwasser* wurde 1957 aufgeführt, gefolgt von *Die Plebejer proben den Aufstand* (1966). 1960 ließ er sich in West-Berlin nieder. Seit 1965 wirbt er im Wahlkampf für die Sozialdemokratische Partei und hat enge Verbindung zu Willy Brandt. Nach dem Erfolg seines ersten Romans wurde er ein international berühmter Schriftsteller. Seine vielen Tätigkeiten, Reisen und Preise können nicht im einzelnen hier aufgeführt werden. Wenn er nicht vom Schreiben längerer Prosaarbeiten in Anspruch genommen ist, zeichnet er weiterhin und schreibt Gedichte. Gedichtbände: *Die Vorzüge der Windhühner* (1956), *Gleisdreieck* (1960), *Ausgefragt* (1967), *Gesammelte Gedichte* (1971) und *Liebe Geprüft* (limitierte Ausgabe mit Radierungen, 1974). Seine Prosaliteratur umfaßt *Katz und Maus* (1961), *Hundejahre* (1963), *Örtlich Betäubt* (1969), und *Aus dem Tagebuch einer Schnecke* (1972). Er veröffentlichte auch Sammlungen seiner Stücke und seiner politischen Reden. Der größte Teil seines Werks ist in englischer Übersetzung zugänglich.

GEÖFFNETER SCHRANK

Unten stehen die Schuhe.
Sie fürchten sich vor einem Käfer
auf dem Hinweg,
vor einem Pfennig auf dem Rückweg,
vor Käfer und Pfennig die sie treten könnten
bis es sich einprägt.
Oben ist die Heimat der Hüte.
Behüte, hüte dich, behutsam.
Unglaubliche Federn,
wie hiess der Vogel,
wohin rollte sein Blick
als er einsah, dass er zu bunt geraten?
Die weissen Kugeln, die in den Taschen schlafen.

< 394 >

GÜNTER GRASS:

Born in Danzig in 1927, he was an Air Force auxiliary and soldier during the war. After hospitalization and a brief internment as a POW, he worked as a farm laborer and in a potash mine before becoming a stonemason's apprentice in 1947. Between 1948 and 1953 he studied painting and sculpture in Düsseldorf and Berlin, and also wrote poetry. His first exhibition took place in 1955, and in the same year he read before the Gruppe 47 in Berlin. In the following year he moved to Paris, where he worked on his first novel, *Die Blechtrommel* (1959). His play, *Hochwasser*, was performed in 1957 and was followed by *Die Plebejer proben den Aufstand* (1966). In 1960 he settled in West Berlin. Since 1965 he has been active as an electioneer for the Social Democratic Party and a close associate of Willy Brandt. He became internationally famous as a writer after the success of his first novel. His many activities, travels, and honors cannot be recorded here. He has continued to produce graphic work and poems when not engaged in the writing of his longer prose works. His books of poems are: *Die Vorzüge der Windhühner* (1956), *Gleisdreieck* (1960), *Ausgefragt* (1967), *Gesammelte Gedichte* (1971), and *Liebe Geprüft* (limited edition with etchings, 1974). His prose fiction includes *Katz und Maus* (1961), *Hundejahre* (1963), *örtlich betäub* (1969), and *Aus dem Tagebuch einer Schnecke* (1972). He has also published collections of plays and political speeches. Most of his work is available in English translation.

OPEN WARDROBE

The shoes are at the bottom.
They are afraid of a beetle
on the way out,
of a penny on the way back,
of a beetle and a penny on which they might tread
till it impresses itself.
At the top is the home of the headgear.
Take heed, be wary, not headstrong.
Incredible feathers,
what was the bird called,
where did its eyes roll
when it knew that its wings were too gaudy?
The white balls asleep in the pockets
dream of moths.
Here a button is missing,

< 395 >

träumen von Motten.
Hier fehlt ein Knopf,
im Gürtel ermüdet die Schlange.
Schmerzliche Seide,
Astern und andere feuergefährliche Blumen,
der Herbst, der zum Kleid wird,
jeden Sonntag mit Fleisch und dem Salz
gefälteter Wäsche gefüllt.
Bevor der Schrank schweigt, Holz wird,
ein entfernter Verwandter der Kiefer,—
wer wird den Mantel tragen
wenn du einmal tot bist?
Seinen Arm im Ärmel bewegen,
zuvorkommend jeder Bewegung?
Wer wird den Kragen hochschlagen,
vor den Bildern stehen bleiben
und alleine sein unter der windigen Glocke?

KLAPPSTÜHLE

Wie traurig sind diese Veränderungen.
Die Leute schrauben ihre Namensschilder ab,
nehmen den Topf mit dem Rotkohl,
wärmen ihn auf, anderen Ortes.

Was sind das für Möbel,
die für den Aufbruch werben?
Die Leute nehmen ihre Klappstühle
und wandern aus.

Mit Heimweh und Brechreiz beladene Schiffe
tragen patentierte Sitzgelegenheiten
und patentlose Besitzer
hin und her.

Auf beiden Seiten des grossen Wassers
stehen nun Klappstühle;
wie traurig sind diese Veränderungen.

< 396 >

in this belt the snake grows weary.
Doleful silk,
asters and other inflammable flowers,
autumn becoming a dress.
Every Sunday filled with flesh
and the salt of creased linen.
Before the wardrobe falls silent, turns into wood,
a distant relation of pine-trees—
who will wear the coat
one day when you're dead?
Who move his arm in the sleeve,
anticipate every movement?
Who will turn up the collar,
stop in front of the pictures
and be alone under the windy cloche?

1956

FOLDING CHAIRS

How sad these changes are.
People unscrew the nameplates from the doors,
take the saucepan of cabbage
and heat it up again, in a different place.

What sort of furniture is this
that advertises departure?
People take up their folding chairs
and emigrate.

Ships laden with homesickness and the urge to vomit
carry patented seating contraptions
and their unpatented owners
to and fro.

Now on both sides of the great ocean
there are folding chairs;
how sad these changes are.

1956: Die Vorzüge der Windhühner

< 397 >

AUSVERKAUF

Ich habe alles verkauft.
Die Leute stiegen vier Treppen hoch,
klingelten zweimal, atemlos
und zahlten mir auf den Fussboden,
weil der Tisch schon verkauft war.

Während ich alles verkaufte,
enteigneten sie fünf oder sechs Strassen weiter
die besitzanzeigenden Fürwörter
und sägten den kleinen harmlosen Männern
den Schatten ab, den privaten.

Ich habe alles verkauft.
Bei mir ist nichts mehr zu holen.
Selbst meinen letzten winzigsten Genitiv,
den ich von früher her anhänglich aufbewahrte,
habe ich günstig verkaufen können.

Alles habe ich verkauft.
Den Stühlen machte ich Beine,
dem Schrank sprach ich das Recht ab,
die Betten stellte ich bloss—
ich legte mich wunschlos daneben.

Am Ende war alles verkauft.
Die Hemden kragen-und hoffnungslos,
die Hosen wussten zuviel,
einem rohen blutjungen Kotelett
schenkte ich meine Bratpfanne

und gleichfalls mein restliches Salz.

IM EI

Wir leben im Ei.
Die Innenseite der Schale

< 398 >

SALE

I've sold out, all I owned, the lot.
Four flights of stairs they came up,
rang the bell twice, out of breath,
and paid down their cash on the floor,
since the table too had been sold.

While I was selling it all,
five or six streets from here they expropriated
all the possessive pronouns
and sawed off the private shadows
of little innocuous men.

I've sold out, all I owned, the lot.
There's no more to be had from me.
Even my last and tiniest genitive,
a keepsake long treasured devoutly,
fetched a good price in the end.

All I owned is sold now, the lot.
My old chairs—I sent them packing.
The wardrobe—I gave it the sack.
The beds—I stripped them, exposed them
and lay down beside them, abstemious.

In the end all I'd owned had been sold.
The shirts were collarless, hopeless,
the trousers by now knew too much;
to a raw and blushing young cutlet
I made a gift of my frying-pan

and all that was left of my salt.

1960: Gleisdreieck

IN THE EGG

We live in the egg.
We have covered the inside wall

< 399 >

haben wir mit unanständigen Zeichnungen
und den Vornamen unserer Feinde bekritzelt.
Wir werden gebrütet.

Wer uns auch brütet,
unseren Bleistift brütet er mit.
Ausgeschlüpft eines Tages,
werden wir uns sofort
ein Bildnis des Brütenden machen.

Wir nehmen an, dass wir gebrütet werden.
Wir stellen uns ein gutmütiges Geflügel vor
und schreiben Schulaufsätze
über Farbe und Rasse
der uns brütenden Henne.

Wann schlüpfen wir aus?
Unsere Propheten im Ei
streiten sich für mittelmässige Bezahlung
über die Dauer der Brutzeit.
Sie nehmen einen Tag X an.

Aus Langeweile und echtem Bedürfnis
haben wir Brutkästen erfunden.
Wir sorgen uns sehr um unseren Nachwuchs im Ei.
Gerne würden wir jener, die über uns wacht
unser Patent empfehlen.

Wir aber haben ein Dach überm Kopf.
Senile Küken,
Embryos mit Sprachkenntnissen
reden den ganzen Tag
und besprechen noch ihre Träume.

Und wenn wir nun nicht gebrütet werden?
Wenn diese Schale niemals ein Loch bekommt?
Wenn unser Horizont nur der Horizont

< 400 >

of the shell with dirty drawings
and the Christian names of our enemies.
We are being hatched.

Whoever is hatching us
is hatching our pencils as well.
Set free from the egg one day
at once we shall draw a picture
of whoever is hatching us.

We assume that we're being hatched.
We imagine some good-natured fowl
and write school essays
about the colour and breed
of the hen that is hatching us.

When shall we break the shell?
Our prophets inside the egg
for a middling salary argue
about the period of incubation.
They posit a day called X.

Out of boredom and genuine need
we have invented incubators.
We are much concerned about our offspring inside the egg.
We should be glad to recommend our patent
to her who looks after us.

But we have a roof over our heads.
Senile chicks,
polyglot embryos
chatter all day
and even discuss their dreams.

And what if we're not being hatched?
If this shell will never break?
If our horizon is only that

<   401   >

unserer Kritzeleien ist und auch bleiben wird?
Wir hoffen, dass wir gebrütet werden.

Wenn wir auch nur noch vom Brüten reden,
bleibt doch zu befürchten, dass jemand,
ausserhalb unserer Schale, Hunger verspürt,
uns in die Pfanne haut und mit Salz bestreut.—
Was machen wir dann, ihr Brüder im Ei?

KÖNIG LEAR

In der Halle,
in jeder Hotelhalle,
in einem eingesessenen Sessel,
Klub-, Leder-, doch niemals Korbsessel,
zwischen verfrühten Kongressteilnehmern
und leeren Sesseln, die Anteil haben,
selten, dann mit Distanz gegrüsst,
sitzt, er, die von Kellnern umsegelte Insel,
und vergisst nichts.

Diese Trauer findet an sich Geschmack
und lacht mit zwölf Muskeln einerseits.
Viel hört er nicht aber alles
und widerlegt den Teppich.
Die Stukkatur denkt er weg
und stemmt seine Brauen gegen.
Bis sich ihr Blattgold löst,
sprechen Barockengel vor.
Die Kirche schickt Spitzel;
ihm fehlen Komparsen.
Vergeblich ahmen zuviele Spiegel ihn nach.
Seine Töchter sind Anekdoten.

Im Hotel Sacher wird nach Herrn Kortner verlangt.
Herr Kortner lässt sagen, er sei auf der Probe.
In der Halle, in seinem Sessel, stellt jemand sich tot
und trifft sich mit Kent auf der Heide.

<   402   >

of our scribbles, and always will be?
We hope that we're being hatched.

Even if we only talk of hatching
there remains the fear that someone
outside our shell will feel hungry
and crack us into the frying pan with a pinch of salt.
What shall we do then, my brethren inside the egg?

1960: *Gleisdreieck*

KING LEAR

In the hall
in any hotel hall
in a chair that sags with long use,
club, leather but never basket chair,
amid premature participants in congresses
and empty armchairs that play their part,
rarely addressed and, if so, with reserve,
he sits,
an island skirted by cruising waiters,
and forgets nothing.

This grief takes pleasure in itself
and laughs with twelve muscles on the one side.
He does not hear much but everything
and refutes the carpet.
His mind rips off the stucco work
and his eyebrows push it away.
Till their gold leaf peels off
baroque angels present themselves.
The church sends informers;
what he lacks is walk-ons.
In vain too many mirrors copy him.
His daughters are anecdotes.

In Hotel Sacher Herr Kortner is paged.
Herr Kortner is busy rehearsing, he has them say.

<   403   >

VORGETRÄUMT

Vorsicht! sage ich, Vorsicht.
Mit dem Wetter schlägt auch das bisschen Vernunft um.
Schon ist Gefühl zu haben, das irgendwie ist:
irgendwie komisch, unheimlich irgendwie.
Wörter, die grad noch brav ihren Sinn machten,
tragen ihr Futter gewendet.
Zeit bricht um.
Wahrsager ambulant.
Zeichen am Himmel—runenhafte, kyrillische—
will wer wo gesehen haben.
Filzschreiber—einer oder ein Kollektiv—verkünden auf Wän-
den
und Plakaten der U-Bahnstationen: glaubt mir glaubt.
Jemand—es kann auch ein Kollektiv sein—hat einen Willen,
den niemand bedacht hat.
Und die ihn fürchten, päppeln ihn hoch mit Furcht.
Und die ihr Vernünftlein noch hüten, schrauben die Funzel
kleiner.
Ausbrüche von Gemütlichkeit.
Gruppendynamische Tastversuche.
Wir rücken zusammen.
Noch vermuten wir uns.
Etwas, eine Kraft, die noch nicht, weil kein Wort taugt,
benannt worden ist, verschiebt, schiebt uns;
und das allgemeine Befinden meint diesen Rutsch
(zugegeben: wir rutschen) mehrmals und angenehm
vorgeträumt zu haben.
Aufwärts! Es geht wieder aufwärts.
Nur ein Kind—es können auch Kinder im Kollektiv sein—
ruft: Da will ich nicht runter. Will ich nicht runter.
Aber es muss.
Und alle reden ihn zu: vernünftig.

< 404 >

In the hall, in his armchair, someone acts dead
and goes to meet Kent on the heath.

1967: Ausgefragt

FOREDREAMED

Careful, I say, Careful.
As the weather turns, so will our bit of good sense.
Already you can buy feelings that are anyhow:
somehow funny, uncannily anyhow.
Words that only now were reliably lugging their sense
wear their lining turned out.
Time goes into reverse.
Clairvoyants all over the place.
Signs in the sky—rune-like, Cyrillic—
somewhere someone claims to have seen.
Felt pens—one or a collective—proclaim on walls
and billboards of underground stations: believe me believe.
Someone—it could be a collective—has a will
that no one has considered.
And those who fear it pamper it fat with their fear.
And those who will guard the bit of good sense lower the splut-
    tering wick.
Eruptions of "gemütlichkeit."
Group-dynamic gropings.
We're moving closer together.
Still we assume one another.
Something, a power that hasn't—because no word serves—
yet been named, shifts and shoves us;
and the general state of mind thinks it has foredreamed this
    slide
(granted that we are sliding)
more than once, and pleasantly.
Upward! An upward trend again.
Only a child—it could be children in the collective—

< 405 >

< 406 >

calls out. I don't want to go down there. Don't want to go
   down.
But he must.
And everyone cajoles him: be sensible.

1974

GÜNTER BRUNO FUCHS:

Geboren 1928 in Berlin, wo er heute noch lebt. Mit 14 wurde er Luftwaffenhelfer, kam dann zum Arbeitsdienst, wurde von den Belgiern gefangengenommen und mit 17 wieder freigelassen. Nach dem Krieg arbeitete er eine Zeitlang im Baugewerbe und auf dem Erziehungssektor in Ost-Berlin. Seit 1952 lebt er als Zeichner und Schriftsteller in West-Berlin. Seine zahlreichen Veröffentlichungen umfassen Erzählungen, Romane, Prosagedichte, Holzschnitte und Radierungen, letztere oft als Illustrationen zu seinen schriftstellerischen Arbeiten. Gedichtbände: *Nach der Haussuchung* (1957), *Brevier eines Degenschluckers* (1960), *Trinkermeditationen* (1962), *Die Meisengeige: zeitgenössische Nonsensverse* (1964), *Pennergesang* (1965), und *Blätter eines Hof-Poeten und andere Gedichte* (1967). 1971 erschien, von Fuchs verfaßt und illustriert, der Roman *Der Bahnwärter Sandomir: seine Abenteuer an der offenen oder geschlossenen Bahnschranke*. 1974 fand eine Ausstellung seiner zeichnerischen Arbeiten in London statt.

DER GROSSE MANN

Der grosse Mann
mit knallender Zigarre,
der grosse Mann
dreht seinen Geschäften
den alten
müden Rücken zu.

Er hat sich
in seine schönste
Zigarrenkiste
gelegt
und wartet sehnsüchtig
auf den grossen
Raucher.

PENNERGESANG

für Manfred Bieler
1
Kneipe,
mein dicker Lumpensammler, schöner Morgen,
der uns umhüllt mit schnapsgetränkten Klamotten,

< 408 >

GÜNTER BRUNO FUCHS:

Born in Berlin in 1928, where he still lives. He was an Air Force auxiliary at fourteen, then in labor service, was taken prisoner by the Belgians, and released at the age of seventeen. After the war he worked for a time in East Berlin, in the building trade and in education. Since 1952 he has lived in West Berlin as a graphic artist and writer. His many publications include stories, novels, and prose poems, as well as woodcuts and etchings, often done as illustrations to his own literary works. His books of poems are: *Nach der Haussuchung* (1957), *Brevier eines Degenschluckers* (1960), *Trinkermeditationen* (1962), *Die Meisengeige: zeitgenössische Nonsenverse* (1964), *Pennergesang* (1965), and *Blätter eines Hof-Poeten und andere Gedichte* (1967). A novel, *Der Bahnwärter Sandomir: seine Abenteuer an der offenen oder geschlossenen Bahnschranke*, written and illustrated by Fuchs, appeared in 1971. His graphic work was exhibited in London in 1974.

THE BIG MAN

The big man
with his banging cigar
the big man
is turning his old
weary back on
his business interests.

He has lain down
in his
very best
cigar box
and longingly awaits
the big
smoker.

1965: *Pennergesang*

SONG OF THE LAY-ABOUTS

for Manfred Bieler

1
Pub,
fat rag and bone collector, lovely morning

< 409 >

du weisst, elendes Loch, wir sind
ein Planschbecken für Krebse und hungrige Möwen,
eine Schlafstelle für den Gesang des Harfenarbeiters:
Freu dich, Fritzchen, morgen gibt's Selleriesalat!—
eine Handvoll Baumblätter,
wir treiben
am Denkmal des grossen Strassenkehrers vorbei,
ein Wurf salutierender Katzen,
wenn zwischen Ober- und Untergebiss
der Alkohol seine stinkende Fahne entrollt.

2

Her mit dem Handwerkszeug!
Die Pulle macht einen Sonntag froh! Kneipe, rostiger
Spiegel, zeig uns die Fratzen deiner Kumpanen!
Wer dir am besten gefällt, wirft heute den Fussboden an:
Pass auf, die Luftschaukel nimmt ihre höflichsten
Diebe an Bord: Jetzt wird der Himmel erleichtert,
sachte von innen nach aussen gekehrt.
Alarm, Ritter der Funkwagenstreife, Alarm!
Pralldicke Tschen voll geklauter Stunden, juckt uns
der weltbewegende Fang: Das Weib hinter der Theke
kann höchstens zwanzig Jahre alt sein! Wir sitzen
auf quietschenden Stühlen, wir dampfen schon ab
mit 'ner Ladung Bettgeschichten frei Haus.

3

In den morgendlichen Kneipen
fällt der Tag über uns her, der wacklige Stehaufmann.
Wenn er zu sprechen beginnt,
schöne alberne Sätze mit Worten aus Hünd Hott,
stellt er draussen die Pferdewagen bereit:
Taxis für Nullkommanichts, Brautkutschen
von Ost nach West, von Bier nach Schnaps—
Klärchens alte Kaschemme auf Rädern.
Wir fahren durch den Tunnel, der uns fressen will.
Kommt näher, Grenzpolizisten, packt euch beim Kragen,

< 410 >

that wraps us up in whisky-sodden togs,
you know, low dive, that we are
      a paddling pool for crayfish and hungry gulls,
a kip-down for the singing of stevedores:
      Remona! we'll have it in before the dawn—
a handful of leaves
      adrift
past the great road-sweeper's monument,
      a litter of saluting cats
when between the upper and the lower denture
      alcohol unfurls his reeking banner.

      2
      Hand us the clobber then!
The bottle cheers up a Sunday! Pub, you rusty
      mirror, show us the mugs of your regulars.
The one that pleases you best will hit the floor tonight:
      Look out, the swing is taking its most well-mannered
thieves on board: now the sky will be made lighter,
      gently turned inside out.
Alarm, you knights of patrol cars, alarm.
      Bulging pockets full of hours we have bagged, we feel
the itch of the worldwide game: That bird behind the bar
      can't be more than twenty. We sit
on squeaking chairs, and we're on our way
      with a load of bedtime stories all on the house.

      3
      In the morning pubs
day attacks us that shaky old stalwart who always lands on his
      feet.
      When he begins to speak,
silly, fine sentences with words made of hey and gee-up,
      he's getting the dray carts ready outside:
taxis for zero point nought, bridal carriages
      from east to west, from beer to whisky—
Cleopatra's old lags' club on wheels.

<   411   >

kommt näher im Gänsemarsch! Die pissbüdenväter
schenken euch alle eine Autogramm.
Bitte nicht drängeln!

4

Hier sind wir, blakenses Licht! Unsre werte
Faulenzerei legt sich neider aufs Stempelkissen—
nach getaner Arbeit, Rücken an Rücken mit uns,
hört sie im Schlaf das Kommando der Aktenzeichen,
unsre Namen werden gebündelt, der vaterländische
Tintenkuli erlässt einen Tagesbefehl!
Kneipe, hier sind wir, lungernde Nacht—
ein verstaubter Satz heiliger Affen—
unser Gelübde, das Maul zu halten, Auge und Ohr
nicht sehen und hören zu lassen:
wir haben alles an deinen Nagel gehängt.
Gib uns ein Stückchen Brot, wir werden essen,
gib uns ein Paar Rabenflügel, wir sagen Adieu!—
gib uns den grossen doppelstöckigen Furz,
damit wir antworten können, wie sich's gehört.

< 412 >

We drive through the tunnel that wants to gobble us up.
Come closer, frontier coppers, grab yourselves by the scruff of
   the neck,
      come closer and make it a goose-step! The piss-house at-
      tendants
will present each one of you with an autograph.
      One at a time, though, please!

4
Here we are, glaring light! Our highly esteemed
laziness lies down on the stamping-pad—
      the day's work over, back to back with us,
in her sleep she hears the orders of office files,
      our names are bundled up, the ministerial
pen-pusher issues a new regulation!
      Pub, here we are, loitering night—
a dusty assortment of holy monkeys—
      our vow to keep our traps shut, to let eye and ear
see nothing, hear nothing, ever:
      we've put all our eggs in your basket.
Give us a bite of bread, and we'll eat,
      give us a pair of ravens' wings, and we'll flit!—
give us the mighty double-barrelled fart,
      so we can answer in the proper manner.

                                    1965: *Pennergesang*

<   413   >

CYRUS ATABAY:

Geboren 1929 in Teheran, Iran. Zog im Alter von 7 Jahren mit seinen Eltern nach Berlin und lebte bis Kriegsende in Deutschland. Danach lebte er im Iran, in der Schweiz und in England. Er schreibt vorwiegend in Deutsch. Seine Gedichtbände umfassen u.a. *Einige Schatten* (1956); *An und Abflüge* (1958); *Meditationen am Webstuhl* (1960) und *Doppelte Wahrheit* (1969). Er veröffentlichte auch deutsche Übersetzungen von Gedichten von Hafiz und anderen persischen Lyrikern (*Gesänge von Morgen* (1968): iranische Lyrik, und *Die Worte der Ameisen* (1971): mystische persische Schriften). Sein neuestes Werk heißt *An diesem Tage lasen wir keine Zeile mehr* (Gedichte), 1974.

BESITZNAHME
Verlässliche Heimstatt, Wortreich,
in das meine Wurzeln tauchten,
sich Wege bahnend
zu dem Born der Namen,
wachsend
mit dem Sprachbaum,
damit er seine Krone breite
über mein
Nirgendhaus.

LIBELLE, GRÜNES FEUER
Libelle, grünes Feuer,
zitternd an der Schwelle
eines Steins,
den deine Liebe
nicht erwecken kann.
Doch deine Unruhe
will sich mit dem Gleichmut
vereinen,
dein Flügel pocjt
an die Pforte,
Einlass suchend
in den kühlen Stein.

< 414 >

CYRUS ATABAY:

Born 1929 in Teheran, Iran. Moved to Berlin with his family at the age of seven and lived in Germany until the end of the war. Since then he has lived in Iran, Switzerland, and England, writing mainly in German. His books of poems include *Einige Schatten* (1956); *An- und Abflüge* (1958); *Meditationen am Webstuhl* (1960); and *Doppelte Wahrheit* (1969). He has also published German translations of poems by Hafiz and other Persian poets (*Gesänge von Morgen* [1968]: poems in Persian, and *Die Worte der Ameisen* [1971]: Persian mystical writings). His latest publication is *An diesem Tage lasen wir keine Zeile mehr* (poems), 1974.

TITLE DEEDS

Reliable homestead, word acre
into which my roots dipped
tunneling ways for themselves
to the wellspring of names,
growing
with the tree of language
that it might spread its crest
over
my nowhere-house.

DRAGONFLY, GREEN FIRE

Dragonfly, green fire
quivering on the threshold
of a stone
which your love
cannot awaken.
Yet your unquiet
desires to fuse
with equanimity,
your wing knocks
on the gate,
seeking entry
into the cool stone.

< 415 >

FOUROUGH ZUM GEDÄCHTNIS

Wiederzuerkennen
im Licht, im freigebigen Licht,
wie du es warst,
wiederzuerkennen
im Geruch der Akazien,
im Kelch der Tulpe,
in dem ich dein Augenpaar sehe.
Abschiednehmend,
bist du zurückgekommen
mit deinen Versen,
mit deiner Stimme,
die Reiser treibt.
In kommenden Tagen,
wenn mich sanftes Licht berührt,
Schwester der Freundlichkeit,
wird es deine Berührung sein.

< 416 >

IN MEMORIAM FOUROUKH

Recognizable
in the light, the generous light,
as you were generous,
recognizable
in the scent of acacias,
in the tulip's calyx
in which I see your two eyes.
Taking leave
you returned
with your verses,
with your voice
that sprouts twigs.
In days to come
when gentle light touches me,
sister of kindness,
it will be your touch.

1969: *Doppelte Wahrheit*

< 417 >

WIELAND SCHMIED:

Geboren 1929 in Frankfurt. Schmied lebte jahrelang in Wien. Er ist Kunsthistoriker und leitete für viele Jahre die Kestner-Gesellschaft in Hannover. Er veröffentlichte Essays über Kunst und Literatur. Gedichtbände: *Landkarte des Windes* (1957), *Der Wein von den Gräbern* (1961), *Seefahrerwind* (1963) und *Worte für Worte* (1964).

EINE HANDVOLL TON

Wir haben kein Leben gehabt mit den Wurzeln in Wasser und
    Schlamm,
kein Leben, in das man seine Finger legen kann,
und langsam mit dem Daumen über die Rinde streichen
(und wie man fährt, ein wenig verweilen in einer greifbaren
    Rinne),
kein Leben mit Romeo und Julia in jeder Bewegung der Lunge
(Liebe zerging uns im Mund wie die Süsse zu früh begehrter
    Frucht).

Wir haben kein Leben gehabt mit einer Strickleiter im Efeu,
über dem ein Vogel kreist, der die Farben
der verbotenen Mythologie in den Fittichen hat,
und in seinem Schnabel den derben Duft harziger Nadeln,
und darum halten wir an einem Machmittag dies Stückchen Ton
    in der Hand
und fragen nach Schönheit, und nach dem, was war.

Denn was von allem, das uns trieb und das schwand, war
    schön?
Dies oder jenes, ein Wort klingt noch nach, irgendein Name,
ein Geschmack aus Spanien, ein Drittelgeschmack aus Wein
    und Schlaf
eine Begegnung, ein offener Marktstand mit Trauben und hel-
    len Orangen,
eine lange Reihe bitterer Kastanienbäume in der Fremde,
oder Verona—was von allem war schön?

Verona? Dieser Bruchteil Nachmittag, frei für die Durchfahrt
    der Züge,

< 418 >

WIELAND SCHMIED:

Born in Frankfurt in 1929, Schmied lived for many years in Vienna. He is an art historian, and for many years he directed the Kestner-Gesellschaft in Hanover. He has published distinguished essays both on art and on literature. His books of poems are *Landkarte des Windes* (1957), *Der Wein von den Gräbern* (1961), *Seefahrerwind* (1963), and *Worte für Worte* (1964).

A HANDFUL OF CLAY

We have had no life without our roots in water and mud,
no life into which one can lay one's fingers
and slowly pass one's thumb over the bark
(and, as one moves on, linger a while in a palpable groove),
no life with Romeo and Juliet in every motion of the lungs
(love melted in our mouths like the sweetness of a fruit craved
    too soon).

We have had no life with a rope ladder in the ivy
over which circles no bird that has the colours
of the forbidden mythology in its wings
and in its beak the harsh odour of resinous needles,
and that is why one afternoon we hold this bit of clay in our
    hands
and ask for beauty and for that which has been.

For what of all that drove us on and vanished was beautiful?
This or that, a word still resounds, some name or other,
a savour from Spain, a third of a savour of wine and sleep,
an encounter, an open market booth with grapes and bright
    oranges
a long row of bitter chestnut trees in a foreign place,
or Verona—what of all that was beautiful?

Verona? That fragment of afternoon, free for trains to pass
    through
that afternoon with alleys and banners?
That had something special about it, something I don't want to
    speak of
(so fleeting it was).

< 419 >

dieser Nachmittag mit Gassen und Fahnen?
An dem noch etwas Besonderes war, etwas, über das ich nicht
    sprechen möchte
(nur so flüchtig war es).
Dieser Nachmittag, verlebt in einer billigen Vorstadt der Welt.
Was von allem: Zypressen, Oliven, oder der gelbe See?
Vielleicht noch: ein rötliches Stück Ton in der Hand, etwas,
    das schmerzt,
eine Milchstrasse von Schmerz, eine Strasse, die in die Ver-
    bannung führt,
bis nichts in der Hand bleibt als der Dolch . . .

SEIT DREISSIG JAHREN

Seit dreissig Jahren
erhebt sich das Gras,
es ist Zeit
aufzustehn und hinauszugehen,
damit es wieder Morgen und Mittag und Abend wird,
richtig zu atmen
und richtig zu hassen,
irgendwo unterzutauchen
in einem Handwerk ohne symbolische Bedeutung,
auf schmutziges Packpapier zu schreiben
und alles zurückzuweisen,
was gegen das Gras ist.
Seit dreissig Jahren
spricht es vom Regen,
aber unsere Kultur
bleibt trocken wie eine ausgepechte Schwarzkiefer.
Ich war taub,
weil ich das Packpapier
und die Sonntagsmaler verachtete,
die mit ihrer Staffelei
nicht über den Gartenzaun sehn.

< 420 >

That afternoon spent in a cheap suburb of the world.
What of it all: cypresses, olives, or the yellow lake?
Perhaps also: a reddish bit of clay in your hand, something that
　　hurts,
a milky way of pain, a road that leads into exile
till there's nothing left in your hand but the dagger . . .

1957: Landkarte des Windes

FOR THIRTY YEARS

For thirty years
the grass has been rising,
it is time
to get up and go out,
so that it will be morning again and noon and evening,
to breathe properly,
to immerse oneself somewhere
in a craft with no symbolic meaning,
to write on dirty wrapping paper
and to reject everything
that is opposed to grass.
For thirty years
it has been talking of rain
but our culture
remains dry as black pine covered in pitch.
I was deaf
because I despised wrapping paper
and Sunday painters
who with their easels
don't look beyond the garden fence.

1963: Frage und Formel

HANS MAGNUS ENZENSBERGER:

Geboren 1929 in Kaufbeuren, Bayern. Er wuchs in Nürnberg auf.
Während seiner Schulzeit arbeitete er nebenher als Übersetzer für die
Amerikaner und als Barkellner. Zwischen 1949 und 1954 studierte er
Fremdsprachen, Linguistik und Philosophie an verschiedenen Univer-
sitäten, u.a. an der Sorbonne. Nach seiner Promotion arbeitete er als
Rundfunkredakteur. Er reiste viel in Skandinavien, den USA, Mexico
und Südamerika, und lebte *jahrelang* in Norwegen. Er arbeitete als
Verlagslektor und als Herausgeber einer einflußreichen Zeitschrift,
Kursbuch, die sich vorwiegend Politik und Soziologie widmet. Er ist
ein hervorragender Kritiker und Übersetzer und arbeitet in allen Medien mit. Seine Gedichtbände: *Verteidigung der Wölfe* (1957), *Landessprache* (1960), *Blindenschrift* (1964) und *Gedichte 1955-1970*
(1971). Die wichtigste Sammlung seiner Essays sind *Einzelheiten I*
(1962) und *Einzelheiten II Poesie und Politik* (1963), und *Politik und
Verbrechen* (1964). *Deutschland, Deutschland unter anderm. Äu-
ßerungen zur Politik* erschien 1967, gefolgt von *Palaver: politische
Überlegungen* (1974). Er veröffentlichte außerdem Hörspiele und
einen Roman, *Der Kurze Sommer der Anarchie* (1972) und viele
Übersetzungen und Anthologien. Seine neueste Publikation trägt den
Titel *Mausoleum* (1975); die englische Übersetzung erschien 1976.
Enzensberger wurde vielfach ins Englische und andere Fremdsprachen
übersetzt: 1974 erschienen *Politics and Crime* und *The Consciousness
Industry: on Literature, Politics and the Media*.

✕ DAS ENDE DER EULEN

ich spreche von euerm nicht,
ich spreche vom ende der eulen.
ich spreche von butt und wal
in ihrem dunkeln haus,
dem siebenfältigen meer,
von den gletschern,
sie werden kalben zu früh,
rab und taube, gefiederten zeugen,
von allem was lebt in lüften
und wäldern, und den flechten im kies,
vom weglosen slebst, und vom grauen moor
und den leeren gebirgen:

auf radarschirmen leuchtend
zum letzten mal, ausgewertet

< 422 >

HANS MAGNUS ENZENSBERGER:

Born in 1929 in Kaufbeuren, Bavaria, he grew up in Nürnberg. While at school he worked part-time as an interpreter for the Americans and as a barman. Between 1949 and 1954 he studied foreign languages, linguistics, and philosophy at various universities, including the Sorbonne. After obtaining a doctorate, he worked as a radio producer. He traveled widely in Scandinavia, the U.S., Mexico, and South America, and lived for many years in Norway. He has worked as a publisher's reader and as the editor of an influential periodical, *Kursbuch*, mainly devoted to politics and sociology. He is eminent as a critic, translator, and contributor to all the media. His books of poems are: *Verteidigung der Wölfe* (1957), *Landessprache* (1960), *Blindenschrift* (1964) and *Gedichte 1955-1970* (1971). His principle collections of essays are *Einzelheiten I* (1962) and *Einzelheiten II, Poesie und Politik* (1963), and *Politik und Verbrechen* (1964). *Deutschland, Deutschland unter anderm. Aüsserungen zur Politik* appeared in 1967, followed by *Palaver: politische Überlegungen* (1974). He has also published radio plays and a novel, *Der kurze Sommer der Anarchie* (1972), as well as many translations and anthologies. His latest book of poems is *Mausoläum* (1975), an English language version of which appeared in 1976. He has been widely translated into English and other languages: *Politics and Crime* appeared in 1974, as did *The Consciousness Industry: on Literature, Politics and the Media*.

THE END OF THE OWLS

i do not speak of what's yours
i speak of the end of the owls.
i speak of turbot and whale
in their glimmering house,
in the sevenfold sea,
of the glaciers—
too soon they will calve—
raven and dove, the feathered witnesses,
of all that lives in the winds
and woods, and the lichen on rock,
of impassable tracts and the gray moors
and the empty mountain ranges:

shining on radar screens
for the last time, recorded,
checked out on consoles, fingered

< 423 >

auf meldetischen, von antennen
tödlich befingert floridas sümpfe
und das sibirische eis, tier
und schilf und schiefer erwürgt
von warnketten, umzingelt
vom letzten manöver, arglos
unter schwebenden feuerglocken,
im ticken des ernstfalls.

wir sind schon vergessen. *wir sind bereits verloren*
sorgt euch nicht um die waisen,
aus dem sinn schlagt euch
die mündelsichern gefühle,
den ruhm, die rostfreien psalmen.
ich spreche nicht mehr von euch,
planern der spurlosen tat,
und von mir nicht, und keinem.
ich spreche von dem was nicht spricht,
von den sprachlosen zeugen,
von ottern und robben,
von den alten eulen der erde.

AUF DAS GRAB EINES FRIEDLICHEN MANNES

dieser da war kein menschenfreund,
mied versammlungen, kaufhäuser, arenen.
seinesgleichen fleisch ass er nicht.

auf den strassen ging die gewalt
lächelnd, nicht nackt.
aber es waren schreie am himmel.

sie schienen zertrümmert,
die gesichter der leute waren nicht deutlich.
noch ehe der schlag gefallen war.

<   424   >

by aerials fatally florida's marshes
and the siberian ice, animal
reed and slate all strangled
by interlinked warnings, encircled
by the last manouevres, guileless
under hovering cones of fire,
while the time-fuses tick.

as for us, we're forgotten.
don't give a thought to the orphans,
expunge from your minds
your gilt-edged security feelings
and fame and the stainless psalms.
i don't speak of you any more,
planners of vanishing actions,
nor of me, nor of anyone.
i speak of that without speech,
of the unspeaking witnesses,
of otters and seals,
of the ancient owls of the earth.

                    1960: *landessprache*

FOR THE GRAVE OF A PEACE-LOVING MAN

this one was no philanthropist,
avoided meetings, stadiums, the large stores.
did not eat the flesh of his own kind.

violence walked the streets,
smiling, not naked.
but there were screams in the sky.

people's faces were not very clear.
they seemed to be battered
even before the blow had struck home.

< 425 >

eines, um das er zeitlebens gekämpft hat,
mit wörtern und zähnen, ingrimmig,
hinterlistig, auf eigene faust:

das ding, das er seine ruhe nannte
da er es hat, nun ist kein mund mehr
an seinem gebein, es zu schmecken.

Kleinschreibung, um das Monotone zu unterstreichen → *Spiel mit der Sprache, normalen, (Fingernägel) alltägliches*

MIDDLE CLASS BLUES

wir können nicht klagen.
wir haben zu tun.
wir sind satt.
wir essen.

hat die notwendigen Dinge, ist aber unzufrieden

alles hat seinen gesunden Lauf

das gras wächst,
das sozialprodukt,
der fingernagel,
die vergangenheit.

Land ist fruchtbar → *Wohlstand* → *Gesundheit*

träges, alltägliches Leben,

die strassen sind leer. →
die abschlüsse sind perfekt. →
die sirenen schweigen.
das geht vorüber.

↳ die unbewältigte Vergangenheit V. Angstgefühl → Trägheit

keine Kinder, keine Autumärsche

alles in bester Ordnung

wird sich ändern, aber jetzt nicht

die toten haben ihr testament gemacht.
der regen hat nachgelassen.
der krieg ist noch nicht erklärt.
das hat keine eile.

> wird Krieg geben, wir kümmern uns aber nicht darüber

wir essen das gras.
wir essen das sozialprodukt.
wir essen die fingernägel.
wir essen die vergangenheit.

man hat Sorgen

> wir leben von dem, was uns unmittelbar umgibt - keine Abwechslu

wir haben nichts zu verheimlichen. – *wir täuschen nichts vor*
wir haben nichts zu versäumen. – *langweilig*

< 426 >

Ein Gedicht zum Gähnen
passive Unzufriedenheit

one thing for which he fought all his life,
with words, tooth and claw, grimly,
cunningly, off his own bat:

the thing which he called his peace,
now that he's got it, there is no longer a mouth
over his bones, to taste it with.

1964: Blindenschrift

MIDDLE CLASS BLUES

we can't complain.
we're not out of work.
we don't go hungry.
we eat.

the grass grows,
the national product,
the finger nail,
the past.

the streets are empty.
the deals are closed.
the sirens are silent.
all that will pass.

the dead have made their wills.
the rain's become a drizzle.
the war's not yet been declared.
there's no hurry for that.

we eat the grass.
we eat the social product.
we eat the fingernails.
we eat the past.

we have nothing to conceal.
we have nothing to miss.

< 427 >

wir haben nichts zu sagen. *- es fehlt der Sinn*
wir haben. *wir haben einfach - materiell, aber*
da Sinn fehlt?

die uhr ist aufgezogen. *- alles läuft planmäßig*
die verhältnisse sind geordnet.
die teller sind abgespült.
der letzte autobus fährt vorbei. *- letzte Möglichkeit wegzukomm*

er ist leer. *- niemand fährt irgendwo hin*
niemand die Möglichkeit
benützt
wir können nicht klagen. *wegzukommen   Eintönigkeit*
warum sollten wir auch?

worauf warten wir noch? *Es muß etwas*
passieren

offenes Ende
DER ANDERE *Wer weiß was!!*

einer lacht
kümmert sich
hält mein gesicht mit haut und haar unter den himmel
lässt wörter rollen aus meinem mund
einer der geld und angst und einen pass hat
einer der streitet und liebt
einer rührt sich
einer zappelt

aber nicht ich
ich bin der andere
der nicht lacht
der kein gesicht unter dem himmel hat
und keine wörter in seinem mund
der unbekannt ist mit sich und mit mir
nicht ich: der andere: immer der andere
der nicht siegt noch besiegt wird
der sich nicht kümmert
der sich nicht rührt

< 428 >

we have nothing to say.
we have.

the watch has been wound up.
the bills have been paid.
the washing up has been done.
the last bus is passing by.

it is empty.

we can't complain.

what are we waiting for?

1964: Blindenschrfit

Handwritten margin note:

Drei besichtspunkte
1. Langeweile
2. Wir haben alles.
3. Wovauf warten wir?
Man muß etwas gegen
die Langweile tun

THE OTHER

one laughs
is worried
under the sky exposes my face and my hair
makes words roll out of my mouth
one who has money and fears and a passport
one who quarrels and loves
one moves
one struggles

but not i
i am the other
who does not laugh
who has no face to expose to the sky
and no words in his mouth
who is unacquainted with me with himself
not i: the other: always the other
who neither wins nor loses
who is not worried
who does not move

< 429 >

der andere
der sich gleichgültig ist
von dem ich nicht weiss
von dem niemand weiss wer er ist
der mich nicht rührt
das bin ich

SCHATTENREICH

i

hier sehe ich noch einen platz,
einen freien platz,
hier im schatten.

ii

dieser schatten
ist nicht zu verkaufen.

iii

auch das meer
wirft vielleicht einen schatten,
auch die zeit.

iv

die kriege der schatten
sind spiele:
kein schatten
steht dem andern im licht.

v

wer im schatten wohnt,
ist schwer zu töten.

< 430 >

the other
indifferent to himself
of whom i know nothing
of whom nobody knows who he is
who does not move me
that is i

1964: *Blindenschrift*

SHADOW REALM

i

here even now i see a place,
a free place,
here in the shadow.

ii

this shadow
is not for sale.

iii

the sea too
casts a shadow perhaps,
and so does time.

iv

the wars of shadows
are games:
no shadow
stands in another's light.

v

those who live in the shadow
are difficult to kill.

< 431 >

vi

für eine weile
trete ich aus meinem schatten,
für eine weile.

vii

wer das licht sehen will
wie es ist
muss zurückweichen
in den schatten.

viii

schatten
heller als diese sonne:
kühler schatten der freiheit.

ix

ganz im schatten
verschwindet mein schatten.

x

im schatten
ist immer noch platz.

DIE MACHT DER GEWOHNHEIT
I

Gewöhnliche Menschen haben für gewöhnlich
für gewöhnliche Menschen nichts übrig.
Und umgekehrt.
Gewöhnliche Menschen finden es ungewöhnlich,

<   432   >

vi

for a while
i step out of my shadow,
for a while.

vii

those who want to see light
as it is
must retire
into the shadow.

viii

shadow
brighter than the sun:
cool shadow of freedom.

ix

completely in the shadow
my shadow disappears.

x

in the shadow
even now there is room.

1964: Blindenschrift

THE FORCE OF HABIT

I

Ordinary people ordinarily do not care
for ordinary people.
And vice versa.
Ordinary people find it extraordinary

< 433 >

dass man sie ungewöhnlich findet.
Schon sind sie keine gewöhnlichen Menschen mehr.
Und umgekehrt.

II

Dass man sich an alles gewöhnt,
daran gewöhnt man sich.
Man nennt das gewöhnlich
einen Lernprozess.

III

Es ist schmerzlich,
wenn der gewohnte Schmerz ausbleibt.
Wie müde ist das aufgeweckte Gemüt
seiner Aufgewecktheit!
Der einfache Mensch da z.B. findet es schwierig,
ein einfacher Mensch zu sein,
während jene komplexe Persönlichkeit
ohre Schwierigkeiten herleiert
wie die Betschwester den Rosenkranz.
Überall diese ewigen Anfänger,
die längst am Ende sind.
Auch der Hass ist eine liebe Gewohnheit.

IV

Das noch nie Dagewesene
sind wir gewohnt.
Das noch nie Dagewesene
ist ein Gewohnheitsrecht.
Ein Gewohnheitstier
trifft an der gewohnten Ecke
einen Gewohnheitsverbrecher.

< 434 >

that people find them extraordinary.
At once they have ceased to be ordinary.
And vice versa.

II

That one gets used to everything—
one gets used to that.
The usual name for it is
a learning process.

III

It is painful
when the habitual pain does not present itself.
How tired the lively mind
is of its liveliness!
The simple person there for instance finds it complicated
to be a simple person,
while that complex character
rattles off his complexity
as nuns do their rosaries.
All these eternal beginners
who long ago reached the end.
Hatred, too, is a precious habit.

IV

The utterly unprecedented—
we are used to that.
The utterly unprecedented
is our habitual right.
A creature of habit
at the usual corner meets
an habitual criminal.

<   435   >

Eine unerhörte Begebenheit.
Die gewöhnliche Scheisse.
Die Klassiker waren gewöhnt,
Novellen daraus zu machen.

V

Sanft ruhet die Gewohnheit der Macht
auf der Macht der Gewohnheit.

< 436 >

An unheard-of occurrence.
The usual shit.
Our "classics" were in the habit
of turning it into stories.

V

Untroubled the habit of force reposes
on the force of habit.

1971: *Gedichte 1955-1970*

< 437 >

WALTER HELMUT FRITZ:

Geboren 1929 in Karlsruhe, wo er heute noch lebt. Er studierte Literatur und Philosophie in Heidelberg. Er schreibt Romane, Kurzgeschichten und Hörspiele: außerdem veröffentlichte er Sammlungen kurze Prosastücker. Gedichtbände: *Achtsam sein* (1956), *Bild und Zeichen* (1958), *Veränderte Jahre* (1963), *Die Zuverlässigkeit der Unruhe* (1966) und *Aus der Nähe* (1972). Er übersetzte aus dem Französischen und veröffentlichte kritische Essays.

MANN IN APULIEN

An niedrigen Steimauern entlang,
zwischen Feigenkakteen und wilden Narzissen,
reitet er auf seinem Esel heim.
Gleichmütiges Leben. Er weiss nicht,
ob ihm die Zukunft etwas bringen wird.
Ein kühler Tag, bald Regen.
Zu Hause bläst er im Kohlenbecken
das schwelende Feuer an.

EIN RÜCKFLUTEN DER WELLE

Der Stein, die Muschel,
das Stück Korkeiche,
ein gebleichter Rückenwirbel,
hinter dem nun
keine Dunkelheit mehr beginnt
wie zu der Zeit,
da er noch Teil eines Körpers war.
Aber ein Rückfluten der Welle
nimmt, was sich eben noch zeigte,
wieder weg.

<   438   >

WALTER HELMUT FRITZ:

Born in Karlsruhe, 1929, where he still lives. He studied literature and philosophy at Heidelberg. He is a novelist, short story writer, and radio dramatist, and has published books of short prose pieces. His books of poems are: *Achtsam sein* (1956), *Bild und Zeichen* (1958), *Veränderte Jahre* (1963), *Die Zuverlässigkeit der Unruhe* (1966), and *Aus der Nähe* (1972). He has translated from the French and published critical essays.

MAN IN APULIA

Along low stone walls,
between prickly pears and wild narcissi
he rides home on his donkey.
An even-tempered life. He does not know
whether the future will bring him anything.
A cool day. With rain to come.
At home he blows the brazier
into smouldering heat.

A WAVE'S RECESSION

The stone, the shell,
the piece of cork,
a blanched vertebra
behind which
no darkness begins now
as it did
when the bone was part of a body.
But a wave's recession
takes away the thing
seen a moment ago.

1972: Aus der Nähe

< 439 >

GÜNTER KUNERT:

Geboren 1929 in Berlin. Während des Krieges befand man ihn wegen seiner teilweise jüdischen Abstammung als dienstuntauglich für die Armee. Nach dem Krieg studierte er Werbekunst, bevor er sich hauptberuflich dem Schreiben widmete. Heute lebt er in Ost-Berlin; er unternahm ausgedehnte Reisen in Europa und Amerika. Er schrieb Romane, Erzählungen, Prosagedichte, Fabeln, Fernsehspiele, Drehbücher und Gedichte. Ein Großteil seines Werks erschien auch in West-Deutschland. Sein Frühwerk ist stark von Brecht beeinflußt. Seine Gedichtbände umfassen u.a.: *Wegschilder und Mauerinschriften* (1950), *Unter diesem Himmel* (1955), *Das kreuzbrave Liederbuch* (1961), *Verkündigung des Wetters* (1966), *Moderne Balladen* (1967), *Warnung vor Spiegeln* (1970), *Offener Ausgang* (1972), und *Im weiteren Fortgang* (1974). Sein Werk ist in der zweisprachigen Anthologie *East German Poetry* vertreten. Seine Erzählungen und Romane umfassen die Titel: *Im Namen der Hüte* (1967) und *Gast aus England* (1973).

ALTES FOTO ALTER STRASSE

Sich einschleichen
in diese vergilbende Gasse,
kopfsteingepflastert, bräunlich
und menschenleer bis auf mich
und winke heraus: Hinter der nächsten,
für euch nicht sichtbaren Ecke
fahre ich sogleich mit der Pferdebahn
heim ins ewige Negativ.

ERINNERN IV

Für Christopher Middleton

Eine Blinde, die Erinnerung heisst,
durch nichts ausgewiesen als durch
ihren Namen, eine Blinde bringt Schätze
herbei, ungreifbar und kostbar.

Aus Blei ist Gold geworden,
zum Erstaunen der Alchemisten: ihnen
gelang nur die Umwandlung
von Menschen in Einwohner, von Völkern

< 440 >

GÜNTER KUNERT:

Born in Berlin in 1929, Kunert was found unfit to serve in the army during the war because of his part-Jewish descent. After the war he studied commercial art before becoming a full-time writer. He now lives in East Berlin, but has traveled widely in Europe and America. He has written novels, stories, prose poems and fables, television plays and film scenarios as well as poems. Most of his work has appeared in West Germany also. Much influenced by Brecht in his early work, his books of poems include: *Wegschilder und Mauerinschriften* (1950), *Unter diesem Himmel* (1955), *Das kreuzbrave Liederbuch* (1961), *Verkündigung des Wetters* (1966), *Moderne Balladen* (1967), *Warnung vor Spiegeln* (1970), *Offener Ausgang* (1972), and *Im weiteren Fortgang* (1974). His work is represented in the bilingual anthology *East German Poetry*. His stories and novels include: *Im Namen der Hüte* (1967) and *Gast aus England* (1973).

OLD PHOTOGRAPH OF AN OLD STREET

To insinuate oneself
into this yellowing street.
Cobbled, brownish
and empty but for me,
and signal out of it: behind
the next, to you invisible, corner
I'm about to take the horse-drawn tram
home into the eternal negative.

REMEMBERING IV

For Christopher Middleton

A blind woman called Memory
with no identification but
her name, a blind woman brings
treasures, impalpable and precious.

Lead has turned into gold,
to the alchemists' amazement: they
achieved no more than the transmutation
of people into inhabitants, of peoples

<   441   >

in Wörter, von Häusern in Kästen,
von Städten in Wüsten, darinnen
Einwohner in Kästen vorkommen und heraus
auf Anordnung der Wörter, ohne Wissen
woher, wohin, wozu.

Eine Blinde, die Erinnering heisst,
hebt einen Spaltbreit das Lid. Indem
sie dich anblickt, ohne dich zu sehen,
erblickst du
im Meer der Kohlenflöze deine Geburt.

Und dass du längst dein Geheimnis verloren:

Denn du bist sichtbar geworden. Was bedeutet:
benützlich.
Dass deine Zukunft mit den Bildern der Zukunft
vergeht und verging immerdar.
Dass du bestenfalls ein Idiot bist. Falls nicht
schlechthin
eine von der Materie abgespaltne Rotation
zur Erzeugung von Material. Also ähnlich
einer Gottheit, die aus Mangel
an Gläubigen sich selber anbetet.
Die Scharen von Mördern mietet.
Die den blinden Blick nicht erträgt,
der alles gesehen hat.

SO SOLL ES SEIN

Zwecklos und sinnvoll
soll es sein
zwecklos und sinnvoll
soll es auftauchen aus dem Schlamm
daraus die Ziegel der grossen Paläste
entstehen und wieder zu Schlamm verfallen
eines sehr schönen Tages

Widerspruch - durch Betonung Wiederholung

selbstverständlich

< 442 >

into words, of houses into boxes,
of cities into deserts where
inhabitants in boxes occur and leave
at the command of words, without knowing
where from, where to, what for.

A blind woman called Memory
opens a chink in one eyelid. As
she looks at you without seeing you
you see
your birth in the ocean of coal seams.

And that long ago you lost your secret:

For you have grown visible. Which means usable.
That your future, with its images of the future,
passes and has always passed.
That at best you are an idiot. If not
indeed
a rotation split off from matter
for the production of matter. Something like
a godhead, then, who for lack
of believers worships himself.
Who hires gangs of killers.
Who cannot bear the blind gaze
which has seen all.

THAT'S HOW IT SHOULD BE

Purposeless and meaningful
it should be
purposeless and meaningful
it should emerge from the mud
out of which the bricks of great palaces
are made—to crumble again into mud
one very fine day

<   443   >

zwecklos und sinnvoll
soll es sein
was für ein unziemliches Werk
wäre das
✳ Zur Unterdrückung nicht brauchbar
von Unterdrückung nicht widerlegbar
zwecklos also
sinnvoll also $\quad >$ einzelne Betonung

wie das Gedicht.

✳ das Leben und sein Verlauf überspielt
die Unterdrückung

Was für die Diktatur nicht als
Unterdrückung dient, ist zwecklos

Gegenüber dem Leben und seinem
Verlauf ist die Unterdrückung unwichtig -
also sinnvoll - das Leben ist sinnvoll

das Gedicht = das Schöpferische
man entgeht der Unterdrückung

die Sprache ist sinnvoll

< 444 >

keine Interpunktion — läuft zusammen -
eine Aussage, mit Punkt am Ende

purposeless and meaningful
it should be
what an unseemly work
it would be
not serviceable for oppression
not controvertible for oppression
therefore purposeless
therefore meaningful

like poetry

1974: *Im weiteren Fortgang*

Gedicht ist zwecklos für das
Regime,

ist aber sinnvoll für den Kreierenden

< 445 >

HORST BIENEK:

Geboren 1930 in Gleiwitz, Oberschlesien. Mit 13 Jahren wurde er Flakhelfer, mit 15 zog man ihn zu Demontagearbeiten an deutschen Industrieanlagen ein, die den Russen in die Hände zu fallen drohten. Mit 17 ging er zurück auf die Schule, mit 19 arbeitete er für eine Zeitung, mit 21 war er Brecht-Schüler, mit 22 Bergarbeiter in einem Sträflingslager in Workuta, zu 25 Jahren Zwangsarbeit verurteilt. Nach vier Jahren wurde er freigelassen, zog nach West-Deutschland, und arbeitete bis 1961 als Rundfunkredakteur. Zur Zeit lebt er als Schriftsteller in München. Er veröffentlichte verschiedene Prosa- und Lyrik-Arbeiten, die auf den Erfahrungen der stalinistischen Repression beruhen; den Anfang bildete *Traumbuch eines Gefangenen* (1957). Gedichtbände: *Was war, was ist* (1966) und *Vorgefundene Gedichte* (1969). Sein Roman *Die Zelle* (1968) wurde in englischer Übersetzung veröffentlicht (1972), ebenso eine Auswahl seiner Gedichte in der Reihe Penguin European Poets; eine kleinere zweisprachige Auswahl erschien in der Reihe Unicorn German 1969 unter dem Titel *Horst Bienek, Poems*. Sein neuester Gedichtband heißt *Die Zeit danach* (1974).

PER SEMPRE

Für Ungaretti

Alter Freund—Giu—
was hast du gemeint
mit deiner letzten Zeile:
FÜR IMMER AUF EWIG VON NUN AN
ALLEZEIT IMMERZEIT ALLZEIT
Wir rätseln
    enträtseln
        verrätseln
sech Übersetzer
zweiundvierzig Rezensenten allein in D.

Du schweigst
für immer
und meinst doch nur:

Der Augenblick
per sempre.

< 446 >

HORST BIENEK:

Born in 1930 in Gleiwitz, Upper Silesia. At the age of thirteen he became an anti-aircraft auxiliary, at fifteen he was called up for demoli-
tion work on German industrial plants about to fall into Russian hands.
At seventeen he went back to school, at nineteen he worked for a
newspaper, at twenty-one he was a student of Brecht's, at twenty-two
a mine worker in a penal camp at Workuta, where he was condemned
to twenty-five years' hard labor. Released after four years, he moved
to West Germany, working as a radio producer until 1961. He now
lives as a writer in Munich. He has published a good deal of prose and
verse based on his experiences of Stalinist repression, beginning with
Traumbuch eines Gefangenen (1957). His books of poems are *Was
war was ist* (1966) and *Vorgefundene Gedichte* (1969). His novel,
Die Zelle (1968), has been published in English translation (1972), and
a selection of his poems in the Penguin European Poets series; a smaller bilingual selection appeared in the Unicorn German Series in 1969
under the title *Horst Bienek: Poems*. His latest book of poetry is called
Die Zeit danach (1974).

PER SEMPRE

For Ungaretti

Old friend—Giu—
what did you mean
by your last line:
FOR EVER ETERNALLY FROM NOW ON
EVERY TIME EVERTIME ALLTIME

We puzzle
        decipher
                encipher

six translators
forty-two book reviewers in G. alone

you keep silent
for ever
and yet only mean:

The moment
per sempre

1969: Jahresring

<   447   >

ANDREAS OKOPENKO:

Geboren 1930 in Kaschau (Kosice) in der Tschechoslowakei. Seine Familie mußte 1939 umziehen und ließ sich in Wien nieder, wo er heute noch lebt. Von seiner Ausbildung her ist er Chemiker. Er schrieb Hörspiele, einen Roman und Kurzgeschichten. Gedichtbände: Grüner November (1957), Seltsame Tage (1963), Warum sind die Latrinen so traurig? (mit dem Untertitel "spleen songs", 1969), und *Orte wechselnden Unbehagens* (1971). 1973 veröffentlichte er einen Band mit Parodien *Der Akasienfresser*, gefolgt von einem Band Kriminalgeschichten *Warnung von Ypsilon* (1974).

ENDE DER TEENAGER

Ich hatte sie nicht verflucht: sie waren ganz herzig
ich hatte meine Schnauze oft in ihr Haar gesehnt
ins lila übergossene wie gesponnener Zucker
in ihre Bonbonschnauze oder unter den Minirock

Ich hatte sie nicht verflucht: das muss wer andrer getan haben
dass Eisen vom Himmel fiel und noch dazu brennendes
ich bin ja kein griesgrämiger menschenfressender Giesser
der die Sachen unzweckmässig anschüttet

Zugegeben: dass ich darunter nicht antraf
Sonja die Raskolnikow zu Sibirien bekehrte
die Immenseesche Elisabeth an der ich was gutmachen wollte
Madame de Staël die es wagte gescheit zu sein

Ich bedaure es indessen dass ich jetzt in Nevada
wohin mich der Weltbebenhimmel verblasen hat
tagelang gehen kann und keinen Teenager finde
nur die mädchenäugige Wüstenspringmaus

ANDREAS OKOPENKO:

Born in Kaschau (Kosice), Czechoslovakia, in 1930. His family was forced to move in 1939 and settled in Vienna, where he now lives. By training he is a chemist. He has written radio plays, a novel, and short stories. His books of poems are: *Grüner November* (1957), *Seltsame Tage* (1963), *Warum sind die Latrinen so traurig?* (sub-titled "spleen songs," 1969), and *Orte wechselnden Unbehagens* (1971). In 1973 he published a volume of parodies, *Der Akasienfresser*, and followed it up by a volume of thrillers, *Warnung vor Ypsilon* (1974).

THE END OF TEENAGERS

I had not cursed them: they were quite attractive
I'd often longed to put my gob in their hair
the mauvely tinted like candyfloss
into their gobstopper gobs or under their miniskirts

I had not cursed them: somebody else must have done it
so that iron fell from the sky, and red-hot at that
after all I'm no grumpy man-eating founder
flinging the stuff about without rhyme or reason

Admittedly, I never discovered among them
Sonia who converted Raskolnikov to Siberia
Elizabeth out of "Immensee" who'd let me make up for some-
    thing
Madame de Staël who dared to be clever

Nonetheless I regret that now in Nevada
where the worldquake wind has blown me for a season
I can walk whole days and not find one teenager
only the girl-eyed desert jerboa-mouse

1965: Einen Affen geschossen

< 449 >

GERHARD RÜHM:

Geboren 1930 in Wien. Als Mitglied der "Wiener Schule" experimentierender Schriftsteller schrieb er konkrete Poesie, experimentierte auch mit unartikulierten Lauten und elektronischen Medien. Er schrieb kurze Stücke und Dialoge, die in "zweifelhaften" Theatern aufgeführt wurden. Zusammen mit Artmann und Achleitner schrieb er Dialektgedichte, gesammelt unter dem Titel *hosn rosn baa* (1959). Seine konkreten Gedichte erschienen 1961 in Eugen Gomringers Reihe. 1968 veröffentlichte er *Farbengedicht*, dem seine *Gesammelten Gedichte und visuellen Texte* (1970) folgten. 1972 erschien *Ophelia und die Wörter; Gesammelte Theaterstücke 1954-1971*. 1973 folgte der Band *Wahnsinn: Litaneien*.

EINIGES

auf dem tisch
ist ein graues tuch
darauf ein geöffnetes päckchen mit zigaretten glänzendes gelb
    zerrissenes blau
daneben eine schachtel streichhölzer
davor eine halbvolle flasche inländer (österreichisches erzeug-
    nis) kirschrum
davor die schreibmaschine mit meinen fingern
links daneben ein kugelschreiber
ein notizheft (orangefarben)
darunter ein weisses blatt papier mit einem gedicht titel februar
daneben (schon am rande des tisches) eine abgenützte mappe
    sie ist geschlossen (aber ich weiss was sie enthält)
und wenn ich nicht tippe mein rechter arm auf der kante des
    tisches
mein gesicht schwebt noch eben darüber
es ist 1 h mittag
das bild des tisches wird sich in kürze verändern

zb werden
unsere gesichter einander gegenüber sein
den mund öffnen und schliessen
die hände gabeln und messer bewegen
unsere augen sich hin und wieder treffen

<   450   >

GERHARD RÜHM:

Born in Vienna in 1930. A member of the "Vienna School" of experimental poets, he has written concrete and near-concrete poems, and has also experimented with inarticulate sounds and electronic media. He has written short plays and dialogues performed in "fringe" theaters. Together with Artmann and Achleitner he wrote dialect poems, collected as *hosn rosn baa* (1959). His concrete poems appeared in Eugen Gromringer's series in 1961. In 1968 he published *Farbengedicht*, which was followed by his collected poems and visual texts under the title: *Gesammelte Gedichte une visuelle Texte* (1970). His collected works for the theater appeared in 1972: *Ophelia und die Wörter; Gesammelte Theaterstücke 1954-1971*. This was followed in 1973 by *Wahnsinn: Litaneien*.

SOME THINGS

on the table
there is a gray cloth
on it an open packet of cigarettes
    shiny yellow torn blue
beside it half a bottle of cherry rum
    (Austrian produce)
in front of it the typewriter with my fingers
to the left of it a ball pen
a notebook (orange)
underneath it a sheet of white paper with a poem
    entitled February
next to it (on the edge of the table) a worn folder
    it is shut (but I know what's inside it)
and when I'm not typing my right arm
    on the corner of the table
my face just floats above it
it is one P.M.
the table's appearance is about to change

e.g., our faces
will be opposite each other
they will open and shut their mouths
our hands move forks and knives
our glances meet from time to time

< 451 >

so wagte ich einige voraussagen für die nächste viertelstunde
und schliesse
mit dem blick auf die *tür*

< 452 >

so I've risked one or two predictions for the next
    quarter of an hour
    and conclude
    with my eyes
    on the door

      1970: *Gesammelte Gedichte und visuelle Texte*

< 453 >

JÖRG STEINER:

Geboren 1930 in Biel in der Schweiz. Nach einem Leben in verschiedenen Orten der Schweiz und im Ausland kehrte er in seine Heimatstadt zurück, arbeitete dort als Lehrer, dann als Schriftsteller und Portner in einer Kunstgalerie, die auf ethnogrphische Arbeit spezialisiert war. Er ist vor allem als Autor von Romanen und Kurzgeschichten bekannt und veröffentlichte nur einen Gedichtband, Der *schwarze Kasten* (1965). 1962 trat er als Romanautor (*Strafarbeit*) in den Vordergrund; daneben schrieb er ein Fernsehspiel, Monologe, und eine Vielzahl kurzer Prosastücke. 1972 wurde der Erzählband *Pele sein Bruder* veröffentlicht, gefolgt von *Schnee bis in die Niederungen* (1973).

IM REGEN

Die Leute auf der Strasse haben Eile,
es regnet auf der Strasse,
die Leute haben Eile, wenn es regnet.

Die Leute in den Häusern haben Zeit,
in den Häusern ist es gemütlich,
die Leute haben Zeit, wenn es regnet.

Die Leute in den Häusern betrachten
die Leute in der Strasse.
Es regnet.

LEBENSLAUF

Die Leute wollen vergnügt leben,
fernsehn und einen Wagen fahren,
ein Haus im Grünen haben.

Die Leute wollen hilfsbereit sein,
dem Blinden über die Strasse helfen, wenn
einmal ein Blinder über die Strasse will.

Die Leute wollen, dass
gut von ihnen geredet werde,
ohne Schmerzen wollen sie leben, lange,

< 454 >

JÖRG STEINER:

Born in 1930 in Biel, Switzerland. After living in various places in Switzerland and abroad, he returned to his home town, working as a schoolteacher, then as a writer and partner in an art gallery specializing in ethnographic work. He is best known as a novelist and short story writer, and has published only one book of poems, *Der schwarze Kasten* (1965). He emerged as a novelist (*Strafarbeit*) in 1962, and has also written a television play, monologues, and a variety of short prose pieces. A volume of stories, *Pele sein Bruder*, was published in 1972 and was followed by *Schnee bis in die Niederungen* (1973).

IN THE RAIN

The people in the street are in a hurry,
it is raining in the street,
people are in a hurry when it's raining.

The people in houses have time,
in the houses it's cosy,
people have time when it's raining.

The people in the houses watch
the people in the street.
It's raining.

CURRICULUM VITAE

People want to live a pleasant life,
watch television and drive a car,
own a house in the green belt.

People want to be helpful,
help the blind man to cross the street, when it happens
that a blind man wants to cross the street.

People want others
to speak well of them,
they want to live without pain, for a long time,

< 455 >

und noch vor dem Tode
ein wenig unsterblich sein.

HIROSHIMA

In der Schule hören die Kinder eine Geschichte,
sie hören die Geschichte von Hiroshima,
Hiroshima ist ein Dorf in der Schweiz.

Hiroshima ist eine keltische Siedlung,
in Hiroshima stehen die Sachen nicht zum besten,
die Bauern in Hiroshima sind unzufrieden.

Hiroshima braucht Industrie,
die Kinder lesen im Chor,
der Lehrer schreibt ein Wort an die Tafel.

SIE FAHREN MORGEN

Sie fahren nicht zur Sonne,
sie fahren zum Mond.
Warum fahren sie zum Mond?
Es gibt nichts Neues unter der Sonne.

Wenn sie zum Mond fahren,
fahren sie nicht zur Sonne.
Wenn sie vom Mond nicht zurückkehren,
geschieht etwas Neues unter der Sonne.

Sie fahren morgen.

< 456 >

and before they die
to be just a little immortal.

HIROSHIMA

At school the children hear a story,
they hear the story of Hiroshima,
Hiroshima is a village in England.

Hiroshima was settled by Celts,
at Hiroshima things are not too good,
the farmers at Hiroshima are dissatisfied.

Hiroshima needs industry,
the children read out in chorus,
the teacher writes a word on the blackboard.

THEY'RE TAKING OFF TOMORROW

They're not taking off for the sun,
they're taking off for the moon.
Why are they taking off for the moon?
There is nothing new under the sun.

If they take off for the moon,
they don't take off for the sun.
If they don't come back from the moon
something new will happen under the sun.

They're taking off tomorrow.

1965: Der schwarze Kasten

HANS JÜRGEN HEUSE:

Geboren 1930 in Bublitz, Pommern. 1959 und 1960 war er Redaktionsmitglied der ostdeutschen Zeitschrift *Sonntag*. Heute lebt er als Lyriker, Übersetzer und Kritiker in Kiel. Er veröffentlichte *Vorboten einer neuen Steppe* (1961), *Wegloser Traum* (1964), *Beschlagener Rückspiegel* (1966), *Worte aus der Zentrifuge* (1966), *Ein bewohnbares Haus* (1968), *Küstenwind* (1969) und *Uhrenvergleich* (1971). Ein Gedichtband erschien in englischer Übersetzung *(Underseas Possessions,* 1972). Außerdem veröffentlichte er Essaysammlungen: *Formprobleme und Substanzfragen der Dichtung* (1972), *Das Profil unter der Maske* (1974) und den Gedichtband *Vom Landurlaub zurück* (1975).

ELEGIE

I

Kohlköpfe haben die Sahara umzingelt,
in Regennächten
rücken sie immer weiter vor.

II

Löwen, ihr kommt,
ausgestopft, ins Museum.
Wüstensand, du musst,
ein Schildchen dran, unter Glas.

HANS JÜRGEN HEISE:

Born in 1930 in Bublitz, Pomerania. In 1959 and 1960 he was on the staff of the East German periodical *Sonntag*. He now lives in Kiel as a poet, translator, and critic. He has published *Vorboten einer neuen Steppe* (1961), *Wegloser Traum* (1964), *Beschlagener Rückspiegel* (1965), *Worte aus der Zentrifuge* (1966), *Ein bewohnbares Haus* (1968), *Küstenwind* (1969), and *Uhrenvergleich* (1971). A book of his poems in English translation appeared in 1972 *(Underseas Possessions)*. He has also published books of essays: *Formprobleme und Substanzfragen der Dichtung* (1972), *Das Profil unter der Maske* (1974). His most recent book of poems is *Vom Landurlauf Zurük* (1975).

ELEGY

I

Cabbage heads have encircled the Sahara
in rainy nights
they advance foot by foot.

II

Lions, they'll put you
in museums, stuffed.
Desert sand, you'll find yourself
under glass, labeled.

1961: *Vorboten einer neuen Steppe*

<   459   >

ADOLF ENDLER:

Geboren 1930 in Düsseldorf. Bevor er, angeklagt wegen subversiver Tätigkeit, 1955 West-Deutschland verließ, arbeitete er als Buchhändlerlehrling, Kranführer und Journalist. In der DDR studierte er am Johannes R. Becher Institut in Leipzig Literatur und arbeitete dann als Herausgeber, Kritiker, Verlagslektor und im öffentlichen Transportwesen. Er lebt in Ost-Berlin. Seine Gedichtbände: *Die Kinder der Nibelungen* (1964) und *Das Sandkorn* (1974). Er übersetzte aus dem Georgischen, Russischen, Armenischen und Bulgarischen.

DER ÄLTESTE MENSCH DER WELT

1

Das alles verdank ich der Presse

2

Nachkommen zählt das Geburtstagskind zweihundertneun
Doch am Mittwoch am kommenden Mittwoch
Zählt er sein einhundertsechsundsechzigstes Jahr
Schir Ali Mislimow der Alte
Er zählt sich lieb nickend zu uns

3

Täglich arbeitet er noch ein wenig im Garten
Lange Spaziergänge führen den Zeitgenossen Napoleons
Oder Goethes bald nach hier bald nach dort hin
Am kommenden Mittwoch bleibt er zu Haus

4

Ich verdanke mein hohes Alter der Sowjetmacht
  Allah
  Der Sowjetmacht
  Der Arbeit
  Allah

< 460 >

ADOLF ENDLER:

Born in 1930 in Düsseldorf. Before leaving West Germany in 1955, charged with subversive activities there, he worked as an apprentice bookseller, crane driver, and journalist. In the GDR he studied literature at the Johannes R. Becher Institute, Leipzig, then worked as an editor, critic, and publisher's reader, and in public transport. He lives in East Berlin. His books of poems are *Die Kinder der Nibelungen* (1964) and *Das Sandkorn* (1974). He has translated from the Georgian, Russian, Armenian, and Bulgarian.

THE OLDEST MAN IN THE WORLD

1

I owe all this to the press

2

Of descendants the man this birthday counts two hundred and
    nine
But on Wednesday next Wednesday
He will count his one hundred and sixty-sixth year
Shir Ali Mislinov the old man
He counts himself one of us with a kindly nod

3

Each day he still does a little work in the garden
Long walks lead Napoleon's or Goethe's
Contemporary now this way now that way
Next Wednesday though he will stay at home

4

I owe my great age to Soviet power
    To Allah
    To Soviet power
    To work
    To Allah

< 461 >

Meinem guten Charakter
Ich habe ein Herz wie ein junger Dshigit

5

Das alles verdank ich der Presse

6

Einhundertsechsundsechzig wird Schir Ali am Mittwoch
Und freut sich auf das Jahr zweitausend schon heut
Älteren Zeitungen entnimmt der Leser voll Neid
Als er einhundertfünfundsechzig wurde hat sich Schir Ali
Hat er sich ah auf den Hundertsten Lenins gefreut

7

Das alles verdank ich der Presse

8

Zweiundachtzig Pulsschläge zählt er in jeder Minute
Sein Blutdruck hundertfünfunddreissigStrichfünfundachtzig

9

Das alles verdank ich der Presse

10

Aber das grösste Glück dieses ältesten Menschen der Welt
Seine Erfahrungen weiterzugeben am kommenden Mittwoch
In Barsawu im Talischgebirge in Aserbeidshan
Seine jahrhundertealten Erfahrungen weiterzugeben
Im Zubereiten von Schaschlyk

< 462 >

To my good character
I have a heart inside me like a young Dshigit's

5

I owe all this to the press

6

One hundred and sixty-six Shir Ali will be on Wednesday
And already today looks forward to the year two thousand
Full of envy the reader gathers from older newspapers
That on his one hundred and sixty-fifth Shir Ali
Looked forward ah to Lenin's hundredth birthday

7

I owe all this to the press

8

Eighty-two pulse beats he counts for every minute
His blood pressure one hundred and thirty-five stroke eighty-
    five

9

I owe all this to the press

10

But the greatest joy of this oldest man in the world
Is to pass on his experience next Wednesday
At Barsavu in the Talish Mountains in Azerbaijan
To pass on his centuries-old experience
In the preparation of shashlik   [1971]; 1974: *Das Sandkorn*

< 463 >

WOHNUNGSÜBERNAHME

Als die Greisin weinte weil sie nun doch noch ins Heim kam
Fühlte ich mich als der neue Mieter einfach dazu verpflichtet
Wie einen Schlagring den Schlüssel zwischen Finger und Bal-
    len gepresst
Hab ich für sie und den Kater habe ICH dann das Taxi bezahlt

< 464 >

TAKING OVER

When the old woman wept because after all she must move to
    a home
As the new tenant I felt I must do the decent thing
With the key clutched tight between finger and thumb like a
    knuckleduster
For her and her tomcat I, yes, I paid the taxi fare.

[1967]; 1974: Das Sandkorn

<   465   >

MANFRED PETER HEIN:

Geboren 1931 in Darkehmen in Ostpreußen. Er studierte deutsche Literatur und Geschichte in Marburg, München und Göttingen. Seit 1958 lebt er in Finnland, wo er als Übersetzer finnischer Prosa und Lyrik arbeitet. Gedichtbände: *Ohne Geleit* (1960), *Taggefälle* (1962) und *Gegenzeichnung* (1974).

DENKMAL

Dies ist ein einfaches Vergahren und nicht der Rede wert
Wenn ich höre wie die Möwen schrein
bewege ich mich auf den Frühling zu

    Und dies ist mein Denkmal

Auf einen sanften Regen verlasse ich mich
mit der hohlen Hand auf den ersten fallenden Tropfen
der den Schnee verkommen lässt im Mai
den weissen heulenden Hund auf dem Dach
des verlassenen Autos an einer Vorortstrasse
mit Zahlen Farben
schwarz von rot bis violett

    Ein Regenbogen
den ich ans Licht bringen will
und seine Skala seine Geschwindigkeit
ans Ende ans Ende ans Ende
wo wie es heisst sich die Zeit überschlägt
wo mein Denkmal stürzt
in die hohle
Hand

Zu lange
vier Milliarden Jahre warte ich
auf die Kontraktion des Weltalls
in einem Punkt
der ich selber bin
der heillose Gegenstand
meiner Träume

MANFRED PETER HEIN:

Born in Darkehmen, East Prussia, in 1931. He studied German literature and history at Marburg, Munich, and Göttingen. Since 1958 he
has lived in Finland, where he works as a translator of Finnish poetry
and prose. His books of poems are *Ohne Geleit* (1960), *Taggefälle*
(1962), and *Gegenzeichnung* (1974).

MONUMENT

This is a simple process And not worth talking about
When I hear the gulls cry
I move toward spring

    And this is my monument

I rely on a gentle rain
with my hollow hand on the first falling drop
that makes the snow perish in May
the white howling dog on the roof
of the abandoned car in a suburban street
with numbers colours
black from red to purple

    A rainbow
that I want to bring to light
and its scale its speed
to the end to the end to the end
where as they say time turns a somersault
where my monument crashes
into the hollow
hand

Too long
four billion years I have been waiting
for the cosmos to contract
within one point
that is myself
the disastrous subject
of my dreams

[1966]; 1974: Gegenzeichnung

THOMAS BERNHARD:

Geboren 1931 bei Maastricht, Holland, als Kind österreichischer Eltern. Bekannt vor allem durch seine Romane und Erzählungen. Den
Anfang bildeten drei Gedichtsammlungen, die 1957 und 1958 veröffentlicht wurden. Seine verschiedenen Romane und Erzählungen umfassen die Titel *Frost* (1963), *Amras* (1964), *Verstörung* (1967), *An
der Baumgrenze* (1969), *Ereignisse* (1969), *Das Kalkwerk* (1970),
Midland in Stilfs (1971) und *Gehen* (1971). Eine englische Übersetzung der *Verstörung* erschien 1970 unter dem Titel *Gargoyles*; 1973
erschien *Das Kalkwerk* unter dem Titel *The Lime Works*. Bernhard lebt
zur Zeit in Österreich und bekam den österreichischen Staatspreis für
Literatur verliehen. Seine neuesten Veröffentlichungen umfassen die
Theaterstücke *Ein Fest für Boris* (1970) und *Die Jagdgesellschaft*
(1974).

JETZT IM FRÜHLING

Jetzt im Frühling
    kann ich die Sprache der Äcker
nicht mehr verstehn
    und die Toten schauen
mit grossen Augen mich an
    und der Weizen schäumt
und der Fluss redet mir vom Himmel . . .
    Wo die Kinder lachen,
da ist mein Land mir
    fremder als alle Länder
der Erde.

AN H. W.

Dreitausend Jahre nach dem Vater
    starb auf dem Hügel ich, der Wind,

verbrannter Schädel, ich, der Norden,
    die Buchstaben Vergils, die Reden grosser Bauern,

dreitausend Jahre nach dem Vater
    geh durch mein Land ich, kränkelnd,

mich fröstelt in den Septemberbetten.

< 468 >

THOMAS BERNHARD:

Born near Maastricht, Holland, in 1931 of Austrian parents. Best known for his novels and stories, he began with collections of poems published in 1957 and 1958. His many novels and stories include *Frost* (1963), *Amras* (1964), *Verstörung* (1967), *An der Baumgrenze* (1969), *Ereignisse* (1969), *Das Kalkwerk* (1970), *Midland in Stilfs* (1971) and *Gehen* (1971). An English translation of *Verstörung* appeared in 1970 under the title *Gargoyles* as well as of *Das Kalkwerk* under the title *The Lime Works* in 1973. He now lives in Austria and has received the Austrian State Prize for Literature. His latest publications include *Ein Fest für Boris* (1970) and *Die Jagdgesellschaft* (1974).

NOW IN SPRING

Now in spring
   I can no longer understand
the language of fields
   and the dead look
at me with wide eyes
   and the wheat foams
and the river speaks to me of heaven . . .
   Where children laugh
my country is stranger
   to me than all the countries
on earth.

TO H.W.

Three thousand years after the father
   on the hill died I, the wind,

burnt skull, I, the north,
   the letters of Vergil, the speeches of great peasants,

three thousand years after the father
   I walk through my country, ailing,

I shiver in the September beds.

1963: Frage und Formel

<   469   >

KONRAD BAYER:

Geboren 1932 in Wien. Er arbeitete als Barmusiker, Bankangestellter und Schauspieler, bevor er sich an Mitglieder der sogenannten Wiener Schule, experimentierende Schriftsteller im Literarischen Kabarett von 1958 und 1959, anschloß. Er schrieb Stücke, experimentelle Drehbücher und Prosatexte, wie z.B. *Der Kopf des Vitus Bering* (1965). 1964 starb Bayer durch Selbstmord. Eine Auswahl seiner Lyrik und Prosa wurde von Gerhard Rühm herausgegeben und 1966 unter dem Titel *der sechste sinn* veröffentlicht.

FÜR JUDITH

wenn der montag die rosen durchs land treibt
steh ich am fenster und warte

wenn der dienstag den regen am ufer zerschlägt
dann steh ich am fenster und tanze

wenn der mittwoch für mittwoch die sonne entzweit
steh ich im fenster und schreie

wenn der donnerstag im park sein kreuz verliert
geh ich vom fenster mit kommenden schritten

wenn der freitag sein kleid in die wolken schlägt
dann steh ich am fenster und verrate dich zweimal

wenn der samstag sein haar im schornstein findet
dann steh im am fenster und singe

wenn der sonntag den tod umsonst verschenkt
dann steh ich am fenster und warte

< 470 >

KONRAD BAYER:

Born in Vienna in 1932. He worked as a bar musician, bank employee, and actor before his association with members of the so-called Vienna School of experimental writers in the Literary Cabaret of 1958 and 1959. He wrote plays and experimental film scenarios, as well as prose texts, such as *Der Kopf des Vitus Bering* (1965). Bayer died by suicide in 1964. A selection of prose and verse texts was edited by Gerhard Rühm and published in 1966 as *der sechste sinn*.

FOR JUDITH

when Monday drives roses across the country
I stand at the window and wait

when Tuesday smashes rain on the river-bank
I stand at the window and dance

when Wednesday for Wednesday splits the sun
I stand at the window and scream

when Tuesday loses its cross in the park
I leave the window with approaching steps

when Friday hurls its clothes at the clouds
I stand at the window and betray you twice

when Saturday finds its hair in the chimney
I stand at the window and sing

when Sunday gives away death for nothing
I stand at the window and wait

[1951]; 1966: der sechste sinn

< 471 >

JÜRGEN BECKER:

Geboren 1932 in Köln, wo er den größten Teil seines Lebens verbrachte. Ein großer Teil seiner Prosa und Lyrik besteht aus detaillierter
Betrachtung der Stadt und Umgebung. Er arbeitete in verschiedenen
Berufen bevor er Schriftsteller wurde. Seine Prosawerke: *Felder*
(1964), *Ränder* (1968) und *Umgebungen* (1970). Er veröffentlichte
einen Band mit Hörspielen, *Bilder, Häuser, Hausfreunde* (1969) und
zwei Gedichtsammlungen, *Schnee* (1971) und *Das Ende der Landschaftsmalerei* (1974). Zur Zeit arbeitet er als Rundfunkredakteur in
Köln. Er veröffentlichte auch einen Photo-Band, *Eine Zeit ohne Wörter* (1971).

BILDBESCHREIBUNG

Das Bild einer Bucht, und die Bucht
ist gewesen, leer, und sanft,
an den Rändern. Der Name sagt
nichts mehr; es gibt keinen Namen,
und das Bild ist erfunden,
unbeschreibbar, wie all das hier herum.

YOU ARE LEAVING THE AMERICAN SECTOR

In memoriam Wolfgang Maier

Zwei Männer auf einem Waldweg; nun
steigen sie über den Zaun
ins Niemandsland, und hier
ist es mucksmäuschenstill, denn
man hört auch das Gras nicht,
das sich aufrichtet, nachdem
die Streife vorbeigefahren ist.

BERLIN-LONDON

Irrtum ziemlich viel; die Jahreszeiten
stimmen noch. Laub. Also
November, November
zwischen Tiergarten und Kensington Gardens;
nutzloser Sommer. Nun auch schon
Schnee, der erste verschwindende Schnee, und
ich bleibe nicht, wo ich bin. Möwen

JÜRGEN BECKER:

Born 1932 in Cologne, where he has spent most of his working life, drawing on detailed observation of the locality for much of his prose and verse. He worked in various professions before becoming a writer. His prose works are *Felder* (1964), *Ränder* (1968), and *Umgebungen* (1970). He has published a book of radio plays, *Bilder Häuser Hausfreunde* (1969) and two collections of poems, *Schnee* (1971) and *Das Ende der Landschaftsmalerei* (1974). At present he works as a radio producer in Cologne. He has also published a book of photographs, *Eine Zeit ohne Wörter* (1971).

DESCRIPTION OF A PICTURE

Picture of a bay, and the bay
was, empty and gentle
around the edges. The name tells us
nothing any more; there is no name,
and the picture is a fiction,
indescribable, like everything hereabouts.

YOU ARE LEAVING THE AMERICAN SECTOR

In memoriam Wolfgang Maier

Two men on a woodland path; now
they climb over the fence
into no man's land, and here
it's quieter than a mouse, for
you don't even hear the grass
straighten again after
the patrol has passed by.

BERLIN-LONDON

Quite a lot of error; the seasons
are still right. Leaves. That means
November. November
between Tiergarten and Kensington Gardens;
useless summer. And now
snow, the first fall that disappears, and
I don't stay where I am. Seagulls

< 473 >

wieder, bleiben den Winter,
Unruhe über der ruhigen Spree. Wer
sprang zuletzt, Sog der Verzweiflung,
nein, Sonne wieder im Gesicht, und
Zärtliches, der Nachmittag. Vergleiche
der Stimmung. Wind. Stundenweise
wechselt der Anteil der Schatten, da,
wechselnde Landschaft, im Kopf und dahinten,
Räumung des Himmels. Jenseits,
ein Wort für etwas, was ich nicht weiss,
wenn ich sage, jenscits
der Irrtums, des Schattens, des Winds.
Noch im November. Es stimmt,
was man sieht, es stimmt nicht,
zum Nutzen der Hoffnung, und
man sieht nicht die Hoffnung,
den Schwindel, aber den Schnee
nun, da unten, verschwindend.

SHAKESPEARE'S LAND

Landschaft zum Spielen; aber
wir spielen nicht; was ist,
fragen wir, mit der Belletristik.
Schafe auf den Hügeln, und Bagger
bewegen die Hügel; es ist
der Gemeinsame Markt. Später
die Huhe des fliessenden Mondes, und
wie der Luftkrieg anfing, denke ich,
Coventry nachts in der Nähe.

< 474 >

again, they stay all winter,
unquiet above the quiet Spree. Who
was the last to jump, slough of despond,
no, sun again on my face, and
something tender, the afternoon. Comparison
of moods. Wind. Hour by hour
the share of shadows changes, over there,
the sky is cleared. Beyond,
a word for something I do not know
when I say, beyond
error, shadow, wind.
Still in November. It's right,
what one sees, it is not right,
to serve hope, and
one does not see hope,
the deception, but the snow
now, down there, disappearing.

SHAKESPEARE'S COUNTRY

Landscape for playing; but
we do not play; how about,
we ask, the state of belles-lettres.
Sheep on the hills; it is
the Common Market. Later
the calm of the flowing moon, and
how the war in the air began. I reflect,
Coventry near me at night.

   1974: *Das Ende der Landschaftsmalerei*

<   475   >

HARALD HARTUNG:

Geboren 1932 in Herne, Westfalen. Hartung studierte deutsche Literatur und Geschichte in München und Münster. Er war Universitätsdozent in Bochum und lebt nun in Berlin, wo er als Literaturkritiker und Lehrer an der Pädagogischen Hochschule tätig ist. Er veröffentlichte zwei Gedichtbände: *Hase und Hegel* (1970) und *Reichsbahngel*ände (1974).

DAS PAAR

das Hand in Hand über
die Wiese hüpft und nicht
still sein kann weil
es sich Zigaretten

anzündet auf dem
federnden grünen
Trampolin
ist glücklich solang

Musik zu hören ist.
Draussen in den Anlagen
das Grün ist schwarz.
In der Stille riecht

man den Tod.
Er ist die Musik
die man nicht mehr
hört.

< 476 >

HARALD HARTUNG:

Born in 1932 in Herne, Westphalia, Hartung studied German literature
and history at Munich and Münster. He was a university lecturer in
Bochum, and now lives in Berlin, where he is active as a literary critic
and teaches at the Pädagogische Hochschule. He has published three
books of poems, *Hase und Hegel* (1970), *Reichsbahngelände* (1974),
and *Das* Licht *Gewihnliche* (1976).

THE COUPLE

who hand in hand hop
across the meadow and can't
keep quiet because
they are lighting

cigarettes on the
springy green
trampoline
are happy as long

as there's music to be heard.
Outside in the parkland
green is black.
In the quietness one

can smell death.
It is the music
one can no longer
hear.

                    1974: *Reichsbahngelände*

< 477 >

REINER KUNZE:

Geboren 1933 in Ölsnitz als Sohn eines Bergmanns. Von 1951 bis 1955 studierte er Philosophie und Journalismus in Leipzig und wurde dann Mitglied der Iakultät der dortigen Karl Marx Universität. Zeitweise arbeitete er auf dem Land, in der Fabrik und als Journalist. 1959 wurde er hauptberuflich Schriftsteller. Er lebte 1961 und 1962 in der Tschechoslowakei, übersetzte Lyrik und Prosa aus dem Tschechischen und hält engen Kontakt mit tschechischen Autoren. Wegen seiner Satiren auf die Bürokratie und seiner Verteidigung Wolf Biermanns— Satiriker wie er—fiel Kunze in Ost-Deutschland in Ungnade und bekam Veröffentlichungsverbot für sein Werk. Seine frühen Sammlungen *Die Zukunft sitzt am Tische* (mit Egon Günther, 1955) und *Vögel über dem Tau* (1959) erschienen in Ost-Deutschland. 1963 wurde ein Lyrikband *Widmungen Veröffentlicht, gefolgt von Sensible Wege* (1969) und *Zimmerlautstärke* (1972) in West-Deutschland. 1973 erschien ein Band ausgewählter Gedichte, *Brief mit blauem Siegel*, in Ost-Deutschland. Im gleichen Jahr erschien auch eine englische Auswahl seiner Gedichte in London.

DIE LIEBE

Die liebe
ist eine wilde rose in uns
Sie schlägt ihre wurzeln
in den augen,
wenn sie dem blick des geliebten begegnen
Sie schlägt ihre wurzeln
in den wangen,
wenn sie den hauch des geliebten spüren
Sie schlägt ihre wurzeln
in der haut des armes,
wenn ihn die hand des geliebten berührt
Sie schlägt ihre wurzeln,
wächst wuchert
und eines abends
oder eines morgens
Fühlen wir nur:
sie verlangt
raum in uns

< 478 >

REINER KUNZE:

Born in 1933 in Ölsnitz as the son of a miner. He studied philosophy and journalism in Leipzig from 1951 to 1955, then joined the faculty of the Karl Marx University there. He did temporary work as a farm laborer, factory worker, and journalist. In 1959 he became a full-time writer. He lived in Czechoslovakia in 1961 and 1962, and has translated poetry and prose from the Czech and maintains close contact with Czech writers. As a satirist of bureaucracy and a defender of Wolf Biermann, a fellow satirist, Kunze fell into disfavor in East Germany and for a long time was forbidden to publish his own work there. His early collections *Die Zukunft sitzt am Tische* (with Egon Günther, 1955) and *Vögel über dem Tau* (1959) appeared in East Germany. A book of poetry, *Widmungen*, was published in 1963, and was followed by *Sensible Wege* (1969) and *Zimmerlautstärke* (1972) in West Germany. In 1973 a book of selected poems, *Brief mit blauem Siegel*, appeared in East Germany. An English selection of poems by Kunze appeared in London in the same year. His work is also represented in *East German Poetry*.

LOVE

Love
is a wild rose inside us
It takes root
in our eyes
when they meet the loved one's gaze
It takes root
in our cheeks
when they sense the loved one's breath
It takes root
in the skin of the arm
touched by the loved one's hand
It takes root,
grows climbs
and one evening
or one morning
we only feel:
it demands
room inside us

< 479 >

Die liebe
ist eine wilde rose in uns,
unerforschbar vom verstand
und ihm nicht untertan
Aber der verstand
ist ein messer in uns

Der verstand
ist ein messer in uns,
zu schneiden der rose
durch hundert zweige
einen himmel

NOCTURNE I

alle nerven sind zündschnuren die
glimmen

Und hinter der herzwand,
geballt,
diese jahre

NOCTURNE II

Schlaf du kommst nicht

Auch du
hast angst

In meinen gedanken erblickst du
den traum deinen
mörder

Love
is a wild rose inside us,
not to be known by reason
and not subject to it
But reason is
a knife inside us

Reason
is a knife inside us
to cut for the rose
through a hundred branches
a patch of sky

[1956]; 1959: *Vögel über dem Tau*

NOCTURNE I

Every nerve is a fuse cord
glowing

And behind the heart's wall,
bundled,
these recent years.

NOCTURNE II

Sleep you don't come

You also
are afraid

In my thoughts you catch sight of
the dream your
murderer.

[1970]; 1973: *Brief mit blauem Siegel*

< 481 >

WULF KIRSTEN:

Geboren 1934 in Klipphausen bei Meißen. Kirsten besuchte die Handelsschule und arbeitete bis 1957 als Buchhalter. 1960 immatrikulierte er sich unch wurde als Deutsch- und Slawisch-Lehrer ausgebildet. Zur Zeit ist er Verlagslektor in Leipzig. Der Großteil seiner Lyrik beruht auf der intensiven Beobachtung seiner unmittelbaren Umgebung. Eine Sammlung seiner Gedichte *Wulf Kirsten* erschien 1968, eine weitere mit dem Titel *Satzanfang* wurde 1970 veröffentlicht.

STUFEN
(Für E.u.R.K.)

die stufen hinaufgehn
zur stadt über der stadt
über einen schweigenden herbst
aus stein,
der zu fliegen beginnt,
wenn der wind
die bäume ihre laubkugeln abrollen heisst.

mit abschüssigen worten
bestreun unsre kehlen
schrittlings den berg.
jede stufe, die sich ausschweigt,
heben wir auf
in die gemeinsame sprache.

<   482   >

WULF KIRSTEN:

Born in Klipphausen, near Meissen, in 1934, Kirsten attended a school of commerce and worked as a bookkeeper until 1957. In 1960 he matriculated, after which he was trained as a teacher of German and Slavic. He is now a publisher's reader in Leipzig. Most of his poetry is based on intense observation of his immediate surroundings. A collection of his poems, *Wulf Kirsten*, appeared in 1968 and another collection, *Satzanfang*, was published in 1970.

STEPS
For E. and R. K.

to walk up the steps
to the city above the city
over a silent autumn
of stone
that begins to fly
when the wind
tells trees to unroll their bales of leaves.

with precipitous words
to spatter our throats
as we pace out the mountain:
each step that keeps silent
we raise up
into our common language.

[1969]; 1970: Satzanfang

<   483   >

YAAK KARSUNKE:

Geboren 1934 in Berlin. Er verbrachte einen Teil seiner Kindheit in der UDSSR, wo sein Vater als Manager eines Industriekonzerns tätig war, den die Deutschen während des Kriegs dort aufgebaut hatten. 1945 kehrte er nach Berlin zurück, und lebte bis 1949 im Ost-Sektor. Er studierte Jura und Theaterwissenschaft, bevor er als ungelernter Arbeiter sieben Jahre lang in verschiedenen Gewerben tätig war. 1966 war er in München einer der Herausgeber der Zeitschrift *Kürbiskern*, die Beiträge aus beiden Teilen Deutschlands herausbrachte. Später arbeitete er in Berlin mit dem Verleger Klaus Wagenbach zusammen, war dann aber unter den Dissidenten, die mit dem Verlagskollektiv brachen. Eine Sammlung vorwiegend politischer und satirischer Gedichte *Kilroy & andere* erschien 1967; eine zweite Sammlung *reden & ausreden* erschien 1969. Das Parabelbuch *Die Apotse kommen* wurde 1972 veröffentlicht, gefolgt von zwei Hörspielen *Versuche aus der Unterklasse auszusteigen* (1973).

HERALDISCH

hier ist eden
neben dem löwen
weidet das einhorn
im lilienfeld

siamesische adler & adler
kreisen über
rosen weiss rosen rot

das einhorn äst
die köpfe der blumen
der guillotinierten

hier
ist eden

< 484 >

YAAK KARSUNKE:

Born in Berlin in 1934, Karsunke spent part of his childhood in Soviet Russia, where his father managed an industrial concern set up there by the Germans during the war. He returned to Berlin in 1945, and lived in the Eastern sector until 1949. He studied law and then drama before working as an unskilled assistant for seven years in various trades. In Munich in 1965, he was one of the editors of the magazine *Kürbis-kern*, which brought together contributions from both Germanys. Later he worked in Berlin with the publisher Klaus Wagenbach, but was one of the dissidents who broke away from this publishing collective. His collection of mainly political and satirical poems, *Kilroy & andere*, appeared in 1967; a second collection, *reden & ausreden*, in 1969. A book of parables, *Die Apotse kommen*, was published in 1972, and was followed by two radio dramas: *Josef Bachmann/Sonny Liston Versuche aus der Unterklasse auszusteigen* (1973).

HERALDIC

here
is eden

next to the lion
grazes the unicorn
in the field of lilies

siamese eagles and eagles
hover above
white roses red roses

the unicorn crops
the heads of the flowers
of the guillotined

here
is eden

< 485 >

HOHL FORM

"but the cup of white gold at Patara
Helen's breasts gave that"
    ——Ezra Pound

vermutlich gab
das weisse gold ihrer brust
der schale zu patara gestalt
& gab troja den tod
(gab den griechen den vorwand)

gab dem blinden Homer
atem für (mindestens)
fünfzehn gesänge
& dem verblendeten Pound
ein bild für zwei zeilen

 : die fast so schön sind
wie Helenas brüste es waren
—die patarische schale es ist—
& fast ebenso leer

<   486   >

HOLLOW

"but the cup of white gold at Patara
Helen's breasts gave that"
                    ——Ezra Pound

presumably the white
gold of her breast
gave shape to the cup at Patara
& gave death to Troy
(gave the Greeks their pretext)

gave blind Homer
breath for (at least)
fifteen cantos
and purblind Pound
an image for two lines

: that are almost as beautiful
as Helen's breasts were
—the cup at Patara is—
& almost as empty

        1967: *Kilroy & andere Gedichte*

KARL MICKEL:

Geboren 1935 in Dresden. Von 1953 bis 1958 studierte er Planökonomie und Wirtschaftsgeschichte in Ost-Berlin. 1958 war er Redaktionsmitglied einer Wirtschaftszeitschrift, von 1959 bis 1963 gab er eine Kunstzeitschrift heraus. Heute liest er als Dozent der Wirtschaftswissenschaften und lebt als Schriftsteller in Berlin. Sein erster Gedichtband *Lobverse und Beschimpfungen* erschien 1963. Sein zweiter Band, ebenfalls in West-Deutschland veröffentlicht, zeigt einen radikalen Wandel von jenen allzu rückhaltlos offenen Lobversen und Beschimpfungen zu subjektiver Beobachtung. Mickel lernte viel von früheren Lyrikern, im Rückgriff auf die Vorbilder des 18. und wohl auch 17. Jahrhunderts. Diese Sammlung mit dem Titel *Vita nova mea* erschien 1966 (westdeutsche Ausgabe 1967). Mickels Werk ist in dem Band *East German Poetry* vertreten.

DEUTSCHE FRAU 1946

Spass muss es machen, sonst machts keinen Spass!
Sagte mein Otto, 's war ein toller Bursche.
Wenn wir im Wald warn, sprach er zu den Bäumen:
Euch hack ich alle klein zu Kinderbetten!
Denn er war Tischler, arbeitslos, Kommune
Und wohnte in der Küche bei den Eltern.
Wenn du 'n Bauch kriegst, gehst du!
Sagte die Gnädige, als Otto mich abholte.
Dann Hitler. Otto sagte: der macht Krieg.
Da wars wieder kein Kind, für die Fleischbank
Wollte ich keins, er wollte eine Tochter.
Dann war der Krieg, Otto im Strafbataillon
Gefangen bei den Russen, Antifaschule
Jetzt kommt er heim, bei mir hats aufgehört

< 488 >

KARL MICKEL:

Born in 1935 in Dresden. From 1953 to 1958 he studied economic planning and economic history in East Berlin. In 1958 he was on the staff of a journal devoted to economics, from 1959 to 1963 he edited a periodical devoted to the arts. Now a lecturer in economics and a writer in Berlin. His first book of poems, *Lobverse und Beschimpfungen*, appeared in 1963. His second, also published in West Germany, showed a radical change from those too patently "committed" eulogies and invectives, a change toward individuality of manner and observation. Mickel had learned a great deal from earlier poets, going back to the eighteenth and (I would guess) seventeenth century for exemplars. This collection, *Vita nova mea*, appeared in 1966 (West German edition 1967). Mickel's work is represented in *East German Poetry*.

GERMAN WOMAN 1946

It must be fun or else it isn't fun,
My Otto said, he was a proper lad.
In woods, out walking, he addressed the trees:
I'll chop the lot of you into baby cots!
He was a carpenter, commune, unemployed,
And living with his parents, in the kitchen.
If you get big, my girl, you'll go,
Said Madam when he came to take me out.
Then Hitler. Otto said: that one means war.
Again there was no child. For slaughtering
I didn't want one. Otto did, a daughter.
Then came the war, the penal battalion,
Prisoner-of-war in Russia, re-education
He's coming home now, and with me it's stopped.

1966: vita nova mea

<   489   >

SARAH KIRSCH:

Geboren 1935 in Limlingerode, Harz. Bevor sie Biologie in Halle studierte, arbeitete sie in einer Zuckerfabrik. Von 1963 bis 1967 studierte sie Literatur in Leipzig. Sie war mit dem Lyriker Rainer Kirsch verheiratet lebt jetzt als Schriftstellerin in Ost-Berlin. Ihr erster Gedichtband *Gespräch mit dem Saurier* (1965) enthielt Arbeiten von ihr und ihrem Mann; ihre zweite Sammlung *Landaufenthalt* erschien 1967. Ein weiterer Band *Gedichte* wurde 1969 veröffentlicht; es folgten *Zaubersprüche* (1973) und *Es war dieser merkwürdige Sommer* (1974). Übersetzungen ihrer Gedichte sind in der Anthologie *East German Poetry* vertreten.

WEITES HAUS

In diesem Winter brauch ich ein Haus
wohnen will ich, kaum reden
unterschiedliche Zimmer
mit verschiedenen Fenstern, eins
hat die Flügel nach Norden, da seh ich
die Wipfel der Bäume Eis in den Zweigen
hüpfende Vögel, die Hunde der Lappen
Schellen in der Schlittenspur
Schnee schmilzt, ich wasche
meinen Mund, die eingefrorenen Briefe
Jäger durcheilen die Landschaft, ihre Gewehre
rauchen, im Rucksack tragen sie Zapfen
willkommne Nahrung fürs Feuer

                                  andere Fenster
zeigen in meine Stadt wo die Kirchen
des Marktes mit verschiedenen Türmen
in hellschwarzen Himmel geht
Karussells rasseln, Weihnachtsdrehorgeln
Wehmut erzeugen
                solln, ich öffne
Türen seh nur noch Raum über die Erde gebreitet
—schwimm gute Kugel noch paar tausend Jahr
kann sein wir lernen was—

                                    ich sitz aufm Bett

SARAH KIRSCH:

Born in 1935 in Limlingerode, Harz. She worked in a sugar factory before studying biology at Halle. From 1963 to 1967 she studied literature in Leipzig. She was married to the poet Rainer Kirsch, and now lives as a writer in East Berlin. Her first book of poems, *Gespräch mit dem Saurier* (1965), contained work by both her and her husband; her second collection, *Landaufenthalt*, appeared in 1967. Another book, *Gedichte*, was published in 1969 and followed by *Zaubersprüche* (1973) and *Es war dieser merkwürdige Sommer* (1974). Translations of her poems are included in the anthology *East German Poetry*.

LARGE HOUSE

This winter I want a house
want to dwell, hardly speak
various rooms
with various windows, one
has glass doors to the north, there I see
the treetops, ice in the boughs
hopping birds, the dogs of the Lapps
bells in the sleigh tracks
snow thaws, I wash
my mouth, the letters frozen stiff
huntsmen rush through the landscape, their guns
smoke, in their rucksacks they carry cones
welcome food for the fire

    other windows
point to my town where the churches
on the marketplace with various towers
rise to a pale black sky
merry-go-rounds rattle, Christmas barrel organs
induce melancholia

    are meant to, I open
doors see only space now spread out over the earth
—drift good sphere for a few more millennia
it could be we'll learn a bit—

    I sit on my bed

< 491 >

entzieh mich den Stiefeln denk mir was aus was
von riesigen Schiffen mit Flügeln, und Vögeln
die fahrn Kabinen über Land, ich sag dem Piloten
die Positionen, er korrigiert meinen Kurs
über Manila weg nach Sibirien
er hat Wimpern wie Gras vorschiesst
wenn es erstmals geregnet hat, in seinem Kopf
könnte ich leben

withdraw from my boots think something up something
about gigantic ships with wings, and birds
that travel in cabins overland, I tell the pilot
our compass bearings he corrects my course
past Manila away to Siberia
he has eyelashes like grass shooting up
after the first rain, in his head
I could live

1968: Saison für Lyrik

< 493 >

CHRISTOPH MECKEL:

Geboren 1935 in Berlin. Meckel studierte Kunst in Freiburg und München und ist heute Maler, Zeichner und Schriftsteller. Er illustriert häufig eigene Bücher und die anderer Autoren. Er unternahm umfangreiche Reisen in Europa, Afrika und Amerika, lebt in Berlin und in Südfrankreich. Er schrieb Erzählungen und Märchen, publizierte 1959 und 1960 vier Bände mit Radierungen und stellte seine Gemälde und Radierungen aus. Seine Gedichtbände umfassen u.a.: *Tarnkappe* (1956), *Hotel für Schlafwandler* (1958), *Nebelhörner* (1959), *Wildnisse* (1962), *Bei Lebzeiten zu singen* (1967), *Die Dummheit liefert uns ans Meer* (1967), und *Wen es angeht* (1974). Die *Balladen des Thomas Balkan* erschienen 1969, gefolgt von einer Sammlung von Erzählungen, *Kranich* (1973), und einem Roman, *Bockshorn* (1973). Andere Gedichtbände: *Jasnandos Nachtlied* (1969) und *Manifest der Toten* (1971). Ein Hörspiel, *Eine Seite aus dem Paradiesbuch*, wurde 1969 veröffentlicht. *Lyrik, Prosa, Graphik aus zehn Jahren* erschien 1965, gefolgt von einer *Werkauswahl: Lyrik, Prosa, Hörspiel* (1971).

DER PFAU

Ich sah aus Deutschlands Asche keinen Phönix steigen.
Räumend mit dem Fuss in der Asche
stiess ich auf kohlende Flossen, auf Hörner und Häute—
doch ich sah einen Pfau, der Asche wirbelnd
mit einem Flügel aus Holz und einem aus Eisen
riesig wachsend die Flocken der Feuerstellen
peitschte und sein Gefieder strählte.

Ich sah aus Deutschlands Asche alte Krähen kriechen
ınd borstige Nachtigallen mit heiseren Kehlen
und Hähne mit Schwertfischschnäbeln und kahlen Kämmen
den Ruhm des Vogels zu pfeifen und zu singen.
Ich sah sie in aller Feuer Asche schnobern,
in die der Wind fuhr, und kalten Rauch
abtrieb über Breiten, wo wenig nur Gold war, was glänzte.

Ich sah aus Deutschlands Asche keinen Phönix steigen;
doch ich sah einen Pfau in der Leuchtzeit seines Gefieders,
ich sah ihn strahlende Räder schlagen
im Gegenlicht eisgrauer Himmel und Wetterleuchten
und hörte den Jubel der Krähen und Spatzen und sah

< 494 >

CHRISTOPH MECKEL:

Born in Berlin in 1935, Meckel studied art at Freiburg and Munich, and is today a painter and graphic artist as well as a writer. He has illustrated many books, his own and other people's. He has also traveled widely in Europe, Africa, and America, and lives in Berlin and in the South of France. He has written stories and fairy tales, and in 1959 and 1960 he published four books of etchings, and has exhibited his paintings and etchings. His books of poems include: *Tarnkappe* (1956), *Hotel für Schlafwandler* (1958), *Nebelhörner* (1959), *Wildnisse* (1962), *Bei Lebzeiten zu singen* (1967), *Die Dummheit liefert uns ans Meer* (1967), and *Wen es angeht* (1974). *Die Balladen des Thomas Balkan* appeared in 1969 and was followed by a collection of stories, *Kranich* (1973), and a novel, *Bockshorn* (1973). Other books of poems are: *Jasnandos Nachtlied* (1969) and *Manifest der Toten* (1971). A radio play, *Eine Seite aus dem Paradieshuch*, was published in 1969. *Lyrik, Prosa, Graphik aus zehn Jahren* appeared in 1965, and was followed by a *Werkauswahl: Lyrik, Prosa, Hörspiel* in 1971.

THE PEACOCK

From Germany's ashes I saw no phoenix rise.
Stirring the ash with my foot
I uncovered glimmering fins, uncovered horns and pelts—
yet I saw a peacock, who whirling ashes
with one wing made of wood and one of iron,
growing gigantic whipped the flaky cinders
wherever fires were alight, and preened his plumage.

From Germany's ashes I saw old crows creep out
and bristly nightingales with throats grown hoarse
and cocks with swordfish beaks and combs grown bald
to whistle and to sing in praise of birds.
I saw them root in ashes of those fires
the wind swept through, and drove cold smoke
over wide spaces where little was gold that glittered.

From Germany's ashes I saw no phoenix rise;
yet saw a peacock in the shining season of his plumage,
and saw the radiance as he spread his tail

<   495   >

Elsternschwärme in seine Goldfedern stürzen
Läuse finster aus seinem Gefieder wachsen
grosse Ameisen seine Augen zerfressen.

FEIERABEND

Und eines Tages erblickten wir ihn
auf dem Rücken des Wals
frierend, durchsichtig, klein
und er rief: ich habe das Meer nicht geschaffen
Menschenbrüder, ich schwör es
und nicht die Springflut und nicht den Taifun
ich hab weder euch noch eure Erde geschaffen
helft mir, beliebt es euch, helft mir an Land!
Aber wir blieben sitzen, wir liessen
das Feuer nicht ausgehn in unsern Pfeifen
und hörten ihn heulen, da draussen, auf seinem Fahrzeug.

BEI KLEINEM FEUER

Und als wir die Erde erledigt hatten
legten wir Gift aus für den Himmel. Der
senkte sich und frass, und die Sonne, befallen
von Übelkeit, übergab sich in unsere Augen.
Die Winde krümmten sich und verpusteten hauchweis; lustig
war der Tag, als der Himmel zu Boden ging
und unsere Messer mit ihm spielten (—bloss
dass kein neuer Tag mehr kommen wollte
und wir, bei kleinem Feuer, im Dunkeln, jetzt—)

WAS DIESES LAND BETRIFFT

Was dieses Land betrifft: hier ist kein Ort, für die Zeit
die kommt, einen Grundstein zu setzen. Dies ist kein Ort
für mehr als ein Dasein in Kälte, ausgeschieden
einsilbig und überstimmt. Wenn dein Knochen wandert
in dir auf der Suche nach Leben und ausbricht, hungrig
nach Freude und Zukunft, aber zurückkehrt
ruhlos, weltwund, todnah—wo ist der Genosse

< 496 >

against a murk of ice-gray skies and northern lights,
and heard the jubilation of crows and sparrows, and saw
flocks of magpies fall on his golden feathers
lice grow darkly out of his plumage
man-sized ants devour his eyes.

1962: Wildnisse

AFTER WORK

And one day we caught sight of him
on the back of the whale
freezing, transparent, small,
and he cried: I didn't create the sea,
fellow men, I swear it,
nor the spring tide nor the typhoon
I did not create either you or your earth,
help me, if that's your wish, help me to land.
But we just sat there, keeping
our pipes alight
and heard him howl, out there, on his vessel.

THE SMALL FIRE

And when we had finished off the earth
we put down poison for the sky. It
descended and ate, and the sun, overcome
by nausea, vomited into our eyes.
The winds writhed and, breath by breath, expired; great
it was, that day when the sky came down
and our knives played with it (—except
that no new day would come
and we by a small fire now, in darkness—)

AS FOR THIS COUNTRY

As for this country, here is no place to put down
a foundation stone for the time to come. This is no place
for more than a cold being there, excluded
monosyllabic and overwrought. When your bone rambles

< 497 >

ohne Vertrag, der Bruder ohne Berechnung? Wer hat
seinen Traum nicht zertrampelt oder verkauft, seine Sprache
nicht abgestimmt auf jedermanns Vorschrift und Vorteil?
Wer hat seinen Kopf nicht eingezogen, wer schleicht nicht
mit halber Sonne unter dem Hut in sein Loch
wo die Ohnmacht Staub ansetzt und die Liebe,
ein Haustier, sich ausschläft. Wo ist ein Mensch
der Handschellen weder trägt noch anlegt, wo ist
der Ort, für die Zeit die kommt, einen Grundstein zu setzen?

Hier bleibst du stehn und lässt dir nicht sagen: verschwinde.

DER TAG WIRD KOMMEN

Und der Tag nach der nächsten Friedensfeier—wird er kommen
    mit einer Taube oder mit einem Schlagring
Und der Tag danach—wird er eintreffen mit einem Spielzeug
    oder wird sich die Hoffnung wieder vertreten lassen
    durch ein Leninzitat
Und der Tag danach—wird er herbeigeschafft werden an den
    Haaren
    in einem Ministersessel, mit einer ganz neuen Be-
    fehlsgewalt
Und der Tag darauf—wird er uns nur den Schlaf kosten, oder
    den Kopf
Und der Tag darauf—wird er sich entschuldigen lassen
    durch ein mittleres Blutbad
Und der Tag darauf—wird er überhaupt erscheinen wollen
    in unserm Neubauviertel, auf unserm Bildschirm
Und der Tag danach, und der Tag nach diesem

Und der Tag nach wievielen Tagen—wird er wieder nur
    GEDENKTAG heissen
    ein Totensonntag sein, ein Papierkrieg, eine Verordnung
Und der letzte Tag—wird er wieder nur eine Atrappe der
    Zukunft sein
    oder endlich Auskunft geben über die Liebe
Und der Tag nach dem letzten Tag—wird er der Tag sein
    an dem wir gelebt und geatmet hätten?

inside you, looking for life, and breaks out, hungry
for joy and future, but then returns
restless, world-sore, close to death—where's the companion
without a contract, the brother without calculation? Who hasn't
stamped on his dream or sold it, tuned his speech
to everyone's prescription and advantage?
Who hasn't retracted his head, who does not creep
with half the sun under his hat into the hole
where powerlessness collects dust and love,
a domestic animal, sleeps? Where's the man or woman
who neither wears nor applies handcuffs, where is
the place to put down a foundation stone for the time to come?

Here you stay put, ignoring the order: Get out!

THE DAY WILL COME

And the day after the next peace celebration—will it come with
a dove or with a knuckle duster
And the day after that—will it arrive with a toy or will hope
once again have itself represented by a Lenin quotation
And the day after that—will it be dragged by the hair on to a
minister's chair, with powers altogether new
And the day after that—will it cost us only our sleep or our
heads
And the day after that—will it excuse itself with a moderate
bloodbath
And the day after that—will it want to come at all to our new
building estate, on to our screens
And the day after that, and the day after that one

And the day after how many days—will it be called only RE-
MEMBRANCE DAY once again, will it be a Sunday of the
dead, a paper war, a proclamation
And the last day—will it be nothing more than a trap for the
future again or at last give us information about love
And the day after the last day—will it be the day on which we
ought to have lived and breathed?

< 499 >

ODYSSEUS

Was bleibt mir zu tun
und wo kann ich hingehn
da doch alles feststeht im Buch des Dichters
das mich überliefert mit meinen Göttern
Häusern, Inseln, Frauen, Adressen.

Bleibt mir zu leben nur ein Echo
wo mein Zuhaus ist: zwischen den Zeilen
stumm und prosaisch
im undeutbaren Rest, im Schweigen
wo sich, Worte reissend, entzieht
der Raubvogel Leben
mein Name, mein Irrweg.

Kann ich nocheinmal anfangen? Untertauchen
hinter dem Rücken des Dichters
mit meinem Namen
ich, Odysseus, unauffindbar
in Büchern, tatenlos ruhmlos schweigend
von Vergleichen nicht mehr getroffen
wirklich zuletzt
und im Fleisch, vorhanden?

Meine Geschichte dauert nur in der Asche.
Wenn vergangen sind Versmass und Götter
endlich vergessen sind die Strophen des Alten
wird auch mein Name frei, und ich
mach mich auf die Socken, ich such mir
eine Heimstatt, gottlos, spurlos
nicht länger Stoff für eine Ballade.

Nicht länger Stoff für irgendetwas
ausser mir selber. Keine Krone
kein Ithaka, und keine Heimkehr
in ein rechtmässiges Bett. Vergänglich

<   500   >

ODYSSEUS

What remains for me to do
and where can I go
when all's been set down in the poet's book
that hands me down with my gods
houses, islands, women, addresses.

Nothing's left to be lived but an echo
where I'm at home: between the lines
dumb and prosaic
in the indecipherable gap, in the silence
where, tearing at words, the bird
of prey life retreats,
my name, my wanderings.

Can I start again? Dive down
behind the poet's back
with my name,
I, Odysseus, not to be found
in books, deedless, fameless, silent,
beyond the reach of comparisons
really, at last,
in the flesh, existing?

My story endures only in ashes.
When metre and gods are gone,
forgotten at last the old man's lines
my name will be free, and I
will be on my way, I'll look
for a homestead, godless, untraced,
no longer stuff for a ballad.

No longer stuff for anything
except myself. No crown,
no Ithaca, and no homecoming
to a lawful bed. Perishable,

< 501 >

ein vom Tod geschüttelter Knochen
Glück oder Unglück
arm, reich, rechtlos
schüttle ich ab, ich schüttle alles ab
und schlag mich durch ins sterbliche Licht
und komme, zu leben!

< 502 >

a bone shaken by death,
fortune or misfortune
poor, rich, without rights
I shake it off, shake everything off
and soldier on into the mortal light
and arrive, to live!

1974: Wen es angeht

< 503 >

HEINZ CZECHOWSKI:

Geboren 1935 in Dresden. Er ist von seiner Ausbildung her Konstruktionszeichner und arbeitete in diesem Beruf, bevor er sich ausschließlich dem Schreiben widmete. Von 1958 bis 1961 studierte er Literatur in Leipzig, wurde dann Verlagslektor in Halle, wo er heute noch lebt. Er veröffentlichte drei Gedichtbände; *Wasserfahrt* (1967), *Nachmittag eines Liebespaars* und *Gedichte, Schafe und Sterne* (1974). *Spruch und Widerspruch*, eine Essaysammlung, erschien 1974.

LIEBESGESPRÄCH

Vor dem Fabriktor stehn sie in der Sonne.
Der Vorstadtnachmittag ist durchkräht von Hähnen.
Im blauen Kittel: sie. Er: auf dem Moped, seine Hände
Sind in den Taschen tief vergraben.
Im Hofe hinten stehn die Späher: schwarze Weiber.
Ich hör die Zungen klirren:
Wie sie auf die Umarmung warten: nacktes Fleisch,
In das sie ihre Küchenmesser stossen . . .
Sie aber steht im blauen Kittel in der Sonne.
Er auf dem Moped hat die Hände tief vergraben.
Der Vorstadtnachmittag ist durchkräht von Hähnen.

< 504 >

HEINZ CZECHOWSKI:

Born in Dresden in 1935. By training he is a draftsman, and worked
as such before becoming a professional writer. From 1958 to 1961 he
studied literature in Leipzig, then became a publisher's reader in
Halle, where he still lives. He has published three books of poems,
Nachmittag eines Liebespaares (1962), *Wasserfahrt* (1967) and *Schafe
une Sterne* (1974). *Spruch und Widerspruch*, a collection of essays,
appeared in 1974.

LOVE TALK

In front of the factory gate they stand in the sun.
Suburban noon is full of the crowing of cocks.
In a blue overall, she. He, on his *moped*, his hands
Are buried deep in his pockets.
In the yard behind them, the spies, women in black.
I hear their tongues tinkle.
How they wait for the embrace: naked flesh
into which they thrust their kitchen knives . . .
But she stands there, sunlit, in her blue overall.
He on the *moped* deeply has buried his hands.
Suburban noon is full of the crowing of cocks.

1970: *Lyrik der DDR*

< 505 >

WOLF BIERMANN:

Geboren 1936 in Hamburg. Sein Vater, der in Ausschwitz starb, war Kommunist. 1953 ging Biermann in die DDR, und studierte Philosophie, Wirtschaftswissenschaften und Mathematik in Ost-Berlin, Geboren 1936 in Hamburg. Sein Vater, der in Ausschwitz starb, war Kommunist. 1953 ging Biermann in die DDR, und studierte Philosophie, Wirtschaftswissenschaften und Mathematik in Ost-Berlin, bevor er mit Brecht beim Berliner Ensemble zusammenarbeitete. Er wurde durch den Vortrag seiner satirischen Lieder und Balladen zu eigener Musik bekannt, bekam aber 1962 Auftrittsverbot. Im Jahr darauf wurde das Verbot aufgehoben, und 1964 besuchte Biermann West-Deutschland, wo er sich ein großes Publikum eroberte. 1965 wurde das Verbot wieder in Kraft gesetzt, und Biermann trat seither weder in der DDR auf, noch veröffentlichte er dort, obwohl er weiterhin in Ost-Berlin lebt. Seine Bücher: *Die Drahtharfe* (1965), eine Sammlung von Balladen, Liedern und Gedichten; *Mit Marx- und Engelszungen* (1968); *Deutschland, Ein Wintermärchen* (1972), *Für meine Genossen* (1972), und ein Stück, *Der Dra-Dra* (1970). Er nahm viele seiner Lieder und Balladen auf Schallplatten auf. Ein Übersetzung seines ersten Gedichtbandes wurde 1968 in Amerika veröffentlicht *(Glass Harp);* eine Auswahl späterer Gedichte erschien in der Anthologie *East German Poetry*.

BRECHT, DEINE NACHGEBORENEN

"Ihr, die ihr auftauchen werdet aus der Flut
In der wir untergegangen sind . . ."

Auf die sich deine Hoffnung gründete
Mit deinen Hoffnungen gehn sie zugrunde
Die es einmal besser machen sollten
Machen die Sache anderer Leute immer besser
Und haben sich in den finsteren Zeiten
Gemütlich eingerichtet mit deinem Gedicht
Die mit dem Spalt zwischen den Augen
Die mit verrammelten Ohren
Die mit der genagelten Zunge

    Brecht, deine Nachgeborenen
    Von Zeit zu Zeit suchen sie
        mich
           heim

WOLF BIERMANN:

Born in Hamburg in 1936. His father was a Communist and died in Auschwitz. In 1953 Biermann went to East Germany, studied philosophy, economics, and mathematics in East Berlin before working with Brecht at the Berliner Ensemble. He became popular as a performer of his satirical songs and ballads, sung to his own music, but he was forbidden to perform them in 1962. In the following year the prohibition was revoked, and in 1964 Biermann visited West Germany, acquiring a large following there. In 1965 the prohibition was re-imposed, and Biermann has neither performed nor published in East Germany since that year, though he continues to live in East Berlin. His books are *Die Drahtharfe* (1965), a collection of ballads, songs, and poems; *Mit Marx- und Engelszungen* (1968), *Deutschland. Ein Wintermärchen* (1972), and *Für meine Genossen* (1972), as well as the play *Der Dra-Dra* (1970). He has also recorded many of his songs and ballads. A translation of his first book of poems was published in America in 1968 *(Wire Harp),* and a selection of later poems appeared in the anthology *East German Poetry*.

BRECHT, YOUR POSTERITY

"You that will emerge from the deluge
In which we drowned . . ."—BRECHT,
To Posterity

Those on whom you founded your hope
With the same hopes as yours they founder
Those who one day were to do better than you
Make the others' cause look better and better
And in those bleak times have settled down
Smugly and snugly to live with your poems
Those with a furrow between the eyes
Those with their ears blocked
Those with their tongues nailed down

> Brecht, your posterity
> From time to time they
> punish
> me.

Broken bits, dreams laid out in front of me
Rubble, expectations piled up in front of me

< 507 >

Scherben, vor mich hingebreitete Träume
Trümmer, vor mir aufgetürmte Erwartungen
Abfall früher Leidenschaften tischen sie mir auf
Schale Reste früheren Zorns schenken sie mir ein
Streun mir aufs Haupt früherer Feuer Asche
Karger Nachlass hängt mir da gegenüber im Sessel
Gebrannt mit den Stempeln der Bürokratie
In die Daumenschrauben eingespannt der Privilegien
Zerkaut und ausgespuckt von der politischen Polizei

    Brecht, deine Nachgeborenen
     Von Zeit zu Zeit suchen sie
          mich
            heim

Und sind wie blind von der Finsternis um sie
Und sind wie taub von dem Schweigen um sie
Und sind wie stumm vom täglichen Siegesschrei
Immer noch feinere Leiden zufügen und
Aushalten, das haben sie gelernt und
Haben den Boden des grossen Topfes noch
Lange nicht erreicht, an Bitternissen
Das bodenlose Angebot an fettiger Armut
Noch lange nicht ausgekostet

    Brecht, deine Nachgeborenen
     Von Zeit zu Zeit suchen sie
          mich
            heim

Auch romantisches Strandgut schwemmt bei mir an
Metapherntriefendes Treibholz der Revolution
Auf Messingsschildern noch immer die grossen Namen
Des 19. Jahrhunderts. Am Wrack noch ahnt man
Das Schiff. Die gesunkenen Planken berichten
Von der abgesoffenen Mannschaft. Der verrottete Hanf
Faselt noch immer von schiffebezwingenden Tauen
Ja, aufgetaucht sind sie aus der Flut, in der ihr
Untergegangen seid und sehn nun kein Land

Refuse of earlier passions they dish up for me
Stale leftovers of earlier anger they pour out for me
Strew on my head the ashes of earlier fires
Sparse remains hang on that armchair facing me
Branded with the stamp of bureaucracy
Clamped into the thumb-screws of privileges
Chewed up and spat out by the political police

> Brecht, your posterity
> From time to time they
>   punish
>   me.

And are as though blind with the darkness around them
And are as though deaf with the silence around them
And are as though dumb with the daily shouts of victory
To inflict ever more subtle pains and
Endure, that's what they have learnt and
Are far still from having reached the
Bottom of the great pot of bitterness
Are far from having eaten up
The bottomless supplies of greasy poverty

> Brecht, your posterity
> From time to time they
>   punish
>   me.

Romantic flotsam too is washed up for me
Metaphor-dripping driftwood of the revolution
On brass plates as ever the great names
Of the 19th century. From the wreckage even one
Can construe the ship. The submerged planks tell
Of the drowned crew. The rotten hemp
Still blathers about the ship-taming ropes
Yes, they've emerged from the deluge in which
You went down and now can see no land

< 509 >

Brecht, deine Nachgeborenen
Von Zeit zu Zeit suchen sie
    mich
      heim

Auch das, Meister, sind—und in Prosa—deine
Nachgeborenen: nachgestorbene Vorgestorbene
Voller Nachsicht nur mit sich selber
Öfter noch als die Schuhe die Haltung wechselnd
Stimmt: ihre Stimme ist nicht mehr heiser
—sie haben ja nichts mehr zu sagen
Nicht mehr verzerrt sind ihre Züge, stimmt:
Denn gesichtslos sind sie geworden. Geworden
Ist endlich der Mensch dem Wolfe ein Wolf

    Brecht, deine Nachgeborenen
    Von Zeit zu Zeit suchen diese
        mich
          heim

Gehn dann endlich die Gäste, betrunken von der irreführenden
Wahrheit meiner Balladen, entzündet auch an der falschen
    Logik
Meiner Gedichte, gehn sie, bewaffnet mit Zuversicht, dann

Bleibe ich zurück: Asche meiner Feuer. Dann
Stehe ich da: ausgeplündertes Arsenal. Und
Ausgeknockt hänge ich in den Saiten meiner Gitarre

Und habe keine Stimme mehr und kein Gesicht
Und bin wie taub vom Reden und wie blind vom Hinsehn
Und fürchte mich vor meiner Furcht und bin

    Brecht, dein Nachgeborener
    Von Zeit zu Zeit suche ich
        mich
          heim

< 510 >

Brecht, your posterity
From time to time they
　　　punish
　　　　　me.

Those too, master, are—and in prose—your
Posterity: post-deceased pre-deceased people
Full of indulgence only for themselves
Changing convictions more often than their shoes
That's right: their voices are no longer hoarse
—since they have nothing more to say
Their features are no longer distorted, right:
For they have grown faceless. At last
Man has become to Wolf a wolf

Brecht, your posterity
From time to time they
　　　punish
　　　　　me

If finally then the guests, drunk with the misleading
Truth of my ballads, inflamed also by the false logic
Of my poems, if they go, armed with confidence, then

I stay behind: ash of my fires. Then
I stand there: a raided arsenal. And
Knocked out I hang in the strings of my guitar.

And I have no voice any more and no face
And am as though deaf with speaking and blind with looking
And am afraid of my fear and am

Brecht, your posterity
From time to time they
　　　punish
　　　　　me

1972: *Für meine Genossen*

< 511 >

KURT BARTSCH:

Geboren 1937 in Berlin; lebt z.Zt. in Ost-Berlin. Arbeitete als Telefonist, Angestellter und Lastwagenbeifahrer, bevor er in Leipzig Literatur studierte. Veröffentlichungen: *Zugluft*, Gedichte (1968), in der DDR, *Poesiealbum 13* (1968) und *Die Lachmaschine* (Gedichte, Lieder und ein Prosafragment) in West-Berlin (1971). Seine überwiegend in Epigrammform gehaltene Lyrik ist in der zweisprachigen Anthologie *East German Poetry* vertreten.

BRECHTS TOD

die graue jacke, dächer, die zigarre,
der rauch fällt in den schnee, zerbricht,
ein schwarzer punkt, leer eine fahnenstange,
nur schnee weht, eine amsel in der luft,
wind springt den rauch an, auch die dächer,
verwischt die amsel, eine schöne spur
und reisst zwei fingern die zigarre aus;
im schnee die rauchfahne weht halbmast.

DER HUMANIST

Das Haus brannte hernieder. Und was
Machte der Humanist?
Er nahm seinen Finger und schrieb
In die kalte Asche: Nie wieder.
Ach, hätte er wenigstens sein Wasser
Abgeschlagen an dem brennenden Haus.

ELAN

Als man endlich auch darüber sprach
Wie schwierig es sein würde
Das Ziel zu erreichen
Spuckten einige in die Hände
Und machten es sich
In den Startlöchern bequem.

< 512 >

KURT BARTSCH:

Born in 1937 in Berlin, presently living in East Berlin. Worked as a
telephone operator, clerk, and truck driver's mate before studying literature in Leipzig. Published *Zugluft,* poems (1968) in East Germany,
as well as *Poesiealbum 13* (1968) and *Die Lachmaschine* (poems,
songs and a prose fragment) in West Berlin (1971). His manly epigrammatic verse is represented in the bilingual anthology *East German
Poetry*.

THE DEATH OF BRECHT

the old gray jacket, roofs, and the cigar,
the smoke falls onto snow, and breaks,
a dot of blackness, bare, a flagpole stands,
nothing but snow blows, a blackbird in the air,
wind pounces on the smoke, and on the roofs,
blots out the blackbird, delicate tracery,
·tears from between two fingers the cigar:
in snow the smoke flag blows at halfmast.

1968: *Saison für Lyrik*

THE HUMANIST

The house burned down. And what
Did the humanist do?
He took his fingers and wrote
Into the cold ash: Never again.
Oh, if at least he had relieved
Himself against the burning house.

VERVE

When at last it came to talking
About how hard it would be
To reach the finishing post
Some spat on their hands
And made themselves
Comfortable in the start-holes.

1971: *Tintenfisch*

< 513 >

NICOLAS BORN:

Geboren 1937 in Duisburg. Er arbeitete in vielen verschiedenen man-
uellen und kirchlichen Berufen, bevor er sich ausschließlich dem
Schreiben widmete. Von seiner Ausbildung her ist er Naturwis-
senschaftler. Er lebte in Essen und West-Berlin. Sein Roman *Der
zweite Tag* erschien 1965. Seine Gedichtbände: *Marktlage* (1967), *Wo
mir der Kopf steht* (1970) und *Das Auge des Entdeckers* (1972). Er
veröffentlichte auch ein Kinderbuch und übersetzte amerikanische
Lyrik. 1972 und 1973 lebte er als Stipendiat in der Villa Massimo in
Rom.

DREI WÜNSCHE

Sind Tatsachen nicht quälend und langweilig?
Ist es nicht besser drei Wünsche zu haben
unter der Bedingung dass sie allen erfüllt werden?
Ich wünsche ein Leben ohne grosse Pausen
in denen die Wände nach Projectilen abgesucht werden
ein Leben das nicht heruntergeblättert wird von Kassierern.
Ich wünsche Briefe zu schreiben in denen ich ganz enthalten
        bin—
wie weit würde ich herumkommen ohne Gewichtsverlust.
Ich wünsche ein Buch in das ihr alle vorn hineingehen und hin-
        ten herauskommen könnt.
Und ich möchte nicht vergessen dass es schöner ist
dich zu lieben als dich nicht zu lieben

DAS VERSCHWINDEN ALLER
IM TOD EINES EINZELNEN

Mache ich mich mit zu grosser Hand?
lebe ich sehr aus der überfüllten Luft
und brauche ich zu viele andere
und schneide ich das Wort ab dem
        der es braucht
und lasse ich es hell und dunkel werden
        in die eigene Tasche?
Ich weiss nicht wie weit die Zukunft
        mir voraus ist
und wie weit ich mir voraus bin.

< 514 >

NICOLAS BORN:

Born in 1937 in Duisburg, he worked in a variety of manual and clerical jobs before becoming a professional writer. By training he is a scientist. He has lived in Essen and in West Berlin. His novel, *Der zweite Tag*, appeared in 1965. His books of poems are *Marktlage* (1967), *Wo mir der Kopf steht* (1970), and *Das Auge des Entdeckers* (1972). He has also published a children's book and translated American poetry. In 1972 and 1973 he held a fellowship at the Villa Massimo in Rome.

THREE WISHES

Facts, are they not painful and boring?
Isn't it better to have three wishes
with the proviso that they will be fulfilled for all?
I wish a life without long intervals
in which the walls are searched for bullets
a life that isn't torn off sheet after sheet by cashiers.
I wish to write letters that contain the whole of me—
how far I should get around without losing weight.
I wish a book which all of you can enter at the front and leave
    at the back.
And I do not wish to forget that it's more pleasant
to love you than not to love you

THE VANISHING OF ALL IN THE DEATH OF ONE

Do I lay it on too thick?
do I live too much on the overcrowded air
and do I need too many others
and do I cut short the words of the man
    who needs them
and do I let it grow light and dark
    to fill my own pocket?
I don't know how far the future
    is ahead of me
and how far ahead I am of myself.
I stand in earth and whenever I take off
    I soon have a crash landing.

< 515 >

Ich stehe in der Erde und wann immer ich abhebe
schlage ich hart wieder auf.
Hier ist mein Fuss der seine eigene
Wirklichkeit hat und seine eigene
Ewigkeit
Fuss du wirst mich verlieren
du wirst bekümmert auftreten
und dann stehenbleiben wie ein Schuh.
Gestern hatten wir eine Tagesschau voll
von Toten
und ein Amerikanisch/Deutsch-Wörterbuch lag
aufgeschlagen auf dem Tisch
und ich lag zugeklappt auf der Couch
während ein verbrecherischer Kommentar
mich segnete
und meine Verbrecherohren spitzte.
Sie packten die Toten bei den Fussgelenken
und schleiften sie zu einem Sammelplatz
die Befehle hatten die Körper verlassen
und es ging auf dreiundzwanzig Uhr.
Ich trank Kaffee und war noch derselbe
ich war nicht mehr derselbe.
Ja vorgestern muss ich auf dir gelegen haben
als jeder andere persönlich starb
aus der Welt fiel durch die Welt hindurch
mit nur noch einem Gefühl einem Wort
einem ganz gewöhnlichen Bild
das sich auflöste
und mit uns allen verschwand.

NATURGEDICHT

Welcher Schmerz zu fliessen
welche Kälte mit dem Feind allein zu sein
welch eine Aufgabe Stickstoff in die Wälder zu blasen!
Das stille Wirken des Blattgrüns im grünen Salat
das lärmende Wirken des grünen Salats in uns.

<   516   >

Here is my foot that has
its own reality and its own
      eternity

Foot you will lose me
you will come down dejectedly
      and be left behind like a shoe.
Yesterday we had a news full
      of dead
and an American-German dictionary lay
      open on the table
and I lay slammed shut on the couch
while a criminal commentary
      blessed me
and pricked my criminal's ears.
They grabbed the dead by their ankles
      and dragged them to a collection point
orders had abandoned their bodies
      and the time was nearly twenty-three hours.
I drank coffee and was still the same person
      I was no longer the same.
Yes the day before yesterday I must have lain on top of you
when everyone else was personally dying
      falling out of the world through the world
with only one feeling left only one word
a quite ordinary image
      that dissolved
and vanished taking us all.

                        1972: *Das Auge des Entdeckers*

NATURE POEM

What a pain to flow
what coldness to be alone with one's enemy
what an assignment to blow nitrogen into woods!
      The quiet working of chlorophyl in the green salad
      the noisy working of green salad inside us.

<   517   >

Ist der Löwenzahn aus unserem Leben verschwunden
 der Huflattich die Grasharfe?
Was verspricht das angelegte Ohr des Pferdes
was bedeuten die Schmerzen in den Armen der Putzfrau
 deren Welt seit zwanzig Jahren im Eimer liegt?
Warum ist die Nelke eine so dumme Blume
 so zackig gehäkelt
und warum fang ich an zu tropfen wenn ich Tulpen sehe?
Was sagt mir die Schwalbe im Tiefflug?
Wer beisst wenn der Hund des Nachbarn knurrt
 er oder ich oder der Nachbar?
Was bedeutet es wenn ich von einem Unbekannten
 einen Tip bekomme und eilig das Haus verlasse?
Wenn die Brauen meines Vaters über Nacht zusammenwachsen
und die Gesichtsnarbe des Abonnentenwerbers rot wird
wenn der Taxifahrer so lange in den Spiegel schaut
 bis der Fahrgast verdächtig ist
und der Dachdecker dem Lehrling einen Tritt geben will
 doch zu spät bemerkt dass er ins Leere tritt
wenn die Teenager im Teenagerclub die Augen verdrehen
 nach der fünften Cola
wenn der Starfighter-Pilot in der Flugpause
 einen langen Roman anfängt
wenn der Grossaktionär in der Jägersuppe
 einen Pferdefuss findet
und der Kassierer der Commerzbank
 mit dem Haushaltsgeld seiner Frau verschwindet
 nachdem er ''Viva Zapata'' gesehen hat?
Die Ruhe vor dem Sturm
der Dorn im Auge
der Balken im Zimmermann
die heissve Liebe mit Siebzehn
die Schwurhand des Vermögensverwalters
Ebbe und Flut
Mini und Maxi
und der Beamte auf dem Sozialamt

Have dandelions disappeared from our lives
  have coltsfoot and meadowsweet?
What does a horse's turned back ear promise
what is the meaning of the ache in the charwoman's arms
  whose world for twenty years has poured down the drain?
Why is the carnation such a stupid flower
  so jaggedly crocheted
and why do I start to drip when I see tulips?
What does the swallow tell me when flying low?
Who bites when the neighbor's dog growls
  the dog or I or the neighbor?
What does it mean when a stranger slips me a tip
  and I hurriedly leave the house?
When my father's eyebrows join up overnight
and the scar on the face of the subscription salesman turns red
when the taxi driver looks so long in his mirror
  that his client grows suspect
and the rooftiler wants to give his apprentice a kick
  but notices too late that he's stepping into the void
when teenagers in the teenager's club roll their eyes
  after their fifth coca-cola
when the starfighter pilot between flights
  starts a long novel
when the tycoon finds a horse's foot
  in his game soup
and the teller at the commercial bank
  does a flit with his wife's housekeeping money
  after seeing "Viva Zapata"?
The hush before a storm
the thorn in the flesh
the beam in the carpenter
ardent love at seventeen
the oath hand of the trustee
ebb and flood
mini and maxi
and the clerk at the labour exchange

< 519 >

der mit Handtuch und Seife das Büro verlässt
    wenn dreissig Leute warten?
Das Montagsauto der umgekippte See
die ungewöhnliche Art in der sich in der Hand
    des Arbeitnehmers Vermögen bildet
die da oben
die da unten
die Talsohle
die Gratwanderung?

Wenn ich dich liebe schneit es auf der Erde
und wenn du mich mit meinem besten Freund verlässt
    dann ist es Frühling
und wenn du völlig mittellos zurückkehrst
    ist es Herbst.
Wenn mir keiner etwas umsonst gibt
    habe ich dann Geld?
Und welchen Sinn hat es als Toter ein Buch über Archäologie
    unterm Kopfkissen zu haben?
Wenn es wahr ist dass Kriege sein müssen
    ist es dann noch wichtig daran teilzunehmen?
Ist es realistisch wenn Mann und Frau
    nach der Hochzeit beschliessen zusammenzuleben?
Wenn sie ihm ein Jahr später ihre Aussteuer
an den Kopf wirft und er ihr
    seinen Wortschatz
und wenn der Fensterputzer oben am IBM-Hochhaus
in den Bann der Lochkarten gerät
aber doch seinem Selbsterhaltungstrieb folgt
    und im letzten Augenblick abspringt?
Was bedeutet es dass ich Gedichte mache
    und dass du lauter Geschichten machst
dass du eine Frau bist und ich beides?

who leaves his office with towel and soap
    when thirty people are waiting?
The Monday motor car the inverted lake
the uncommon way in which wealth accumulates
    in the employer's hand
those up there
those down there
the foot of the valley
the excursion over the ridge?
When I love you it snows on earth
and when you leave me for my best friend
    it is spring
and when you come back without a penny
    it is autumn.
When no one will give me anything for nothing
    do I have any money?
And what is the point of a dead man's keeping a book
    on archeology under his pillow?
If it's true that there have to be wars
is it still important to take part in them?
Is it realistic if a man and a woman
    decide after marrying to live together?
If a year later she uses
    her dowry as a weapon and he
    the whole of his vocabulary
and if the window-cleaner up on the IBM skyscraper
succumbs to the lure of perforated cards
yet still obeys his instinct of self-preservation
    and at the last moment jumps off?
What does it mean that I make poems
    and that you give rise to stories
that you are a woman and I am both?

1972: *Das Auge des Entdeckers*

< 521 >

KITO LORENC:

Geboren 1938 in Schleife in Lausitz. Lorenc ist serbischer Abstammung. Er studierte slawische Sprachen und arbeitete nach 1961 am Institut für Serbische Forschung in Bautzen. Viele seiner Gedichte waren ursprünglich in Serbisch geschrieben, einer slawischen Sprache, die von einer kleinen ethnischen Gruppe in Ost-Deutschland gesprochen wird. Er war auch in einer serbischen Theatergruppe tätig. Wie Wulf Kirsten ist auch Lorenc ein bewußt regional orientierter Lyriker. Sein erster Gedichtband *Struga* (1967) enthielt deutsche und serbische Texte. Seine spätere Sammlung *Flurbereinigung* (1973) richtet sich an eine größere und deutschsprachige Leserschaft.

DAS WORT

Das Wort eine Nuss
das Wort eine eiserne Nuss
zwischen den Zähnen
Und die tiefen, ertrunkenen Brunnen
des Schweigens

Es gab, sagt man,
eine seidige Sprache, weiss
wie des Morgens Haut, juchten- und saffianduftend
Es gab angeblich
Gespräche, die noch verliefen
im Sande wie Kinderspiel
Und Abende wie Pfauen sollen gewesen sein
mit tausend beredten Blicken
und Nachtmären atmend Mohnblüten
vordem

Ich, gekrümmt eine Sichel,
die Lippen voll Spinnweb, hör
nur fallen das Laub. Das
gibt einen Laut, einsilbig
auf dem Wasser. Darauf
schreib ich, und ein Gähnen
geht um in den Windbergen der Lüge

< 522 >

KITO LORENC:

Born in 1938 in Schleife, Lausitz, of Sorbian descent. He studied
Slavic languages, and after 1961 worked at the Institute for Sorbian
Research at Bautzen. Many of his poems were originally written in
Sorbian, a Slavic language spoken by a small ethnic group in East
Germany. He has also been active in a Sorbian theater group. Like
Wulf Kirsten, Lorenc is a deliberately regional poet. His first book of
poems, *Struga* (1967), contained German and Sorbic texts. His later
collection, *Flurbereinigung* (1973), is intended for a larger, German-
speaking readership.

THE WORD

The word a nut
the word an iron nut
between the teeth
And the deep, drowned wells
of silence

There was, they say,
a silken language, white
as the skin of morning, Russian leather, morocco-scented
They say there were
conversations that seeped
into sand like children's games
And evenings like peacocks, they say,
with a thousand eloquent glances
and nightmares breathing poppies
at one time

I, a sickle curved,
my lips full of cobwebs, only
hear leaves fall. That
yields a sound, monosyllabic
on water. On that
I write, and a yawn
spreads in the windyards of lies

< 523 >

Mach doch Holz aus der Asche, nur
zerhack nicht die Fiedel
Heiz doch dein Zimmer mit dem Mond, nur
hetz nicht den Hund auf ihn

Da fliehen die Frösche, durchlöchert,
das Stoppelfeld
Zurück stürzen die Krebse
aus ihrem Fledermausflug
Nicht mehr zittern
die Herzen der Steine
Dem Dunkel darin sie stak
entfällt die Axt

So ist es gut, ruhig
treiben die Schmetterlinge des Winters,
sinkt in meinen Adern
das Wasser
Die Erde, aus verdorrter Hülle
braunrunzlich eine Nuss, rollt
unter den Hirtenstern
Die Erde ein Wort
mit den gebenedeiten Hemisphären des Hirns
in der Schale, rauh
und diesem kostbaren Nussgeschmack
der sich nun nicht mehr
vergisst

< 524 >

Make words, then, out of ashes, only
don't chop up the fiddle
Heat your room with the moon, then, only
don't set the dog at the moon

Then the frogs flee, riddled,
the stubble-field
Back the crayfish hurtle
from their bat flight
No longer tremble
the hearts of stones
From the darkness in which it stuck
the axe drops

That's how it should be, calmly
drift winter's butterflies,
in my arteries
water ebbs
The earth out of its parched wrapping
with brown wrinkles a nut, rolls
under the shepherd's star
The earth a word
with the brain's blessed hemispheres
in its shell, rough
and this delicious taste of nuts
that now becomes
unforgettable

1972: *Flurbereinigung*

< 525 >

VOLKER BRAUN:

Geboren 1939 in Dresden. Er arbeitete als Drucker, Bauunternehmer und Machinenfacharbeiter. Nach einem Philosophiestudium in Leipzig arbeitete er als Assistent beim Berliner Ensemble und wurde 1967 freier Schriftsteller. In West-Deutschland, wo 1966 sein Gedichtband *Vorläufiges* und 1967 *Provokation für mich* erschienen, wurde viel von ihm veröffentlicht. Spätere Sammlungen: *Wir und nicht sie* (1970), die Auswahl *Gedichte* (1972), und *Gegen die symmetrische Welt* (1974). Seine Prosawerke umfassen einen Roman, *Das ungezwungene Leben Kasts* (1972), und das Stück *Die Kipper* (1972). Seine Lyrik ist in der zweisprachigen Anthologie *East German Poetry* vertreten.

LANDWÜST

Natur, wie zieht mich, mit grüner Schlinge
Das Blühen an, das Lodern
Des Winds auf den kahlen Kuppen
Und die harten halten mich, die verbohrten
Kirschbäume, auf den Schiefern!

Aber ich geh
In die Wälder, wo sie am dichtesten sind
Auf die gelassene Erde
Und seh sie gedreht und gewendet
Von Hand, und der Hang menschlich
Bestanden mit grüner Erfahrung.
Noch unter dem Dorf
Unter Brachdisteln und Fladern verschollen
Spür ich ein Dorf
Meiner Vorvoreltern Schlag
Und aufgebrannt der Welt ein Fleck
Zum Leben.

Und der Berg, herzieht der mich: abgerichtet
Für Galgen, Fingerhut
Welch blutiges Rot! Den harten Zügen
Folge ich, in der Gegend herum, Haufen
Leichnamen der geschlachteten Bauern.
Eisern noch
Strahlt der Morgenstern hier. Und ungestalt

< 526 >

VOLKER BRAUN:

Born in 1939 in Dresden. He has worked as a printer, builder, and as a skilled machine worker. After studying philosophy at Leipzig, he worked as an assistant at the Berliner Ensemble, becoming a free-lance writer in 1967. He has been widely published in West Germany where his book of poems *Vorläufiges* appeared in 1966 and *Provokation für mich* in 1967. His later collections are *Wir und nicht sie* (1970), the selection *Gedichte* (1972), and *Gegen die symmetrische Welt* (1974). His prose works include a novel, *Das ungezwungene Leben Kasts* (1972), and the play *Die Kipper* (1972). His poetry is represented in the bilingual anthology *East German Poetry*.

LANDWILD

How with green tendrils, nature, blossoming
Snares me, the flaring up
Of the wind on the bare hilltops
And those hard ones hold me, the cracked
Cherry trees, on the slates!

But I go
Into the woods, where they are thickest
On to composed earth
And see it turned and inverted
By hand, the slope humanly
Planted with green experience.
Under the village even
Under wasteland thistles and sycamores, lost
I sense a village
My forefathers' kind
And branded upon the world a plot
On which to live.

And the mountain, it draws me on: trained
for gallows. Foxglove
What a bloody red: The harsh traits
I follow, around these parts, heaps
Of corpses of the butchered peasants.
Steely even
The morning star shines here. And misshapen

< 527 >

Scheint alles Leben, wild
Und unbetreten die Tage.

Natürlich bleibt nichts.
Nichts bleibt natürlich.
Die Signale wachsen grün, die Weichen
Der Äcker. Ich, der Nachfahr
Lauf über die grauen Entwürfe
Ohne Geduld. Langsam
Steigen die Stallungen herauf
Zu den Burgen der Silos, Traktoren
Traben unter den Peitschenlampen.
Ich geh, in diesem Dorf
Mit zureichendem Grund
Aus mir heraus.

Wirtsberg
Rundblick 360 Grad
Der volle Winkel der Zukunft: gefüllt schon
Ein Streif.

< 528 >

All life seems, wild
And untrodden the days.

Naturally nothing remains.
Nothing remains natural.
The signals grow green, the sidings
Of the fields. I, the descendant
Walk across the gray sketches
Without patience. Slowly
The stable blocks rise up
To the silo castles, tractors
Trot under the whip lights.
In this village I
With adequate grounds
Go out of myself.

Wirtsberg
Perspective 360 degrees
The future's entire angle: one strip
Already filled.

1972: Gedichte

< 529 >

ROLF DIETER BRINKMANN:

Geboren 1940 in Vechta. Vor seiner Ausbildung zum Volksschullehrer arbeitete er von 1959 bis 1962 in einer Buchhandlung in Essen. Nach 1962 lebte er vorwiegend in Köln. 1972/73 lebte er in Rom und Olevano. Er war 1974 visiting poet in Austin, Texas. Im April 1975 wurde Brinkmann nach der Teilnahme am Cambridge Poetry Festival in London von einem Auto getötet. Sein Werk ist stark von amerikanischen Modellen und Einflüssen geprägt. Er übersetzte Gedichte von Frank O'Hara und gab eine zweisprachige Anthologie zeitgenössischer amerikanischer Lyrik heraus. Seine Gedichtbände: *Ohne Neger* (1965), *Was fraglich ist wofür* (1967), *Die Piloten* (1968), *Godzilla* (1968), *Standfotos* (1969), *Gras* (1970), und *Westwärts 1 & 2* (1975). Ein Roman, *Keiner weiß mehr* erschien 1968.

DIE ORANGENSAFTMASCHINE

dreht sich & Es ist gut, dass der Barmann
zuerst auf die nackten Stellen eines
Mädchens schaut, das ein Glas kalten

Tees trinkt. ''Ist hier sehr heiss,
nicht?'' sagt er, eine Frage, die
den Raum etwas dekoriert,

was sonst? Sie hat einen kräftigen
Körper, und als sie den Arm
ausstreckt, das Glas auf

die Glasplatte zurückstellt,
einen schwitzenden, haarigen
Fleck unterm Arm, was den Raum

einen Moment lang verändert, die
Gedanken nicht. Und jeder sieht, dass
ihr's Spass macht, sich zu bewegen

auf diese Art, was den Barmann
auf Trab bringt nach einer langen
Pause, in der nur der Ventilator

< 530 >

ROLF DIETER BRINKMANN:

Born in 1940 in Vechta. He worked in a bookshop in Essen from 1959 to 1962 before training as a primary school teacher. After 1962 he lived mainly in Cologne. In 1972-73 he lived in Rome and Olevano. He was Visiting Poet in Austin, Texas, in 1974. In April, 1975, after taking part in the Cambridge Poetry Festival, Brinkmann was killed by a car in London. His work owes much to American models and influences. He translated poems by Frank O'Hara and edited a bilingual anthology of contemporary American verse. His books of poems are *Ohne Neger* (1965), *Was fraglich ist wofür* (1967), *Die Piloten* (1968), *Godzilla* (1968), *Standfotos* (1969), *Gras* (1970), and *Westwärts 1 & 2* (1975). A novel, *Keiner weiss mehr*, appeared in 1968.

THE ORANGE JUICE MACHINE

revolves & it's good that the barman
first looks at the bare parts of a
girl who is drinking a glass of

cold tea. "Pretty hot in here,
don't you think?" he says, a question
that adds a bit to the room's decoration,

what else? She has a strapping
body, and when she extends her
arm to put her glass back

on the glass top of the bar
a sweaty, hairy patch
under her arm, which for a

moment changes the place, but not
one's thoughts. And all can see that
it gives her pleasure to move

in this way, which sets the barman
off again after a long
pause in which only

< 531 >

zu hören gewesen ist wie
immer, oder meistens, um
diese Tageszeit.

EINEN JENER KLASSISCHEN

schwarzen Tangos in Köln, Ende des
Monats August, da der Sommer schon

ganz verstaubt ist, kurz nach Laden
Schluss aus der offenen Tür einer

dunklen Wirtschaft, die einem
Griechen gehört, hören, ist beinahe

ein Wunder: für einen Moment eine
Überraschung, für einen Moment

Aufatmen, für einen Moment
eine Pause in dieser Strasse,

die niemand liebt und atemlos
macht, beim Hindurchgehen. Ich

schrieb das schnell auf, bevor
der Moment in der verfluchten

dunstigen Abgestorbenheit Kölns
wieder erlosch.

< 532 >

the ventilator was to be heard as
ever, or usually, at
this time of day.

TO HEAR ONE OF THOSE

classical black tangos in Cologne, end of
August, when the summer's already

turned all dusty, soon after the
shops close, from the open door of a

dark restaurant that belongs
to a Greek, is almost a

miracle, for a moment a
surprise, for a moment

a taking of breath, for a moment
an interval in this street

that nobody loves and makes
breathless, walking through. I

quickly jotted that down, before
the moment went out again

in this damned smoggy lifelessness
of Cologne.

1975: *Westwärts 1 & 2*

<   533   >

BERND JENTZSCH:

Geboren 1940 in Plauen. Er wuchs in Chemnitz in Sachsen auf. Nach seiner Schulzeit folgte die Dienstzeit in der ostdeutschen Armee. Von 1960 bis 1965 studierte er Deutsch und Kunstgeschichte in Leipzig und Jena. Seit dieser Zeit arbeitet er für einen Verlag in Ost-Berlin, und gibt daneben eine Reihe lyrischer Pamphlete *Poesiealbum* heraus. 1961 veröffentlichte er einen frühen Gedichtband *Alphabet des Morgens*. Seither erschienen seine Gedichte nur in Zeitschriften und Anthologien. Er gab außerdem verschiede Anthologien heraus und übersetzte aus vielen europäischen Sprachen. Sein Kurzgeschichtenband *Jungfer im Grünen* wurde 1973 in West-Deutschland veröffentlicht. 1973 erschien ein Band mit freien Wiedergaben von Gedichten, *Die Henker des Lebenstraums*.

TEREZÍN, DAS GRÄBERFELD

Für Robert Desnos

Vorausgesetzt,
Das die Belegschaft des Friedhofs Ruhe bewahrt
Und nicht die achtzig Zentimeter fremder Erde
Aufbricht, sondern
Durchschläft und den üppigen Efeu weiterhin
Von unten betrachtet. Vorausgesetzt,
Dass die Opfer, leichtfertig unsterblich geheissen,
Uns nicht, dich nicht, mich nicht,
Beim Wort nehmen und eines beliebigen jüngsten Tages
Vor der Tür stehen, ohne weiteres, und
Sich räuspern. Für den Fall,
Dass die bröckelnden Särge nicht hochsteigen
Mit dem, was Strassennamen liefert, Kränze
Kostet und, wie es heisst, emotional allmählich
Abhanden kommt. Vorausgesetzt also,
Dass die gerühmte Belegschaft des Friedhofs,
Angesichts der makellosen Reisebusse,
Wirkliche Ruhe bewahrt,
Schrei ich:
Den da,
An Händen und Füssen,
Ergreift. Einer,
Und das ist zu viel, einer

< 534 >

BERND JENTZSCH:

Born in 1940 in Plauen, he grew up in Chemnitz, Saxony. After school he served in the East German army. From 1960 to 1965 he studied German and history of art at Leipzig and Jena. Since then he has worked for a publishing house in East Berlin, also editing the series of poetry pamphlets *Poesiealbum*. He published an early book of poems, *Alphabet des Morgens*, in 1961. Since then his poems have appeared only in periodicals and anthologies. He has also edited several anthologies and translated from many European languages. His book of short stories, *Jungfer im Grünen*, was published in West Germany in 1973, *Die Henker des Lebenstraums*, a volume of free renderings of poems, appeared in 1973.

TEREZÍN, THE GRAVES

For Robert Desnos

Provided
that the occupiers of the graveyards keep quiet
And do not break up the eighty centimeters
Of foreign soil, but
Remain asleep and continue to observe the luxuriant
Ivy from below. Provided
That the victims, so glibly called immortal,
Do not take us, take you, take me
At our, your, my word and at some judgment day or other
Stand at the door, just like that, and
Clear their throats. Always assuming
that the crumbling coffins don't rise
With that which provides street names, costs
Wreaths and, so they say, is gradually losing
Its emotional grip. Provided, then,
That the much-praised occupiers of the graveyards,
In view of the flawless coaches,
Keep really quiet,
I cry:
That one,
By his hands and feet
Seize him. One,
And that is too many, one
Stands here and is not

< 535 >

Steht hier und ist nicht
Bewegt, hat alles,
Im allgemeinen, entschieden
Vergessen.

< 536 >

Moved, on the whole,
Decidedly has forgotten
It all.

1970: *Lyrik der DDR*

< 537 >

GUNTRAM VESPER:

Geboren 1941 in Frohberg bei Leipzig. Vesper zog 1957 nach West-Deutschland. Er arbeitete in Fabriken, auf dem Land und im Baugewerbe, bevor er in Göttingen Medizen studierte. Er ist einer der vielen jüngeren Lyriker, die in den sechziger Jahren mit einer kargen, fast epigrammartigen, sozial und politisch engagierten Lyrik auf-tauchten. (Andere Autoren, die sich aus verschiedenen Gründen als weniger leicht übersetzbar erwiesen, sind Arnfried Astel und Volker von Törne). Ein früher Gedichtband *Fahrplan* erschien 1964, gefolgt von einer Sammlung mit dem Titel *Gedichte* im Jahr darauf (1965). 1970 wurde ein Prosaband, *Kriegerdenkmal ganz hinten*, veröf-fentlicht.

NICHTS ZU BEFÜRCHTEN

Eingemietet
bei einer freundlichen Familie
sehe ich dem Winter entgegen
ohne kleinliche Bedenken.
Erfriert eine Hand
bleibt mir die zweite.
Fällt mir das Dach auf den Kopf
werden meine Füsse nicht verderben.
Und wenn unversehens
der nächste Sommer ausbleibt
weil geschehen ist
was kein Baum überblebt nun
so tröstet mich die Aussicht
auf Vergeltung.

BEKANNTE NACHRICHTEN

Während ich esse,
erzählt man
von Krisen.
Wenns nur das ist.
Ich lege verärgert
die Gabel zur Seite:
Der Sprecher meint,
das Wetter werde schlecht.

< 538 >

GUNTRAM VESPER:

Born in 1941 in Frohburg near Leipzig, Vesper moved to West Germany in 1957. He worked in factories, on the land, and in the building trade before studying medicine at Göttingen. One of many younger poets who emerged in the 'sixties with a spare, almost epigrammatic poetry of social and political comment. (Others, who proved less translatable for various reasons, are Arnfried Astel and Volker von Toerne.) An early book of poems was published in 1964 (*Fahrplan*), followed the next year by a collection entitled *Gedichte* (1965). A book of prose, *Kriegerdenkmal ganz hinten*, appeared in 1970.

NOTHING TO FEAR

Lodging
with a friendly family
I await winter
with no petty misgivings.
If one hand freezes
I still have the other.
If the roof falls on my head
my feet will not perish.
And if inadvertently
next summer fails to come
because that has happened
which no tree survives—well
then I'll take cheer at the prospect
of retribution.

FAMILIAR NEWS

While I'm eating
they talk
of crises.
If that's all.
Annoyed I lay down
my fork:
The speaker believes
the weather is turning bad.

< 539 >

Das ist es seit
langem.

ALLTÄGLICHER VORFALL

Dachte ich es
stark zu machen.

Sagte ich
Dreckskommunist.

Trat er mir ins
Gekröse.

Hatte ich ihn
verwechselt.

War er ein
Kirchgänger.

It's been so
for a long time.

EVERYDAY HAPPENING

Wanted to
play it rough.

Said to him
commy swine.

Kicked him
in the guts.

Had picked on
the wrong guy.

Was a
church-goer.

1966: *Aussichten*

< 541 >

PETER HANDKE:

Geboren 1942 in Griffen, Kärnten. Er trat in den sechziger Jahren als der meistdiskutierte deutsche Schriftsteller, Dramatiker, Romanautor, Lyriker und Autobiograph seiner Generation in den Vordergrund. Nach einem Jurastudium lebte er eine Zeitlang in Düsseldorf. Zur Zeit lebt er in Paris. Seine quantitativ große Produktion umfaßt die Stücke *Publikumsbeschimpfung* (1966), *Kaspar* (1968), *Das Mündel will Vormund sein* (1969), *Quodlibet* (1970) und *Der Ritt über den Bodensee* (1970). Seine Stücke und Hörspiele sind in verschiedenen Bänden gesammelt: *Wind und Meer* (4 Hörspiele) erschien 1970. Seine Romane une Erzählungen umfassen: *Die Hornissen* (1966), *Der Hausierer* (1967), *Die Angst des Tormanns beim Elfmeter* (1970), *Der kurze Brief zum langen Abschied* (1971), *Chronik der laufenden Ereignisse* (1971), *Ich bin ein Bewohner des Elfenbeinturms* (1972), *Wunschloses Unglück* (1972) und *Die Unvernünftigen sterben aus* (1973). Seine Gedichte erschienen in drei Sammlungen: *Die Innenwelt der Aussenwelt der Innenwelt* (1969), *Deutsche Gedichte* (1969) und *Als das Wünschen noch geholfen hat* (1974). Eine englische Übersetzung *The Inner World of the Outer World of the Inner World* von Michael Roloff erschien 1974, ebenso eine englische Übersetzung von *Als das Wünschen noch gehofen hat* (*Nonsense and Happiness*, 1976).

DIE VERKEHRTE WELT

Eingeschlafen wache ich auf:
Ich schaue nicht auf die Gegenstände, und die Gegenstände
    schauen mich an;
Ich bewege mich nicht, und der Boden unter meinen Füssen
    bewegt mich;
Ich sehe mich nicht im Spiegel, und ich im Spiegel sehe mich
    an;
Ich spreche nicht Wörter, und Wörter sprechen mich aus;
Ich gehe zum Fenster und werde geöffnet.

Aufgestanden liege ich da:
Ich schlage die Augen nicht auf, sondern die Augen schlagen
    mich auf;
Ich horche nicht auf die Geräusche, sondern die Geräusche hor-
    chen auf mich;
Ich schlucke das Wasser nicht, sondern das Wasser schluckt
    mich;
Ich greife nicht nach den Gegenständen, sondern die

< 542 >

PETER HANDKE:

Born in 1942 in Griffen, Carinthia, he emerged in the 'sixties as the most widely discussed German writer, dramatist, novelist, poet, and autobiographer of his generation. After law studies he lived for a time in Düsseldorf. At present he lives in Paris. His prolific output includes the plays *Publikumsbeschimpfung* (1966), *Kaspar* (1968), *Das Mündel will Vormund sein* (1969), *Quodlibet* (1970), and *Der Ritt über den Bodensee* (1970). His plays and radio plays have been collected in various volumes: *Wind und Meer* (four radio plays) appeared in 1970. His novels and stories include: *Die Hornissen* (1966), *Der Hausierer* (1967), *Die Angst des Tormanns beim Elfmeter* (1970), *Der kurze Brief zum langen Abschied* (1971), *Chronik der laufenden Ereignisse* (1971), *Ich bin ein Bewohner des Elfenbeinturms* (1972), and *Wunschloses Unglück* (1972), and *Die Unvernünftigen sterben aus* (1973). His poems have appeared in three collections: *Die Innenwelt der Aussenwelt der Innenwelt* (1969), *Deutsche Gedichte* (1969), and *Als das Wünschen noch geholfen hat* (1974). An English verson of *The Inner World of the Outer World of the Inner World* translated by Michael Roloff, appeared in 1974, and also an English version of *Als das Wünschen noch geholfen hat (Nonsense and Happiness,* 1976).

THE WRONG WAY ROUND

Gone to sleep I wake up:
I do not look at things, and things look at me;
I do not move, and the floor under my feet moves me;
I do not see myself in the mirror, and I in the mirror look at
    me;
I do not speak words, and words pronounce me;
I go to the window and am opened.

Having got up I lie there:
I do not open my eyes, but my eyes open me;
I do not listen to sounds, but the sounds listen to me;
I do not swallow water, but the water swallows me;
I do not reach out for things, but things attack me;
I do not take off my clothes, but my clothes take off from me;
I do not persuade myself with words, but words dissuade me
    from me;
I go to the door, and the handle depresses me.
The rolling blind is raised, and night falls, and to snatch air I
    submerge myself in water.

< 543 >

Gegenstände greifen mich an;
Ich entledige mich nicht der Kleider, sondern die Kleider ent-
ledigen sich meiner;
Ich rede mir nicht Wörter ein, sondern Wörter reden mich mir
aus;
Ich gehe zur Tür, und die Klinke drückt mich nieder.
Die Rollbalken werden hinaufgelassen, und es wird
Nacht, und um nach Luft zu schnappen, tauche ich unters Was-
ser:

Ich trete auf den Steinboden und sinke knöcheltief ein;
Ich sitze auf dem Bock einer Kutsche und setze einen Fuss vor
den andern;
Ich sehe eine Frau mit einem Sonnenschirm, und der
Nachtschweiss bricht mir aus;
Ich strecke den Arm in die Luft, und er fängt Feuer;
Ich greife nach einem Apfel und werde gebissen;
Ich gehe mit blossen Füssen und spüre einen Stein im Schuh;
Ich reisse das Pflaster von der Wunde, und die Wunde ist im
Pflaster;
Ich kaufe eine Zeitung und werde überflogen;
Ich erschrecke jemanden zu Tode und kann nicht mehr reden;
Ich stecke mir Watte in die Ohren und schreie;
Ich höre die Sirenen heulen, und der Fronleichnamszug führt an
mir vorbei;
Ich spanne den Regenschirm auf, und der Boden brennt mir
unter den Füssen;
Ich laufe ins Freie und werde verhaftet.

Über den Parkettboden stolpere ich,
mit weit offenem Mund führe ich Konversation,
mit den Handballen kratze ich,
mit der Trillerpfeife lache ich,
aus den Haarspitzen blute ich,
am Aufschlagen der Zeitung ersticke ich,
wohlriechende Speisen erbreche ich,
von der Zukunft erzähle ich,

< 544 >

I tread on the stone floor and sink up to my ankles;
I sit on the driving-seat of a coach and place one foot in front
    of the other;
I see a woman with a parasol and night sweat breaks out of me;
I extend one arm into the air and it catches fire;
I reach out for an apple and am bitten;
I walk barefoot, and feel a stone in my shoe;
I tear the plaster off my wound, and the wound is in the plas-
    ter;
I buy a newspaper and am skimmed;
I frighten someone to death and can no longer speak;
I stuff cotton wool into my ears and scream;
I hear the sirens howl, and the Corpus Christi procession pass-
    es;
I open my umbrella, and the ground burns under my feet;
I run out into the open and am arrested.

Over the parquet floor I stumble,
with my mouth agape I make conversation,
with the balls of my thumbs I scratch,
with my policeman's whistle I laugh,
from the tips of my hair I bleed,
on the opening of the newspaper I choke.
food with an attractive smell I spew up.
about the future I tell stories.
To things I speak.
me I see through.
dead people I kill.

And I see sparrows shoot at guns;
and I see the despairing man being happy;
and I see the suckling baby harbour desires;
and I see the milkman in the evening.

: and the postman? asks for mail;
and the preacher? is shaken up;
and the execution squad? lines up against the wall;

< 545 >

zu Sachen rede ich,
mich durchschaue ich,
Tote töte ich.

Und die Spatzen sehe ich auf die Kanonen schiessen;
und den Verzweifelten sehe ich glücklich sein;
und den Säugling sehe ich Wünsche haben;
und den Milchmann sehe ich am Abend:

:und der Briefträger? fragt nach Post;
und der Prediger? wird aufgerüttelt;
und das Erschiessungskommando? stellt sich an die Wand;
und der Clown? wirft eine Granate unter die Zuschauer;
und der Mord? geschieht erst beim Lokalaugenschein.

Und der Leichenbestatter feuert seine Fussballmannschaft an;
Und das Staatsoberhaupt verübt ein Attentat auf den Bäcker-
     lehrling;
Und der Feldherr wird nach einer Gasse benannt;
Und die Natur wird getreu nach einem Bild gemalt;
Und der Papst wird stehend ausgezählt—

und hör! Die Uhr geht ausserhalb ihrer selbst!
Und schau! Die herabbrennenden Kerzen werden grösser!
Und hör! Der Schrei wird geflüstert!
Und schau! Der Wind versteinert das Gras!
Und hör! Das Volkslied wird gebrüllt!
Und schau! Der erhobene Arm weist nach unten!
Und hör! Das Fragezeichen wird befohlen!
Und schau! Der Verhungerte ist fett!
Und riech! Der Schnee fault!

Und es neigt sich der Morgen,
und auf einem Bein steht der Tisch,
und im Schneidersitz sitzt der Flüchtling,
und im obersten Stockwerk befindet sich die Haltestelle der
     Strassenbahn:

and the clown? throws a hand grenade into the audience;
and murder? does not happen till there are witnesses.

And the undertaker eggs on his football team;
And the head of state assassinates the baker's boy;
And the general is named after a street;
And nature is painted faithfully after a picture;
And the Pope is counted out on his feet—

and listen: The watch runs outside itself!
And look: The candles burning down grow longer!
And listen: The scream is whispered!
And look: The wind petrifies the grass!
And listen: The folk song is roared out!
And look: The raised arm points down!
And listen: The question mark is commanded!
And look: The starved man is fat!
And smell: The snow is rotting!

And morning sets,
and the table stands on one leg,
and the refugee sits crosslegged like a tailor,
and on the top floor you'll find the bus stop:

Listen: It's deathly quiet!—It's rush hour.

Gone to sleep I wake up
and escape from the unbearable dream into gentle reality
and merrily hum: Stop thief! Murder!—
listen how my mouth waters: I see a corpse!

1967: *Die Innenwelt der Aussenwelt der Innenwelt*

FRANKENSTEIN'S MONSTER'S MONSTER
FRANKENSTEIN

Ah!
Under the straw in the stable lies Frankenstein's monster.
In Charleswell lives a doctor called Stein.

Horch! Es ist totenstill!—Es ist Hauptgeschäftszeit!

Aufgewacht bin ich eingeschlafen
und flüchte mich aus dem unerträglichen Traum in die sanfte
Wirklichkeit
und summe fröhlich Zeter und Mordio—
horch, wie mir das Wasser im Mund zusammenrinnt: ich sehe
eine Leiche!

FRANKENSTEINS MONSTERS MONSTER FRANKEN-STEIN

Ah! Unter dem Stroh im Stall liegt Frankensteins Monster.
In Carlsbrunn wohnt ein Doktor namens Stein.
Frankensteins Tochter fährt in der Kutsche zur Kur nach Insbad
(oder nach Inzbad).
Die Burschen im Dort heissen Fritz, Karl, Otto und Hans.
Im Stall über dem Stroh hängt ein ziemlich schwarzer Reifen
aus Holz.
Der Pförtner ist das erste Opfer des Monsters, das zweite Opfer
heisst Gerda.
Im Stall unterm Stroh liegt Frankenstein, Frankensteins Mon-
ster.

Im Herrschaftshaus spielt das Quartett einen echt
englischen Komponisten, aber auf Wunsch der Dame des
Hauses folgt Händel darauf.
Im Wirtshaus sind die Tischtücher so weissblau kariert, dass
man Heimweh kriegt.
Im Keller nimmt der Doktor dem erschrockenen Assistenten
den Handschuh aus der Hand.
Es gibt auch eine Stadt namens Frankenstein.
Im Wald schläft Frankensteins Monster weinend unter dem
Farnkraut.
Der Geliebte von Frankensteins Tochter heisst Hans.
Frankensteins Monster steht auf dem Altan des
Herrschaftshauses.

< 548 >

Frankenstein's daughter travels by coach to take the water at
Bath.

The village boys are called Fred, Charles, William, and John.

In the stable above the straw hangs a rather black wooden
hoop.

The porter is the monster's first victim, the second is called
Gerda.

In the stable under the straw lies Frankenstein, Frankenstein's
monster.

In the mansion a quartet plays a genuinely English composer,
but the lady of the house has them switch to Handel.

At the inn the tablecloths are so white and blue checked that
they make one feel homesick.

In the cellar the doctor snatches the glove from his startled assistant's hand.

There is a town called Frankenstein.

In the wood Frankenstein's monster sleeps weeping under the
bracken.

Frankenstein's daughter's lover is called John.

Frankenstein's monster stands on the balcony of the mansion.

Doctor Stein visits a patient.

The lovers are called Gerda and Frank, they sit under the
shrubs in the middle of the night, counting ants.

The groom hangs in the stable from a rather black wooden
hoop.

Frankenstein's monster used to be called John.

The scream of the lady of the house puts out the candle for the
string quartet's music.

Frankenstein's monster has hidden under the bracken.

Frankenstein's daughter wore a crinoline from Bath.

John and Frankenstein's daughter often used to sit together in
the grass, eating from the picnic basket that stood between them in the grass.

The lady of the house holds a fan between fingers and thumb.

< 549 >

,Der Doktor Stein macht eine Krankenvisite.

Das Liebespaar heisst Gerda und Franz, sitzt mitten in der
Nacht unterm Gebüsch und zählt Ameisen.

Der Stallknecht hängt im Stall an einem ziemlich schwarzen
Reifen aus Holz.

Frankensteins Monster hiess früher Hans.

Der Schrei der Dame des Hauses löscht die Kerze für die Par-
titur des Streichquartetts aus.

Frankensteins Monster hat sich unter das Farnkraut verkrochen.

Frankensteins Tochter trug einen Reifrock aus Inzbad (oder aus
Insbad).

Hans und Frankensteins Tochter sassen oft miteinander im Gras
und assen aus dem Jausenkorb, der zwischen ihnen im
Gras stand.

Die Dame des Hauses hat einen Fächer zwischen Daumen und
Fingern.

Frankensteins Monster, in seiner Verzweiflung,
hat den Hemdkragen offen.

"Ihr seid so gut zu mir!" sagte Hans.

Der Mann aus dem Volke reibt sich den Bauch.

"Ich bin immer nur angestarrt worden!" sagt Frankensteins
Monster.

Der Doktor Stein heisst jetzt Doktor Franck und hat eine Praxis
in London West, Harley Street.

Frankenstein's monster, in his despair, wears his shirt collar
open.

"You are so good to me!" said John.
The man of the people rubs his belly.
"All the time people have done nothing but stare at me" says
Frankenstein's monster.
Doctor Stein is now called Dr. Frank and has a practice in Har-
ley Street, London W.1.

1967: *Die Innenwelt der Aussenwelt der Innenwelt*

< 551 >

FRIEDRICH CHRISTIAN DELIUS:

Geboren 1943 in Rom. Er wuchs in Hessen auf; studierte an der Freien Universität in West-Berlin, wo er heute noch lebt. Bekannt ist er vor allem als Kommentator und Satiriker der westdeutschen politischen Szene, wie z.B. seine dokumentarische Prosa-Polemik *Wir Unternehmer* (1966) zeigt. Seine Gedichtbände: *Kerbholz* (1965) und *Wenn wir, bei Rot* (1969). Er beschäftigte sich auch mit Literaturkritik und veröffentlichte, u.a. *Der Held und sein Wetter; ein Kunstmittel und sein ideologischer Gebrauch im Roman des bürgerlichen Realismus* (1971). Seine zweite Prosa-Polemik mit dem Untertitel 'Festschrift' war *Unsere Siemens-Welt* (1972); eine Sammlung von Gedichten und Reiseberichten *Ein Bankier auf der Flucht* (1975).

GEBURTSTAG

Meine Angst hat
im Februar Geburtstag.
Zur Feier zeche ich
mit all meinen Feinden
abendlang—
und abwechselnd
deuten wir blasse Orakel
aus leeren Gläsern.

Auch die Behüter der Ordnung
sind meine Feinde.
Sie verhängen einen prächtigen
Ausnahmezustand,
während wir meine Angst
hoch leben lassen dreimal,
dreimal hoch.

Am Morgen machen
meine Feinde den schweren
Kopf leicht (denn
deshalb sind sie geladen)
sie reichen mir Glückwünsche:
Ich möge zufrieden sein und
meine wieder so reich beschenkte Angst
zurücklegen ins Herz.

< 552 >

FRIEDRICH CHRISTIAN DELIUS:

Born in Rome in 1943, he grew up in Hessen. He studied at the Free University, West Berlin, where he still lives. He is best known as a commentator on, and satirist of, the West German political scene, as in his documentary polemic in prose, *Wir Unternehmer* (1966), shows. His books of poems are *Kerbholz* (1965) and *Wenn wir, bei Rot* (1969). He has also written critical books on literature, among them *Der Held und sein Wetter; ein Kunstmittel und sein ideologischer Gebrauch im Roman des bürgerlichen Realismus* (1971). His second prose polemic, subtitled "Festschrift," was *Unsere Siemens-Welt* (1972), followed by a collection of poems and travel sketches *Ein Bankier auf der Flucht* (1975).

BIRTHDAY

My fear's birthday
falls in February.
To celebrate it I spend
the evening
drinking with all my enemies—
and each in turn
we interpret pale oracles
in empty glasses.

The guardians of order too
are my enemies.
They proclaim a splendid
state of emergency
while three times we drink
to the health of
my fear.

In the morning my enemies
make light
my heavy head (since that's
what I invited them for),
they hand me congratulations:
I'm to be content and
put the fear once more so richly provided with presents
away again in my heart.

<   553   >

GEDICHT FÜR KATZEN

Dämmrung ist die Stunde der Katzen;
sie atmen den Tag aus,
schleichen schwarz übern Weg,
spielen Eisenbahn mit ihren Augen.

Die Katzen tragen den Mond fort.
Sie sprechen in Bildern,
lachen auf Dächern den Unfug aus,
verspotten den alternden Wind.

Die Jagd auf Vögel ist verschoben,
die Katzen wissen, was recht ist:
Sie stürmen mein Kartenhaus,
verschlingen, ungelesen, meine Briefe.

Ich schreibe: Wir sollten die Katzen
loben in der Stunde der Dämmrung.

< 554 >

POEM FOR CATS

Dusk is the hour of cats:
they exhale the day,
slink blackly across the road,
play railway trains with their eyes.

Cats carry the moon away.
They speak in images,
laugh at mischief on roofs,
make fun of the aging wind.

Their bird hunt has been postponed,
cats know what's right:
They assault my house of cards,
gulp down my letters unread.

I write: we ought to praise
cats at the hour of dusk.

1965: *Kerbholz*

< 555 >

JÜRGEN THEOBALDY:

Geboren 1944 in Straßburg. Er lebt heute in Berlin und Heidelberg. Er veröffentlichte die Sammlung *Sperrsitz* (1973), wovon ein Teil in die spätere Sammlung *Blaue Flecken* (1974) aufgenommen wurde. Er übersetzte aus dem Englischen und anderen Sprachen.

EINE ART NÄCHSTENLIEBE

Du willst mich anrufen um zu sagen
ich solle später kommen so gegen zehn
aber ich bin schon weg
komme zu dir
und so ein Typ sitzt herum
völlig stoned
grinsend glucksend
und als wir ihn
gegen elf draussen haben
sind sckon zwei andere da
nicht so stoned
aber auch kaputt
jemand ruft an: er habe
die Pulsadern schon geöffnet
neue Aufregungen . . .
gegen halb eins dann dieser Psychologe
und sein Gerede über Gruppentherapie
als wir sie alle gegen drei
aus dem Zimmer kriegen
bin ich konfus genug um mitzugehen
du holst mich zurück
wir machen eine Dose auf
rauchen
trinken
und liegen glücklich um vier im Bett
ich meine endlich

GEDICHT VON DER KÜCHENFRONT

Ich öffne den Kühlschrank, blicke
hinein, er ist kalt und leer!
Er ist kalt und leer, und sein Weiss

< 556 >

JÜRGEN THEOBALDY:

Born in 1944 in Strasbourg, he now lives in Berlin and Heidelberg. He has published the collection *Sperrsitz* (1973), part of which was incorporated in the later collection *Blaue Flecken* (1974). He has translated from the English and from other languages.

A SORT OF LOVE OF ONE'S NEIGHBOR

You want to ring me up to say
I am to come later round about ten
but I have already left
arrive at your place
and some type is sitting around
completely stoned
grinning and clucking
and by the time
we have got him out round about eleven
two others have turned up
not quite as stoned
but all freaked out too
someone rings up saying
he has already slashed his wrists
more excitement . . .
round about ten thirty comes this psychologist
with his talk of group therapy
by the time we have got them all
out of the room round about three
I'm confused enough to go with them
you fetch me back
we open a tin
smoke
drink
and by four we are safely in bed
about time I think

POEM ABOUT THE KITCHEN FRONT

I open the refrigerator, look
inside, it's cold and empty.
It's cold and empty, and its whiteness

< 557 >

erinnert mich an nordische Landschaften
voll Schnee und verschont, weil dort
nichts Brauchbares wächst.
Wenn die Preise weiter steigen, wird es
auch hier überall schneien.
Wir werden eine Eiszeit der Preise haben
eine Landschaft mit leeren Kühlschränken.
Wir werden kälter werden, noch kälter.
Was wir essen, wird nicht in der Küche
entschieden, auch nicht im Kühlschrank.
Vielleicht ist das ein kluger Gedanke
— entscheide dich, Leser! — vielleicht
hilft er mir durch dieses Gedicht.
Doch im Augenblick und erst recht morgen
würde ich lieber die Pfanne
für ein Schnitzel richten, wäre mir nicht
das Blut in den Adern gefroren als
die Metzgersfrau den Preis nannte!

<   558   >

reminds me of northern landscapes
full of snow and left intact
because nothing useful grows there.
If the prices keep on rising here too
it will be snowing everywhere.
We shall have an ice age of prices
a landscape with empty refrigerators.
We shall get colder, even colder than now.
What we eat is not decided
in the kitchen, nor in the refrigerator.
Maybe that's a clever thought —
decide for yourself, reader! — maybe
it will help me through this poem.
But at the moment and even tomorrow
I'd rather get the frying-pan
ready for a chop, if the blood
hadn't frozen in my veins when
the butcher told me the price.

1974: *Blaue Flecken*